BRITISH POLICY TOWARDS IRELAND
1921–1941

British Policy Towards
IRELAND
1921–1941

PAUL CANNING

CLARENDON PRESS · OXFORD
1985

Oxford University Press, Walton Street, Oxford OX2 6DP

London New York Toronto
Delhi Bombay Calcutta Madras Karachi
Kuala Lumpur Singapore Hong Kong Tokyo
Nairobi Dar es Salaam Cape Town
Melbourne Auckland

and associated companies in
Beirut Berlin Ibadan Mexico City Nicosia

Oxford is a trade mark of Oxford University Press

Published in the United States
by Oxford University Press, New York

© Paul Canning 1985

British Library Cataloguing in Publication Data
Canning, Paul
British policy towards Ireland 1921–1941.
1. Great Britain——Foreign relations——Ireland
2. Ireland——Foreign relations——Great Britain
I. Title
327.410417   DA47.9.175
ISBN 0-19-820068-4

Set by Butler & Tanner Ltd, Frome and London
Printed in Great Britain
at the University Press, Oxford
by David Stanford
Printer to the University

To My Mother
and the
Memory of My Father

Preface

THIS work aims to provide a general account of British policy towards Ireland from 1921 to 1941. That no such account has previously been produced is remarkable, not only because of the intrinsic interest and importance of the subject, but also for the example it set. The lesson of Ireland, as every Dominions Secretary and Secretary for India knew, was not lost on the other subjects of the Empire.

Defeat in war, such as the British suffered at the hands of the Irish guerrillas from 1919 to 1921, is often the occasion for national soul-searching. Witness the United States since the end of the Vietnam War. Not so for the British after 1921. Though the Irish question had dominated British politics from 1918 to 1922, not to mention much of the preceding half-century and, as Asquith had said as recently as 1920, things were being done in Ireland 'which would disgrace the blackest annals of the lowest despotism in Europe', once peace was concluded, the whole affair was soon forgotten. While a few personal accounts were published, not for almost fifteen years did a serious study of the negotiations leading up to the Irish Treaty of 1921 appear.[1] And not until the mid-1970s did a scholarly account of British policy from 1919 to 1921 become available.[2] Yet the twenty years following the Treaty have been even more neglected. Not until the revival of 'the Troubles' in Northern Ireland during the 1970s did British, Irish, and American historians begin taking a more active interest in this later phase of Anglo-Irish relations. Even now, when most of the British archives covering this period have been open for over a decade, there has been no attempt to cover the entire inter-war period of Anglo-Irish relations.[3] This work intends to help fill that gap.

[1] Frank Pakenham (Earl of Longford), *Peace by Ordeal* (London, 1935).

[2] Charles Townshend, *The British Campaign in Ireland 1919–1921* (Oxford Historical Monographs: Oxford, 1975).

[3] D.W. Harkness, *The Restless Dominion: The Irish Free State and the British Commonwealth of Nations, 1921–31* (London, 1969), focused on the constitutional issues, but

This study does not purport to be a comprehensive treatment of Anglo-Irish relations from 1921 to 1941. It is rather an attempt to explain what the Irish dimension meant to British policy-makers, how perceptions of it changed, and how British policy was formulated during this period. As such it concerns attitudes, politics, and how governments work. There was a remarkable continuity about British politics from the 1920s through the 1930s. The men whose opinions about Ireland mattered in the 1930s would not have had trouble recognizing those who had made peace with Ireland in 1921. They were the same men! Most of the attitudes, ideas, and prejudices of those at the top were formed during the late Victorian heyday. The process by which they changed and accommodated themselves to the underlying and constantly shifting realities and personal alignments is the stuff of politics. Back-benchers and party opinion, the press and pressure groups—all were important, but mainly in so far as politicians deemed them to be so. Civil servants, expecially influential ones like Thomas Jones, Sir Maurice Hankey, Sir Horace Wilson, and Sir Warren Fisher, also had roles to play, and often important ones. But the fundamental reality behind British policy-making on Ireland, as with other important issues of the day, lay with the interactions between the politicians who mattered. Mutual distrust and contempt, as well as self-interest, frequently were the prime motivators. Shared assumptions—not always having much to do with the objective situations about which they were concerned—were often the main obstacles to be overcome. It was from these politicians that almost all initiatives on Ireland came.[4]

They did not, however, live in isolation. Outside the cloisters of Whitehall and Westminster there was a world that had to be taken into consideration. In particular, there were two

---

was written before most of the official archives for the period was opened to the public. Deirdre McMahon has written a thesis on 'Anglo-Irish Relations: 1932–38' (Ph.D. Thesis, Cambridge University, 1979). The war years have been covered in several recent studies, most recently and comprehensively by Robert Fisk, *In Time of War: Ireland, Ulster and the Price of Neutrality 1939–45* (London and Philadelphia, 1983).

[4] For a fuller discussion of 'politics on the top', see the two stimulating works on this period by Maurice Cowling, *The Impact of Labour, 1920–1924* (Cambridge University Press, 1971), pp. 1–12; and *The Impact of Hitler: British Politics and British Policy, 1933–1940* (Cambridge University Press, 1975).

disagreeable realities which kept intruding upon them. One was the growing nationalism within the Empire–Commonwealth which would not be quieted, and of which Ireland was simply the nearest example. The other was the decline of British power.

British policy towards Ireland must be seen as part of a general policy of appeasement that marked the conduct of Britain's foreign and imperial relations after the war. Britain's leaders were acutely conscious that, though the Empire was vast, it was overextended and Britain did not have the resources to defend it. Between 1921 and 1941 Britain's relations with the Dominions were profoundly altered, to a degree that made these two decades a transitional period of the greatest importance in the history of the Empire–Commonwealth. During this time the former colonial appendages were formally recognized as independent states comprising the British Commonwealth of Nations. Although in retrospect the transition from Empire to Commonwealth was a swift one, at the time it seemed so gradual and natural an evolution that many scarcely noticed that it was occurring—a fact reflected in the marked tendency of politicians, civil servants, and military men to continue referring to the Dominions during the inter-war years as part of the Empire.

At the forefront of this change was Ireland. As the 'restless Dominion' under Cosgrave during the 1920s, and even more so later under the more extreme nationalism of de Valera during the 1930s and 1940s, Ireland was by far the most assertive of the Dominions as regards imperial questions. Beginning with the Irish Treaty of 1921—where the term 'Dominion' was first used in an official document—down to the final acceptance of Ireland's right to remain neutral during the Second World War, Ireland's attitudes and preoccupations—even when not fully shared by the other Dominions—inevitably stimulated, and to a large degree determined, the broad trend of developments in the Dominions' fundamental relationship with Great Britain. Thus Anglo-Irish relations during these years were particularly traumatic for Britain's rulers, not only because of the intense emotions with which they were as always fraught, but also because they were symptomatic of that decline which began with Ireland and led

inevitably to the dissolution of the Empire after the Second
World War.

This study is based primarily upon the records preserved in
the Public Record Office and on the letters and diaries written
by politicians and civil servants and preserved in the collections listed in the bibliography. I am grateful to the Controller
of HM Stationery Office for permission to quote from
Crown-Copyright records, and also to the many owners of
copyright material who have graciously granted me permission to use it. I apologize to any whom I have failed to consult.

In particular, I would like to thank Lord Simon for kind-
ness and hospitality in allowing access to the papers of his
father, Lord Salisbury for access to his family's papers, David
Marquand for the use of Ramsay MacDonald's papers while
they were under his control, and A.J.P. Taylor and the staff
of the late lamented Beaverbrook Library for generous assistance while examining the collection under their care. I am
also indebted to Lord Longford and the late Rt. Hon. Malcolm MacDonald for taking the time to share some of their
reminiscences with me.

Among others too numerous to mention individually, but
to whom I am equally grateful, I wish to thank the staffs of
the Public Record Office, the British Library, the Cambridge
University Library, the Bodleian, the Scottish Public Record
Office, the House of Lords Record Office, the National Li-
brary of Scotland, the National Library of Wales, the National
Register of Archives, the National Maritime Museum, the
Public Record Office of Northern Ireland, the Shropshire
Records Office, the Durham County Record Office, and the
libraries of the London School of Economics, Newcastle University, Nuffield College, Churchill College, Birmingham
University, Gonzaga University, Marymount College, and the
University of Washington. In addition, I would like to thank
the staff of the Oxford University Press for their generous
assistance in the preparation of this book, and the editors of
Albion and of the *International History Review* for permission to
republish material in chapters eight and nine which originally
appeared in their journals.

Lastly, and most of all, I want to thank my dear friend and
mentor, Professor Giovanni Costigan, for his constant encour-

agement and patient criticism over the years, and Barbara Wheaton and my mother, Mary Canning, for their help and inspiration in general without which this book would never have been completed.

April *1984*

Contents

Abbreviations

ADM	Admiralty document in the Public Record Office of series indicated
BT	Board of Trade document in PRO of series indicated
CAB	Cabinet paper in PRO (followed by suffix indicating series and number)
CID	Committee of Imperial Defence
CIGS	Chief of the Imperial General Staff
CP	Cabinet Paper in PRO of series indicated
CO	Colonial Office document in PRO of series indicated
COS	Chiefs of Staff Subcommittee of the CID
DCOS	Deputy Chiefs of Staff Subcommittee of the CID
DO	Dominions Office document in PRO of series indicated
FO	Foreign Office document in PRO (followed by series number)
GOC-in-C	General Officer Commanding-in-Chief
HO	Home Office document in PRO of series indicated
INF	Ministry of Information document in PRO of series indicated
IRA	Irish Republican Army
ISC	Irish Situation Committee

Parl. Deb.	Parliamentary Debates (*Hansard*, Lords or Commons as indicated)
PREM	Premier: Prime Minister's Private Office correspondence in PRO
PRO	Public Record Office
T	Treasury document in PRO of series indicated
WM	War Cabinet Minute (1939-45)
WO	War Office document in PRO of series indicated
WP	War Cabinet Paper in PRO of series indicated

PROLOGUE

THE IRISH TREATY

IRELAND

I

The Triumph of
Lloyd George

This surrender to assassination is appalling—far worse than I expected. It is the beginning of the end of this Empire.

I earnestly hope that an opportunity will be given for the die-hards in the House of Lords to record their votes against this intolerably humiliating and dishonouring betrayal. The House is doomed, and it surely might bear on its records the fact that a number of peers would not bend their knee to Baal.

Sydenham to Salisbury, 7 December 1921

Yes! I would have voted with the Government, but much *à contre cœur*. It is a miserable business, and the 'Treaty' (my blood boils at the use of the word) is the only way out—(given a British public with a weak stomach, and a tendency to hysteria whenever an old woman happens to get shot or a farm building set on fire).

Lansdowne to Salisbury, 27 December 1921

AT the end of 1921 the British Coalition Government led by Prime Minister David Lloyd George made two far-reaching decisions regarding Ireland. One was to grant that country Dominion status under the terms of the Agreement signed on 6 December 1921. The second was to allow Ulster[1] to 'opt out' of a united Ireland and remain an integral part of the United Kingdom. Both decisions were made under duress: the first because of the failure of the British campaign against Sinn Féin from 1919 to 1921, the second from reluctance to confront the Ulster Protestants and their supporters in Britain. The

---

[1] For the sake of convenience the term 'Ireland' has been taken in this study to refer generally to the present twenty-six county area of Southern Ireland known from 1922 to 1937 as the Irish Free State and thereafter as Éire, while the term 'Irish' is taken to signify citizens of that state unless otherwise made clear. Similarly, Ulster is used not in the strictly geographical sense, but to refer to the six-county area known officially as Northern Ireland.

next twenty years of Anglo-Irish relations are in large part the history of the attempt to reconcile these two decisions.

The Irish Treaty signed in December 1921 was the direct result of the abrupt reversal in policy by the British Government the previous June. Ever since the proclamation of the Irish Republic on 21 January 1919, and indeed since the 1916 Easter Rising, the Government had been employing the traditional method of dealing with Ireland—alternating conciliation with coercion. These efforts did not prove as effective as had others in the past. On the one hand, Sinn Féin was not only irreconcilable, but better organized and more popular than previous nationalist groups. On the other, there were limits to how far the Government was willing or able to use coercion as an instrument of policy. In early 1921, when the Government began extending martial law and 'authorized reprisals' throughout Ireland, it faced an immediate storm from the press and public in England. The Labour Party charged that 'things are being done in the name of Britain which must make our name stink in the nostrils of the whole world'; while a short time later the Government found its Irish policy condemned in the House of Lords by the Archbishop of Canterbury.[2]

Nor were these the only problems facing Lloyd George. Repression was an expensive business. Even during the postwar boom the government had felt the constraints imposed against it by the need for budgetary restraint, having for instance to jettison Lloyd George's promise to the returning veterans of 'homes fit for heroes'. Then in 1921 the economy suddenly slumped disastrously[3] and every department had to face the prospect of drastic cutbacks. With retrenchment in the air, and the Army already over-committed in Ireland and elsewhere throughout the Empire,[4] a quick victory over the Irish Republican Army (IRA) was needed. But such a victory was proving as elusive as ever. In May 1921 the Commander-in-Chief in Ireland, Sir Nevil Macready, warned

[2] Charles Loch Mowat, *Britain Between the Wars, 1918–1940*, (Boston, paperback edn., 1971), pp. 82–3.

[3] 'Not for a hundred years has British finance and commerce experienced such a disappointing year as 1921', reported the *Annual Register* (1921), II, p. 69.

[4] See Brian Bond, *British Military Policy Between the Two World Wars* (Oxford, 1980), pp. 10–34.

that the stress and strain which the nature of the Irish conflict imposed on both officers and men was so great that unless a settlement had been achieved by October practically all the troops would have to be withdrawn, even if there were no other troops to replace them.[5] Meanwhile, Sir Henry Wilson, Chief of the Imperial General Staff (CIGS), was warning that Ireland could be reconquered only by full-scale war, an army of 100,000 men, and the proclamation of martial law throughout the country.[6] Under the circumstances, even a politician less adroit than Lloyd George might have been looking for a way out.

The difficulty lay in persuading his colleagues of the wisdom of such a course. As early as January 1921 Lloyd George told Andrew Bonar Law, the Conservative leader, that 'in the interests of Peace with America' he thought that they 'ought to see de Valera [President of the Irish Provisional Republic] and try to get a settlement'. At the time this conversation only prompted the disgruntled Law to comment to Thomas Jones, the Assistant Secretary to the Cabinet and Lloyd George's personal adviser on Irish affairs, that he had come to the conclusion 'that the Irish were an inferior race'.[7] But it is probable that Law's growing frustration with the Irish question was not unrelated to his sudden retirement from political life two months later.[8] Whereas for Lloyd George Ireland was just one of a host of problems, to be settled as expediently as possible, to Law it was an emotional issue. Born in Canada, the son of a Presbyterian minister from Northern Ireland, he had built his career around a fanatical attachment to Ulster and opposition to Home Rule. As Conservative leader before the First World War, he had not hesitated to push opposition to the Third Home Rule Bill to the brink of civil war. But 1921 was a world removed from 1914, and de Valera bore little resemblance to John Redmond. Worn-out, ill, and disgusted, Bonar Law sought a way out of the Irish imbroglio. Unlike Lloyd George, he found it in the South of France. By removing himself from the Government, Law made it possible

[5] Townshend, p. 182.
[6] A.J.P. Taylor, *English History 1914–1945* (Oxford, 1965), p. 156.
[7] Thomas Jones, *Whitehall Diary*, iii, *Ireland, 1916–26* (London, 1971), p. 49.
[8] For evidence that Law's illness was at least partly psychosomatic, see A.J.P. Taylor (ed.) *Lloyd George: A Diary by Frances Stevenson* (New York, 1971), p. 236.

for Lloyd George to seek a settlement with Sinn Féin without his blocking the way, and ensured that, unlike other Coalition Conservatives, he would not be implicated. In so doing, though he did not know this at the time, Law virtually guaranteed that he would be the next Conservative Prime Minister.

In March 1921, all this lay in the future. With Law out of sight, if not out of mind, Lloyd George could now move forward on Ireland. In July he succeeded in opening negotiations with de Valera, taking care in doing so to involve Winston Churchill and Lord Birkenhead.

Lloyd George had two alternatives. He could either work with the Conservatives to reach a settlement along the lines of the Government of Ireland Act of 1920 which, while giving the South considerably more autonomy than had originally been intended, would still guarantee separate parliaments in both North and South, thereby assuring Ulster's continued attachment to the United Kingdom; or, if faced with either Conservative refusal to make concessions to Sinn Féin, or a refusal of Sinn Féin to give way on Ulster, he could force an election on the old pre-war programme of maintaining Irish unity against Ulster and Conservative intransigents. A campaign waged along such lines would have the added benefit of reuniting the Liberals under his banner.[9]

From July until November Lloyd George conducted negotiations with these two options in mind. Whether he would ever have called an election on an anti-Ulster ticket, or was simply using this threat as a means of blackmailing the Conservatives, is uncertain; they came along willingly in any event, and he did not have to show his hand.

In November he ran into difficulties. Although de Valera was proving inflexible, Lloyd George had been able to persuade Arthur Griffith to agree that Ireland would remain in the Commonwealth and recognize the Crown as its head, provided Irish unity was preserved in a single Dominion under an all-Irish parliament. For a time Lloyd George may have thought he could pressure Sir James Craig, the Prime Minister of Northern Ireland, into a united Ireland by insisting that Ulster would have to pay British income tax if she remained part of the United Kingdom.[10] If so, he was thwarted by

[9] Cowling, *Impact of Labour*, pp. 122-3.   [10] Ibid. pp. 124-5.

Bonar Law, who had returned from France in September and now threatened to reinvolve himself in politics unless Lloyd George renounced any intention to coerce Ulster.[11]

If Ulster could not be persuaded to join a unified Irish state, as seemed clear after Law's intervention, there remained only one avenue of escape short of calling off the negotiations or forcing an election: Sinn Féin must be persuaded to accept Dominion status for the South without Ulster. To make this more palatable to Arthur Griffith and the Irish delegation, Lloyd George devised a Boundary Commission whose duty it would be at some later date to redraw the borders of Northern Ireland in keeping with the wishes of the inhabitants.[12] Since the counties of Fermanagh and Tyrone were predominantly Catholic, this allowed the Irish delegation to accept division in principle, while still believing that it would not work in practice, as it was thought that, without Fermanagh and Tyrone, Northern Ireland would be too small to be a viable state. (At the same time Lloyd George had to assure Craig and his Conservative backers in England that the Boundary Commission posed no threat to Ulster.) To this was added the not altogether credible threat of a resumption of the war if the terms were not accepted. Finally, in the early hours of 6 December, the Irish delegation resigned itself to the consequences, and, together with their British counterparts, signed the 'Articles of Agreement for a Treaty between Great Britain and Ireland'.

The Treaty provided that Ireland should have the same constitutional status in the Empire as the other Dominions.[13] It was to be called the Irish Free State, and its position in relation to the Imperial Parliament and Government would be the same as that of Canada, including a Governor-General as the representative of the Crown. Other provisions called for the swearing of an oath to the Crown by the members of the

[11] Stevenson diary, 9 Nov. 1921 (*Lloyd George: A Diary*, pp. 235-6).
[12] The idea of setting up a Boundary Commission to examine the distribution of population along the borders of the six counties was first suggested by Craig in Dec. 1919. Presumably he had adjustments rather than any substantial changes in mind. Nicholas Mansergh, 'The Influence of the Past' in David Watt (ed.), *The Constitution of Northern Ireland: Problems and Prospects* (London, 1981), p. 17.
[13] Edmund Curtis and R.B. McDowell, (eds.) *Irish Historical Documents 1172-1922* New York, 1968 edn., pp. 322-3.

Irish Free State Parliament, forbade religious discrimination
in North and South, and made the Irish Free State liable for
its share of the public debt of the United Kingdom as of the
signing of the Treaty. The sixth and seventh articles dealt
with naval issues, providing that, 'until an arrangement has
been made between the British and Irish Governments whereby the Irish Free State undertakes her own coastal defence',
the naval defence of the British Isles would be undertaken by
Great Britain. This provision was subject to review after five
years. In peacetime the Admiralty was to retain the ports of
Berehaven, Queenstown (Cobh), and Lough Swilly in the
South, as well as Belfast Lough in the North; and in wartime
'such harbour and other facilities as the British Government
may require'. Finally, Northern Ireland was granted the right
to 'opt out' of the Irish Free State if it so desired. If this option
were exercised, a Boundary Commission was to be set up to
determine the border between North and South.

In England the Treaty was welcomed with relief by virtually all shades of opinion.[14] The debates in both Houses
from 14 to 16 December were triumphs for the Government,
its first in many months. Lloyd George, although still ex-
hausted from his part in the 'peace by ordeal',[15] nevertheless
demonstrated in a resounding *tour de force* how both sides had
secured what they needed from the Treaty: for the British
there was 'allegiance to the Crown, partnership in the Empire,
security of our shores, non-coercion of Ulster'; for the Irish,
freedom 'to work out their own national destiny'.[16] Similarly,
in one of his best speeches, Churchill expressed his hope that
Ulster would join the South, 'and that the national unity of
Ireland within the British Empire would be attained'. It was
this dream of a united Ireland, and not the threat of continued
war, which had motivated the Irish to accept allegiance to
the Crown, he maintained.[17]

On the left, support for the Treaty was forthcoming from
the Asquithian Liberals and the Labour Party, who tended to
view it as a lasting settlement between the two nations which

[14] *Daily Telegraph*, 8 Dec. 1921; *The Times*, 9 Dec. 1921; *Daily Express*, 9 Dec. 1921.
[15] Jones to Hankey, 13 Dec. 1921 (Jones, iii, pp. 187-8).
[16] *Parl. Deb. Commons*, vol. 149, cols. 29-39 of 14 Dec. 1921.
[17] Ibid. cols. 175-83 of 15 Dec. 1921.

would afford 'the fullest scope for every manifestation of Irish nationhood'.[18] The main reservation was the fear that only a united Ireland would become fully reconciled to friendship with Britain.

Opposition to the Treaty came only from the small group of diehards led by John Gretton and Lord Salisbury, supported by H.A. Gwynne and the *Morning Post*. It was based on moral principle, strategic considerations, empathy for Ulster, and dislike of Lloyd George, but was not widespread enough to pose any real threat. Crucial in this regard was the attitude of Bonar Law who, though he did not like the Treaty, accepted it, knowing that it was favoured by a majority of the Conservative Party and by 'the overwhelming mass of the people'. While disclaiming responsibility for the Treaty, he expressed his belief that Northern Ireland would receive fair treatment under it, and would be making a mistake if she rejected it. To him this was all that mattered. His indifference to the fate of the South allowed him to view its future relationship with the Empire with more detachment, and consequently more realism, than most. The only thing that mattered in Ireland, he told the House, was goodwill. If Southern Ireland were hostile, it would not make much difference whether it was called a Republic or a Dominion.[19]

In the House of Lords the drama centred around Lord Carson, who bitterly flailed his former colleagues, in particular his old friend Birkenhead, the 'galloper' of the volunteer days, as traitors. Carson's invective had little effect, and Birkenhead's devastating reply proved to be the most articulate defence of the Government's policy heard in either House. While allowing that the Irish were a 'very strange, wayward, and incalculable people', the Lord Chancellor nevertheless claimed that the Treaty offered the best chance to satisfy their sentiment of nationhood, while at the same time removing gradually the animosities which had poisoned public life in England. 'Is it your alternative that we should resume the war', he asked the diehards,

and take and break this people as we can with our military strength? When we have done that, shall we be any better off? Shall we be

[18] Ibid. (Clynes), col. 20 of 14 Dec. 1921.   [19] Ibid. cols. 197–206 of 15 Dec. 1921.

nearer a settlement when Lord Salisbury, if he becomes Prime Minister, has raised the army, carried fire and sword into every village
in Ireland, and brought back a new laurel to add to the military
standards of the great war? There is no one listening to me who does
not know that on the conclusion of that war, with memories a
thousand times more bitterly inflamed, Lord Salisbury would have
to do what we have done now, enter into negotiations with these
people and define the conditions under which they and we will live
our lives.

Birkenhead concluded his speech with an appeal to their
Lordships to vote 'not confident, but still hoping that we shall
see in the future an Ireland which will at last, after centuries,
be reconciled with this country ...'.[20] It was this hope, as
much as anything, that carried the day for the Government.
In the end the Treaty was approved by a vote of 401 to 58 in
the Commons, and 166 to 47 in the Lords.

The Treaty was to have far-reaching effects: in Ireland it led
within a few months to civil war between pro-Treaty and
anti-Treaty factions of Sinn Féin; in England it lent impetus to
the diehard movement which contributed to the overthrow of
the Coalition within the coming year. For some time it was
by no means clear whether the Treaty would even last. Only
with the passage of time could it be seen that it had in fact
established the basis for a new and stable Anglo-Irish relationship.

    In the short term, both Lloyd George and Birkenhead
hoped to capitalize on the Treaty by calling a general election.
In this they were thwarted by Conservative opposition, led by
Tory Central Office. While the Prime Minister's defeat on the
election issue had more to do with Conservative dislike of his
continued leadership of the Coalition than with Ireland, the
situation there presented for many the most convenient focus
of attack. Claiming that 'neither wing' of the Government's
supporters was 'really proud of the achievements of the Coalition', and that neither Ireland nor Washington would be
electoral assets, Malcolm Fraser, the chief party agent, warned

[20] *Parl. Deb. Lords*, vol. 48, cols. 16–35 of 14 Dec. 1921.

that an appeal to the country 'would split the Unionist Party from top to toe'.[21]

The confused situation in Ireland and the renewed impetus it had given to the diehard movement also alarmed the Coalition's supporters. Citing this as a major reason why he opposed an immediate election, Sir Austen Chamberlain, Conservative Party leader and Leader of the House of Commons (who, together with Churchill, Birkenhead, and Sir Robert Horne, the Chancellor of the Exchequer, were popularly thought to make up an 'inner Cabinet' or 'directorate') argued that it would be 'taking grave and unjustifiable risks to leave the new Irish policy incomplete and exposed to all the accidents of the weeks in which every member of the Government would have to be stumping the country instead of governing it'.[22] Lord Derby similarly warned against an election, giving the delay by the Dáil in ratifying the Treaty as his reason. He felt that there was no doubt the delay had 'strengthened the case of the Diehards', and was 'making a lot of waverers incline more to their side, because if what is a great gift on the part of England is not to be received in the spirit in which it is given, it does not look as if there would be any real peace in Ireland'. Derby gathered 'that the Delegates are doing their best to get it accepted but it certainly is a case of looking a gift horse in the mouth'.[23]

In the long term the Irish Treaty weakened Lloyd George's hold over his own Cabinet, as evidenced first by his defeat over the election issue, and then again in March when he was voted down on the question of recognition of Russia at the forthcoming Genoa Conference. Henceforth not only was Lloyd George's personal ascendancy over the Cabinet no longer unchallenged, but the centrifugal forces already at play within the Conservative Party were enlarged. As conditions in Ireland deteriorated after the Treaty, and the Government's policy came under almost incessant attack from the Conser-

[21] Kenneth O. Morgan, *Consensus and Disunity: The Lloyd George Coalition Government, 1918–1922* (Oxford, 1979), p. 273.

[22] Sir Charles Petrie, *The Life and Letters of Sir Austen Chamberlain*, ii, (London, 1940), p. 170. C.P. Scott also opposed an early election (C.P. Scott diary, entries for 7–20 Jan. 1922; Scott diaries, 50906, vi, p. 134).

[23] Derby to Lloyd George, 22 Dec. 1921 (J.C.C. Davidson papers, Box 19122 (uncatalogued)).

vative benches, the Prime Minister's Conservative colleagues began to lose control of their party organization. The Liberal leader of a predominantly Conservative Coalition, Lloyd George could do little to restrain Conservative back-benchers. For this he had to rely on Chamberlain. But Chamberlain was unable even to control Sir George Younger, the Party Chairman, who was now strongly opposed to the Coalition.

To Churchill as Colonial Secretary fell the duty of implementing the Treaty; he accepted his new assignment with characteristic gusto. Earlier, while engaged in the effort to suppress the Sinn Féin 'murder-gang', Churchill had detected a 'diabolical streak' in the Irish character which had 'done them in in the bygone ages of history and prevented them from being a great responsible nation with stability and prosperity'.[24] Now he pronounced himself 'full of hope and confidence about Ireland' and certain that 'we are going to reap a rich reward all over the world and at home'.[25] Others were less optimistic. While Lloyd George and Churchill had developed a sympathy for the Irish leaders during the treaty negotiations and had confidence that Collins and Griffith possessed 'moral courage' and were 'men of their word', Chamberlain still entertained doubts. During the negotiations he had not been favourably impressed by the Irish delegates, finding them 'not very clever and some ... very stupid'.[26] Afterwards he wished he 'knew anyone who really knows Ireland and the Irish'. Chamberlain mistrusted 'every interpretation of fact or character' that he saw. While de Valera gave him 'the impression of a beaten man', and he hoped 'that the prolongation of the struggle was steadily reducing his influence in Ireland', he nevertheless wondered 'who shall say what that strange people thinks or who guarantee that what they think, they will do?'[27]

During 1921 British policy towards Ireland had been formulated at the highest level of the Cabinet. After the Treaty

[24] Churchill to Clementine Churchill, 31 Mar. 1920, quoted in Martin Gilbert, *Winston S. Churchill*, iv, *The Stricken World 1916–1922* (Boston, 1975), p. 449.

[25] Churchill to the Prince of Wales, 2 Jan. 1922 (ibid. pp. 682–3).

[26] Chamberlain to Lady Chamberlain, 23 Nov. 1921 (Austen Chamberlain papers, AC 6/1/470).

[27] Chamberlain to Lady Chamberlain, 7 Jan. 1922 (Austen Chamberlain papers, AC 6/1/473).

this was no longer the case. Although important decisions were still referred back to the Cabinet, more routine matters were now handled by a Cabinet Committee on the Irish Provisional Government. Besides Churchill, as chairman, this consisted of Sir Hamar Greenwood, Chief Secretary for Ireland, Lord Fitzalan, Irish Viceroy, Sir Gordon Hewart, Attorney-General, Sir Laming Worthington-Evans, Secretary of State for War, and the Service chiefs, with others sitting in as the situation required. As 1922 progressed the Irish Government was gradually dismantled and its powers transferred to the Provisional Government set up in Dublin at the beginning of the year. In fact it had already lost much of its influence. At the head of the Irish Government stood the Viceroy or Lord-Lieutenant (he answered to either title). He was assisted in his duties by a Chief Secretary, who moved between his office in Dublin Castle and the Irish Office in Whitehall, managing the various departments under him and answering to Parliament on Ireland. Ordinarily the duties of the Viceroy were largely ceremonial, and most of the responsibility for Ireland rested with the Chief Secretary. But in 1921 this had gone somewhat topsy-turvy. Lloyd George, no respecter of persons, especially discredited ones, paid little heed to Greenwood in arranging the truce with de Valera or in the negotiations that followed. After the Treaty, though sitting on the Irish Committee, Greenwood devoted most of his attention to administrative duties, such as looking after the pension rights of the Royal Irish Constabulary. Fitzalan, on the other hand—whose appointment as a Catholic Viceroy known to oppose the 'Black and Tan' policy had been an adroit bit of window-dressing on Lloyd George's part—counted among his close friends the king and prominent diehards like Salisbury and Sir James Craig. Though his duties were few, this political influence earned him seats both in the Cabinet and on the Irish Committee.

Between Churchill and Greenwood there was no problem; the former simply appropriated to himself any responsibilities concerning Ireland which interested him; the rest he left to the Chief Secretary. Administratively, this added to the confusion surrounding Irish affairs because Churchill, as Colonial Secretary, naturally tended to look to his own officials to deal with Irish affairs. But many of the duties for which he was now responsible were still being handled by the Irish Office, where more than half of the staff were soon engaged on work for him rather than for Greenwood. Although this was a source of considerable frustration and annoyance for the civil servants involved[28]—not to be ended until the Irish Office was abolished and its staff absorbed into the Colonial Office in October 1922— it did not bother Churchill unduly.

Like Lloyd George, Churchill did not have an undue regard for civil servants in general, regarding them often as obstacles to be over-ridden or circumvented whenever possible. Nor was he one to pay much attention to details, especially if they happened to get in the way of whatever policy he was intent upon pursuing. For advice on Ireland, Churchill relied on a most unusual civil servant, Lionel Curtis. A graduate of New College, Oxford, and a member of Milner's 'Kindergarten' in South Africa after the Boer War, Curtis had been instrumental in the founding of the *Round Table*, and was the foremost advocate in England of imperial unity through a Commonwealth of Nations. In September 1921 Lloyd George had summoned Curtis from All Souls to serve as his personal adviser and secretary during the Irish negotiations. After the Treaty was concluded, Churchill moved him to the Colonial Office, where for the next three years he served as 'adviser on Irish affairs'.[29]

Curtis and Churchill tended to view Ireland through the lens of Britain's South African experience—which they regarded as a triumph of liberal statesmanship—with Collins and Griffith clearly cast for the role of Botha and Smuts. Both thought that Ireland, like South Africa, would embrace the imperial connection if she were dealt with firmly, yet fairly. Later, Churchill never forgave the Irish for not conforming to his expectations.

With Churchill in the South of France on holiday, Curtis monitored the debates in the Dáil on the Irish Treaty. They struck him as a sign of 'how terribly deep-seated is the de-

---

[28] G. Whiskard minute to Mark Sturgis, 28 June 1922 (CO (Colonial Office) 739/12/35095)

[29] Curtis to Shawn (his niece), 25 Dec. 1948 (H.A.L. Fisher papers, Box 49).

moralization from which the Irish are suffering'. On the whole, he found the speeches in favour of the Treaty even 'more deplorable' than those against it. What concerned him most was how many

frankly took the line that the Treaty should be accepted because it was the best which Ireland could get for the moment. Among other things she would get an army which would enable her later on to exact further demands. ... All this seems quite compatible in the Irish mind with the frequent references to England as a notorious breaker of treaties. It is the most amazing piece of unconscious self-revelation I ever remember to have seen.

But Curtis did not take the debates 'too tragically'. That the Irish were discussing the issues in the Dáil was a relief in itself. He compared Ireland to an uninhabited room, 'the windows and doors of which have been closed shut for years. When at last they are opened the atmosphere which comes out of them is not likely to smell particularly sweet or wholesome. It will clear itself in time.' Curtis believed that the line taken by the pro-Treaty speakers in the Dáil was dictated by the unrepresentative nature of the 'Khaki Parliament'. If an election for a new legislature were to take place, he was convinced that the 'saner element of Irish life' would assert itself, and the resulting government would assume the British position 'that the Treaty represents a final settlement'. His biggest worry was that the split between the pro-Treaty and the anti-Treaty factions might be repaired. Fears in Dublin that civil war might break out, he told Edward Grigg, considerably relieved 'the anxiety with which we have watched the developments since the Dáil met ... From all we can gather the split between the "rats" and the "anti-rats" goes as deep as anything can go.'[30]

Even after the Treaty was passed by the Dáil, the attempts by Collins to reconcile the two Irish groups were looked upon with distrust by Curtis and Churchill, who feared that such a grouping might try to assert its right to become the Provisional Government. It thus became one of the paramount objectives of British policy during 1922 to see that such a *rapprochement*

---

[30] Curtis to Edward Grigg, Jan. 1922 (Thomas Jones papers, Class 6: Ireland, iii, 1).

did not occur, and to promote by whatever means possible the elimination of de Valera and the republican faction associated with him. This eventually proved to be the decisive factor in the outbreak of the Irish civil war.

2

The Threat From
Salisbury

You say we might 'have conceivably a Mond–Montagu–Samuel–
Sassoon government.' Is that not very much what we *have* got?
Jews have lost us India. A Jew has played the devil in Palestine.
Who appointed these persons? How could they have attained immense power if the government was not of their complexion? And
why are most important Conferences held at Lympne under Sassoon's auspices, if this is not the case?

Sydenham to Strachey, June 18, 1921

BRITISH policy towards Ireland during 1922 cannot be fully
explained without some reference to the diehard movement.[1]
Although composed of many disparate elements, it found its
inspiration in Ireland; and although never strong enough to
determine Government policy on Ireland, by its very existence
it exerted a profound influence on the nature of that policy.

The diehard movement had its roots in the conservative
reaction to the revolutionary surge sweeping Europe in the
wake of the Bolshevik Revolution in Russia in 1917.[2] Within
the movement there was a widespread fear that international
Communism lay at the root of the problems facing the Empire
in India, Palestine, Egypt, and Ireland. The more frenetic
diehards were even convinced that Communists and Jews (the
two terms were interchangeable) had infiltrated the Government and were undermining the Empire from within. The
septuagenarian Lord Sydenham, a former Governor of Mad-

---

[1] For the diehard impact on Conservative policy after the First World War, see
David Close, 'Conservatives and Coalition after the First World War', *Journal of
Modern History*, 45, 2(1973), 240–60.
[2] The clash between the so-called 'parties of movement' and the 'parties of order'
has been stimulatingly and exhaustively chronicled in Arno Mayer's *Political Origins
of the New Diplomacy, 1917–1918* (New Haven, 1959), and *Politics and Diplomacy of
Peacemaking* (New York, 1967).

ras and Secretary of the Committee of Imperial Defence, was
one of the foremost proponents of this view. In his mind de
Valera was transformed into a 'Spanish Jew' and any concession to Sinn Féin 'assassins' was seen as a disaster for England
and the Empire. 'If we are ever to know what Ireland really
wants,' he told Salisbury in August 1921, 'the Terror must be
broken up at any cost. It is all very like Russia, and at the
back of the IRA is Bolshevism. A Red Army in Ireland could
set up a Soviet and proceed to loot in the best Russo-Jewish
style.' Sydenham further warned that the country was in the
hands of Jews who were 'withholding the truth in order to
create an atmosphere favourable to the P.M.'s concessions'.[3]

The settlement with Sinn Féin in December did nothing to
assuage diehard fears. 'If fighting begins the loyalists are
doomed,' the Duke of Northumberland warned Salisbury five
months later.

Our first duty is to them. The next step is to warn the country of
the real nature of the Irish danger, i.e. that it is an attempt on the
part of the international revolutionism [sic] to turn Ireland into a
Western Russia—an advanced base for an attack on the British
Empire. There will be a Soviet terror in Ireland in the course of two
or three months. The intention is to extend that Terror to these
shores by a campaign of sabotage, etc. the machinery for which
exists in the shape of the Irish Self-Determination League and the
Communist Societies. There is an immense amount of money available in America in the hands of German Jews for supporting this
movement. You know I have always said this would happen and it
is all coming true.

The third step is to reconquer Ireland and crush the terror. But
this can only be done when the British people are convinced of the
danger.[4]

Had these been the views of isolated eccentrics, they would
be of little significance. But Sydenham was a respected elder
statesman and Northumberland a politician of considerable
ability who, had his views been not quite so extreme, might
have risen to high office. As it was, Northumberland was
widely sought after as a speaker for public meetings, and in

---

[3] Sydenham to Salisbury, 19 Aug. 1921 (Salisbury papers, S(4), Box 22, Bundle 98/59).
[4] Northumberland to Salisbury, 30 May 1922 (Salisbury papers, S(4), 22/101/139).

1923 he was elected President of the Conservative Party's National Union. He also found ventilation for his opinions in the *National Review* and the *Morning Post*. The latter, the leading diehard daily, was edited by H.A. Gwynne, an imperialist of the Joseph Chamberlain school, and owned until 1924 by Lady Bathurst, when it was bought by a group of right-wing Conservatives led and financed by Northumberland. (Many of the paper's leaders were written by Ian Colvin, who later was chosen fittingly to write the official biography of Edward Carson, while the vitriolic outpourings of its Irish correspondent, C.H. Bretherton, were later collected in a book entitled *The Real Ireland*.)[5]

There was just enough truth in the diehard claims about Ireland to lend them credibility, especially to those who needed little convincing in the first place. While the main Sinn Féin leaders, whether Collins and Griffith on the right, or de Valera on the left, showed no interest in transforming the nationalist struggle against Britain into a revolutionary crusade against imperialistic capitalism, there were some within Sinn Féin who did think along those lines.[6] And while the political approach of Irish labour leaders tended to be reformist or mildly syndicalist, despite their professed attachment to James Connolly's Marxist gospel, the memory of fiery Jim Larkin—temporarily domiciled in a New York jail—had not entirely faded with the years. Nor were the diehards the only ones to see international conspiracies at work in Ireland. Philip Kerr, one of Lloyd George's close personal advisers, also thought he detected an international conspiracy at work trying to undermine the British Empire. But he located the source as being the Anglo-Irish community in the United States rather than the Bolsheviks in Russia.[7] Similarly, Churchill, never one to minimize the threat from international Bolshevism and organ-

---

[5] The reactionary views of the *Morning Post* and the *National Review* were reinforced by the influential *Spectator*, edited by John St. Loe Strachey, who predicted that, without the British in control, 'Southern Ireland is probably condemned to be one of the worst governed states in the world—a land of civil disorder and intimidation, over-shadowed by the selfish and suffocating power of a reactionary sacerdotal caste.' (*Spectator*, 10 Dec. 1921.)

[6] See e.g. C. Desmond Greaves, *Liam Mellows and the Irish Revolution* (London, 1971); and Donal Nevin, 'Radical Movements in the Twenties and Thirties' in T. Desmond Williams (ed.), *Secret Societies in Ireland* (New York, 1973), pp. 166-79.

[7] Kerr to Lloyd George, 14 Sept. 1921 (Lloyd George papers, F/34/2/7).

ized labour—the two threats tended to blend in his mind—
often failed to distinguish Sinn Féin from Bolshevism. When so
intelligent and well-informed a man could hold such views, it
is not at all surprising that dyed-in-the-wool Tories like the
diehards would share them. Finally, despite the efforts of the
Provisional Government to put them down, agrarian disturbances remained fairly widespread in Ireland through 1922,
causing exaggerated fright in the diehard camp, many of
whom had large landholdings in Ireland and England.

The diehards were a very English group. Most were country
gentry and ex-army officers. They generally represented tradi-
tionally Conservative rural and south-eastern districts, and
were especially heavily concentrated in the West End of London. What diehard sentiment there was in the North was
centred around Liverpool and Glasgow, cities with a large
percentage of Irish immigrants, and a correspondingly high
rate of anti-Irish backlash.[8] University seats were also extremely conservative. Four holders of English and Scottish
University seats—three of whom were diehards—voted
against the Irish Treaty.

Although opposition to the Coalition Government was the
main unifying element in their policy, it was the Irish question
which first caused them to coalesce into an organized group.
On 31 October 1921, thirty-two diehard MPs supported a
motion of non-confidence on the Government's policy of negotiations with Sinn Féin. As virtually all other Conservative MPs
supported the Government on the issue (the total vote was
441 to 45 in its favour), this marks the beginning of the diehard revolt. During the next nine months, five of the eight
main diehard divisions concerned Ireland. While this shows
that the diehards were able to unite on Ireland more easily
than on any other issue, the fact that few non-diehards joined
them in these divisions also demonstrates how isolated they
were from their party.[9]

---

[8] Three Conservative MPs representing Liverpool voted against the Treaty, as did
one from Glasgow. Sir Archibald Salvidge, the leading Liverpool Conservative, described one of these, the diehard retired naval officer Hall, as 'a perfect enigma. He
seems to live in a world of his own, entirely peopled by spies. Everyone who is not a
Tory is either a German, a Sinn Feiner, or a Bolshevik.' (Michael Kinnear, *The Fall
of Lloyd George: The Political Crisis of 1922* (Toronto, 1973), p. 80.)

[9] Kinnear, p. 84.

Ireland became the main diehard grievance against the Coalition for a number of reasons. For some, such as Sydenham and Northumberland, it was the fear of the international Jewish–Bolshevik conspiracy gaining a foothold on Britain's doorstep. For others, like the Cecils, opposition to Celtic nationalism was a matter of principle and family tradition. But most diehards were motivated by a close personal relationship with Ireland. At least half of the diehard MPs were Irishmen or had close Irish connections such as Irish parents.[10]

The leader of this small band of right-wingers was Colonel John Gretton, a brewer who had been in Parliament since 1895, but had never held office, a common diehard grievance. Though he appears to have been alienated from the Coalition by its efforts to appease the Temperance movement, he did not renounce the Conservative whip until July 1921, when Lloyd George began negotiating with Sinn Féin. Steeped in Irish Protestant folklore, Gretton was convinced that Sinn Féin was the latest in a long line of Catholic conspiracies aimed at nothing less than the total extermination of the Protestants in Ireland.[11]

During 1922 Gretton's group of diehards merged with the remnants of Henry Page Croft's National Party on the Irish issue.[12] Since its founding in 1917, the National Party had campaigned energetically for a wide range of reactionary issues, including the repression of Sinn Féin. Although this new group had Northumberland as its public symbol, and the *National Review* and the *Morning Post* as its organs, by itself it carried little political weight in the Conservative Party. What made the diehards matter was the adherence of Salisbury.

James Edward Hubert Gascoyne-Cecil, fourth Marquess of Salisbury, was important because of his vast network of connections. Not only was he on close terms with men like Bonar Law, but, as head of one of England's great aristocratic families, he was related to many of the most powerful peers in the realm. From his father, the last peer ever to be prime minister, the 60-year-old Salisbury inherited the 'Cecil tradition of con-

[10] Ibid. p. 79.
[11] Gretton to Churchill, 26 July 1922 (CO 739/15/35922).
[12] See William D. Rubinstein, 'Henry Page Croft and the National Party, 1917–22', *Journal of Contemporary History*, 9 (1974), 129–48.

tempt for the Irish as a Celtic Catholic race'.[13] An honest if
tactless parliamentarian, and an uncompromising enemy of
Irish nationalism in any guise, Salisbury personified the protest of the old landed classes against the new industrial and
more progressive spirit in the Conservative Party. Even when
he knew he was beaten, he felt obliged to vote against the
Treaty.[14] During 1922 Salisbury served as a bridge between
the diehards and the rest of the Conservative Party. Although
always voting with the diehards, he was careful to keep his
rhetoric restrained and to see that his views on Ireland did
not separate him from those who, like Bonar Law, were taking
a more moderate stand. He was to be rewarded for his pains
when the Coalition finally collapsed in October.

Salisbury's younger brothers, Robert and Hugh, shared
with him an almost quixotic devotion to Conservative ideals.
All were men of pronounced views, with a religious, almost
clerical cast to their ideas and even their appearances (another
brother became a bishop, and Robert always had a cross
hanging from his waistcoat pocket). They considered the
Coalition Government unprincipled and looked forward to its
early demise. Of the three, Robert Cecil had the most liberal
outlook, and did not vote against the Treaty. (His passion was
the League of Nations, and from 1923 to 1945 he was the
President of the League of Nations Union.) Hugh Cecil, on
the other hand, was an outspoken diehard opponent of the
Treaty. Regarding the Irish question as a 'moral question and
not a political question', he maintained that the only hope of
its ever being solved was 'the hope that is always before man-
kind of some moral improvement'. Asking 'Ulstermen to come
under a Government which is dominated by murder', he asserted, was 'asking them to take a step down in civilization'.[15]

In addition to his brothers, Salisbury's family connections
included his cousin, Arthur James Balfour (created Earl of
Balfour in 1922), and his brother-in-law, William Waldegrave
Palmer, the second Earl of Selborne. One of the few English
politicians ever to have benefited politically from governing
Ireland, 'Bloody Balfour' had advanced from Chief Secretary

---

[13] J.L. Hammond to Gilbert Murray, 15 Apr. 1922 (Hammond papers, Box 2).
[14] Salisbury to Bonar Law, 12 Dec. 1921 (Bonar Law papers, 107/1/92).
[15] *Parl. Deb. Commons*, vol. 149, col. 72 of 14 Dec. 1921.

eventually to succeed his uncle, the third Marquess of Salisbury, as prime minister from 1901 to 1905. As Lord President of the Council, and distinguished elder statesman in the Cabinet, Balfour had considerable influence on Government policy. Despite a well-deserved reputation for taking everything philosophically, he generally favoured a strong line on Ireland and on the question of Ulster.

At sixty-two, Selborne also had an impressive career behind him, including service as Under-Secretary to Joseph Chamberlain at the Colonial Office, First Lord of the Admiralty under Balfour, and High Commissioner for South Africa from 1905 to 1910. One of the first to earn the epithet 'diehard' for opposition to the Parliament Act of 1911, Selborne resigned from the Coalition Government in 1916 over its attempt to reach an Irish settlement. His deep aversion to Lloyd George caused him subsequently to decline offers from him of the Viceroyalty of India, the Viceroyalty of Ireland, and a marquessate. After 1921, though accepting that a majority in the country and in the Conservative Party backed Lloyd George in offering Dominion status to Ireland, he supported Craig because 'an Ulster government and parliament could alone save us from the worse consequences of their [the Government's] policy, the independence of any part of Ireland, and I think we are now saved from that'. The time for the diehards' policy would come only if the Irish proved either utterly intransigent in their demands for independence, or incapable of governing. 'Then', he assured Salisbury, 'the position could be retrieved thru' the bridgehead of Ulster. You and I think that the [Government] policy cannot possibly succeed ... I think the Irish are an utterly irrational, incomprehensible and contemptible race, and I do not regard it as [?] impossible that they may be slobbering the King with loyalty (!) before twelve months are passed.'[16]

Of the remaining diehards little need be said. Sir Wilfred Ashley, the son-in-law of Sir Ernest Cassel, was a wealthy country squire with an estate in Ireland which had once belonged to Palmerston (where Ashley's son-in-law, the Earl Mountbatten of Burma, was later murdered). Ashley performed various functions such as chairman of the Anti-Socialist

[16] Selborne to Salisbury, 19 July 1921 (Salisbury papers, S(4) 22/97/90-3).

Union and president of the Navy League. Ronald McNeill (later Lord Cushendun), an Ulster Unionist of Scotch-Irish descent and the author of *Ulster's Stand for Union*, had won acclaim for hurling a blue book at Churchill during a pre-war debate on Home Rule. He later held minor posts in government after the fall of Lloyd George.

By itself, the diehard movement would never have amounted to much. But the mere fact of its existence, at a time when there was already serious disaffection within the ranks of the Coalition, severely constrained the range of policy options on Ireland open to the Government. Any thought of coercing Ulster, for example, was almost out of the question with Bonar Law holding such a pivotal position between the diehards and the rest of the Conservative Party. Diehard pressure on the Government from without also tended to reinforce the influence within the Cabinet of ministers like Churchill, who favoured a right-wing approach on most issues, at the expense of Lloyd George, who might otherwise have been more flexible.

The diehards might have had even more influence on Government policy had not the great majority of the Irish peers and those peers having a vested interest in Ireland followed the lead of Lords Midleton and Lansdowne in supporting the Treaty.[17] Lansdowne, former Foreign Secretary and Viceroy of India, who had been instrumental in blocking the attempted Home Rule settlement in 1916,[18] supported the Treaty only because he felt there was no other choice.[19] Similarly, Midleton, leader of the Irish Unionists in the House of Lords, thought the outlook 'nearly hopeless' just after the Treaty was signed, and fed Salisbury's fears

[17] The following Irish peers, or peers having interests in Ireland, voted for the Treaty: the Earls of Brandon, Desart, Drogheda, Donoughmore, Dunraven, Midleton, Pirrie, Wicklow, Oransmore, and Browne; Lords Castlemaine, Fingall, Hemphill, McDonnell, and Monteagle; the Marquess of Sligo and the Lord-Lieutenant, Viscount Fitzalan.

[18] See David W. Savage, 'The Attempted Home Rule Settlement of 1916', *Éire-Ireland*, 2, 3 (1967), 132-45. Lansdowne inherited 94,983 acres in Co. Kerry alone, together with sizeable additional holdings in Co. Meath, Queen's Co., Dublin, and Limerick. See John Bateman, *The Great Landowners of Great Britain and Ireland* (London, 1883, rep. New York, 1970). Much of Lansdowne's holdings had presumably been sold off under the terms of the various land acts.

[19] Lansdowne to Salisbury, 27 Dec. 1921 (Salisbury papers, S(4) 22/99/183-5).

by wailing that the South of Ireland was a 'prey to chaos and plunder'.[20] Yet these same Unionists gathered together in January to pledge their support to the new Provisional Government.

By their support of the Treaty, the Anglo-Irish peers performed a valuable service: they undermined the diehard argument that the British Government was 'selling out' the loyalists in the South of Ireland. In so doing they greatly assisted the Provisional Government in its attempt to restore order and stability in the South, since a disproportionate amount of commerce and industry was owned by the Anglo-Irish. In return, they were allotted a small political role in the Free State Senate (later abolished by de Valera). But far more important—and almost unique following revolutionary disturbances in modern times—they were allowed to retain their old estates and way of life as best they could in the face of the onslaught of the twentieth century without having to contend with any serious ill-feeling from the Irish Government and people.

The diehards could pose a serious threat to the Government's Irish policy only if there was a major shift in English public opinion which would enable them to combine with the more moderate Conservative elements under Bonar Law. Despite the ambiguous nature of the debates in the Dáil on the Treaty—which gave the *Morning Post* ample scope for its fulminations[21]—no such change appeared likely in early 1922. The mood in the British press was generally one of sympathy for the pro-Treaty faction and hope for peace. 'As far as England is concerned,' commented the Conservative *Daily Mail*, 'there is only one feeling and hope: that the experiment now about to begin may bring happiness and prosperity to Ireland.'[22] Despite de Valera's 'perversity of thought', which, according to the Liberal *Westminster Gazette*, had 'so often in the last six months come near to wrecking all our hopes of peace',[23] the press on the whole remained optimistic.

[20] Midleton to Salisbury, 28 Dec. 1921 (Salisbury papers, S(4) 22/99/187-8).
[21] *Morning Post*, 7 Jan. 1922.
[22] *Daily Mail*, 9 Jan. 1922.
[23] *Westminster Gazette*, 9 Jan. 1922.

They were not alone. 'We must now await developments in Ireland,' wrote Walter Long to Bonar Law, 'but I really believe there is a prospect of Peace—a wonderful result after all those years.'[24]

[24] Walter Long to Bonar Law, 3 Jan. 1922 (Bonar Law papers, 107/2/2).

PART I

THE TREATY PRESERVED

3

Defending the Treaty

> If I were asked to suggest how and why the treaty survived the turmoil of 1922, I should say owing to your personal success in making Irishmen for the first time in History feel that Englishmen were to be trusted to keep faith.
>
> Lionel Curtis to Churchill, 18 November 1928

> The session closed peacefully with a quiet Irish debate. I think things may yet turn out well there. Extraordinary people! They are all paying their taxes. Revenue is up to the mark: cattle trade roaring. Record entries for the horse show. And civil war galore! All that they cd. desire.
>
> Churchill to Clementine Churchill, 4 August 1922

ON 7 January 1922 the Dáil approved the Treaty by a vote of 64 to 57. De Valera immediately resigned. Although the margin was not as wide as had been hoped, the British Government was confident that the split between the pro-Treaty and anti-Treaty factions was deep and lasting, and was pleased with the composition of the Provisional Government, headed by Collins and Griffith, which according to the Treaty would serve as a caretaker government until new elections could be held to replace the old Dáil.[1] A short time later, Dublin Castle, symbol of British authority in Ireland, was formally turned over to the new Government. Announcing that 'We do not wish to continue responsible one day longer than is absolutely necessary,' Churchill ordered that 'ostentatious' preparations to quit Ireland begin everywhere.[2]

---

[1] A departmental committee at the Colonial Office had estimated that the Dáil would ratify the Treaty by a majority of about 20. Tom Jones to Hankey, 30 Dec. 1921 (Jones, iii, p. 191); Curtis to Grigg, Jan. 1922 (Thomas Jones papers, Class G; Ireland, iii, 1); and Chamberlain to Lady Chamberlain, 8 Jan. 1922 (Austen Chamberlain papers, AC 6/1/476).

[2] Winston S. Churchill, *The World Crisis: The Aftermath* (London, 1929), p. 330.

With the Treaty accepted, the British had two paramount
objectives in Ireland. The first was to see that a responsible
government with a mandate from the people was established
in the South. This could be accomplished only if the Provisional Government could establish its authority and hold an
election. The second was to ensure the survival of the Government of Northern Ireland by preventing its overthrow by the
IRA. For Churchill the two objectives went hand in hand. He
did not believe that the North would be secure until the Provisional Government got the situation in hand in the South.
Nor, so long as pogroms were taking place against the Catholics in Belfast, could the Provisional Government be expected
to restrain the IRA from intervening in the North.

At first things did not seem unhopeful. On 21 January Collins and Sir James Craig met at the Colonial Office in London
under Churchill's auspices to see if they could reconcile their
differences. Both men had good reason to seek an accord.
Craig needed a respite from IRA attacks while the Northern
Government attempted to re-establish order. Moreover, he
hoped to end the disruptive boycott of Belfast goods which the
South had imposed in retaliation for the anti-Catholic attacks
in the North. For his part, Collins wanted to see his co-reli-
gionists in the North protected while his government was
establishing order in the South.

The two men reached agreement in what was called the
Craig–Collins pact. Craig agreed to safeguard the Northern
Catholics from persecution; Collins to end the boycott of Belfast goods. The pact was widely hailed by the British press as
a step towards Irish unity.[3] Nor was optimism over the accord
limited to the press. 'What a confirmation of our hopes! What
a justification for our action!', exulted the normally restrained
Austen Chamberlain to his sister. 'I can think of nothing else.
I knew that it must come, but I did not dare to expect it so
soon ... Collins and Craig to make their own treaty. Thank
God for that.'[4]

The optimism was premature. Within a week the Craig–
Collins pact dissolved amid mutual recriminations. The problem concerned the proposed Boundary Commission. While

---

[3] *Liverpool Post*, 23 Jan. 1922.
[4] Chamberlain to Ida, 21 Jan. 1922 (Austen Chamberlain papers, AC 5/1/225).

Collins hoped the Commission would reduce the size of Northern Ireland by at least two counties, Craig refused to accept
that its terms of reference would allow it to make anything
more than minor border rectifications.

On 2 February Collins and Craig met again in an attempt
to break the deadlock, but neither would give way on a matter
each considered of vital importance. This placed the British
Government in an embarrassing position. While it dared not
pressure Craig, neither could it put overt pressure on Collins
because of the 'serious risk that Mr. Griffith and Mr. Collins
will share the fate of Mr. Redmond and Mr. Dillon'.[5] The
Liberal press, led by the *Daily News*, was adamant that the
boundary question was a matter for the Irish themselves to
settle, and that 'on no account should the Government suffer
itself to be dragged back again at the bidding of Sir James
Craig or another into this vortex of Irish politics'.[6] But Conservative support for Craig was even stronger in the face of
what was widely interpreted as a threat to Ulster's survival as
a state. The Conservative *Sunday Express* questioned whether
the Conservative ministers could carry the majority of their
own supporters on a proposal which meant giving Ulster
counties or parts of counties a kind of local option to leave
Ulster and join the South. 'It is not too much to say', it
commented, 'that the very existence of the Government is
menaced by the dreadful alternative of a complete breakdown
of the Irish settlement on the one hand, or a devastating
Conservative revolt on the other.'[7]

Churchill worked skillfully to defuse the rising diehard agitation over Ireland. Even the mounting list of casualties in
Belfast—where thirty people were killed between 11 and 16
February—left him undismayed. 'These theatrical Irishmen
are enjoying themselves enormously,' he reassured his wife,

& apart from a few cruel things vy little blood is shed.
Our position is a vy strong one, *so long* as we adhere to the Treaty.
And Ulster's position is a vy strong one *so long as she respects the Law*.
I have made it clear I will defend or conceal no illegalities or irre-
gularities of any kind. I will expose them coldly to Parliament

[5] Memo by Curtis for the Irish Technical Committee at the Colonial Office, 4
Feb. 1922 (CO 739/5/17115).
[6] *Daily News*, 4 Feb. 1922.   [7] *Sunday Express*, 5 Feb. 1922.

whoever is guilty. We must not get back into that hideous bog of reprisals, from which we have saved ourselves.[8]

On 16 February Churchill introduced the Irish Free State Bill implementing the Treaty. Despite the hostility generated by the boundary controversy, the bill passed easily by 302 votes to 60. But this was not the end of the matter. Although Churchill was able to persuade Collins to tone down his rhetoric on the boundary question, disaffection in the Conservative Party over the issue continued to spread, causing even the usually placid Balfour to begin to wonder exactly what the Government had committed itself to with the Boundary Commission. Birkenhead assured him that Collins was exaggerating the likely results for political reasons, and that this had no foundation whatever 'except in his over-heated imagination'. If and when Collins and Griffith obtained a majority and a 'sane' parliament, the Lord Chancellor thought it likely they would come to terms with Craig. If not, he was convinced 'that the Tribunal, not being presided over by a lunatic, will reach a rational conclusion'.[9] Similarly, Churchill urged upon Salisbury the need for restraint until passions had cooled, at which time the border issue could be amicably settled along the lines of the Craig–Collins Pact.[10]

Fortunately for the Government, this was also the line being taken by Bonar Law, who considered any attempt to define the terms of reference of the Boundary Commission to be 'the height of folly, not only from the point of view of the United Kingdom, but of Ulster itself'. Law feared that British intervention over the Commission would bring chaos in the South and the recrudescence of problems with the United States and the Dominions. Far better for the South to break the Treaty, in which case they could hope for 'a pretty universal feeling in this country in favour of Ulster'.[11]

The Treaty envisioned the surrender of British military installations and bases to the armed forces of a democratically elected government in the South of Ireland. But what would

[8] Quoted by Gilbert, *Churchill*, iv, p. 689.
[9] Birkenhead to Balfour, 3 Mar. 1922 (Austen Chamberlain papers, AC 30/1/27).
[10] Churchill to Salisbury, 24 Mar. 1922 (Salisbury papers, S(4) 22/100/120).
[11] Bonar Law to Charles Ker, 9 Mar. 1922 (Bonar Law papers, 107/4/27).

be the Government's response to a *coup d'état* by de Valera before the elections, or if he won a majority in favour of a republic at the elections? These were questions raised on 14 February by General Sir Nevil Macready, the British Commander-in-Chief in Ireland, whose job it was to supervise the withdrawal of British troops from the South. Unless instructed otherwise, Macready intended to set the Provisional Government aside immediately and declare martial law in Dublin.[12]

A good administrator, with a demonstrated ability for adapting to unfamiliar and complicated situations, Macready was no alarmist.[13] Unlike most British officers, he had Liberal sympathies and had deplored the unconstitutional behaviour of the Unionists in 1914. He had been disgusted, moreover, by the activities of the Black and Tans, and was a consistent advocate of Home Rule throughout the struggle of 1920–1. But his experience in command of British troops in Belfast during the crisis of 1914 and as Commander-in-Chief in Ireland since April 1920 had imbued him with a distaste for Irish affairs and an exaggerated contempt for politicians and their doings.[14] During February and March of 1922 Macready was growing increasingly concerned about the inability or unwillingness of the Provisional Government to assert its control in the South and to restrain the IRA in Ulster.[15]

Until 18 February Macready's superior was Sir Henry Wilson. A man of strong passions, and much given to intrigue, Wilson came from an Irish Protestant background in County Longford. His devotion to Ulster had carried him to the point of treason—some say beyond—against the Liberal Government during the Ulster crisis in 1914. So flagrant was his contempt for Irish Catholics ('natives') and politicians ('frocks') that by 1922 he had almost totally estranged himself from the Cabinet. His solution to the Irish question was the

[12] Gilbert, *Churchill*, iv, p. 689.

[13] He did, however, disagree with Churchill upon occasion, who in a moment of pique wrote, 'I have never thought much of Macready's work in Ireland'. Churchill to Sir Laming Worthington-Evans: not sent. 25 Feb. 1922 (Martin Gilbert (ed.), *Winston S. Churchill, Companion*, iv, 3 (Documents 1921–1922) (London, 1978).

[14] Townshend, pp. 74–5.

[15] Report by the GOC-in-C Ireland (Macready) on the Situation in Ireland, for the week ending 18 Mar. 1922, CP (Cabinet Paper) 3879 of 2 Mar. 1922 (CAB 24/134).

reconquest of the South. Although he recognized that this would not be feasible until British public opinion had been won over, in the meantime he wanted the British troops being withdrawn from the South to be stationed in Ulster rather than returned to Britain. When he did not get his way, he retired from the Army and went to Ulster to offer the Northern Government military advice and to enter politics.[16]

The Earl of Cavan, Wilson's replacement as CIGS, provided an almost total contrast with his flamboyant predecessor. Mild and unassuming, with no pretensions to brilliance or desire for intrigue, Cavan was content to leave politics to the politicians. Convinced of the need for retrenchment of an army overstretched on almost every front, he tended to view Ireland almost entirely in military terms as a burden on limited resources, the sooner ended the better, rather than as a field for eventual reconquest.

During March Macready began concentrating his remaining troops in Ireland in the vicinity of Dublin and the Curragh to await the results of the upcoming election in the South. Despite despondent reports on the situation emanating from Macready, Churchill remained optimistic about the eventual outcome. 'There is no doubt Ireland is settling down in many ways', he wrote to Lloyd George on 8 March, 'and the Provisional Government are getting a stronger grip every day. . . . All I can hear points to a heavy defeat of De Valera at the polls. A decisive pronouncement by the Irish People in favour of the Free State and against a Republic will be a dazzling event . . .[17]

The rising tide of murders and outrages against the Catholics in Belfast—some perpetrated by the quasi-military Protestant B Specials—together with continued IRA activities in the North prompted Churchill at the end of March to organize an elaborate conference at the Colonial Office with the object of ending the violence and settling the details of the relationship between North and South. While an accord was reached there on 30 March, it had little practical effect, and violence in the North only increased.

---

[16] Bernard Ash, *The Lost Dictator: A Biography of Field Marshall Sir Henry Wilson* (London, 1968), p. 176.
[17] Quoted by Gilbert, *Churchill*, iv, p. 697.

Nor were things any better in the South. Despite the existence of two separate armies, one loyal to the Provisional Government and the other to the IRA Executive, the lines between the two were not always easily drawn, and neither side wanted a real split if it could be avoided. But compromise continued to be what the British feared most.

By early April Churchill had lost much of his earlier optimism. Although still professing confidence in the good faith of the leaders of the Provisional Government, he felt that they were 'obviously afraid of a breach with their extremists and have not shown themselves on any single important occasion capable of standing up to them'. There was no doubt that the Irish had 'a genius for conspiracy rather than for government. The Government is feeble, apologetic, expostulatory; the conspirators, active, audacious and utterly shameless.' He now feared a Republican revolution in Dublin, in which the Provisional Government 'would no doubt go on parleying until they were bundled into prison or, what is not impossible, make terms with the victorious Republicans'. Taking it for granted that Britain would not recognize a republic under any circumstances, and that 'the mere fact of its being brought into being would constitute an act of war between it and the British Empire', Churchill drew up plans to meet such a contingency. In the event of a war between Britain and an Irish republic, he envisioned the British holding Dublin and possibly certain other ports, with a military line protecting the North, while simultaneously imposing a blockade on the republic and using aerodromes around Dublin and in the North to attack hostile concentrations. In that posture he thought that they 'could sit down for a considerable time until Ireland came to her senses, without any great expense or inconvenience'.[18]

The Cabinet discussed the Irish situation on 5 April. In the face of mounting criticism from within the Coalition, Lloyd George's attitude was stiffening. The Cabinet agreed that an Irish republic was out of the question, but there was some doubt as to the practicability of applying military pressure on the Provisional Government for fear the situation might revert to what it had been before the truce in 1921. Economic

---

[18] Churchill, draft Cabinet memo of 4 Apr. 1922, later circulated to the Cabinet on 11 Apr. 1922 (Gilbert, *Churchill, Companion* iv, 3, pp. 1846–50).

pressure in the form of a blockade was considered, but there was concern that foreign countries might exploit the opportunity to increase their own trade with Ireland and thus defeat its purpose. The Cabinet finally decided to approve the issue to the Provisional Government of further consignments of arms as recommended by Macready, and to authorize the appointment of a CID subcommittee to consider the Irish situation and what military measures might be necessary 'to meet certain contingencies'.[19]

Meanwhile the War Office had become alarmed at the prospect of renewed military involvement in Ireland. Cavan thought that Churchill did not take sufficiently seriously the enormity of the problems involved in such a task. Just to hold down important centres in Ireland, he pointed out at a meeting of the Irish Situation Committee on 10 April, would require an addition of 100,000 men to the Army, provided that the opposing forces did not concentrate themselves into commandos.[20] Two days later the CIGS submitted a memorandum to the Committee refuting Churchill's idea of using flying columns against Irish Republicans, arguing that they would be merely 'beating the air'. Cavan was convinced that, if a blockade failed, nothing would bring the Republicans to their senses except 'a large and comprehensive scheme involving the use of very large numbers of troops and the systematic clearing of Ireland area by area and district by district'.[21] This was Macready's view also. On 20 April he told the Irish Committee that, without reinforcements of an additional twenty companies, he would be unable to enforce martial law in Dublin if a republic were declared and generally supported by the Free State.[22]

The War Office's concern about the demands that would be made on the Army in the event of an Irish republic being declared was shared by the Admiralty, whose fears in that regard were heightened during April by reports from the District Intelligence Officer at Queenstown that the split in Sinn Féin was merely bluff, and that an Irish republic would be

declared with the connivance of the Provisional Government
as soon as all the British troops had been withdrawn from
Southern Ireland.[23]

Within Conservative political circles there was some doubt
whether the Coalition Government could 'survive the shock'
of a declaration of an Irish republic.[24] Churchill and the rest
of the Cabinet remained worried that the breach in Sinn Féin
might somehow be healed, or the Provisional Government be
overthrown by the Republicans. They were less concerned
about a violent action than a gradual withering of resolve on
the part of the Provisional Government.[25]

A test of this resolve seemed to come on 14 April, when a
force of Republicans led by Rory O'Connor seized the Four
Courts—the Law Courts of Dublin. Worried that Griffith and
Collins might bow to Republican pressure and postpone elections indefinitely,[26] Churchill urged Cope (former Assistant
Under-Secretary for Ireland, then serving as Chief British liaison with the Provisional Government), to do his utmost to
dissuade them 'from making such a pitiful surrender to a man
[de Valera] who has already broken faith with them and does
not pretend to control his extremists'.[27] Only with difficulty
did Cope restrain Churchill, telling him that public opinion
in Dublin was behind the Provisional Government, which did
not want to create 'dramatic effects and funeral orations';
while the Irregulars, on the other hand, were making themselves very unpopular by their actions, especially in comman-
deering food from the local shops.[28] Writing in a similar vein
on 16 April, Macready assured Churchill that the time would
soon come when Collins and Griffith would be able to 'put
their foot down and assert their authority strongly'.[29] This
convinced Churchill, who was soon informing Lloyd George
that the personal prestige of Collins and Griffith had been
'greatly enhanced by recent events', and that the Provisional

[23] G.M. Crick (District Intelligence Officer) to M.S. Fitzmaurice (Director of Naval Intelligence), 6 Apr. 1922 (CO 739/3/17296).

[24] J.C.C. Davidson (Baldwin's Parliamentary Private Secretary) to Richard Dickinson, 11 Apr. 1922 (Davidson papers).

[25] Fisher to Gilbert Murray, 18 Apr. 1922 (Fisher papers, Box 7).

[26] Gilbert, *Churchill*, iv, p. 709.

[27] Churchill to Cope, 17 Apr. 1922 (CO 739/13/37032).

[28] Cope to Churchill, 14 and 18 Apr. 1922 (ibid.).

[29] Gilbert, *Churchill*, iv, p. 710.

Government was wise to put up with the occupation of the Four Courts 'until public opinion is exasperated with the raiders'.[30]

Again Churchill's optimism was short-lived. During April the Irish Cabinet and its advisers were preoccupied with drafting a constitution for the new Free State. Before long, concern about its eventual nature began dislodging the issue of the Four Courts from Churchill's mind. Any real compromise with de Valera on its drafting would result in a republican constitution and effect a violation of the Treaty. On 29 April Churchill wrote to Collins praising him and Griffith for the development of 'strong, bold, romantic personalities' at the head of the Provisional Government, and urging moderation as the key to Irish unity. 'On both sides the wreckers dread any approach to the idea of a united Ireland as the one fatal blow at their destructive schemes,' he said, adding that while Craig meant to play 'fair and straight', he did not think that Collins would find 'such another man in the whole of the North'. Moreover, Churchill warned, the Ulstermen 'are in a very strong, and in fact inexpugnable, position; and they hold in their hands the key to Irish unity'.[31]

While it was about extremists on both sides that Churchill cautioned Collins, it was an accord between the latter and de Valera that the British wanted most to prevent. 'I am not sorry to see that de Valera and Arthur Griffith are at daggers drawn,' Tom Jones wrote to Hankey on 28 April. 'What I should most fear would be an attempt by Collins to buy De Valera's support by twisting the Constitution into something which we could not possibly accept.'[32] As a warning, Churchill ordered that the rate of evacuation of British troops from Ireland be reduced to only one battalion every three weeks.[33]

On 12 May Churchill held an important conference with Cope and Macready on the Irish situation. Cope said that in his view the 'rebel' IRA was daily gaining strength, and would

---

[30] Churchill to Lloyd George, 19 Apr. 1922 (quoted by Gilbert, *Churchill*, iv, p. 710).

[31] Churchill to Collins, 29 Apr. 1922 (CO 739/13/21011).

[32] Jones, iii, p. 198.

[33] 4th Meeting of ISC, 4 May 1922 (CAB 16/42).

soon be able to involve the British troops in hostilities with all IRA forces. Churchill objected strongly to any further granting of arms to the Provisional Government unless they were used to clear the Irregulars from Dublin, saying that he would regard Collins's attitude towards this proposal as a test of his good faith and a proof of his willingness to re-establish order even at the cost of bloodshed.[34]

The following day Churchill was outraged by the news that negotiations had begun between Collins and de Valera for 'an agreed election'. So great was his excitement that his advisers began to fear that he might do something rash while Lloyd George was away in Genoa and unable to restrain him. Tom Jones noted this concern in his diary:

Curtis came in. He and Masterton-Smith are worried about Churchill. So long as matters seemed to be going smoothly in the early days after the Treaty Churchill was splendid. But he is now so disappointed with the situation that he wants to pull the whole plant out of the ground. It therefore becomes doubly important to secure the early return of the P.M. and I shall write in this sense to Hankey to-day. Meanwhile Curtis and Masterton-Smith will try to get Churchill sent on a holiday.[35]

Churchill was not the only one disappointed with the performance of the Provisional Government. Chamberlain, under mounting Conservative pressure, agreed that the time had come 'to put it across them straight'.[36] On 16 May Chamberlain presided over a Cabinet meeting in Lloyd George's absence during which Churchill was allowed full scope for his anger. After giving the Cabinet his view of the situation, Churchill warned that they might have to re-establish an English 'pale' around Dublin prior to the reconquest of Ireland. 'We must put it to the Provisional Government that they must take effective action to meet the republican challenge to their authority,' he insisted. Chamberlain agreed, while Fitzalan thought that, if anything, Churchill's gloomy description of the state of Ireland underestimated the process of degeneration. Although the Church was in solid support of

[34] Tom Jones diary, 12 May 1922 (Jones, iii, p. 200).
[35] Tom Jones, 15 May 1922 (ibid.).
[36] Chamberlain to Hilda, 13 May 1922 (AC 5/1/237).

the Free State, its influence was no longer very strong, and only a free election could save the situation.[37]

Despite warnings from Churchill that such an election 'would be received with world-wide ridicule and reprobation', and 'be an outrage upon democratic principles',[38] Collins signed a pact with de Valera on 20 May by which it was agreed that the forthcoming election should not be taken as deciding the issue of the Treaty, but as creating a government to preserve peace. The *status quo ante* in the Dáil was to be preserved, and the new ministry would consist of four Republicans and five pro-Treaty members, with the President elected by the Dáil and the Minister for Defence elected by the Army.

Churchill reacted to the Collins–de Valera agreement by summoning Griffith and Collins to London for consultation. It was, he told his colleagues, a case of 'dog won't eat dog'.[39] Although, as Curtis pointed out, there was nothing contrary to the letter of the Treaty in the agreement to 'fake' an election, and the British had themselves set an embarrassing precedent for the pact in their last 'coupon' election, it nevertheless appeared that Collins had 'clearly capitulated' to the Republicans. Since members of the new ministry would presumably be responsible to the new legislature, and must, according to the Treaty, take an oath to the king to which the Republicans could not subscribe, it followed that Collins had agreed with de Valera to establish a government after the elections of a character contrary to the letter of the Treaty. With confidence in Collins abandoned, at least for the moment, Curtis now hoped that Griffith would dissociate himself from the compact and become the 'nucleus for a genuinely constitutional movement'.[40]

In a conference held on 23 May to discuss the new situation resulting from the pact, it soon became clear that Churchill and Curtis were not the only ones whose faith in Collins had been shaken by it. Chamberlain had never really trusted him. Even Macready now asserted that Collins '[was] not playing

[37] Cabinet conclusions of 16 May 1922 (CAB 23/27).
[38] Churchill to Collins, 15 May 1922, quoted by Gilbert, *Churchill*, iv, p. 715.
[39] Meeting of British Signatories to the Treaty with Ireland, 23 May 1922 (CAB 43/1).
[40] Memo by Curtis, 21 May 1922 (CO 739/5/24517).

the game'. While he did not believe Collins deliberately treacherous, Macready thought that by letting matters drift he had fallen into the hands of de Valera, and that until he was prepared to kill things would not be put right. Both Macready and Sir Laming Worthington-Evans, Secretary of State for War, feared that further reprisals against the Nationalists in the North by Craig might have the effect of rallying together the two parties in the South. This also worried Lloyd George, who warned his colleagues that they were drifting into a position of having either to abandon or to reconquer Ireland, and cautioned against any precipitate action such as Churchill appeared to be contemplating. Should it become necessary to act, he argued, it must come on a clear issue on which they could count on the support not only of the British people, but also of the Dominions and America. In his opinion the only thing on which they could fight with the whole Empire behind them was on the issue of allegiance to the king.[41]

On 27 May Collins and Griffith arrived in London with the draft Free State Constitution. It proved to be as extreme as the British had feared. The Crown was reduced to a cipher, the oath was dropped, appeal to the Judicial Committee of the Privy Council was excluded, the right of making their own treaties was claimed, and the special position of Ulster was not recognized. Chamberlain expressed his feelings on the matter to his sister:

Ireland, always Ireland. What a people! It is impossible to explain them or to make them credible. Here have they brought over the draft constitution, and for the moment every other complaint or remonstrance is laid aside, for this is a republic scarcely covered with the monarchial varnish. It is flagrantly at issue with the Treaty in half a dozen vital points. And they seem—nay they are—genuinely surprised that we view it so gravely. They meant it to be the Treaty—of course, the Treaty stretched as far as it can go in their sense—but still the Treaty. If we show them that it is not the Treaty, it shall be changed, but why, oh why, are we so meticulous and pernickety?[42]

For a time it appeared that the situation might be more serious than Chamberlain at first imagined. Collins attempted

[41] Meeting of British Signatories, 23 May 1922 (CAB 43/1).
[42] Chamberlain to Hilda, 28 May 1922 (AC 5/1/240).

to link the Constitution with the state of affairs in Northern Ireland. When Lloyd George threatened a break over the former, Collins flew into a rage, accused him of being incredibly callous about the murders of Ulster Catholics, and even threatened to go back to fight with his old comrades.[43]

Collins's accusations were not lacking in substance, as Lloyd George recognized. While generous in its financial and military support of the Northern Government, the Prime Minister noted, they had done almost nothing to ensure the protection of the Catholic minority in the North. Saying he was 'profoundly concerned with the public presentation of the trouble when it came', he warned the Cabinet that he was 'not sure that Collins was not manoeuvring us into a position where our case was weak'. He 'strongly urged that they should take such steps as would eliminate the Ulster issue and leave a clear issue of Republic versus British Empire', suggesting that this could be done by means of a Judicial Enquiry.[44]

Churchill, on the other hand, took a sterner line against the Provisional Government. While Lloyd George was anxious to secure Liberal support in case of a break, Churchill was increasingly leaning towards the Conservatives. In Cabinet he spoke out strongly in support of the Northern Government, blaming most of the troubles in Ulster on the situation in the South.[45] In the House of Commons Churchill tried to strike a balance between the Provisional and the Ulster Governments by conveniently blaming de Valera for everything from the Ulster boycott to the violence in Belfast, even asserting without any reliable evidence that the IRA in the North was entirely under his control.[46]

Churchill's efforts to dampen the spreading hostility towards the Government's Irish policy were only partially successful. While the Government could still count on the support of the Liberals and Labour, the Conservative camp was becoming increasingly restive.[47] Among others, Sir Samuel Hoare, a prominent Conservative back-bencher who had ex-

[43] Tom Jones diary, 30 May 1922 (Jones, iii, p. 203).
[44] Cabinet conclusions 36(22) 30 May 1922 (CAB 23/30).
[45] Ibid.
[46] *Par. Deb. Commons*, vol. 154, col. 2128 of 31 May 1922.
[47] Chamberlain to Churchill, 11 May 1922 (Gilbert, *Churchill, Companion* iv, 3, p. 1888).

pressed liberal sentiments on Ireland in the past, and who had
moved the address on the Irish Treaty Bill in December, now
spoke out strongly in support of Ulster, urging the Government to 'bring matters to an issue' with Collins.[48]

Rising diehard sentiment in the House of Commons
strengthened Churchill's hand within the Cabinet. As negotiations with the Provisional Government over the Constitution
dragged on into June, the split in the Cabinet between Lloyd
George and .Churchill widened. With Cabinet approval,
Churchill began preparing plans for bringing pressure to bear
on the Provisional Government. 'When we begin to act,' he
told the Irish Committee on 1 June, 'we must act like a sledge
hammer, so as to cause bewilderment and consternation
among the people in Southern Ireland.'[49] Lloyd George
quailed at such talk, earning for himself the retort from
Chamberlain that 'the Irish were fortunate in having a Celt
in the Cabinet to put their case against England'.[50]

The contention between Lloyd George and Churchill was
over tactics, not policy, for neither wanted a break with the
Provisional Government if it could be avoided. Of the two,
Churchill was far more willing to adopt a threatening posture.
The dispute came to a head on 8 June when Churchill sent
7,000 men to recapture the small towns of Pettigo and Belleek
on the northern side of the border, which had been seized a
few days earlier by the IRA, and threatened to resign if Lloyd
George interfered.[51] Fearful that the Government was being
manœuvred into war by border incidents for which he thought
de Valera and Sir Henry Wilson largely responsible, Lloyd
George tried fruitlessly to countermand the order.[52] In private
he compared Churchill to 'a chauffeur who apparently is

[48] *Parl. Deb. Commons*, vol. 154, col. 2128 of 31 May 1922.
[49] 6th Meeting of CID Sub-committee on Ireland, 1 June 1922 (CAB 16/42).
[50] Tom Jones diary, 2 June 1922 (Jones, iii, p. 208).
[51] In this Churchill may have been swayed by personal considerations. His aunt,
Lady Leslie (née Leonie Jerome) lived with her husband Sir John Leslie in Glaslough
Castle, on the Leslie estate in County Monaghan, which covered 32,000 acres and
included much of the town of Pettigo itself. Lady Leslie was just recovering from a
serious illness, and earlier Churchill had expressed alarm to Collins and Griffith after
hearing reports that the IRA had seized the castle. Churchill to Collins and Griffith:
telegram, 20 Mar. 1922 (Gilbert, *Churchill, Companion* iv, 3, p. 1813).
[52] Lloyd George to Churchill: message dictated over the telephone, 8 June 1922
(ibid. p. 1914).

perfectly sane and drives with great skill for months, then
suddenly he takes you over a precipice ... there was a strain
of lunacy'. Moreover, Lloyd George imagined that he detected
in Churchill's behaviour a ploy to win the backing of the
diehards. 'No Churchill was ever loyal,' he told Tom Jones.
'Churchill is fancying himself as a leader of a Tory revolt. He
is trying to copy Disraeli.'[53]

Lloyd George's fears were exaggerated. Belleek was occupied by British troops without loss of life on either side, and
a week later agreement was reached on the new Constitution.
On 16 June Ireland went to the polls. The results seemed to
justify Collins's tactics. Fifty-eight pro-Treaty representatives
were elected against only 35 anti-Treaty, and 34 others.

Just as it appeared that Anglo-Irish relations might be
approaching a more normal footing, violence once again dis-
torted the pattern of events. On 22 June Sir Henry Wilson
(now an Ulster MP) was assassinated by an IRA gunman on
his own doorstep in Eaton Place in London, not far from
the home of his friend Bonar Law. Sir Maurice Hankey, the
Secretary of the Cabinet, who spent the hours following the
assassination with Lloyd George, sent this account to his wife
that same night:

I fear Henry Wilson brought this on himself by his bitter attitude
towards the Irish policy of the Govt. and he was suspected by the
extremists of having caused the anti-Sinn Fein pogroms in Belfast.
He was probably urged on to all this by his wife who is a rabid
fanatic. To Ll. G.'s telegram of sympathy tonight she replied in her
own hand that Henry Wilson's death lies at his door. ... The P.M.
took it very well ... Personally I believe the assassination, though
political, was personal to Henry Wilson, and I don't believe it is
part of any general plot. No one can tell what the political effect
will be. It might mean a stampede of Unionists against the Coalition, but personally I am convinced it will not, unless followed by
other murders ...[54]

The British Government reacted to Wilson's murder by
entreating Collins to break the power of the IRA and in particular to put an end to the continuing Republican occupation
of the Four Courts in Dublin.[55] In a debate in the House of

[53] Tom Jones diary, 8 June 1922 (Jones, iii, p. 212).

[54] Stephen Roskill, *Hankey: Man of Secrets*, ii (London, 1972, p. 265).

[55] Gilbert, *Churchill*, iv, pp. 733–4.

Commons on 26 June Churchill delivered what was widely 'interpreted as an ultimatum' to Griffith and Collins.[56]

As expected, the diehards attempted to seize upon Wilson's assassination as an excuse to bring down the Government, but failed. Even when unhappy with the Government's Irish policy, most Conservatives were not prepared to abandon it when the only likely alternative was a return to the even more distasteful situation that preceded the armistice in 1921. In the end, a motion of censure against the Government was defeated by a vote of 342 to 75. While this represented a considerable weakening of the Government's position since the vote on the Irish Treaty in December, it showed that there was no immediate danger of a serious challenge to its Irish policy being mounted in the House of Commons. An analysis of the voting on the two occasions shows that there was a net change in the voting patterns of only 17 out of over 400. In all, 29 MPs who had abstained or voted with the Government on Ireland in December voted against it in June; while 12 who earlier had opposed the Treaty either abstained or voted with the Government in June. Of the 29 who voted against the Government's Irish policy for the first time on 26 June, 11 were diehards and 12 were military men whose votes may have been swayed at least in part by the temporary emotional issue of a respected Field Marshal's assassination. Only three were of any importance: Ashley, Sir William Joynson-Hicks, an evangelical solicitor, and Lord Eustace Percy, Northumberland's brother and the nephew of the Duke of Argyll, another prominent diehard. A breakdown of the voting on 26 June into percentages shows that only among the diehards was there serious opposition to the Government's policy.[57]

Even for the diehards, general disenchantment with the Coalition Government, rather than just disagreement over its Irish policy, was the strongest motivating factor behind their voting on 26 June. According to Hugh Cecil,

It was not a question of whether the Provisional Government maintain their good faith to restore order. ... We should vote to turn out

[56] *Annual Register* (1922), p. 64.

[57] *Parl. Deb. Commons*, vol. 154, cols. 1699–1808, of 16 June 1922. For a comparison of voting on 26 June with that on other occasions, see Close, 'Conservatives and Coalition after the First World War', p. 253.

the Government because, whatever policy you pursue, they are incompetent to carry it out. . . . They have failed in everything . . .

You are going downhill because you have not got any moral
character . . .[58]

Much as they might deplore the Government's Irish policy,
most diehards realized that there was no going back on it. But
this did not prevent them from using Ireland as a convenient
stick with which to beat the Government. Once again, the
attitude of Bonar Law was crucial. So long as he and other
moderate Conservative leaders in the House of Lords like
Derby and the Duke of Devonshire continued to support the
Treaty, opposition to the Government's Irish policy would not
go beyond threats.

Whether or not the killing of Wilson actually posed a serious
threat to the survival of the Government, Churchill was determined to use it as an excuse for forcing the issue of the Four
Courts. But another pretext for action was provided on 27
June when the Republicans kidnapped the Assistant Chief of
Staff of the Free State Army. Collins retaliated by attacking
the Four Courts the next day.

Churchill received the news of the fighting in Dublin with
ill-concealed excitement. Once the Provisional Government
had committed itself and 'blood [had] flowed in the quarrel',
there was no limit to the support he was willing to lend it. He
immediately implored Macready to turn over his arms and
even tanks to the Provisional Government if he thought they
would know how to use them,[59] while also urging Collins to
distribute arms to the citizens of Dublin and to anyone who
would volunteer to help.[60] In Dublin, Cope was pressing the
Provisional Government 'to get on with it and finish it',[61] but
at the same time telling Curtis that they were 'not anxious to
destroy the whole blooming city'.[62]

In his enthusiasm to support Collins, Churchill overcame
problems of supply and over-rode resistance from the War
Office and the Admiralty, neither of which shared his un-

[58] *Parl. Deb. Commons*, vol. 154, cols. 1806–1808 of 26 June 1922.
[59] Churchill to Macready, 1 July 1922 (CO 739/6/32291).
[60] Churchill to Collins, 2 July 1922 (ibid.).
[61] Cope to Sturgis, 2 July 1922 (ibid.).
[62] Cope to Curtis, 2 July 1922 (ibid.).

bounded confidence in the wisdom of turning over large quantities of weapons to the Provisional Government, and from the Treasury, which doubted whether the cost of the weapons would ever be retrieved by the Exchequer. Churchill characteristically would not be bothered by such matters. His policy, Curtis told Otto Niemeyer, the Controller of Finance at the Treasury, 'now that the Provisional Government have committed themselves to definite action with the rebels is to give them every possible assistance and avoid troubling them with details while the fighting goes on'.[63]

For Churchill it was not enough that fighting had finally broken out in Dublin. He was eager to see British forces become involved at the first sign of any faltering by the Free State troops. Stressing the need to end the fighting in Dublin as soon as possible in order to avert the danger of civil war breaking out throughout Ireland, Churchill suggested to the Irish Committee on 29 June that, if things went badly for the Free State troops, the British should support them by opening fire upon the Four Courts with 6-inch howitzers in Phoenix Park without making any previous announcement of their intentions. Such action might, he thought, tip the scale in favour of the Free State troops and should at least be tried before the British undertook the capture of the Four Courts by definite military operations. In addition, he proposed that the Royal Air Force lend the Free State planes and pilots for use against the Four Courts. This idea met with the approval of Sir Hugh Trenchard, Chief of the Air Staff, who suggested that heavy bombs with delayed action fuses be used which would enable them to penetrate the building and burst for maximum effect. When Cavan objected that such action by the British would create 'a new situation',[64] Churchill turned to the Cabinet for authorization for British troops to assist Free State troops irrespective of the requests or the wishes of the Free State Government.[65] But British intervention proved unnecessary. On 30 June the Republicans in the Four Courts set fire to the building and surrendered. Within a few days the

---

[63] Curtis to Niemeyer, 5 July 1922 (CO 739/6/32291).

[64] 9th Meeting of CID Sub-committee on Ireland, 29 June 1922 (CAB 16/42). In light of such talk, it is ironic to find Churchill later lamenting the loss of historical records in the destruction of the Four Courts (Churchill, *Aftermath*, p. 364).

[65] Tom Jones diary, 29 June 1922 (Jones, iii, p. 213).

Free State Government had Dublin secured, and by the end
of July most of the principal cities in Ireland likewise.

The attack on the Four Courts thus turned out to be the
watershed in Anglo-Irish relations during 1922. Although the
Free State did not come into formal existence for almost
another six months—until 6 December—after the fight for
the Four Courts, there could be no turning back for either
side. Even the death by heart attack of Arthur Griffith on
12 August, followed ten days later by the death by ambush
of Michael Collins, did not disrupt the pattern of events.

Churchill's main bugbear remained the fear of a *rapprochement* between the Republicans and the Free State Government. After the death of Collins he warned Cope:

The danger to be avoided is a sloppy accommodation with a
quasi-repentent De Valera. It may well be that he will take advantage of the present situation to try to get back from the position of
a hunted rebel to that of a political negotiator. You should do
everything in your power to frustrate this ...

The surrender of the rebels or rebel leaders would of course be all
to the good, but it ought not to be in any circumstances followed by
the immediate reappearance of these men defeated in the field as
Members of the Assembly. Having appealed to the sword and having been defeated, they are out of politics for the time being and
ought to be rigorously shut out. Never fail to point out in your
communications with Cosgrave [Acting Chairman of the Provisional
Government], Mulcahy [Minister of Defence and Commander-in-
Chief of Free State Forces] and others that the only hope of a
friendly settlement with the North and of ultimate Irish unity lies in
a clear line being drawn between the Treaty party and the Republicans. Any temporary accommodation which might ease the
situation in the South will be obtained only through the raising up
of a lasting barrier between the North and the South, whereas firmness may easily make the life-sacrifice of Michael Collins a bond of
future Irish unity. Use your utmost endeavours to keep this position
constantly before their eyes, making it clear that you have my
authority for speaking in this sense.[66]

Churchill's anxiety was unnecessary. The new leaders of the
Provisional Government had no intention of compromising
with the Republicans. The debates in the newly elected Dáil
made this clear. The British were especially impressed by the

[66] Churchill to Cope, 24 Aug. 1922 (CO 739/6/43249).

resolution shown by the young Kevin O'Higgins. 'His [O'Higgins's] performance has been admirable!' Sir Francis Greer, the chief legal adviser to the Colonial Office, wrote to Curtis. 'I am amazed by the firmness and loyalty he has shown in taking his stand on the Treaty. Except for the suggestion that the Irish people could repudiate the Treaty?? his attitude has been just what we would have dictated, had we been in a position to do so.'[67]

The civil war in Ireland dragged on until April 1923, outlasting the Coalition Government by six months. Although the war was more destructive and caused greater loss of life than the previous 'Troubles' with Britain had done, and despite Churchill's repeated assurances to the contrary, it did nothing to win over the diehards in Britain or Ulster who, despite all evidence to the contrary, continued to regard the fighting as a 'sham' and 'mainly a farce',[68] and the leaders of the Provisional Government as 'disloyal to the Crown and Empire'.[69] In the end, the events of 1922 left as deep and lasting an imprint on British policy towards Ulster as they did on British relations with the South. Although this study is primarily concerned with British policy towards Southern Ireland, the problems that they encountered in their dealings with the South cannot be appreciated without some account of the influence exerted by continued British involvement in Northern Ireland.

[67] Greer to Curtis, 27 Sept. 1922 (CO 739/15/32939).
[68] Milner diary, 3 July 1922 (Milner papers, 182); 'Memo [by Salisbury?] on Present Position', 5 July 1922 (S(4) 102/22); Londonderry to Masterton-Smith (copy), 19 July 1922 (Londonderry papers, D/LO/C242(9).
[69] Londonderry to Marsh (for Churchill), 7 Oct. 1922 (D/LO/C242(1)).

4

Northern Ireland:
The Politics of Siege

> You ought not to send us a telegram asking for help on the largest possible scale and announce an intention to defy the Imperial Parliament on the same day.
>
> Churchill to Craig, 25 May 1922

> Indeed, I don't think Winston takes any interest in public affairs unless they involve the possibility of bloodshed.
>
> Robert Cecil to Edward Wood, 7 January 1927

THE Government of Northern Ireland was established in May 1921 under the terms of the Government of Ireland Act of 1920. In theory that Act had been intended to confer Home Rule upon the whole of Ireland, but in fact it had provided for separate executives and separate parliaments in the twenty-six counties and in the six counties. A single Lord-Lieutenant to represent the king in both areas, however, and a proposed Council of Ireland consisting of twenty representatives from each parliament were intended to provide the framework for gradual reconciliation and eventual unity between North and South. In the South Home Rule was already a dead issue by the time the Act was passed. In the North it was accepted reluctantly as the only alternative to rule by Dublin.[1]

The basic principle underlying the Constitution of Northern Ireland was that of devolution. Northern Ireland was not a sovereign state. It resembled in some respects a United King-

---

[1] For a good introduction to the problem of Northern Ireland, see F.S.L. Lyons, *Ireland Since the Famine* (London, paperback edn., 1973), pp. 695-780. See also Patrick Buckland, *The Factory of Grievances: Devolved Government in Northern Ireland 1921-1939* (Dublin, 1979); Nicholas Mansergh, *The Government of Northern Ireland: A Study in Devolution* (London, 1936).

dom in miniature. The Sovereign was represented by the Governor who summoned, prorogued, and dissolved Parliament in the king's name and gave royal assent to bills. In theory the Governor, as was the case with the Governors-General in the Dominions, complied with any instructions issued by the Crown in respect of any bill, and could, if so directed, reserve the royal assent. In practice this was attempted only once— in 1922—when the British Government retreated almost immediately in the face of a bitter backlash in the Northern Ireland Parliament.

The Ulster Parliament was composed of two houses, a House of Commons and a Senate, of which the former was by far the more important. In an attempt to protect the rights of minorities, the Government of Ireland Act provided that elections for the House of Commons were to be conducted on a basis of proportional representation. This procedure was abolished by the Ulster Government—first for local elections in 1922, and then for national elections in 1929—on the grounds that it tended to create a multiplicity of parties. That action had the intended effect of further solidifying the already deep sectarian division of Ulster politics between the official Unionist Party and the Nationalists. The Senate, in turn, was elected by the members of the House of Commons.

Broadly speaking, the powers of the Parliament of Northern Ireland were restricted to matters of local concern, while imperial matters were expressly reserved to the Parliament at Westminster. But the borderline between transferred and reserved matters was not always very clear, and occasionally gave rise to difficulties. Questions of law and order, for example, supposedly were entirely under the jurisdiction of the Northern Government, but it was never definitely decided whether suppression of the IRA should be undertaken by the British Army or by the Ulster police with British financial assistance. The intermediary between the Northern Government and the United Kingdom Government, whose responsibility it was to sort out some of these difficulties, was the British Home Secretary. Among other things, his function, according to the official history of the Home Office, was 'to watch Northern Ireland's interests generally', and 'to ensure that the views of the Government of Northern Ireland on matters affecting them are made known to the Government of the United Kingdom'.[2]

During this period, and indeed down almost to the present, the Home Office interpreted its responsibilities regarding Ulster in a narrow light. While every effort was made to retain the goodwill of the Northern Government, this was always accomplished—and could only be accomplished—at the expense of the Catholic minority in Ulster. Thus the Home Office not only permitted relatively minor inequities to exist at the United Kingdom and provincial levels of government in Northern Ireland (e.g. property qualifications, plural voting, and the abolition of proportional representation), but also stood idly by and let the most egregious discrimination occur at the local level. Besides gross gerrymandering of electoral districts in favour of the Protestants, the Northern Government enforced property restrictions for voting in local elections which weighed more heavily on the Catholics as the relatively poorer element of the population, and allowed discrimination against Catholics in the allocation of local government-provided housing. Similarly, discrimination was evident in appointments by local government bodies and in appointments to the Northern Ireland civil service. To take but two examples: although approximately one-third of the population of Northern Ireland was Catholic, in 1922, 681 out of 714 officials employed by the Belfast Corporation were Protestants; and in 1927, of the 229 highest appointees in the Northern Ireland civil service, 215 were Protestant.[3]

Although some of the disparity between Catholics and Protestants could be, and was, explained away by one reason or another, the pattern of pervasive discrimination is nevertheless clear. From the point of view of this study, the important question is why the British Government allowed this situation to develop. The answer, of course, lies in the realm of politics. Although the Government of Ireland Act expressly outlawed religious discrimination, and the British were careful to ensure that no patterns of discrimination were allowed to develop in those branches of the United Kingdom civil service which

[2] Sir Frank Newsam, *The Home Office* (London, 2nd ed. rev., 1955), pp. 168-9.
[3] Donald H. Akenson, *Education and Enmity: The Control of Schooling in Northern Ireland, 1920-1950* (New York, 1973), p. 34.

operated in Northern Ireland, such as the post and telegraph services,[4] Whitehall was not anxious to provoke an outcry by looking too closely into Ulster's internal affairs unless there was a powerful reason for doing so. The moral issue alone did not provide sufficient justification. Except in times of crisis, few in Britain showed much interest in the plight of the Catholic minority in Northern Ireland. British politicians and civil servants tended to reflect this lack of concern. A convention was established—not broken until the disturbances of 1968–9—that ministerial responsibility for transferred matters rested solely with the Parliament of Northern Ireland and thus were not the proper object of concern for the Parliament at Westminster.

Not that the British Government lacked for leverage against the Ulster Government. Besides the ultimate threat of suspension, the Northern Government was dependent upon handouts from the British Treasury almost from the start; first, because of the civil disturbances in Northern Ireland during 1922, and then because the decline of Northern Ireland's staple industries of linen and shipbuilding caused her to fall farther and farther behind the rest of the United Kingdom economically.[5] But there were limits to how far this leverage could be used. As Lloyd George had discovered during the negotiations with Sinn Féin in 1921, and Asquith before him, the Ulster Protestants would accept the authority of the British Government only as long as it championed their own interest; otherwise they would defy it. Which was, after all, why they had their own state in the first place. Moreover, they were encouraged in their defiance by virtually all right-wing Conservative politicians.

The Ulster Government was not reluctant to play upon its links with Conservative politicians in Britain. Sir James Craig (created Viscount Craigavon, 1927), elected what was to be in effect Prime Minister of Northern Ireland for life—for this was not a state much given to political change—was no stranger on the English political scene. Although born in Belfast,

[4] D. Barrett and C.F. Curtis, *The Northern Ireland Problem* (Oxford, 1962). This conclusion was drawn from evidence gathered in the late 1950s, but it probably holds true for the earlier years as well.

[5] See R.J. Lawrence, *The Government of Northern Ireland: Public Finance and Public Service, 1921–1964* (Oxford, 1965).

he had been educated in Edinburgh, and had served as an MP at Westminster for fifteen years before resigning his post as Financial Secretary to the Admiralty to head the Ulster Government. This background served him well in his efforts to uphold the interests of the North in the years to come. He understood British politics and was on intimate terms with many influential Conservative politicians. Even his schooling in Edinburgh proved an invaluable bond between him and the influential Permanent Under-Secretary at the Home Office, Sir John Anderson.[6] A competent, if unimaginative, administrator, and a straightforward, though narrow, politician, Craig's strongest political asset was a streak of moral ernestness that never failed to impress upon British politicians of whatever stamp a conviction that, whatever his public utterances might imply, he was in reality a basically moderate and conciliatory man who was not a free agent, and who was, moreover, all that stood between them and the really intractable body of Protestant extremists in Northern Ireland.[7]

In striking contrast to the prosaic Craig was Northern Ireland's other important link to the Conservatives in Britain, the dashing, young Charles Stewart Henry Vane-Tempest-Stewart, seventh Marquess of Londonderry. Educated at Eton and Sandhurst, heir to a great title and vast wealth in the shape of English coal mines and numerous estates (including Mount Stewart near Belfast), Londonderry interrupted a promising career in British politics by resigning his post as Under-Secretary of State for Air in order to become Minister of Education and Leader of the Senate in the new Government. In addition to wealth and titles, Londonderry inherited a family tradition of uncompromising hostility to Irish aspirations dating back to Castlereagh, who was responsible for the original Act of Union back in 1800. It was thus with a certain sense of *noblesse oblige* that Londonderry assumed his new role in Northern Ireland. Although he was to perform creditably as Minister of Education in the new Government,[8] his main concern always was to use his influence in aristocratic and Conservative circles—and not least with his cousin Churchill—

---

[6] Sir John Wheeler-Bennett, *John Anderson, Viscount Waverly* (London, 1962), p. 92.

[7] e.g. H. A. L. Fisher to Gilbert Murray, 6 Dec. 1921 (Fisher papers, Box 7).

[8] Akenson, p. 41.

to see that the interests of Ulster were safeguarded. This he did unflaggingly for the rest of his life. Although he never made any great mark in British politics, and there is no reason to think that his own frequently expressed views on Anglo-Irish relations had any important effect on British policy, he nevertheless served the interests of the Ulster Government well by providing an avenue via which its views were kept constantly at the attention of prominent British politicians. Tiresome and predictable as those views might be, they could not be safely ignored by any British Government during these years.

During 1922 Northern Ireland was in a state of siege. The very existence of the state was threatened at its inception by a combination of the IRA operating along the borders and sometimes within the North, and by civil strife between Protestants and Catholics, especially in Belfast. By the end of the year at least 232 people had been killed in the North and nearly 1,000 wounded. The Northern Government survived, partly with the aid of the British Army, partly by the use of emergency powers and the creation of the Special Constabulary, and most of all, perhaps, because the outbreak of the Civil War in the South relieved much of the pressure.[9]

The major concern of the Ulster Government during 1922—outweighing the violence in Belfast—was the proposed Boundary Commission. During the Debate on the Irish Treaty Craig had warned Chamberlain that local feeling in the North was so intensely aroused by the provisions of the Commission that he and his colleagues might be swept off their feet, and the 'Loyalists may declare independence on their own behalf, seize the Customs and the Government Departments and set up an authority of their own. Many already believe that violence is the only language understood by Mr. Lloyd George and his Ministers.'[10] Two days earlier Craig had written in a similar vein to Bonar Law, saying that he could 'place no reliance on the personal assurance of Mr. Lloyd George', and that unless it was stipulated that only minor adjustments in the boundary were contemplated 'the Ulster Cabinet will

[9] Lyons, *Ireland Since the famine*, p. 716.
[10] Sir James Craig to Austen Chamberlain, 15 Dec. 1921. Tom Jones diary, 15 Dec. 1921 (Jones, iii, p. 190).

refuse to take part in the Boundary Commission and will proceed to any length that is necessary' to maintain their rights.[11]
   Neither Chamberlain nor Bonar Law were unduly alarmed
by this talk of rebellion. For the Unionists the language of
treason and confrontation had become a habit; they found it
difficult to speak otherwise. And they might be forgiven for
thinking that the British Government understood no other
language when it came to Ireland. After assuring Bonar Law
that the Cabinet was not contemplating coercion of Ulster,
Chamberlain mildly reproved Craig, telling him that he could
not believe 'that men whose loyalty is their pride are contemplating acts of war against the King'.[12]
   This reprimand from Chamberlain did nothing to stop
Craig's conspiring with the diehards against the British
Government. His efforts met with some success. On the reas-
sembling of Parliament in February, Chamberlain had an
interview with the diehards but was unable to reassure them
about the Government's intentions with regard to Ireland.
The diehard demonstration against the second reading of the
Irish Bill, though smaller than expected, mustered 60 votes.
More ominously, the Conservative junior ministers decided as
a body to prevent the Boundary Commission claiming power
to remove any substantial part of the six counties.[13]
   The problem with Craig was that he did not trust the
British Government to carry out its unwritten assurances to
him. For this he had some reason. Lloyd George's mutually
contradictory promises to Craig and Collins could only be
explained away on grounds of political expediency. While this
might suit Lloyd George, it provided little in the way of reassurance for the followers of Craig or Collins. Nor were Craig
or the diehards apt to put much trust in Churchill's hint that
the setting up of a Boundary Commission might be avoided
altogether by an agreement on the boundary question along
the lines of the Craig–Collins Pact.[14] Though this plan might
seem to offer the easiest solution to the problem, the fate of
the earlier agreement left little ground for optimism.

[11] Craig to Bonar Law, 13 Dec. 1921 (copy in ABL papers, 107/1/93).
[12] Chamberlain to Craig, 16 Dec. 1921 (copy in ABL papers, 107/1/98).
[13] Cowling, *Impact of Labour*, p. 154.
[14] Churchill to Salisbury, 24 Mar. 1922 (S(4) 22/100/120).

Besides the Boundary Commission, the next most pressing problem facing the Northern Government was the restoration of order in Ulster. Under Wilson's instructions, the Northern Government planned to accomplish this by reorganizing and taking control of a paramilitary police force based on the earlier Ulster Volunteer Force. This new force, the Ulster Special Constabulary, was divided into classes (A, B, or C, depending upon whether full-time, part-time, or reserve) and used to support the regular police force—the Royal Ulster Constabulary, which had replaced the former Royal Irish Constabulary in Northern Ireland.

Craig was right in suspecting that his new and expensive instrument of repression would not be popular with the British Government. But this did not daunt him. In March he told Balfour that his Cabinet was determined to carry out Wilson's recommendations regardless of cost. 'When the crisis is over,' he added, 'I propose to ask you and my old Unionist colleagues to re-imburse us from the British Exchequer for all such emergency expenditures.' His reasons for not publicly announcing this course of action, he explained, were that it would lead to extravagance in Northern Ireland and might also embarrass the British Government in its dealings with the Provisional Government.[15]

The major opposition to Craig's proposal came from outside the Cabinet: from the Treasury, which objected to the large sums involved and the lack of strict accountability;[16] and from the Army, which found the lack of discipline of the Special Constabulary distasteful, and considered the existence of a paramilitary force in Ulster a source of possible conflict with themselves. Macready, in particular, was known to have a very low regard for the Specials. On 8 March he reported that from 10 February to 6 March 12 Protestants had been killed in Belfast and 51 wounded. In the same period, casualties for the Catholics were 25 killed and 71 wounded. Those figures, Macready argued, showed that, whatever Craig and his cabinet might argue, 'the balance for making trouble is due to the so-called Protestants'.

Although Macready was not prepared to use British troops

[15] Craig to Balfour, 12 Mar. 1922 (AC 30/1/33).
[16] Minute by Otto Niemeyer of 26 May 1922 (T (Treasury) 163/6/g256/049).

as police, he had no faith in the Special Constabulary or its leaders, being 'very doubtful whether it is not a fact that the "B" and "C" Specials when off duty take part in a little sniping of their own'. He thought that only stern military measures would have any effect, but doubted whether Craig was really in earnest about stopping what was going on in Belfast. 'All this talk of R.O.I.A. [Restoration of Order in Ireland Act] and Martial Law is perfect nonsense. ... The fact remains that if they did so a greater number of Protestants would probably have to be executed than Catholics, and we all know what that means.'

Nor was Macready impressed by what he knew of the Northern Government. Dawson Bates, the Minister of Home Affairs (who had control of the Special Constabulary), he considered 'both a physical and moral coward'. While believing that 'four-fifths of the trouble in the Six Counties is entirely due to the presence there of recognized Divisions of the IRA who owe allegiance to Griffith', Macready nevertheless opposed the granting of any more arms to the Northern Government because of his contempt for their existing organization, but was himself unwilling 'to advise the army of a whole lot of undisciplined scallywags'.[17]

Macready and the officials in the Treasury were not alone in opposing the expansion of the Special Constabulary at British expense. On 17 March Tom Jones warned Lloyd George that the Unionists were 'bringing us back to the position we were in in 1914, with the advantage that the Field-Marshal is making his preparations legally with the money of the British Government and without protest'. In his view Britain would be departing from the spirit of the Treaty with the South and could be charged by the world with 'one more breach of faith' if it continued paying for the Special Constabulary, thereby allowing Ulster to cloak 'a military force under the guise of a police force'.[18] Moreover, Jones and Curtis argued the next day, in the face of language like that of Craig's correspondence with Chamberlain, it was 'impossible to assume that the formidable forces now being organized under the guise of police are directed solely against the danger

17 Macready to Worthington-Evans, 8 Mar. 1922 (CO 739/1/13691).
18 Tom Jones to Lloyd George, 17 Mar. 1922 (Jones, iii, p. 194).

of invasion from the South'. An equivalent force of police in Great Britain, they pointed out, would number at least 800,000 men. 'The British Government', they concluded,

has armed and is paying for forces which, it is told by the one who controls them, will in certain eventualities be turned against itself. If Ulster does not accept the award of the Boundary Commission the British Government will either have to pour in overwhelming forces to engage on a civil war of the most hateful kind, or else be accused in the presence of the civilized world of connivance with Ulster in creating a position in advance which must render nugatory the most vital provisions of the Treaty . . .[19]

In the end, the political situation at home outweighed all other considerations. This reflected the decline of Lloyd George, who was in no position to stand up to diehard demands in dealing with Ulster. He could no longer get his way by threatening to resign because he could not even be sure of carrying his fellow Coalition Liberals with him, much less his Conservative colleagues. In large part this was due to Churchill. While in no position to displace Lloyd George from the premiership, even had he so desired, Churchill was unquestionably second in importance among the Coalition Liberals, and was in a position to destroy the group if Lloyd George tried to remove it united from the Coalition. The Prime Minister viewed him as a rival who would be likely to exploit his resignation as an opportunity to join with the Liberals in a new coalition government with the Conservatives.[20]

Lloyd George's fears were not without some basis. During 1922 Churchill adopted a progressively more reactionary stance towards both domestic and foreign affairs. On socialism and India his attitudes were scarcely distinguishable from those of the diehards. His staunch support of Ulster made him more popular with the Ulstermen than any of the regular Conservative leaders.[21] In March he led the opposition in the Cabinet against Lloyd George's policy of recognition for Russia, causing many to think that he might destroy the Coalition by resigning over the issue of recognition and join the

[19] 'Memorandum on the Present Position of the Imperial Government in Northern Ireland', by Tom Jones and Curtis, 18 Mar. 1922 (CO 906/30).

[20] Sir Philip Sassoon to Lloyd George, 13 Feb. 1922 (Gilbert, *Churchill, Companion* iv, 3, pp. 1172-3).

[21] Churchill to Clementine Churchill, 10 Feb. 1922 (ibid. p. 1766).

diehards.[22] Churchill's strident rhetoric on Ireland and other issues was not prompted solely by reasons of political expediency. Many of his deepest instincts and feelings pushed him in the direction of the diehard camp. Had he not convinced himself that the Southern Irish would remain loyal members of the Empire, he might have sided with the diehards on Ireland too. As it was, he had a deep and abiding sympathy for the 'loyalists' of Ulster.

In his swing towards the right in early 1922, Churchill carried the whole Cabinet with him. In the interests of party unity, Chamberlain was not prepared to take any action that might be construed by the diehards as being anti-Ulster. Despite the objections of Macready, Jones, Curtis and the Treasury officials, therefore, the Ulster Government was assured of receiving at least some of the funds necessary to support the Special Constabulary.

What the extent of that support would be remained a matter of dispute throughout the next two months. On the one side was Lloyd George, supported generally by Worthington-Evans, Horne, and H.A.L. Fisher, the President of the Board of Education. On the other was Churchill, reinforced by Balfour and Chamberlain. Unlike Churchill, Lloyd George was trying to broaden his appeal to Liberal opinion, and continued to be influenced by Tom Jones, who was convinced that it was the intention of 'Henry Wilson and Co.' to embroil the British in a renewal of war with the South.[23] Horne, as Chancellor of the Exchequer, was worried about the cost of the Specials; Worthington-Evans spoke for the Army, which resented the tendency of Wilson and General Sir Richard Solly-Flood, his right-hand man (and since 11 April the official Military Adviser to the Northern Ireland Government), to go behind Macready's back and deal directly with General Cameron, British Commander in Northern Ireland, or with the British supply agencies, as well as their habit of dealing directly with politicians and with the Committee of Imperial Defence (CID).[24]

[22] Sassoon to Lloyd George, 24 Mar. 1922 (ibid. p. 1826); see Cowling, *Impact of Labour*, pp. 168-9.

[23] Tom Jones diary, 27 May 1922 (Jones, iii, p. 202).

[24] 6th Meeting of ISC, 26 May 1922 (CAB 16/42). Both Wilson, after his retirement as CIGS, and Solly-Flood maintained close contacts with leading diehards. For

Matters came to a head in late May, when Londonderry arrived in London to press the case for increased British aid to Ulster. At a meeting of the Irish Committee on 22 May, during which Londonderry painted a bleak picture of the condition of Northern Ireland, Churchill over-rode the objections of Macready to increased British support. Arguing that further army reinforcements were required in Ulster 'as part of the Government's general political plan', he said that developments in the South pointed to an attempt to force the North into an All-Ireland Government. Until adequate army reinforcements could be stationed in Ulster, it was essential that the Ulster Constabulary be developed into a well-organized gendarmerie.[25] When British signatories to the Treaty met to discuss the matter on the following day, they agreed that Northern Ireland should be lent the arms and equipment requested, and that the cost of maintaining the police forces in Ulster should be shared equally between Northern Ireland and Britain.[26]

Three days later the controversy over the Special Constabulary flared up anew when Collins and Griffith arrived in London to defend the proposed Free State Constitution.[27] In negotiations with the British, Collins adroitly attempted to divert the issue from the proposed Constitution itself to the chaotic situation in Belfast. Both he and Griffith insisted that there be an impartial enquiry into the outrages in Belfast, and that the British Army proclaim martial law in the city.[28] In the meantime Craig did not make the position of his supporters in the British Government any easier by declaring that in no circumstances would the Northern Government accept any rectification of the frontier or any Boundary Commission as provided for in the Treaty.

The British were now in a quandary. Macready was prepared to proclaim martial law in Belfast, but was opposed by

the short-lived career of Solly-Flood as Military Adviser to the Northern Ireland Government see Paul Bew, Peter Gibbon, and Henry Patterson, *The State in Northern Ireland, 1921-72: Political Forces and Social Classes* (New York, 1979), pp. 57-62.

[25] 5th meeting of ISC, 22 May 1922 (CAB 16/42).

[26] 22nd conclusions of Meeting of British Signatories to the Treaty with Ireland, 23 May 1922 (CAB 43/1).

[27] See pp. 41-2. [28] 6th Meeting of ISC, 26 May 1922 (CAB 16/42).

the Ulster Government, which insisted that this would be a confession that it could not govern.[29] Lloyd George, concerned about the position Collins was manœuvring them into, supported his demand for a judicial enquiry, claiming that the 48,000 Specials were in fact an army similar to the Fascists in Italy. He warned his colleagues that, if they broke with the Provisional Government on the issue of 'Republic versus Monarchy', they could count on solid support from the United States and the Dominions, but if they broke on the question of Ulster, they would have a very weak case. But faced with opposition from Churchill, Balfour, and Chamberlain, and supported only by H. A. L. Fisher, his fellow Coalition Liberal, Lloyd George could not carry the Cabinet.[30]

Two days later Lloyd George again pushed for a judicial enquiry, this time receiving support from Hankey, who, in one of his rare recorded intrusions into Cabinet deliberations, voiced misgivings as to whether the moral position of the British Government was fully realized in the United States and the Dominions.[31] With the outcry in the Liberal press intensifying as the killing in Belfast continued unabated, even Churchill began to waver in his opposition to a judicial enquiry.[32] In its June issue, the influential *Round Table* carried an article, probably written by or at the behest of Curtis, which condemned the violence in Ulster and called in effect for the ending of partition. Faction fights in Belfast were nothing new, it noted, but never before had there been 'disturbances of the nature or the scale which have disgraced its name before the world in the present year'. The article concluded by calling on Ulster to take some risks on the boundary question for the sake of Irish unity, and on Craig to seize the opportunity to prove himself 'the leader of Imperial vision that we have already reason to think him'.[33]

Such thoughts could not have been further from Craig's

---

[29] 6th Meeting of ISC, 26 May 1922 (CAB 16/42).

[30] Cabinet conclusions 30(22) of 30 May 1922 (CAB 23/29).

[31] Cabinet conclusions 31(22) of 2 June 1922 (CAB 23/29).

[32] A leader from the *Manchester Guardian* of 7 June entitled 'The Danger in Northern Ireland', which argued that the boundary between the six counties and the rest of the country was artificial, and also attacked the Special Constables, particularly caught the attention of the officials in the Colonial Office (CO 739/13/27197).

[33] *Round Table*, 47 (June, 1922), pp. 524–36.

mind. Behind the 'orgy of crime', he informed Balfour, there was a tremendous conspiracy, working with great skill on Catholic feelings, which he felt Solly-Flood was gradually unravelling. The working of a commission, he feared, might affect the morale of the Ulster police and call into question the very strength and judgement of the Northern Government itself. Far better, if something needed to be done, to have the British Government send an agent to Belfast to investigate the situation and furnish an unbiased report. To Lloyd George and Churchill's objection that an agent would be of no use from a public opinion point of view, Craig replied that he was not impressed by figures (furnished by Lloyd George) showing that some 380 Catholics had been killed in Ulster since 1920, and thousands more thrown out of work, since there were, he ventured, many cases of Catholics being killed by their own people. In the end Craig overcame all objections simply by threatening to resign. Bowing to his wishes, Churchill suggested Sir Stephen Tallents, Lord Fitzalan's private secretary and a member of the Irish Committee, as the British agent to send to Belfast. In return, Craig acceded to Lloyd George's demand that there be an enquiry if Tallent's report should prove unsatisfactory.[34]

The thirty-eight-year-old Oxford-educated Tallents proved an excellent choice for the job. Like Cope, he had served under Lloyd George at the Ministry of Munitions during the War, after which he had distinguished himself as British Commissioner in the chaotic Baltic states. Gervas Huxley, who served under him later on the Empire Marketing Board, described him as a 'shy man whose aloofness and reserve of manner discouraged intimacy and made many people find him cold and awe inspiring', but possessed of 'an imagination completely unfettered in red tape'.[35] He was probably as fair-minded and capable an agent as the British could have found for the assignment, and his reports provide a valuable source of information about the conditions existing in Northern Ireland during 1922 as viewed through the eyes of a well-informed and relatively unbiased observer. Tallents was

---

[34] 31st conclusions of Meeting of British Signatories to the Treaty with Ireland, 16 June 1922 (CAB 43/1).
[35] Gervas Huxley, *Both Hands: An Autobiography* (London, 1970), p. 129.

not long in his new assignment before he had formed a
generally low opinion of the Ulster Government, and particularly of Dawson Bates. He was not impressed with Solly-
Flood's programme, and thought that the Special Constabulary should be placed forthwith under the Royal Ulster Constabulary. 'Today the feeling against the Specials and the "B"
in particular', he reported ominously, 'is more bitter than
against the Black and Tans.'[36] Even prominent Unionists were
telling him 'that this purely partisan and insufferably
[un]disciplined force [B Specials] was sowing feuds in the
countryside which would not be eradicated for generations'.[37]

Despite his frequently disparaging remarks about the
Northern Government, Tallents recognized that it was la-
bouring under particularly trying conditions. It trembled over
the Boundary Commission and found it difficult to cope with
the 'conspiracy of murder and violence' of the IRA.[38] Moreover, Tallents warned, if Craig went he would not be replaced
by a moderate like Hugh Pollock, the Minister of Finance,
but by an extremist like Henry Wilson.[39]

Tallents eventually concluded that an independent judicial
enquiry into events in Belfast should not be held because 'It
would lead to a revival of propaganda about matters that are
best forgotten. Inadvertently it would encourage the Northern
Catholics in their refusal to recognize the Northern Government.'[40] Though small consolation to the Catholic minority,
this advice was welcome to the British, for by July the fighting
in the South had diverted much of the attention and pressure
from the North, thereby removing any pressing need for a
judicial enquiry into the affairs of Northern Ireland. A relieved Government retained Tallents in Ulster for the next
four years as Imperial Secretary responsible for certain reserved services and acting as liaison officer with the Ulster
Parliament.

During 1922 the British had one other opportunity to demonstrate their concern for the welfare of the Catholics in North-

[36] Report by Tallents of July 1922 (CO 906/27).
[37] Tallents to Masterton-Smith (Colonial Office), July 1922 (CO 906/30).
[38] Note by Tallents on 'The Situation in Northern Ireland', June 1922 (ibid.).
[39] Note by Tallents of June 1922 (CO 906/24).
[40] Tallents to Masterton-Smith, 4 July 1922 (CO 906/30).

ern Ireland. Proportional representation was specifically written into the Government of Ireland Act in order to safeguard
the rights of minorities throughout the island. But when it was
seen to work against the Unionists—as in the local elections of
1920, when the Nationalists took control of Londonderry for
the first time since 1689—the Unionist-dominated Northern
Parliament immediately passed a bill altering the local fran-
chise from proportional representation to a simple majority.
This embarrassed the British, for Collins protested vehemently
against the bill, and Churchill dared not offend him when
matters had not yet been finally resolved between the Provisional Government and the Republican Irregulars. Moreover,
when asked for a ruling, the legal experts at the Colonial and
Home Offices determined that the bill was a proper matter
for the reservation of the Royal Assent. In their opinion, the
security of minorities was a vital question; the hopes of any
lasting peace in Northern Ireland depended to a large extent
on the minority being brought to recognize the Northern Parliament and Government as their Parliament and Government, and to take their part in the public business of the
country. 'The present Bill,' they concluded, 'rightly or
wrongly, is regarded as an abrogation of the rights of the
Northern minority, and its enactment would intensify suspicion and distrust and be a fatal obstacle to conciliatory efforts
on the above lines.'[41]

Unwilling to confront the Ulstermen, Churchill played for
time. After a personal appeal to Craig to take into consideration the position of the Loyalists in the South failed,[42] he sent
Curtis and Cope to Belfast to plead the case for postponing
the operation of the act for a few months. The proverbial
stone wall would have been as easy to budge as Craig, who
was himself under pressure from the Unionist Constituency
parties; indeed, in his report, Curtis remarked that 'there is an
anthracite quality about these Ulstermen'.[43]

Once again, Craig held all the best cards. If the British did
not give in, he would simply resign. The ensuing election

[41] 'Legal opinion of Sir Frederick Liddell, Sir Francis Greer, Sir John Risley, and
Sir John Anderson on the Bill to abolish proportional representation in Northern
Ireland', July 1922. Appendix C to 67th conclusions of 31 July 1922 (CAB 43/2).
[42] Churchill to Craig, July 1922 (CO 739/14/31545).
[43] Curtis to Churchill, 1 Sept. 1922 (ibid.).

would merely endorse his actions, and they would then be
confronted with an impasse. The suppression of the disorders
in Belfast, according to Cope, had given Craig a new sense of
confidence. Rather than becoming more amenable to compromise, as some had hoped, he and Curtis both got the impression that in recent months the feelings of Craig and of the
dominant classes in the North had definitely hardened against
inclusion in the Free State. For the first time in Curtis's experience, Craig refused even to refer to union as the consum-
mation to be worked for. Nor did he make any attempt to
conceal his expectation that the proposed voting change
would result in increasing Unionist majorities. Yet he seemed
to have no difficulty in reconciling this belief with a professed
and apparently sincere desire (or so it seemed to Curtis) to
reconcile the Catholic minority to the system.[44]

Though Craig had still to confer with the Cabinet in London, the issue was no longer in doubt, if indeed it ever had
been. In July Churchill—no believer in proportional representation himself—told Collins that he was satisfied from consultations with the Ulster Government 'that their object in
promoting the Bill was not to deprive any minority of its due
representation, but to save the expense and other administrative drawbacks which ... accompany the use of the system of
Proportional Representation in the Six Counties.'[45]

The British learned much from this encounter with Craig.
Never again did they attempt to use the Royal prerogative to
hold up Northern Ireland legislation; not even when, seven
years later, the Ulster Government abolished proportional representation for parliamentary elections as well. It was to be
almost another fifty years before the British Government made
any serious attempt to intervene with the Ulster Government
on behalf of the Catholic minority. By then it was too late.[46]

[44] Curtis to Churchill, 1 Sept. 1922 (ibid.).

[45] Churchill to Collins, 31 July 1922. Appendix D to 67th conclusions of 31 July
1922 (CAB 43/2).

[46] On rare occasions the British Government did try to influence the Ulster
Government on certain measures, as when, for example, Churchill complained about
the severe and biased enforcement of the Civil Authorities (Special Powers) Bill,
commonly known to Nationalists as the 'Flogging Bill'. Such remonstrances, however,
generally had little effect and were made more for political than humanitarian
reasons. See CO 739/1/46127; and Londonderry papers (DLO/6242 (1)).

5

The Return of Bonar Law

Ireland about wh you praise me is I think going to save itself. No one else is going to. They are a proud and gifted race & they are up against the grimmest facts. I do not believe they will succumb. But the pangs will be cruel and long.

Churchill to the Countess of Lytton, 12 September 1922

ON 19 October 1922, at a meeting at the Carlton Club, the Conservative MPs voted by 187 votes to 87 in favour of contesting the next election as an independent party. The Coalition was at an end; Lloyd George resigned that same day; four days later Bonar Law became Prime Minister of a Conservative Government.

Ireland is widely considered to have been the main reason for the fall of the Lloyd George Coalition.[1] Like many other historical legends, this one fades under close scrutiny. While there is no doubt that it was an emotive issue for many Conservatives, particularly the diehards, its importance in the overthrow of the Coalition can easily be exaggerated. The revolt at the Carlton Club was over personalities, not policies. It was a repudiation by the rank and file of the leadership of Chamberlain, Birkenhead, Balfour and Lloyd George. In the last analysis, concludes a recent historian of the Coalition Government, it was 'a reassertion of the autonomy of party for its own sake'.[2] Bonar Law, the most crucial figure in the voting, specifically disclaimed any difference over principle as a reason for his break with the Coalition. He was heavily

[1] See e.g. Robert Blake, *The Unknown Prime Minister: The Life and Times of Andrew Bonar Law, 1858–1923* (London, 1955), p. 436; Taylor, *English History 1914–1945*, p. 161; and Kinnear, p. 15.

[2] Morgan, p. 355.

influenced by Lord Beaverbrook and Henry Wickham Steed,
the editor of *The Times*, both of whom were strong supporters
of the Government's Irish policy. Of the non-diehards who
voted against continuing the Coalition, only three mentioned
Ireland as a major reason for their break, while the diehards,
the only group that had consistently if not unanimously
opposed the Government's Irish policy, agreed among themselves beforehand not to speak at the Carlton Club meeting for
fear their intervention would only prove counter-productive.[3]

Nor was Ireland a primary issue for the members of the
Coalition Government who rejected Lloyd George. While
some junior ministers, like Leopold Amery, objected to certain
parts of the Government's Irish policy, other issues bothered
them even more, and their real complaint was the haughty
attitude of the Coalition's leaders.[4] Of the four Cabinet ministers who rebelled, none did so because of Ireland. Two of
them in fact—Baldwin and Curzon—had spoken strongly in
support of the Treaty the previous December.[5] Moreover, to
form a Government, Bonar Law would have to include Derby
and the Duke of Devonshire to make up for the loss of the
Conservative leaders who remained loyal to Lloyd George.
While both had many complaints against Coalition policy—
each had refused to join the Government in March—Ireland
was not among them. On this issue their attitude can only be
described as moderate.

If the outcry over Ireland was thus more a symptom of the
Coalition's decline than the cause of it, how then did the
legend arise that the Irish settlement brought down the
Government? The main propagator of this myth appears to
have been Churchill. In the ensuing election he faced a serious
challenge in Dundee, a seat he had represented for fourteen
years. He was opposed by five other candidates, including E.D.
Morel and the Communist Willie Gallacher, who was a strong
advocate of self-determination for Ireland. Finding his Irish
record under constant attack—though this time the attack
came not from the right, but from the left—Churchill had to

[3] Kinnear, p. 87.

[4] L.S. Amery, *My Political Life*, ii (London, 1953), p. 233.

[5] *Parl. Deb. Commons*, vol. 149, cols. 119-22 of 14 Dec. 1921; *Parl. Deb. Lords*, vol.
48, cols. 26-35 of 14 Dec. 1921.

stress the liberal side of his role in the Irish settlement. Before long he was claiming that the major reason for the fall of the Coalition was the Irish settlement. 'I attribute', he said in a speech a few days before the election, 'the fall of the government—more than anything else, far more than all other causes put together—to the resentment and fury of the so-called diehard party against the men who made the Irish settlement.'[6] Churchill's efforts were unavailing. His earlier role as the oppressor of Ireland was not forgotten. Whenever he tried to defend his Irish record hecklers would howl him down with cries like: 'What about the Black and Tans?' By the eve of the poll the invective had become so overpowering that he could not even complete a speech.[7] The next day he went down to overwhelming defeat.

Churchill's part in the Irish settlement did not save him at Dundee; nor had it ruined him in England. On the whole, the British people welcomed the Treaty, despite its vicissitudes, and the Conservative Party tended to mirror this acceptance. But for Churchill, Ireland remained the best explanation for the fall of the Coalition, and he never relinquished it.[8]

Upon taking office, Bonar Law soon made it clear that as Prime Minister he would faithfully implement the Irish Treaty. Virtually everyone from whom he solicited advice on policy stressed the need for repose and the avoidance of foreign adventure. On Ireland, Amery, soon to become First Lord of the Admiralty in the new Government, maintained that the country's

earnest desire for national stability imposes on the Government, and indeed on every citizen, whatever his personal feelings may be, the duty of fulfilling this Country's treaty with the Irish Free State. Both in the letter and in the spirit it will respect the agreement and, recognizing the difficulties which face those at the head of affairs in Southern Ireland, it is the Government's intention to approach its future relations with the New Dominion with patience and forebearance.[9]

[6] Election Address, Caird Hall, Dundee, 11 Nov. 1922 Winston S. Churchill, *Complete Speeches*, iv, ed. Robert Rhodes James (New York, 1974), p. 3376.

[7] Ibid. p. 3379.

[8] See Winston S. Churchill, *The Second World War*, i, *The Gathering Storm* (Boston, 1948), p. 20.

[9] Memo by Amery, 24 Oct. 1922 (ABL papers, 110/1/1).

Sir Arthur Griffith-Boscawen, the former Coalition Minister of Agriculture, who was slated to join Law's Government as Minister of Health, expressed similar hopes, but also emphasized that 'the Government must insist on the protection of the Unionist minority and on full compensation for damage done. There must be no interference with the rights and position of Ulster.'[10] Even Salisbury, who was invited to join the Government as Lord President of the Council and Chairman of the CID, agreed with Law 'that the Provisional Government must be treated with liberal patience so long as they are doing their best to carry out the Treaty'.[11]

The part that the diehards had played in the undermining of the Coalition, and the refusal of most of the former Conservative leadership to serve with Bonar Law—out of seventeen former Conservative ministers in Lloyd George's last Cabinet, only four were willing to serve under Law—gave rise to fears in moderate Conservative circles that the new Government would be dominated by the right wing of the Party.[12] Such was not to be the case.[13] Law's most important appointments were men of moderate persuasions: Baldwin as Chancellor of the Exchequer, Derby as Secretary for War, the Duke of Devonshire as Colonial Secretary, and Curzon as Foreign Secretary.

Of these, Stanley Baldwin, the surprise choice as Chancellor of the Exchequer, was a relative unknown who had not entered Parliament until 1908, after twenty years in his family's iron manufacturing business, and who was already fifty-three when he first joined the Cabinet as President of the Board of Trade in 1921. Ordinarily cautious and easy going, Baldwin had nevertheless played an important role in the overthrow of Lloyd George, for whom he had conceived a profound and lasting distrust.

---

[10] Memo by Griffith-Boscawen, 25 Oct. 1922 (ibid.).

[11] Salisbury to Bonar Law, 22 Oct. 1922 (ABL papers, 111/29/137).

[12] Edward Grigg, e.g., felt 'no interest in a Conservative party which panders to the Diehards and ... would rather not be in politics than sit on the back benches behind any of the men who spoke of the Irish Treaty and those who made it as the Right wing of the Conservative party did' (Grigg to Lady Astor, 21 Oct. 1922, quoted by Cowling, *Impact of Labour*, p. 215).

[13] Many right-wing Conservatives and diehards, including Lord Hugh Cecil, were conspicuously excluded from the Government, despite Salisbury's efforts on their behalf. Salisbury to Bonar Law, 23 Oct. 1922 (ABL papers, 109/2/37).

Derby and Devonshire, on the other hand, were two of the wealthiest and most influential peers in the kingdom. The former owned much of Lancashire, which formed his main base of operations, while the latter, the son-in-law of Lord Lansdowne, had great estates and houses sprinkled over much of England and Ireland, where he spent a considerable portion of his time riding to hounds. Of the two, Derby was the more important. Still exuberant at fifty-seven, he had already served as Secretary for War from 1916 to 1918, and had since turned down many offers to rejoin the Coalition Government, preferring instead to preach moderation from outside. In March 1921 Lloyd George had chosen him to serve as an intermediary in a vain attempt to initiate negotiations with de Valera. In the interests of Anglo-American harmony and Lancashire trading interests, as well as of peace within the Conservative Party, Derby was an advocate of reconciliation with Ireland.

Churchill's replacement at the Colonial Office, Victor Cavendish, ninth Duke of Devonshire, was the nephew of that Lord Frederick Cavendish who had been murdered in Phoenix Park on his arrival in Dublin as Chief Secretary in 1882. Although lacking his predecessor's drive and imagination, Devonshire was a good choice for his post. Conservative enough not to offend the diehards, he could also be counted on to deal fairly with the Free State.

While they did not dominate the new Government, the diehards were not without significant representation in it, especially at the lower levels. Thus, though Salisbury was the only diehard in the Cabinet, five diehards formerly in opposition were made junior ministers—McNeill, Wolmer, Ashley, Joynson-Hicks, and Linlithgow. Of these, only McNeill—perhaps because his house at Cushendun in Northern Ireland had just been burned down by the I R A—proved disconcerting to the Government when he remained publicly outspoken against the Treaty even after taking office. In one important respect, Law's appointments did not bode well for the future of Anglo-Irish relations, despite the relative exclusion of diehards from important posts in the government. Although, as with the other Dominions, final appeal in the Irish Free State was to the British Privy Council, three of the Law Lords on the Council—Carson, Sumner, and Cave—had spoken against the Treaty in the House of Lords. Curtis considered it a constitutional calamity 'that at this juncture the Court, which we have always stipulated must be the supreme arbiter in interpreting the Treaty, should have been exposed to the profound distrust of a most suspicious people by the fact that three of its members plunged into party politics'.[14] Moreover Cave, the new Lord Chancellor, was known mainly to the Irish for his having been the presiding judge in the trial of Sir Roger Casement for high treason in 1916. Under the circumstances it is not surprising that the Free State Government should have considered the deck stacked against them when it came to appeals to the Privy Council, and that they would struggle against that provision in their Constitution from the start.

On 24 October the Irish Ministers arrived in London to meet the new Prime Minister. Curtis had already written to Cope telling him that he anticipated a stiffer attitude in Whitehall and suggesting that he advise the Provisional Government 'to take cognizance of a definite change in political facts and shape their course wisely in view of it'.[15] In a meeting at the Board of Trade Cosgrave voiced optimism about what the future held. He told Law that de Valera was believed to be in Dublin disguised as a clergyman, but that he was not worth arresting as the Irregulars no longer took orders from him. Kevin O'Higgins, the Free State Minister of Home Affairs, assured Law that the British had nothing to fear from reports of peace negotiations between the Provisional Government and the rebels, as public opinion in Ireland would now condemn anything of the nature of the Collins–de Valera pact.[16]

If the advent of a Conservative Government to power in Britain was viewed with some consternation in Dublin, in Belfast it was welcomed with undisguised relief. The Ulster Government had never felt comfortable dealing with the Coalition led by Lloyd George; from a Conservative Government led by Bonar Law great things were expected. Craig made no attempt to conceal these expectations.[17] While it was not im-

[14] Curtis to Churchill, 20 Sept. 1922 (CO 739/7/47027).

[15] Curtis to Cope, 2 Oct. 1922 (CO 739/7/44746).

[16] 'Minutes of a Meeting between Bonar Law and the Irish Ministers at the Board of Trade', 24 Oct. 1922 (CO 739/7/54174).

[17] Craig to Devonshire, 6 Nov. 1922 (CO 739/1/55311).

mediately evident, the coming to power of the Conservatives
did in fact bring about a fundamental change in British policy
towards Ireland. Heretofore the ostensible aim had always
been, as Churchill told Cosgrave upon resigning, to promote
'a true and lasting unity' in Ireland.[18] Despite the tactical
twists and turns taken by the Government during the preceding year, the ultimate reunion of Ireland within the British
Empire was the goal consistently held out to the Provisional
Government as the prize awaiting them once they had sup-
pressed the Republican Irregulars. After the Conservatives
came to power this changed. Henceforth British policy was
directed almost solely towards preserving the *status quo* in Ireland.

The change was more real than apparent. Until he left
Ireland for good at the end of the year, Cope continued to
conduct his operations as though there were still some hope of
eventual Irish unity, as did Loughnane, his successor as British
liaison to the Free State Government. Within the Colonial
Office, Curtis similarly continued to work for the unity not
only of Ireland, but of the whole British Isles, hoping that 'in
time both communities will find that the links which bind
them are so close that some new political synthesis will have to
be devised with the consent of both'. In his view, the whole
object of British policy should be to preserve and strengthen
those threads which bound the two countries together.[19]

Although some imperialists in the new Government, such
as Amery, shared this view, it was not the prevailing attitude
in the Government as a whole, nor was it the view taken by
Bonar Law. While Curtis was convinced that the Irish would
eventually become reconciled to the Empire if treated fairly,
Law suffered under no such illusion. He believed that the
Irish would be satisfied with nothing less than a republic. But
this did not greatly concern him. He cared only for Ulster.
With his understanding of the Orange mentality (which he
shared), he knew that the Ulstermen would never willingly
subject themselves to rule by Dublin. His aim was to see that
they would never have to do so.

Despite his sentimental attraction to Ulster, Law was deter-

[18] Churchill to Cosgrave, 25 Oct. 1922 (CO 739/2/54170).
[19] Minute by Curtis to Devonshire, 11 Dec. 1922 (CO 739/8/62076).

mined to be scrupulously correct in his policy towards the Free State. Although he was in office for only seven months, his premiership was important in regard to Ireland: it saw the carrying into law of the Bill formally setting up the Irish Free State, the appointment of its first Governor-General, and the end of the civil war.

In the elections of 4 November, the Conservatives were returned with a large majority. With 344 seats, they had a majority of 77 over all other parties combined. The Labour Party almost doubled its previous strength to 138 seats, while the Asquithian Liberals won 60 seats and the Lloyd George Liberals slumped to 57. Two Communists were elected also, both outspoken advocates of Sinn Féin and the Irish Republic. Having campaigned on a platform calling for tranquillity and stability both at home and abroad, the new Conservative Government determined to carry out its Irish Treaty obligations 'not only in the letter but in the spirit'.[20]

On Ireland the new Government was influenced primarily by Tom Jones and Curtis. Jones was careful to see that Bonar Law always understood the situation and did nothing to disrupt the good relations being so carefully fostered with the Free State. To Curtis fell the more difficult task of dealing with the various departments on a day to day basis and trying to persuade them to treat the Irish Free State on a basis of equality with the other Dominions. His success was such that by February the reactionary *Morning Post* was grumbling about Colonial Office partiality to the Free State and 'sighing for the days of Winston'.[21]

One point on which Jones and Curtis got their way was the appointment of a Governor-General for the Irish Free State. Although it was not common practice in the other Dominions to choose a native for the post of Governor-General, the Colonial Office was strongly of the opinion that only a native Catholic Irishman in that post would hold out the hope of winning the Irish to a 'serious united allegiance to the Crown'.[22] Jones and Curtis eventually secured the position for

[20] Conclusions of a conference on the Irish Free State Bill held on 22 Nov. 1922 (CO 739/8/56786).

[21] Tom Jones diary, 9 Feb. 1923 (Jones, iii, p. 220).

[22] Memo by R. Pope-Hennessy on the 'Appointment of the first Governor-General of Ireland under the new Constitution', 21 Aug. 1922 (CO 739/16/43763).

Tim Healy—a former Nationalist MP and a friend of Beaverbrook's—but only over the initial objections of Bonar Law, who regarded Healy as too impulsive and 'too heavy a drinker of whiskey'.[23] Healy also had to pledge in writing that he would not give the Royal Assent to any bill passed by the Parliament of the Irish Free State if there existed the smallest doubt as to whether it fell within the constitutional power of that Parliament, unless he first consulted with the Colonial Secretary.[24]

On 5 December the Royal Assent was given to the two Irish Acts giving effect to the Treaty and the Free State Constitution. Northern Ireland immediately exercised its right to vote itself out of the Irish Free State. A decision then had to be reached about what to do with the British troops remaining in Ireland. These forces had been retained—mainly around Dublin and in Northern Ireland—as an encouragement to the Provisional Government not to relapse into an agreement with the Republican Irregulars to make common cause against Northern Ireland. Since the outbreak of the civil war, the British had been generous in their supply of munitions to the Provisional Government Army—a policy continued under Bonar Law—but caution had always been taken to ensure that these supplies did not put it in a position of superiority over the British garrison in Dublin, for few in Whitehall thought that the Provisional Government was fighting because it wanted to.[25] Even Curtis, as late as the end of October, still believed that a large number of those supporting the Treaty did so only because they had no choice. He hoped, however, that if Britain scrupulously adhered to its side of the bargain Irish sentiment could be changed. 'The settlement embodied in the Treaty will become real and binding', he told Devonshire, 'only in so far as the people of Ireland learn to regard it as something too sacred to be broken whenever Great Britain happens to be in a position of embarrassment.'[26]

The War Office was also anxious to see strict adherence to

[23] Tom Jones diary, 16 Nov. 1922 (Jones, iii, p. 218).
[24] Extract of Cabinet conclusions of 29 Nov. 1922 and correspondence with Healy (CO 739/7/59788).
[25] Memo by Curtis on 'War Material for the Provisional Government', 25 Oct. 1922 (CO 739/7/54475).
[26] Minute by Curtis to Devonshire, 26 Oct. 1922 (CO 739/7/54174).

the Treaty on Britain's part, not out of confidence in the
Provisional Government's Army, of which it had little, but
out of fear of possible repercussions if any other policy were
pursued. A report circulated to the Cabinet in September
1922 by Major W.E. Whitaker predicted that the Provisional
Government would try and break away from England as soon
as it had succeeded in restoring peace. He nevertheless saw no
alternative to continued support for it, because for the British
to restore peace in Ireland would require an army of at least
200,000 men. Even this would be merely an army of occupation, for the people would never be sympathetic to English
rule.[27]

As it gradually became clear that the Republicans were
fighting a lost cause, British confidence in the Provisional
Government grew. By late November Derby was anxious to
have the remaining British troops withdrawn from the South
as soon as possible out of concern for their morale and fear
that their presence was an open invitation to attack by the
Irregulars.[28] He wanted also to see British troops withdrawn
from Ulster because he did not approve of their living conditions and because he thought that in an emergency they could
be more easily concentrated in England. Moreover, he had no
confidence in the Special Constabulary, which he considered
a waste of British money, and he felt that the Northern
Government would never get organized so long as it thought
it could depend on British troops.[29]

Circumstances favoured Derby's efforts. With each passing
month the position of the Republicans in the South was growing more desperate. In November and early December some
of their leaders were captured and executed by the Provisional
Government—including Erskine Childers, for possession of
firearms, and Rory O'Connor and Liam Mellows, in reprisal
for the murder of a member of the Dáil. News of the execu-

[27] Report by Major W.E. Whitaker on the 'Position of the Irish Provisional
Government', CP 4229 of 19 Sept. 1922 (CAB 24/139). This report characterized the
Irish as a 'suspicious and cowardly lot ... possessed of little inherent regard for
human life', showing that the attitude of at least some British officers had not changed
much since the days of Essex and Mountjoy.

[28] Derby to King George V, 28 Nov. 1922 (Derby correspondence, WO (War
Office) 137/4/4).

[29] Derby to W.C. Bridgeman, 18 Dec. 1922 (WO 137/4/11).

tions was received with satisfaction in the Colonial Office. Curtis, who had been trying without success to persuade the Provisional Government to use part of the island of St Helena as an internment camp for Republicans,[30] applauded the actions taken by the Provisional Government. Childers he considered 'one of the people responsible in the first degree for the bloodshed in Ireland', and the others 'undoubtedly deserving of death in any civilized state' for their part in 'precipitating and initiating this bloody struggle'.[31]

With the gradual winding down of the civil war the removal of British troops from the South could be completed. In the North, violence was also fading from the streets of Belfast. In December, Solly-Flood, who by then had been fully discredited in the eyes of the Northern Government, resigned amidst bitter recriminations on both sides[32] and Derby was able to win Craig's acquiescence to a gradual reduction of British troops from sixteen battalions to five.[33]

Besides continuing the supply of munitions for use against the Republicans,[34] the Government of Bonar Law made one other important contribution towards ensuring the survival and stability of the new Irish Free State: it provided financial aid. Although the civil war dragged on until May 1923, by December it was already clear that in the new year the major problems facing the Free State Government would be not military but financial—indeed, bankruptcy appeared imminent. This prospect fanned hopes among the diehards that the Free State might yet be undone and the Union restored, and the *Morning Post* and Lord Rothermere's *Daily Mail* began a campaign with this idea in mind. The demand for high compensation for damages incurred during the civil war became one of the great rallying cries of the diehard movement throughout much of 1923.

This outcry was not taken lightly, either by the British Government, which was also facing a reparations crisis in

[30] Curtis to Ceylon Dept., 20 Nov. 1922, and minute by Masterton-Smith to Devonshire, 20 Nov. 1922 (CO 739/7/56786).

[31] Curtis to Loughnane, 11 Dec. 1922 (CO 739/2/60975).

[32] Tallents to Masterton-Smith, 6 Dec. 1922 (CO 739/1/55311); Solly-Flood to Salisbury, 6 Dec. 1922 (S(4) 103/162).

[33] Derby to Bonar Law, 9 Dec. 1922 (WO 137/4/6).

[34] Baldwin to Devonshire, 18 Dec. 1922 (WO 137/4/24).

Europe at this time, or by the Irish Government, which encouraged Beaverbrook to counter it in his newspapers.[35] In
the Colonial Office, Curtis dismissed the initial stages of the
diehard campaign with scorn. To him the only alternative to
British financial assistance to the Free State was the reconquest of Ireland. Although this might be just what the
diehards wanted, not only would the cost be prohibitive, but
the military effort necessary would be crippling for the imperial power in Europe, and be the swiftest 'road to a revolution in this country'. But Curtis did not underestimate the
problems facing the Free State in the financial sphere.
Alarmed by the threat of its impending bankruptcy, he encouraged the Treasury to help stabilize the situation. Not only
did he fear the loss of English markets and consequent higher
unemployment in Britain should the Free State collapse, but
he was also concerned that the example of a successful campaign of sabotage waged by the Republicans in Ireland might
be emulated in Britain.[36]

The Treasury was not unsympathetic to these views. It
recognized that it was almost as much in Britain's interest as
the Free State Government's to see that Ireland got back on
a sound financial footing. But it did not consider the situation
as dire as Curtis made it out to be. While acknowledging
damage to property, in particular railroads, had been extensive, Niemeyer, the Controller of Finance, argued that the
problems facing the Free State were 'by no means insuperable,
and in fact far less than those of the greater number of countries in Europe'. Moreover, though anxious to help, the Treasury was scrupulous about recognizing Ireland's new status as
a Dominion, fearing that any overt British action might be
self-defeating. Instead, working informally through the semi-
official channels that bound the Bank of Ireland with the Bank
of England, the Treasury attempted to prod the Irish Banks
into buying Irish securities. Although Niemeyer anticipated
that the effort would 'not be popular with the Banks, who are
not over-patriotic and would get a better investment in Eng-

[35] Blythe to Healy, 21 Oct. 1923; Healy to Beaverbrook, 31 Oct. 1923; and Beaverbrook to Healy, 1 Nov. 1923 (Beaverbrook papers).
[36] Curtis to Masterton-Smith, 15 Jan. 1923 (Tom Jones papers, TJ G./iv4/3/3).

land', in the end it was successful.[37] In the meantime the
Treasury also had direct dealings of its own with the Free
State. In February a secret agreement was concluded with
Cosgrave which provided, among other things, for the Free
State Government to accept the liability for the Land Purchase Annuities, which were annual instalments paid by Irish
tenant farmers purchasing their land through loans advanced
by the British Government under the Land Purchase Acts of
1870-1909. The agreement was not a very generous one on
the part of the British Government and, although subsequently revised, it was never formally accepted by the Dáil.
This was to lead to major complications in Anglo-Irish relations after the fall of the Cosgrave Government in 1932.

In one respect Bonar Law's Government overstepped the
bounds of legality in its effort to support the Free State. A
section on Irish Revolutionary Activities had long formed an
integral part of the weekly report on 'Revolutionary Organizations in the United Kingdom' compiled under the Home
Office Directorate of Intelligence, largely by Sir Basil Thom-
son, head of the Special Branch. These reports were routinely
circulated to the Cabinet during Lloyd George's premiership,
and the practice was continued under Bonar Law. Although
occasionally enlivened by the doings of Countess Markiewicz,
they were generally pretty routine and focused mainly on the
activities of the Irish Self-Determination League and its few
supporters. Art O'Brien, who besides being president of the
League, was the Irish Republican representative in Britain
from 1919 to 1924, as well as the president of the Gaelic
League and the Sinn Féin Council of Great Britain, under-
standably figures prominently in the reports. Labour Party
leaders who had in the past occasionally spoken out for the
Irish Republicans were also included, but by 1922 the only
active supporter in Parliament that the Republicans could
count on was Saklatvala, the wealthy Parsee Communist returned in the previous election as the official Labour candidate from North Battersea. As his influence in Parliament was

---

[37] Memo by Niemeyer, 9 May 1923 (CO 739/20/21871). Henry Guinness, the
Governor of the Bank of Ireland, and Andrew Jamison, owner of Jamison's Irish
Whiskey and an influential director of the Bank of Ireland, were in close contact with
the bank of England and the British Treasury throughout this period.

negligible, the only purpose he served was to link the whole
Gaelic movement with Communism in the eyes of the diehards
and Scotland Yard. This was more than enough to damn it
with the Government, and led to some rather hasty action in
the spring.

It started with the 198th report on 'Revolutionary Organizations in the United Kingdom' of 8 March 1923, which
concluded that the I R A in Britain were 'gathering their forces
so as to put their full weight behind the blow to be struck
against the Free State this spring'.[38] Since by then the cause
of the Irregulars in Ireland was visibly crumbling, which was
clearly having its effect on the morale of their supporters in
Britain, where Countess Markiewicz's efforts to rally the faith-
ful were meeting with small success ('Art O'Brien's attempt to
boom Countess Markiewicz is falling flat; her presence arouses
no enthusiasm in the London Irish, who mostly regard her as
mad'[39]), it is difficult to see how there was much cause for
alarm. The Government nevertheless decided to act, partly to
provide assistance to the Free State, which was convinced that
plots against it were being hatched in Britain, but also to rid
itself of a presence it found noxious. On 11 March over 100
men and women, including Art O'Brien, were arrested and
subsequently deported to Dublin. Although the deportees
were later returned to Britain and released after it was ruled
that they had been arrested illegally, by then the civil war in
Ireland was virtually over, and the danger to the Free State,
such as it was, had passed.

In this small matter, as well as in the more important ones
involving military and financial support, the Government of
Bonar Law demonstrated that British adherence to the letter
and spirit of the Irish Treaty was not subject to the vagaries
of fluctuating majorities at Westminster. So long as the Free
State Government stood by the Treaty, it could count on the
British Government to do the same. Or, so it seemed, with
one possible exception. This was the problem of Ulster and
the Boundary Commission. So long as civil war raged in the
South, the question lay in abeyance; with the restoration of

---

[38] Report No. 198 on 'Revolutionary Organisations in the United Kingdom', 8
Mar. 1923 (CAB 24/159).
[39] Ibid.

peace in May, it was only a matter of time before it would again be raised. By then, however, Bonar Law was no longer Prime Minister.

Law resigned in May for reasons of ill health, and died shortly thereafter. Baldwin, his successor, was equally committed to the Treaty and determined to see its provisions carried out, but it appeared for a time that the diehards were determined to use his inexperience and their strength on the Cabinet's Irish Affairs Committee to wreck the Treaty.[40] Salisbury led the attack. The target was the Irish Land Bill and the issue was the familiar one of the 'betrayal' of the Irish Loyalists. Earlier he had made it clear that he would oppose any assistance to the Free State unless they conformed completely to British wishes on land purchase and compensation.[41] Although the Irish Land Bill proved more generous than the Loyalists had expected, as even the landowners in the Irish Senate admitted, this did not dissuade the diehards from denouncing it as confiscation, nor Salisbury from clamouring for a policy which, as it appeared to Jones, 'would not only wreck the Treaty but would smash this Government'.[42]

In the end, the diehards got nowhere. Neville Chamberlain, who had succeeded Baldwin as Chancellor of the Exchequer, proved impervious to their pressures. Salisbury was even deserted by his own son-in-law, William Ormsby-Gore (later Lord Harlech), the Under-Secretary of State at the Colonial Office, who returned from a visit to Ireland in July convinced that if the Free State received generous co-operation from Britain she would 'in a very short time establish herself firmly as a loyal member of the British Empire'.[43]

By the summer of 1922 a far more important issue was threatening to resurface, one on which the diehards could count on receiving strong support from within the Conservative Party. In June Cosgrave warned Baldwin that he would

---

[40] Jones diary, 8 June 1923 (Jones, iii, p. 220). The Irish Affairs Committee numbered among its members three diehards: Salisbury, Cave, and Joynson-Hicks; in addition to Devonshire (chairman), Curtis (secretary), and Ormsby-Gore.

[41] Minute by Salisbury on Land Purchase Memorandum, 23 Apr. 1923 (CO 739/20/21846).

[42] Salisbury to Bridgeman, 3 June 1923 (CO 739/25/18130); Tom Jones diary, 8 June 1923 (Jones, iii, p. 220).

[43] Ormsby-Gore to Devonshire, 9 July 1923 (CO 739/20/44907).

have to demand the appointment of a Boundary Commission.[44] Just over a year earlier the junior ministers of the Coalition Government—several of whom were now in the Cabinet—had pledged not to allow the Commission to operate. Any attempt to coerce Ulster into accepting it might bring down the Government.

Under the circumstances, Baldwin had only three real alternatives. First, he could try to postpone the Commission indefinitely, as Tom Jones suggested,[45] hoping that somehow the problem would go away. As Cosgrave proved insistent, this did not work. Secondly, he could invite Cosgrave and Craig to London to work out a settlement along the lines of the Craig–Collins Pact, which would avoid the necessity of appointing a Commission. Cosgrave accepted, but the project had to be shelved when Craig refused to have anything to do with it.[46] As a third resort, he could break the deadlock by an Act of Parliament which either would provide that the Commission was duly constituted even though the Ulster Government did not appoint a Commissioner by a certain date, or else would authorize the British Government to appoint a member to act on behalf of the Government of Northern Ireland. The obvious drawback to this option, as Curtis pointed out to Devonshire, was that 'such a proposal might seriously divide the Government's supporters and even the Cabinet'.[47]

Baldwin had other things on his mind. He was considering the possibility of appealing to the country on the issue of Protection. This alone was virtually guaranteed to split both the Cabinet and the Conservative Party; the last thing he wanted was to confuse the issue and divide the Party further by bringing on a crisis over the Boundary Commission. As he bluntly warned Craig a short time later: 'I do not want the Irish conflict revived in the House of Commons in any shape or form if it can justly be avoided.'[48] This was to remain his policy through the years.

Fortunately for Baldwin, there were other distractions to

[44] Cosgrave to Baldwin, 9 June 1923 (Jones, iii, p. 221).
[45] Tom Jones diary, 10 June 1923 (ibid.).
[46] Devonshire to Baldwin, 20 July 1923 (CO 739/18/36328).
[47] Minute by Curtis to Devonshire, 10 Sept. 1923 (CO 739/20/49361).
[48] Baldwin to Craig, copy with no date, 14(?) Jan. 1924 (Baldwin papers, 101 E.4.15 21/197).

keep the Cosgrave Government busy during the autumn of 1923. Besides the work of rebuilding their country, they had to prepare for entry to the League of Nations Assembly in September, and for their first participation in an Imperial Conference in October. By the time the Boundary Commission again became a serious issue, the Conservatives were no longer in power.

The British Government viewed Ireland's first tentative steps on the international stage—where over the next fifty years she was to play a role out of all proportion to her size—with mixed feelings. The Foreign Office always tended to regard the assertion of independence in foreign affairs by any of the Dominions as a nuisance and an impediment to its ability to speak for a united Empire; Ireland was no exception. Irish membership in the League of Nations also made it all that more imperative that the Boundary Question be resolved as soon as possible lest Ireland exercise its right to appeal to the League for arbitration. Curtis, on the other hand, regarded the Free State's adhesion to the League as a 'clear gain' for Great Britain. In Geneva for the ceremonies marking Ireland's admission to the League, he watched the Irish delegates having 'the time of their lives listening to it all', and concluded optimistically that 'their immersion in this centre of world troubles has made them realize that there are other things which matter than the questions which have obsessed the Irish mind'.[49]

Curtis also placed great importance on the appearance of Cosgrave at the Imperial Conference in October. He thought that this would serve both to moderate the attitude of the right-wing press in Britain towards the Free State, and to help convince the Irish leaders that the rights accorded to them as a Dominion under the Treaty would be observed in the spirit as well as the letter.[50] Although Cosgrave did come to the Conference, he was inexperienced and did not play an important part in the proceedings.[51]

---

[49] Minute by Curtis to Devonshire, 19 Sept. 1923 (CO 739/20/49361).
[50] Curtis to Loughnane, 18 Apr. 1923 (CO 739/20/21846).
[51] Tom Jones diary, 1 Oct. 1923 (Jones, i, *1916-25* (London, 1969), p. 245).

Under Bonar Law and Baldwin, British policy towards Ireland remained on an even keel partly because there were no new problems of consequence, and partly because it continued in effect to be laid down and administered by Tom Jones, Curtis, Sir James Masterton-Smith, the Permanent Under-Secretary at the Colonial Office, and their associates in the civil service.[52] While this had certain obvious advantages, and may well have secured the best possible British policy available at the time, it also had one grave defect. So long as civil servants were administering Irish policy, there could be no new initiatives, for only politicians could accept the political risks attendant upon these. The result was that British policy towards Ireland calcified after 1922. Most politicians were as anxious as Baldwin to keep Ireland out of party politics. After the many years of strife, the public was bored with Ireland, and for the most part looked upon the 1921 Treaty as the final resolution of the Irish question. British politicians tended to reflect this general view. Not only would intervention in the affairs of Northern Ireland have been politically risky, but there was very little pressure on the British Government to act. After 1922 the Catholics in Northern Ireland split into two groups. The Nationalists, the largest group, decided on 'constitutional' opposition. They took their seats in Parliament, participated in local government, closely associated themselves with the Catholic Church, and were so deeply conservative as to present a very 'respectable' and almost totally unthreatening pressure group both at Stormont and at Westminster. The Republicans, on the other hand, continued to refuse to participate in governing Northern Ireland. But their refusal to take their seats in Parliament and their association with the violence of the I R A put them beyond the pale as far as British politicians were concerned. Also, after the resolution of the dispute over the Boundary Commission in 1925, the Free State tended to acquiesce in the *status quo* as far

[52] The new style in government is reflected by Hankey's comments following the Imperial Conference of 1923: 'Throughout the conference I don't think Baldwin uttered one sentence, unless prompted by the Colonial Office or myself ... It was essentially a "Permanent Official" conference. Our politicians only read out what the officials—mainly Masterton-Smith and myself—told them to say. It was a deplorable spectacle compared with Lloyd George & Co.' Hankey diary, 11 Nov. 1923 (Roskill, *Hankey*, ii, p. 349).

as Northern Ireland was concerned. Not until the rise to power of de Valera did the Irish Government begin again to put serious pressure on the British Government to rethink its policy towards Northern Ireland. But even then the issue was addressed largely in political terms. The oppressed Catholic minority in the North remained quiescent partly because they had no effective champions until the rise of their own indigenous Civil Rights Movement in the 1960s. This explains, even if it does not exonerate, the British Government's neglect of that minority during the period between the wars.

6

The Advent of Labour
The Boundary Crisis (I)

Ulster and the *Morning Post* are on the war-path; L.G. feels that
'all's right with the world' again, and I am terribly gloomy. S.B.
is either dishonest or he absolutely agrees with me, but has he the
clearness of conviction and the force of will to impress his views on
the Ulstermen? It will be a miracle if we keep our ship off the
rocks. And again I say that if it comes to a fight, I don't see how
I can fight on either side.

Chamberlain to Lady Chamberlain, 1 August 1924

An independent all-Irish Republic with Ulster forever alienated
as a spear-point of anti-British hostility planted between Great
Britain and the Atlantic is a very thinkable result of these tran-
sactions.

J.L. Garvin in *The Observer*, 3 August 1924

The breakdown of the Treaty means for sure and certain war with
Ireland, if that breakdown is really attributable to a failure of faith
on our part. It will be a war which cannot be terminated by
another Treaty because no one in Ireland will ever trust us again
. . .
  For you of all men to forget what you had done and turn to
smashing your own handiwork would break my heart.

Curtis to Churchill, 31 August 1924

I am really hopeful after all I have heard that we may succeed in
preventing the Irish Treaty from becoming an issue at the election.
It would only divide friends and unite enemies. The Russian issue
is the one, and with good handling might well be decisive.

Churchill to Sir Robert Horne, 30 August 1924

If the Commission should give away counties, then of course Ulster
couldn't accept it and we should back her.

Baldwin to Edward Wood, 6 September 1924

IN December 1923 Britain went to the polls in what amounted to a vote on Protection. The Conservatives, who favoured it, were defeated—losing over 90 seats and dropping to 258. Although still the largest party in the House of Commons, they were no longer a majority. The Liberals and Labour, joined together in an uneasy alliance under the banner of Free Trade, were victorious—emerging with 159 and 191 seats respectively. On 22 January 1924 the first Labour Government was formed with Liberal support.

James Ramsay MacDonald, the new Prime Minister, had not expected to win the election and had no policy other than to show that Labour could govern, and perhaps accomplish something in foreign affairs. A lowland Scot, illegitimate and largely self-educated, the 58-year-old MacDonald was one of the founding fathers of the Labour Party. As Secretary of the Labour Representation Committee, and later as Chairman of the Labour Party, he had always shown a willingness to work with the other parties to further Labour's interests. After resigning the chairmanship of the Party in 1914 in opposition to the war, MacDonald had re-emerged as its leader in 1922 just in time to become the first Labour Prime Minister. Although capable and hard-working, he was also vain and stand-offish, and not without strong prejudices. He disliked Asquith and loathed Lloyd George with a vehemence rivalling Baldwin's. Though dependent on the Liberals for support, he felt more at home with the Conservatives; though leader of the most left-wing party in the country, he was anything but a radical.[1]

Facing the new Labour Government were two pressing problems: the reparations crisis in Europe, and the Boundary Commission dispute. MacDonald opted to deal with the former, taking for himself the office of Foreign Secretary, where his expertise would be of some use. Ireland had never much interested him. He shared the typical lowland Scot's distaste for the Irish and contempt for their Roman Catholic faith,[2] and had a feeling of kinship with the Ulster Protestants. He thus felt a close affinity with Craig, and whenever he travelled to Ireland in the coming years it was always to

[1] David Marquand, *Ramsay MacDonald* (London, 1977), p. 320.
[2] Emmanuel Shinwell, *I've Lived Through it All* (London, 1973), p. 53; and Robert Keith Middlemas, *The Clydesiders* (London, 1965), p. 110.

Northern Ireland that he went, and then to stay at Mount Stewart with his good friends the Londonderrys, whose views on Ireland were not far different from his own.[3]

To deal with Ireland, MacDonald appointed as Colonial Secretary the 49-year-old head of the National Union of Railwaymen (NUR), J.H. Thomas. Like MacDonald, largely self-educated, 'Jimmy' Thomas was a good-humoured, hard-drinking, picturesque individual whose jingoistic patriotism and unabashed imperialism heartened the Conservatives and dismayed the radicals.[4] Unlike MacDonald, Thomas had always taken a keen interest in Irish affairs; before the war, when working to strengthen the railwaymen's union in Ireland, and later, during 'the Troubles', when organizing labour opposition to the reprisals of the Lloyd George Government. Despite these activities, and his genuine sympathy for the Irish people, Thomas was, like most trade union men, fundamentally conservative. Jim Larkin's brand of revolutionary syndicalism had shocked him; he had helped see to it that British labour withheld its support from him during the Dublin general strike in 1913. Similarly, during the summer of 1920, when the Hands Off Russia Movement was supplemented by a Hands Off Ireland Movement, the British NUR, of which Thomas was the head, made no effort to bestir itself on behalf of its Irish confrères.[5] And the following year, when the Labour Party conference passed, over his strenuous opposition, a resolution calling for independence for Ireland, he persuaded the more conservative Trades Union Congress (TUC) conference the following week to pass a motion demanding only Dominion status for Ireland together with the withdrawal of British troops.[6] As head of the TUC Parliamentary Com-

---

[3] MacDonald was much criticized, then and later, for his tendency 'to surround himself with "well-bred men, in spite of their reactionary attitude towards affairs"' (Beatrice Webb diary, 15 Feb. 1924). In her memoirs, Lady Londonderry had this to say about the Irish: 'Democracy as the British know it is not for Southern Ireland. They are of a different race. They want firm, wise but powerful control, to prevent them from trying to eat each other up.' (Marchioness of Londonderry, *Retrospect* (London, 1938), p. 189.)

[4] See Earl of Birkenhead, *Contemporary Personalities* (London, 1924), p. 234; Amery, ii, p. 502; and Egon Wertheimer, *Portrait of the Labour Party* (London, 1929), pp. 178-9.

[5] Greaves, p. 190.

[6] Gregory Blaxland, *J.H. Thomas: A Life for Unity* (London, 1964), pp. 143-4.

mittee, he assured Lloyd George that the majority of the trade unionists were opposed not only to complete independence for Ireland, but to coercion of Ulster as well.[7]

In constructing a Cabinet, MacDonald made few concessions to the left wing of his Party. Several of his appointees were ex-Liberals, like Haldane, who became Lord Chancellor, a post he had held under Asquith. Lansbury was excluded. J.R. Clynes, the son of an evicted Irish farmworker who had emigrated to Lancashire, and the man whom MacDonald had defeated for the Party leadership in 1922, was made Deputy Leader of the House, where his influence waned rapidly. Henderson was made Home Secretary, though he was more interested in foreign affairs, and Snowden, an austere teetotaler, was given the Exchequer, where he was certain to be a bastion of conservative orthodoxy. The only radical in the group was the Clydesider John Wheatley, who was to prove an outstanding success as Minister of Health. Wheatley had strong feelings about Ireland. Irish by birth, and married to an Irishwoman, he had had Nationalist politics bred into him from an early age. Among the frequent visitors to the family home had been James Connolly, whose *Labour and Irish History* deeply influenced the young Wheatley.[8] But MacDonald liked neither Wheatley nor his politics, and perhaps in part because the latter's views on Ireland were so pronounced, the subject was almost never discussed openly in the Cabinet. MacDonald preferred to let Thomas handle Irish affairs almost singlehandedly, referring matters to the Cabinet only when absolutely necessary, and then only to ratify a decision that had in effect already been made. So isolated did MacDonald become from some of his ministers that, during the height of the crisis over the Boundary Commission in July, even Haldane found it virtually impossible to obtain a private meeting with him to discuss the issue.[9]

At first Thomas hoped that a way around the Boundary Commission could be found by using Clause 14 of the Treaty. By this means an All-Ireland Council would come into being,

[7] Minutes of a meeting of a deputation to Lloyd George from the Trades Union Congress Parliamentary Committee, 22 July 1920 (Thomas papers, U. 1625/011).

[8] Middlemas, pp. 35-6.

[9] Beatrice Webb diary, 11 July 1924 (Beatrice Webb papers).

with very limited powers at first, but which could gradually be expanded. Cosgrave and Craig met in London in February to discuss this plan, but it collapsed when the latter insisted that the representation on such a Council be on a fifty-fifty basis.[10] The resulting deadlock further unsettled the political situation in the South. Loughnane estimated that 40 per cent of the South was Republican, which might in certain untoward circumstances rise to 60 per cent. He believed that many in the South supported Cosgrave only as a matter of honour because a pledge to stand by the Treaty had been given. If the British were to break the Treaty, he felt that a motion would be put through the Dáil abolishing the office of Governor-General and the oath, thus virtually setting up a republic.[11]

The situation was allowed to drift through the spring. MacDonald may have seriously considered putting financial pressure on Ulster and the Free State in an attempt to force them to compromise.[12] If so, he soon discarded the idea. Instead, he sent Jones over to Dublin to try to persuade Cosgrave to resume negotiations with Craig in one last attempt at a solution.[13] Cosgrave agreed, but only on condition that, if the conference failed, the British Government would exercise its powers under Article 12 of the Treaty to set up a Boundary Commission. Cosgrave and Craig resumed their negotiations on 24 April, but made no headway. The Labour Government seemed now to have no recourse but to seek legislation to break the impasse. The risk was that this would thrust Irish affairs back into British party politics. This MacDonald and Thomas wished to avoid, fearing that it might serve as an effective rallying point for Lloyd George and the Liberals against the Conservatives, leaving Labour out in the cold.

Tom Jones and Curtis were convinced that Craig placed his hopes on splitting the parties in England as had been done

[10] According to Tallents, Craig and Londonderry were both prepared to make real concessions in the hope of a compromise on the Boundary issue, but were prevented from doing so by extremists in their own party, in particular Pollock. Tallents to Anderson, 18 Feb. 1924 (CO 739/26/8694).

[11] Jones, iii, p. 226.

[12] C.P. Scott diary, 2-3 Feb. 1924 (Scott papers, 50907, vii, p. 92).

[13] MacDonald considered Cosgrave 'a weak man, but one who would fight hard if driven into a corner' (ibid. p. 40).

before the war. They urged MacDonald and Thomas to counter the threat by calling together Asquith, Lloyd George, and Baldwin in an all-party meeting to discuss the Irish problem.[14] When Thomas proved reluctant to go along with this suggestion, Curtis complained that the Colonial Secretary was 'under Craig's thumb', and prepared to resign because he felt that the Government was no longer making an honest effort to put the Treaty through.[15]

On 15 May, in anticipation of the setting up of a Boundary Commission, Curtis circulated a report on the political situation in Ireland that he had prepared for the War Office 'in view of the grave contingencies involved in the present position', and in order that 'the events of 1914 might not be repeated'. In it he warned that, if the decision of the Boundary Commission went against the South—that is, if Northern Ireland were not emasculated by the transfer of the whole of Fermanagh and Tyrone, as well as Derry and Newry to the Free State—it was 'not improbable that a Republic would be declared, followed by an outbreak of disorder between Catholics and Protestants in the North'. In such a case, the British should not attempt the reconquest of Ireland, but should resort to a blockade. This, he supposed, would somehow enable Cosgrave to regain control and reconstitute the Free State. But the gravest contingency for the Army to consider was the situation that would arise if the Commission decided to conduct a plebiscite along the boundary. In that case the British were 'certain to meet with the armed resistance of the Protestant majority throughout Northern Ireland'.[16]

The General Staff also worried about a return to the conditions of 1914. It estimated that, if a plebiscite were to be held, at least three divisions, a brigade of cavalry, and some armoured cars would be needed to cordon off Tyrone, Fermanagh, and Armagh, and prevent outside interference from either Northern Ireland or the Free State. In the event of a decision going against the Free State and a republic being proclaimed, the Army estimated it would require two divi-

---

[14] Jones, iii, p. 226.
[15] Ibid. p. 231.
[16] 'An Appreciation of the Present Political Position in Ireland', by Curtis, 9 May 1924 (CAB 21/281).

sions, a cavalry brigade, and some tanks and armoured cars in addition to the five battalions already in Northern Ireland. In either case, the Empire would be deprived for an indefinite period of its only mobile reserves at a time when serious problems were threatening in Iraq and Egypt. Moreover, if the Army were required to act against Northern Ireland, there would be a 'strain on discipline and morale', as 'a great majority would have to act contrary to their convictions', while, if the decision went against the South, the efficacy of a blockade in restoring moderate government was doubted, in which case it might be necessary to consider reconquest. In either case, the General Staff feared that the commitment of the Army would be unlimited and 'fraught with serious danger both for the army itself and for Imperial defence'.[17]

Geoffrey Whiskard, the Colonial Office's specialist on Irish affairs, did not take such a pessimistic view of the situation. He thought it unlikely that the Army would have to employ force against Ulster. He also ruled out reconquest in the event a republic was declared in the South. He opposed even a blockade, arguing that the result 'might well be that after a year or more of a very costly blockade, a stalemate would be produced carrying with it the final ruin of the "loyalists" and the destruction for years to come of one of Great Britain's best markets'. In addition, a blockade might resuscitate 'intense anti-British propaganda abroad, and it is not inconceivable that in such circumstances the United States might recognize an Irish Republic'. He favoured non-recognition instead, in which case 'Ireland would sink at once from her position as a member of the League of Nations and the equal of the Dominions to a position of complete unimportance in world affairs.'[18]

Had a republic been declared in the South, it is likely that the Government would have followed Whiskard's advice. Little support would have been forthcoming for any stronger course of action. Even Salisbury viewed 'with great apprehension' the prospect of renewed warfare against the South. As

---

[17] Note by the General Staff on the Colonial Office memo on Ireland, 11 June 1924 (ibid.).

[18] Whiskard to Hankey, 28 July 1924, and 'Note (by Whiskard) on the Situation in Ireland with Special Reference to Curtis' memo of 9 May 1924 and the General Staff note of 11 June 1924' (ibid.).

he warned his brother Robert, 'Unless the greatest of self-restraint is exercised at the earlier stages so as to put the Free State flagrantly in the wrong, the fact of reconquering a self-governing Dominion by the Mother Country might have a deplorable reaction elsewhere.'[19]

But even non-recognition had its risks. The only hope to avoid such a situation arising was to appoint a Boundary Commission and hope that its decision would somehow prove acceptable to both parties. This the Government belatedly determined to do.

Much depended upon who was chosen to be the Chairman of the Boundary Commission. The Government first asked Sir Robert Borden, a former Conservative Prime Minister of Canada, of Scottish and English descent, who said he would accept provided that both Irish governments agreed beforehand to recognize the Commission and to appoint their respective representatives. As the Ulster Government refused to comply, the British turned next to Richard Feetham, a judge of the South African Supreme Court, who accepted without any conditions.[20]

At first glance, Feetham might have seemed an odd choice for a Labour Government to make. Like Curtis, one of Milner's protégés, Feetham was a confirmed imperialist who retained close friendships with many prominent Conservatives in England. But this was in fact exactly what the Government was looking for in order to ward off any attack from the right. What is surprising is the Cosgrave Government's letting the appointment of Feetham pass without any protest.

In retrospect, it is interesting to speculate on what the difference might have been had Borden rather than Feetham been Chairman of the Commission. Feetham, as the British expected, interpreted its powers very narrowly. Borden, on the other hand, became convinced that the opportunity should be utilized to bring about a united Ireland. In early June he sent Thomas a proposal for a united Ireland along

---

[19] Salisbury to Robert Cecil, 22 May 1924 (Cecil of Chelwood papers, 51085).

[20] The correspondence concerning the appointment of a chairman for the Boundary Commission is in HO (Home Office) 45/12296, Part I 46/3600/5. The correspondence between Borden and Thomas on this matter was withheld from the Command Paper at the former's request.

Canadian lines, with the assurance of the British connection and full protection for all minorities. There would be a federal parliament and executive similar to Canada's, and each of the four ancient provinces of Ireland would have its own provincial legislature and executive similar to those of the Canadian provinces. Borden warned of the danger to Anglo-American relations if an amicable settlement of the boundary dispute were not found soon.[21]

Thomas ignored Borden's proposal, no doubt feeling that it would serve only to arouse emotions on both sides. But cautious as was his approach to the boundary problem, by July it looked as if a domestic political crisis was nevertheless brewing. The danger lay in the possibility of an election being forced on the Irish question, giving Lloyd George an opening to reforge the old pre-war Liberal–Labour alliance against the Conservatives and Ulster intransigence. This was what MacDonald and Baldwin feared most. On nothing did they see more eye to eye than the need to keep 'the Goat' in the wilderness. It was with this aim in mind that much of the behind-the-scenes manoeuvring during 1924 was directed.

As long as there was still hope of mutual agreement between the Free State and Ulster the Conservative leadership avoided making any public pronouncements on the matter. But once it became clear that a Boundary Commission would have to be constituted, feeling in the Conservative Party began to mount. The renewed offensive against the Treaty was launched by the *Morning Post*, which had never regarded it as anything less than a betrayal of Ulster. In April Rothermere's *Daily Mail* joined in with editorials openly advocating the breaking of the Treaty in respect of the Boundary Commission,[22] followed by *The Times*, which in early May asserted that 'any suggestion ... that Ulster is going to cede counties or towns ... should be ruled out in advance'.[23]

Soon Baldwin was being made to feel the pressure. On 9 May Lord Robert Cecil enquired what Conservative policy would be in the event of negotiations breaking down, Cosgrave

[21] Borden to Thomas, 2 June 1924 (Beaverbrook papers, BBK C/164).
[22] *Daily Mail*, 30 Apr. 1924.
[23] *The Times*, 2 May 1924.

being overthrown, and a republic set up in the South. While reconquest seemed out of the question, Cecil thought it 'inadmissible to desert or coerce Ulster or do anything to hamper or destroy the admirable government that at present exists in North Ireland. The administration there appears to be excellent.'[24] Salisbury was also concerned, though he doubted that 'even the lunatics of the F.S. would attack Ulster', since 'the Southern Irish are not really a brave people'. The most they would be capable of would be 'outrage raids', which he felt confident the Ulster Government could repress, with British assistance if necessary.[25]

Tension increased in late July, when it became clear that the Judicial Committee of the Privy Council would rule that a majority vote of the Boundary Commission would serve to give effect to its ruling, and that legislation was required to enable the British Government to appoint the third commissioner on behalf of Northern Ireland. This prompted MacDonald finally to accept Tom Jones's idea of holding an all-party conference of party leaders and the signatories to the Treaty who were still members of either house of Parliament.[26] The conference was held at the end of the month. As expected, MacDonald announced that the Government would call Parliament together for a special session in order to provide legislation for the appointment of a commissioner for Ulster. Lloyd George (who was the only Liberal present, as Asquith was ill and Churchill and Greenwood had been defeated at the last election) pledged the support of the Liberal Party for the undertaking, but pressed MacDonald to force the bill through before Parliament adjourned rather than wait for a special session.[27]

Lloyd George's proposal further agitated the Conservatives. If the necessary legislation were passed through the Commons at the end of the session, the Lords would probably reject it, thus precipitating an election on Ireland. Austen Chamberlain described his old chief as 'just bursting with new-born hope'.

[24] Lord Robert Cecil to Baldwin, 9 May 1924 (S(4) 23/109/45).
[25] Salisbury to Cecil, 12 May 1924 (Cecil of Chelwood papers 51085).
[26] C. P. Duff to Lloyd George, 30 July 1924 (Lloyd George papers, G/13/21).
[27] Tom Jones found Baldwin in an unusually belligerent mood before the conference, saying that 'It is difficult to forgive assassination and to forget their behaviour in the war.' (Jones, iii, p. 233).

In such an election, Chamberlain was convinced, the Conservatives 'would get a smashing defeat, and Labour might very likely get a clear majority'. Craig he saw as the key to the situation. 'If Craig will not or cannot carry any compromise with his followers,' he lamented, 'he has the party in a cleft stick and nothing but crushing disaster awaits us.' Chamberlain depicted Baldwin as seeing himself 'confronted with disaster'. Everything depended upon 'Baldwin's power to carry his old colleagues unitedly with him in putting pressure on Craig and upon the success of that pressure'. If it failed, and an election were to be held on the 'fatal issue' of the Boundary Commission, he was seriously considering withdrawing permanently from politics.[28]

But Chamberlain was unwilling to see his work on the Irish Treaty go down in ruin if he could prevent it. While Baldwin worked on Amery, Cave, Salisbury, and other prominent Conservatives, trying to get them to use their influence to moderate Craig's attitude, he turned his attention to the Conservative press. His main grievance was against *The Times*, whose championing of Ulster was growing progressively more strident. To its editor, Geoffrey Dawson, he sent a 'grave private remonstrance' for allowing *The Times* to print an editorial carrying the 'wholly confounded and most mischievous charges that there had been trickery' involved in the making of the Irish Treaty.[29] But it was in J.L. Garvin, the editor of *The Observer*, that Chamberlain placed most hope; he was not disappointed. On 2 August Garvin came out with a long editorial on 'The Irish Crisis' in which he excoriated both the Irish Republicans on the one hand, and on the other 'the fatal faction of the Conservative Diehards, always tempted to play with fire', while praising MacDonald: 'the electioneering temptation which Mr. Lloyd George holds out to the Labour Government is strong, and may in the end be overpowering', fortunately MacDonald 'is not the one to sell his soul for a majority'. Fearing that such an election might cause Ulster to forsake Great Britain, Garvin urged that 'Placed in this emergency, involving issues which reduce party interests to insignificance, the business of Unionists is to shun the Diehard

[28] Chamberlain to Lady Chamberlain, 29 July 1924 (AC 6/1/543).
[29] Ibid.

spirit like the plague. Above all, Ulster's fate will depend largely upon its own power of self-control.'[30]

Garvin's article reflects the dominant mood in the Conservative Party during this period, that Ulster should be retained as an adjunct to Great Britain for both strategic and sentimental reasons, but that this should be done in a way that would be least injurious to Anglo-Irish relations. Not all Conservatives were convinced that an election on Ireland would necessarily redound to the advantage of the Liberals and Labour. Amery doubted whether the 'Irish business' would come to a head before the autumn. 'When it does', he wrote Baldwin, 'we shall have to face the possibility of the Goat trying to lead a raging campaign against Ulster in the hope of bringing about a Liberal socialist combination and swamping us. It won't come off.'[31]

This also was MacDonald's view. Unmoved by Cosgrave's plea that he did not think he could survive in office if two months were allowed to elapse before the enactment of a bill that would enable the British Government to appoint a commissioner for Northern Ireland, the Cabinet decided on 4 August to run the risk of a republic being set up in Ireland during the adjournment rather than chance an election by trying to force a bill through during the present session.[32] Four days later, after 'protracted and difficult' negotiations in Dublin between Thomas, Henderson, and Cosgrave, the Cabinet reluctantly agreed to have a special session of Parliament summoned on 30 September to appoint a commissioner for Ulster.[33]

When announcing the Cabinet's decision to the House on the following day, Thomas appealed to the press and people of England to refrain during the interval before the special session from any action that might awaken old suspicions or inflame old prejudices. His wishes were not granted. Speaking for the Liberals, Sir John Simon promised support for the Government's policy, but went on to enquire whether Thomas

---

[30] Article by Garvin in the *Observer* enclosed in a letter from Chamberlain to Lady Chamberlain, 3 Aug. 1924 (AC 6/1/557).

[31] Amery to Baldwin, 3 Aug. 1924 (Baldwin papers, 7/118–119).

[32] Cabinet conclusions 46(24) of 4 Aug. 1924 (CAB 23/48).

[33] Cabinet conclusions 48(24) of 8 Aug. 1924 (CAB 23/48).

had pointed out to the Ulster Government that under the Act of 1922 the opportunity to contract out of the Irish Treaty was given it by the same article as provided for the Boundary Commission, so that it was claiming to accept the advantage of that article without the burden imposed by it. 'Ominous cries arose from the Conservative benches at this home-thrust', records the *Annual Register*, 'and to prevent a tumult the Speaker judged it advisable to disallow all further questions.'[34] No one was more indignant than MacDonald, who, as usual, found the behaviour of the Liberals far more reprehensible than that of the Conservatives.[35]

Within the Conservative Party opinion was running strongly in favour of supporting Ulster rather than placating the Free State at her expense. The threat of a republic in the South was widely interpreted as a bluff intended to force the Labour Government to give the Free State 'as much of Ulster as they can get without fighting for it'.[36] Baldwin could not swim against the pro-Ulster tide, even if he wanted to. But neither could he expect to retain the Party leadership if he led it to another defeat at the polls. Fortunately Craig and Londonderry were not blind to the danger that might result if the Conservatives were to be defeated on the issue of standing by Ulster. During the Parliamentary recess Baldwin travelled to Belfast and extracted from Craig a promise of moderation. In return he promised Craig his support if the decision of the Boundary Commission went against the North. From his customary holiday retreat at Aix-les-Bains in the South of France, Baldwin later described the situation to Edward Wood (later Lord Halifax):

Craig is willing to accept, 'under duress', as he puts it, the new Act, relying on the interpretation of the Treaty as expounded by the signatories in Parliament. If the Commission should give away counties, then of course Ulster couldn't accept it and we should back her. But the Government will nominate a proper representative and we hope that he and Feetham will do what is right ...

The Lords are the curse. They will never let the Bill through

[34] *Annual Register* (1924), p. 88.
[35] MacDonald to King George v, 5 Aug. 1924 (MacDonald papers, 1/228).
[36] Memo by Moyle to Colonel Storr (Unionist Central Office), 7 Aug. 1924 (Baldwin papers, 7/120).

except on the definite assurance that Ulster will accept it. Craig's first idea was to fight the Bill along the line; the Lords to let it through at the last. But I showed him the snag and I told him that he would have to consider at his leisure whether some pronouncement should be made by the 30th [of September] so that the Bill could be let through. If the Lords once reject it, we may be in grave difficulties.[37]

In the end, fear of electoral disaster, more than anything else, convinced the Conservatives not to oppose the Government's Bill.[38] Wood urged Baldwin to use

whatever influence you have with Craig in the direction of persuading him to be very careful how he talks about resistance to what we all suppose to be an improbable verdict by the Boundary Commission, if and when established. He can say the same thing in other words, but I suspect the British law abiding temperament was more shocked than we always recognised by Carson's performance and Ulster will lose sympathy if she appears to be following that line.[39]

Meanwhile, Londonderry was also preaching moderation.[40] By the time Parliament reconvened on 30 September Baldwin had Salisbury's assurance that he would help put the Irish Bill through the Lords.[41]

The Irish Bill passed without any difficulty. An Ulster-sponsored amendment aimed at limiting the scope of the Boundary Commission did not receive the support of the Conservative leadership and was easily defeated, although it did get 124 out of the 415 votes cast—symbolic of the enduring emotional commitment to Ulster within the Conservative Party. Craig's grudging acceptance of the Bill deprived the Liberals of any chance of making Ireland an issue in the upcoming elections. During the special session only the radical non-conformist Liberal William Wedgwood Benn urged that the crisis be settled by an approach towards Irish unity. He received no support,

[37] Baldwin to Edward Wood, 6 Sept. 1924 (Halifax papers, A 4/410/41/1).
[38] Derby to Baldwin, 4 Sept. 1924 (Baldwin papers, 7/130-131); Churchill to Sir Harry Goschen, 11, 19, and 28 Aug. 1924; Churchill to Colonel Jackson, 14 and 19 Aug. 1924; Churchill to Sir Robert Horne, 30 Aug. 1924; Churchill to Balfour and Carson, 1 Sept. 1924 (Gilbert, *Churchill, Companion* v, 1, pp. 174-7, 183-4, 185, 190).
[39] Wood to Baldwin, 9 Sept. 1924 (Halifax papers, A 4/410/1).
[40] Londonderry to Baldwin, 27 Aug. 1924 (Baldwin papers, 7/128-29).
[41] Salisbury to Baldwin, 25 Aug. 1924 (Baldwin papers, 7/122-126).

and was rebuked by Austen Chamberlain for 'stirring up strife'.[42]

The Irish policy of the first Labour Government, as of the previous Conservative Governments, owed less to the realities of the situation in Ireland than it did to the political situation at home. From the beginning, MacDonald had been determined to stay in office as long as possible to prove that Labour could govern. To do so without becoming dependent upon the Liberals, whom he despised, it was necessary to stay on good terms with the Conservatives. He and Baldwin had a mutual interest in keeping Ireland out of British politics. An election on Ulster might backfire against the Conservatives and cost Baldwin his position as Party leader. It might also galvanize the faltering Liberals as a viable party on the left and provide an opening for Lloyd George, thereby undermining the hopes of Labour of replacing the Liberals as the leading radical party. It was in order to prevent this happening that MacDonald and Baldwin combined to avoid a crisis over the Boundary Commission. This left the Liberals with no place to go. It also meant that the Irish policy of the first Labour Government was no different from that which a Conservative Government would have pursued under the same circumstances. This was seen when the Conservatives returned to power under Baldwin in November.

[42] *Parl. Deb. Commons*, vol. 177, cols. 159-60 of 20 Sept. 1924.

7

The Return of Baldwin:
The Boundary Crisis (II)

On 8 October 1924 the Liberals and Conservatives combined to defeat the Government on a vote of no confidence on the Campbell case.[1] MacDonald resigned immediately and on 29 October the British people went to the polls for the third time in as many years. Except in heavily Irish areas, Ireland was not an issue in the election.[2] The result was a triumph for the Conservatives, who returned 419 members out of 615. Labour lost 40 seats, dropping to 151. But the Liberals suffered worst, losing 116 seats and being reduced to a rump of 40 members in the House of Commons under the uneasy leadership of Lloyd George and Simon. The leader now of a united party with an unshakeable majority, Baldwin welcomed magnanimously the repentant Coalitionists back into the fold: Birkenhead as Secretary of State for India and Austen Chamberlain as Foreign Secretary. Most surprising of all, Churchill, who had completed his metamorphosis back into a Conservative, was rewarded with the Exchequer. In addition, the two Cecils remained in the Cabinet, as did Cave (Woolsack), Joynson-Hicks (Home Office), and Amery (Colonial Secretary). Important

---

[1] J.R. Campbell, the Communist editor of the *Workers' Weekly*, had published an article calling on soldiers not to obey the orders of their officers. In September 1924 Ramsay MacDonald had agreed to drop the Government's prosecution of Campbell. On 8 October the House of Commons debated the Campbell case. Asquith, who demanded a Select Committee, was supported by Baldwin, and the Labour Government was defeated by 364 votes to 198. MacDonald at once called for a general election.

[2] Hugh Dalton ascribed his victory at Peckham to a large Irish Catholic vote against his Tory opponent, Archer Shee, who, although a Catholic, had opposed the Irish Treaty. Hugh Dalton, *Call Back Yesterday 1887–1931* (London, 1953), p. 153. Churchill, on the other hand, before being accepted by the Conservatives as a candidate for Epping, was asked by the local constituency leaders to give 'a pledge on Ulster, to the effect that no boundary changes would be made without the approval of the Ulster Parliament' (Gilbert, *Churchill* v *The Prophet of Truth 1922–1939* (Boston, 1977), p. 46.

additions included Edward Wood, Lord Eustace Percy, Arthur Steel-Maitland, and Sir Douglas Hogg.

With the appointment by the British Government of J.R. Fisher, a prominent Ulster Unionist, to represent the Ulster Government, the Boundary Commission was formally constituted. It spent much of 1925 in deliberations. The proceedings were supposed to be confidential until the release of the final report. Eoin MacNeill, the Free State representative on the Commission, followed this injunction so faithfully that the Cosgrave Government was caught completely unawares when it learned the results. Fisher, on the other hand, appears to have kept his friends in the North well-informed of the proceedings.[3] How much of this the British were aware of is uncertain. Certainly few in the Government thought that there was much cause for anxiety. The presence of Feetham as chairman was reassuring. In addition, F.B. Bourdillon, the former Oxford don appointed as secretary to the Commission, who had had prior experience with the Upper Silesian Commission, made it clear beforehand that he did not regard religion, even in the case of Ireland, to be of much, if any, importance in regard to the delimitation of a boundary.[4]

But until near the end, no one could say for certain what the Commission would determine or how the three governments involved would react to that determination. In the summer of 1925 British and Irish officials began meeting to discuss the administrative steps to be taken to implement the Commission's decision. These efforts were hampered by British reluctance to make serious preparations for the transfer of large segments of territory, which they did not anticipate, but which they felt the Irish representatives 'will no doubt pretend to expect'. The Treasury, for example, hoped that 'the questions will be confined to a few postmen at most'.[5]

On 25 October, with the proceedings of the Commission

[3] See the introduction by Geoffrey Hand to the *Report of the Boundary Commission* (Shannon, 1969). See also the essay by the same author on 'MacNeill and the Boundary Commission' in F.X. Martin and F.J. Byrne (edd.), *The Scholar Revolutionary: Eoin MacNeill, 1867–1945, and the Making of the New Ireland* (Shannon, 1973), pp. 201–75; and Michael Tierney, *Eoin MacNeill: Scholar and Man of Action, 1867–1945* (Oxford, 1980), pp. 340–59.
[4] Memo by F.B. Bourdillon, n.d. (CO 537/1079).
[5] Treasury to Dominions Office, 3 Aug. 1925 (CO 537/1073).

nearing an end, Amery prepared a memorandum on the situation for circulation to the Cabinet. In it he stated: 'We are
under an absolute obligation to place the Government of the
Irish Free State, at their request, in possession of the portions
of Northern Ireland, however large they may be, which may
be transferred by the determination of the Commission to the
Irish Free State.' Amery did not expect that the determination
of the Commission when made would be 'obviously outrageous or unreasonable'. He considered it impossible, for
example, that the Commission would transfer the city of
Londonderry or the whole of Tyrone or Fermanagh, though he
did think it possible that the town of Newry and an appreciable
amount of those two counties might be transferred. He also
expected that the whole of the area conveyed to the Free State
would exceed that of the Free State transferred to Northern
Ireland. Arguing that the consequences of any violation of the
Treaty by Great Britain would be 'more disastrous than an
open and violent breach with Northern Ireland', Amery suggested that a 'clear and unequivocal' statement made by the
British Government to Northern Ireland would greatly strengthen the position of Craig *vis-à-vis* his own colleagues and
people. If it were made clear that the two alternatives before
Northern Ireland were either to co-operate with the British
Government in carrying out the determination, or else to go
into open rebellion, they would choose the former. 'But if by
hesitating or hedging we give Northern Ireland any ground
to believe that if their protest is loud enough we will accept it,
we may get into a position of the gravest difficulty.' Even if
the determination should be one which the Government of
Northern Ireland could obviously not accept, 'the British
Government is nevertheless, in our opinion, bound in the last
resort to give effect to it'.[6]

This was strong language, stronger perhaps than Amery
himself had intended, and too forceful for Joynson-Hicks, the
diehard Home Secretary, whose name was also on the memorandum. Refusing to 'add or subtract' from the assurances he
had already given to Ulster, Joynson-Hicks had Sir John Anderson, the Permanent Under-Secretary at the Home Office,

[6] Draft memo by Amery and Joynson-Hicks, 25 Oct. 1925 (CO 537/1089).

tone down the Colonial Office draft for submission to the Cabinet. The final draft included the warning:

> If this expectation [of a reasonable settlement] were falsified and the award were manifestly one which could not be carried out without grave risks of widespread disorder and possibly bloodshed, we should still be free to point out to the Free State that in the interests of Ireland as much as of this country, decisive action could not immediately be taken and that, while fully recognising our obligation, we must have time to cast about for means of discharging them without entailing such consequences as no responsible Government could deliberately contemplate.[7]

Even this proved too much for some of the Cabinet, including Joynson-Hicks and Salisbury, and touched off a dispute between the civil servants struggling to uphold the Treaty and the politicians committed to Ulster. Tom Jones, Baldwin's closest adviser on such matters, urged the Prime Minister to side with the departmental advisers, calling it 'one more crucial case for your own personal courage'.[8] Baldwin was not equal to the challenge. 'I could not do right off what you wanted about Ireland,' he later confessed. 'The moment the subject was mentioned at the Cabinet they all got excited; Salisbury and Jix [Joynson-Hicks] were bursting their buttons with eagerness to talk so I am going to see Feetham.'[9] But later Baldwin told the Cabinet that, having learned of the pledge undertaken by the commissioners to maintain secrecy, he had decided not to see him.[10]

In the meantime, Joynson-Hicks had been to Belfast to discuss the situation with Craig, whom he had found in an unusually co-operative mood. The Ulster Prime Minister not only agreed to abide by a reasonable settlement, but urged the Unionist members of the Northern Parliament from the border areas to do likewise. Even the Grand Master of the Orange Order was reported to be urging his followers to refrain from publishing inflammatory resolutions denouncing the Commission's report in advance.[11] Craig's surprising good

[7] CO 537/190. The revised memo was circulated to the Cabinet as CP 445 of 26 Oct. 1925 (CAB 24/175).

[8] Tom Jones to Baldwin, 28 Oct. 1925 (Jones, iii, p. 236).

[9] Tom Jones diary, 28 Oct. 1925 (ibid.).

[10] Cabinet conclusions 52(25) of 11 Nov. 1925 (CAB 23/51).

[11] Tallents to Anderson, 30 Oct. 1925 (CO 537/1072).

humour was based, we now know, on the knowledge that Ulster had nothing to fear from the Commission. How much of this he let on to Joynson-Hicks is unclear. Perhaps not very much, for he hoped to extract from Britain an exemption for Ulster from its annual imperial contribution to the British Exchequer as a reward for the sacrifices it was making in the cause of amicable Anglo-Irish relations.[12]

The as yet unresolved question whether the British should enforce the determination of the Boundary Commission, regardless of its findings,[13] took a new twist when, on 7 November, the *Morning Post* published an apparently inspired statement to the effect that the Commission would leave the frontier much as before. Two weeks later MacNeill, under pressure, resigned from the Commission. Events now took a volte-face. Ulster began pressing for the promulgation of the report so that it could exchange certain heavily Catholic portions of Fermanagh and Armagh for Protestant eastern Donegal,[14] while Cosgrave's Government appeared likely to collapse if it were published. Cosgrave's most probable replacement would be a Labour–Republican coalition in which the Republicans would probably enter the Dáil and the government without taking the oath. Not only would this be 'very embarrassing', observed Whiskard, but it 'might easily lead to a *coup d'état* which would bring the whole of the old Irish question back on our heads'.[15]

To forestall such a development, the British invited the Irish leaders to London on 24 November for a conference. To Austen Chamberlain Cosgrave appeared a man 'very puzzled to know how to deal with the situation, but a man anxious for peace'.[16] The British gave the Irish two choices: either to accept the award of the Commission or to keep the existing boundary. While opting for the latter, the Irish insisted that in exchange the North should make a complete restitution of

[12] Note of conversation between Craig and Joynson-Hicks, 4 Nov. 1925 (CO 537/1095).

[13] Minutes and draft memos by Whiskard, Nov. 1925 (CO 537/1096); memo by Amery of 18 Nov. 1925 (CAB 27/295).

[14] 1st Meeting of the Committee on Irish Affairs, 23 Nov. 1925 (CAB 27/295); and minutes by Whiskard, Nov. 1925 (CO 537/1103 and 1106).

[15] Minute by Whiskard (ibid.).

[16] 3rd Meeting of Committee on Irish Affairs, 26 Nov. 1925 (CAB 27/295).

civil rights to the Catholic minority, including the release of
political prisoners. They threatened that otherwise they might
have to appeal to the League of Nations or, what was more
likely, that they would be 'swept out of office and replaced by
a more irreconcilable Government'.[17]

The British were prepared to make concessions. Craig, who
was in London for the negotiations, was also prepared to be
generous, though at British expense. He insisted upon scrap-
ping the Council of Ireland altogether, and in addition asked
for a £4 million subsidy for the North, and that the British
forgo Ulster's annual imperial contribution for the next two
years. In return, he agreed to release a few prisoners.[18] While
the Irish committee initially appeared fully prepared to meet
all of Craig's demands, it found itself over-ruled by the civil
servants. Anderson thought it would be best if the award of
the Commission were 'washed out' and the present boundary
allowed to stand. He believed that Craig had weakened his
tactical position by asking not only for execution of the award,
but also for compensation and the disappearance of the Council of Ireland. The Dominions Office officials felt the Free
State's surrendering of its rights under the Council of Ireland
would be concession enough.[19] A compromise was found
when, after private conversations between Craig and Kevin
O'Higgins, it was discovered that the Free State might also
like to be relieved of some of its financial obligations under
the Treaty, in particular its liability under Article 5 for a
share of the national debt of the United Kingdom as of the
signing of the Treaty.[20] In return for promises from the Irish
ministers not to meddle any longer in the internal affairs of
Northern Ireland on behalf of the Catholic minority, Craig
agreed that the determination of the Boundary Commission
should remain a secret. Churchill's failure to persuade the

---

[17] Report by Baldwin on matters relating to Irish affairs, Cabinet Conclusions
55(25) of 30 Nov. 1925 (CAB 23/51).

[18] Ibid. and 3rd Meeting of Committee on Irish Affairs, 26 Nov. 1925 (CAB 27/
295).

[19] Attending the meeting on 26 Nov. in addition to Anderson were Charles Davis,
the Permanent Under-Secretary at the Dominions Office, Harding, and Whiskard
(CO 537/1104).

[20] Report by Baldwin of 30 Nov. 1925, Cabinet conclusions 55/25 of 30 Nov. 1925
(CAB 23/51).

Irish leaders on either side to sign an agreement calling for joint action in the future passed almost unnoticed amidst the euphoria generated by the happy ending to the dispute.[21]

The final result was widely hailed by the British press. *The Times* expressed the general hope that the abrogation of the boundary clause of the Treaty would bring a sense of security and relief to Ulster, 'and in the end a greater readiness to accept the Catholic minority of Northern Ireland as fellow citizens rather than as enemy outposts'.[22]

These hopes were not realized. As usual, no sooner had Craig returned to Belfast than he reverted to his old ways. A number of prisoners were released from gaols in Northern Ireland in accordance with a supplementary agreement reached in London, only to be served immediately with orders to remove themselves from Ulster. Baldwin chided Craig for failing to live up to the spirit of the recent agreement and for action which 'might justly be deemed oppressive',[23] but to no effect.

In March 1926 accord was reached on the so-called Ultimate Financial Agreement between Great Britain and the Irish Free State. In return for being relieved of some of its financial obligations under the Treaty, the Cosgrave Government agreed to resume payments of land annuities. This pact, which lasted only as long as Cosgrave remained in power, was never submitted to the Dáil for approval, and was to become a source of bitter contention between the British and Irish Governments when de Valera returned to power in 1932.

Settlement with Ulster was more difficult to achieve. Because of the decline of its staple industries of linen and shipbuilding, Northern Ireland throughout the inter-war years was dependent upon the British Treasury for subsidies. But from the beginning, Ulster strove for parity in unemployment benefits for itself in relation to the rest of the United Kingdom.[24] While not an unreasonable goal, it was neverthe-

[21] 'Report of a Meeting between Churchill, Salisbury, Birkenhead, Craig and the Free State Ministers', 1 Dec. 1925; 3rd report to the Irish Affairs Committee (CAB 27/295); Cabinet conclusions 56(25) of 2 Dec. 1925 (CAB 23/51).

[22] *The Times*, 5 Dec. 1925.

[23] Baldwin to Craig, copy of telegram appended to CP 18 of 1926 (CAB 24/178).

[24] Buckland, *Factory of Grievances*, pp. 81-129; and, more generally, Lawrence, *Government of Northern Ireland*.

less fraught with considerable political implications, for the more the British subsidized Northern Ireland, the wider would be the gap between its social services and those of the South, whose economy during this period was also none too robust. Consequently, British subsidies to Ulster would have the effect of reducing the inclination of Ulster to merge with the South, thereby becoming an additional stumbling block to Irish unity. This could easily be construed as a violation of the spirit, if not the letter, of the Irish Treaty.

Such was the line taken by the British Treasury, which consistently opposed parity for the social services of Ulster with those of the rest of the United Kingdom. It argued that, if the Parliament of Northern Ireland were to adopt all the legislative measures passed in Great Britain, and if the cost of doing so where it was not covered by revenue measures corresponding to those passed in Great Britain were to be paid by the British taxpayer, then the autonomy of Northern Ireland would become purely nominal. While not unwilling to concede that the poorer country should derive certain advantages from union with her richer neighbour, the Treasury thought that fair compensation had already been given in the form of the free gift of the land annuities, amounting in Northern Ireland's case to £600,000 a year. 'To give them the Land Annuities and at the same time provide at the expense of the British taxpayer for keeping all services up to the British level is to let them eat their cake and have it.'[25]

Even more important, the Treasury argued, were the political implications of such action. The application of the Act of 1920 to Northern Ireland was part of the terms of the Treaty with the Free State.

The Act itself was intended to offer certain inducements to the two portions of Ireland to unite. Any concession which makes separate existence more attractive to Northern Ireland than the Act intended is a breach of this condition of the Treaty. A concession in the present case would furnish a precedent for similar concessions of which the total effect might be a complete transformation of the whole basis of the Act.[26]

[25] Memo by Treasury, Sept. 1923 (HO 45/13743/466247/2).
[26] Ibid.

Although Ulster won some concessions from the British Government—the most important being the decision of the Colwyn Committee that the imperial contribution should no longer be the first charge on the revenue of Northern Ireland, but instead the residue left over after domestic expenditures had been met—the Treasury was for some time able to rebuff its demands for parity. The Chancellors of the Exchequer during these years accepted the argument of Sir Warren Fisher, the powerful Permanent Under-Secretary of the Treasury, that concessions on the question of parity were impossible because the matter could not be dealt with in isolation. In 1924 Neville Chamberlain accordingly told Craig that he doubted whether he could 'in any circumstances' admit the claim for parity 'which would involve a fundamental amendment of the Government of Ireland Act, 1920'.[27] Similarly, Philip Snowden, as Labour Chancellor of the Exchequer, refused to admit parity for Northern Ireland or to accept the Special Constabulary as a regular charge on the British Exchequer.[28]

But in 1925 the Baldwin Government took a new departure. Despite objections from the Treasury, a Cabinet Committee chaired by Cave recommended in May that the political reasons for strengthening Northern Ireland made it desirable that Britain accept in principle that 'amalgamation of the unemployment funds of Northern Ireland with those of the rest of the United Kingdom must be the object of British policy'.[29] On 28 May the Cabinet accordingly appointed a subcommittee under Sir John Anderson to study the practicability of achieving this goal. But the report of the subcommittee issued on 15 July voiced certain 'grave objections' to the proposed amalgamation of social services. Not the least of these were political in nature. 'It seems to us certain', the report concluded,

that they [Irish Free State Government] would equally claim that any *diminution* of those powers [of Northern Ireland], tending as it would towards the ultimate reinclusion of Northern Ireland in the

[27] Chamberlain to Craig, 3 Jan. 1924 (ibid.).
[28] Sir William Graham (Financial Secretary to the Treasury) to Pollock (Northern Ireland Minister of Finance), 5 Sept. 1924 (ibid.).
[29] Cabinet conclusions 17(25) of 20 March 1925 (CAB 23/49).

political system of Great Britain, was a violation of the Treaty. It is
by no means certain that such a claim would be upheld; but we
submit that it would be in the highest degree undesirable that, if it
can be reasonably avoided, the issue should be raised.[30]

The findings of the Anderson subcommittee were upheld in
principle. Ulster had never made any secret of the fact that
one of its main reasons for seeking amalgamation of its social
services with those of Great Britain was a political one, 'the
desire of the Government and people of Northern Ireland to
remain in the closest possible association with Great Britain'.[31]
But it was precisely for this reason that amalgamation was
rejected. In 1925 the British Government still accepted that
any financial agreement which would tend to bind Northern
Ireland permanently to the United Kingdom at the expense
of its connections with the South was a violation of the spirit
of the Government of Ireland Act, 1920, and of the Irish
Treaty. Nevertheless, by providing that the unemployment
funds of the two parts of the United Kingdom be kept in a
state of parity by grants to the poorer fund, the Unemployment Insurance Agreement concluded with Northern Ireland
in 1926 took a giant stride in that direction. Ostensibly reciprocal, it in fact amounted to a permanent subsidy by Great
Britain to Northern Ireland. This established the precedent
for what amounted, by 1938, to full parity in the social services
between Northern Ireland and the rest of the United Kingdom. Thus did the British Government gradually yield in
practice what it refused, at least in the beginning, to yield in
principle.

With the successful settlement of the boundary dispute,
Anglo-Irish relations entered into their most harmonious
period between the wars. The high point in these relations
was reached at the Imperial Conference of 1926, during which
the concept of equality between the Dominions was first

[30] Report of Sub-committee on Amalgamation of Social Services, 15 July 1925,
appended to the minutes of the 4th Meeting of the Cabinet Committee on Northern
Ireland Unemployment Fund (CAB 27/279).

[31] Memo by the Government of Northern Ireland on 'Reasons Why the Government of Northern Ireland desires to be included in the British scheme', 1925 (CAB
27/279).

broadly stated. Problems still remained—especially after de Valera's new party (Fianna Fáil) entered the Dáil in 1926 as a 'constitutional' opposition—but there was considerable hope and optimism on both sides that peaceful solutions could be found to the issues that still divided the two nations. Since the constitutional development of the British Commonwealth, and the role of the Irish Free State in that process, has already been the object of numerous studies,[32] it need not detain us long here. But because of its intrinsic importance, some notice of British attitudes towards these events must be taken.

On the whole, the British were favourably impressed by the role played by the Free State representatives at the Imperial Conference in 1926, especially by their head delegate, Kevin O'Higgins.[33] Hankey found them surprisingly conciliatory,[34] as did Austen Chamberlain, who was 'confirmed in [his] belief that only time is needed to bring them heartily on our side'.[35] This was largely because the Free State delegates were content to support General Hertzog, the South African Prime Minister, from the sidelines, rather than adopt any independent initiatives themselves.[36] While some wondered what would become of the Irish Treaty once it was accepted that all the Dominions were equal, and their parliaments completely autonomous and independent,[37] that was a question the British chose not to confront at the time. When, for example, Balfour objected to the term 'freely associated' in the statement which was to become one of the great landmarks in the constitutional history of the Empire-Commonwealth, pointing out that 'if we were freely associated we might equally easily be freely disassociated, and it was undesirable to introduce this idea', he was persuaded by Birkenhead and Amery that,

[32] See especially, Harkness, *The Restless Dominion.*
[33] Hankey to Baldwin, 'Report on Meeting of Lord Balfour's Committee of Prime Ministers on Inter-Imperial Relations', 1 Nov. 1926 (DO (Dominions Office) 117/48/D12602).
[34] Roskill, *Hankey*, ii, p. 248.
[35] Petrie, ii, p. 308.
[36] Imperial Conference 1926, stenographic notes of meetings (CAB 32/46).
[37] Minute by Edward Harding, 27 Oct. 1926 (DO 117/35/D11377). The Dominions Office was separated from the Colonial Office in 1925, and remained separate until it was integrated with the Foreign Office in 1968. But until 1929 Amery served as Secretary of State for both the Colonial and the Dominions Office.

if they accepted the argument of equality of status, the point must be conceded.[38]

The Imperial Conference of 1926 laid the groundwork for the one of 1930 and the Statute of Westminster in the following year in which was made clear the extent of the powers enjoyed by the Dominion parliaments. In the future, legislation by the Parliament of the United Kingdom could only apply to Dominions at their request and with their consent. In addition, Dominions would henceforth be competent to legislate in those matters affecting them which had previously been regulated by the legislation of the United Kingdom Parliament, and they would have the power to repeal existing legislation by that Parliament on such matters. Moreover, they would have full authority to make laws having extra-territorial operation.[39]

Despite the spirit of optimism engendered by the Conference of 1926, the legacy of distrust still pervading Anglo-Irish relations did not vanish overnight. It remained especially strong in the Services. The Admiralty, which wished to retain its control over the Irish ports, is a special case, and will be considered in Chapter 9. But distrust of the Irish was also strong in the War Office, as was evidenced, for example, in 1926, when an application by the Free State for a light tank for its army was turned down at Cabinet level after Worthington-Evans, the Secretary of State for War, successfully opposed the request on the grounds that 'technical details might become known to foreign officials'.[40] Suspicion of the Free State was also rife at the highest level of defence planning, the CID. Papers routinely circulated to the other Dominions were withheld from it as a matter of course, nor was it invited to send representatives to attend meetings as were the other Dominions. Hankey suggested that it should be accorded the same treatment as Newfoundland.[41] The Dominions Office rarely objected because it thought the Treaty precluded full Dominion status for the Free State regarding

---

[38] Report on meeting of Lord Balfour's Committee (DO 117/48/D12602).

[39] K.C. Wheare, *The Statute of Westminster and Dominion Status* (London, 1949).

[40] CP 381 of 12 Nov. 1926 (CAB 24/182).

[41] Memo by Hankey on 'The Circulation of Documents to the Dominions', 7 May 1929 (DO 117/147/D6059).

defence, and because the Free State Government did not seem to mind.[42]

Almost as suspicious of the Free State as the Service departments was the Foreign Office. Neither Sir Eyre Crowe, Permanent Under-Secretary for Foreign Affairs until his death in 1925, nor his somewhat more conciliatory and Catholic successor, Sir William Tyrell, had much confidence in the ability of the Free State Government to keep Foreign Office circulars confidential.[43] Nor did their chiefs, Curzon and MacDonald, think highly of the Free State. Not until 1927, when Austen Chamberlain was Foreign Secretary, did the Foreign Office agree that Cosgrave should receive the Foreign Office lists routinely circulated to the prime ministers of the other Dominions.[44] Foreign Office distrust of the Free State may have been based in part on resentment towards its apparent determination to play an independent role in world affairs, whether by taking an active part in the League of Nations, or by establishing its own consulates and embassies—as it did in Washington in 1924 (thereby becoming the first Dominion to open its own embassy in a foreign country). Here the Foreign Office was fighting a losing battle to preserve a unified (its own) voice in imperial affairs, and wanted the Irish, as Curtis put it, to 'be content to run like good dogs after the British coach'.[45]

Despite their general improvement during the 1920s, by 1930 Anglo-Irish relations were again beginning to sour. This was due mainly to the domestic political situation in Ireland, where Cosgrave was being forced to move to the left to counter de Valera. As early as September 1930, before the Imperial Conference of that year, the British Trade Commissioner in Dublin, William Peters, had begun to warn of this danger. The political situation was slowly becoming more

[42] Minute by Harding, 27 Oct. 1926 (DO 117/35/D11377).

[43] Curtis to Devonshire, 9 Sept. 1923 (CO 739/20/49361).

[44] Prior to this they were held in the Vice Regal Lodge. Sir Robert Vansittart, private secretary to Curzon from 1920 to 1924, and later to Baldwin and MacDonald, before serving as Permanent Under-Secretary at the Foreign Office from 1930 to 1938, also had a strong distrust of the Irish and made no secret of his preference for the Ulstermen. Lord Vansittart, *The Mist Procession* (London, 1958), p. 265.

[45] Curtis to Devonshire, 9 Sept. 1923 (CO 739/20/49361).

unfavourable for the Cosgrave Government, he reported, in part because many moderate voters who sympathized with the Fianna Fáil programme and who in the past had abstained from voting or even voted for Cosgrave's Party simply because they were afraid that the advent of de Valera to power meant 'a second round with England', were beginning to feel that a change of Government was possible without a violent up-heaval, and were voting accordingly. Peters warned that sentimental attachment to the Empire was a negligible factor in Ireland, and suggested that debating points might be taken away from Fianna Fáil if the British accepted Ireland's 'right to secede'.[46]

But the British Government was as yet unprepared to make such a concession. One of its major concerns in preparing for the Imperial Conference was that General Hertzog of South Africa would press for just such a statement on the right of secession. The British regarded the issue as 'a trap'. 'If we agree in the right of secession', Hankey warned MacDonald, 'de Valera will exercise it. If we refuse to admit it, we shall have no end of trouble.'[47] To the Government's relief, the point was not raised at the Conference. Yet, unlike the Imperial Conference of 1926, when the Free State had been content to follow Hertzog's lead, at the Conference of 1930 it was the Free State delegates who dominated proceedings and who took the most pronounced 'anti-British' pose. Hankey's prediction was prophetic, as the question of the right of secession remained a convenient issue for de Valera to use against both Cosgrave and Britain.

The onset of the Great Depression, which brought down governments all over the world, including the Labour Government in Britain and the Cosgrave Government in Ireland, contributed greatly to the deterioration in Anglo-Irish relations from 1929 to 1931. Besides throwing Cosgrave on to the defensive in Irish domestic politics, thereby forcing him to the left in imperial relations, it also exacerbated other tensions

[46] British Trade Commissioner in Dublin (Peters) to Dominions Office 'Regarding the attitude likely to be adopted by the Irish Free State delegation at the Imperial Conference', 27 Sept. 1930 (MacDonald papers, 1/347).
[47] Hankey to MacDonald, 10 Aug. 1930 (MacDonald papers, 1/357).

between Britain and Ireland. In Ireland economic nationalism, as preached by Fianna Fáil, including higher tariffs on
British goods, was beginning to gain wider appeal. In Britain,
higher unemployment, which had already been running at
approximately 10 per cent of the working population during
the 1920s, put added pressure on the Government to restrict
Irish immigration. This pressure was strongest where unemployment was heaviest, mainly in the North and the Celtic
fringe, where the old declining industries—coal, shipping,
linen, and steel—were concentrated. Irish immigrants had
long made up a significant percentage of the population in
these areas, and they continued to cross over to Britain during
the 1920s, though in much smaller numbers than before.[48]
The problem was worst in Scotland, where long-standing religious and racial prejudice heightened the awareness of the
economic problem.[49]

The Scottish Presbyterian Church, and others worried
about Irish immigration, found a sympathetic listener in
Joynson-Hicks, the Conservative Home Secretary. An evangelical teetotaler, member in good standing of the Church
Assembly, past president of the National Church League, and
one of the heroes in the defeat of the Prayer Book measure in
1927, Joynson-Hicks was easily persuaded of the advantages
of limiting further Irish immigration into Great Britain.[50] But
after considerable study of the matter by the departments
concerned, even he had to admit in March 1929 that the
available evidence indicated that the immigration of Irish
nationals into Scotland was not at the time significant enough
to affect materially the position of the Irish population in
Scotland. Instead, he complained of the problems arising from
the number of Irish already settled in Scotland, and suggested
the repatriation of Irish on the dole and an appeal to Scottish

[48] The rate of immigration from Ireland to Great Britain appears to have reached
a low of little more than 20,000 a year by 1920, after which the number rose slowly
throughout the 1920s, only to drop again just prior to the outbreak of war in 1939.
See Kevin O'Connor, *The Irish in Britain* (London, 1972), p. 177; Sean Glynn, 'Irish
Immigration to Britain 1911–1951: Patterns and Policy', *Irish Economic and Social
History*. viii (1981), pp. 50–69.
[49] See James Edmund Handley, *The Irish in Modern Scotland* (Cork University Press,
1947), pp. 305–9.
[50] Cabinet conclusions 41 (48) of 23 July 1928 (CAB 23/58).

employers to give preference to Scottish rather than Irish labourers. Moreover, given the high rate of immigration of Irish into Britain (by his estimate 20,000 in 1928), and the criminal inclinations of the Irish, he suggested that the Dominions Secretary should press Cosgrave on the repatriation of immigrants from Southern Ireland who became a charge on the Poor Law.[51] But before the matter could be settled, the Conservatives found themselves turned out of office.

For those involved, including Joynson-Hicks, the crusade against Irish immigration was largely an emotional issue. As a practical matter, given the common citizenship between the two countries, and barring the unlikely possibility of an agreement with Cosgrave, it would have been almost impossible to propose legislation aimed solely at preventing the immigration of citizens of the Irish Free State. The senior officials of the Home and Dominions Offices realized this, and could see no way around it.[52] With the return of Labour to power in 1929, the issue might have been dropped (as Clynes, the new Home Secretary, was himself the son of an Irish immigrant) had it not been taken up personally by the Prime Minister. Spurred by the Protestant Scottish Churches, MacDonald, himself a Scot, urged his colleagues to give 'the most careful consideration' to the problem of Irish immigration 'which presented serious aspects from the point of view of social conditions in Scotland'.[53]

Three weeks later, Adamson, the Secretary of State for Scotland, submitted a report to the Cabinet indicating that the number of persons of Irish birth in Scotland had been steadily declining since 1911. The report also took issue with the frequent charge that people of Irish descent were both less independent and more criminally inclined than the native population, producing tables indicating that the percentage of Irish pauperism in relation to total pauperism was steadily declining from its 1911 level, and that from 1925 onwards the

[51] Cabinet conclusions 10(29) of 6 Mar. 1929 (CAB 23/60).

[52] Anderson to Harding, 10 May 1929, and Harding to Anderson, 1 May 1929 (DO 117/140/D.5149).

[53] Cabinet conclusions 35(30) of 2 July 1930 (CAB 23/64); and memo by Minister of Labour on 'Migration from Ireland into Scotland', CP 220 of 1 July 1930 (CAB 24/72).

proportion of Irish crimes to total crimes in Scotland had been steadily diminishing.[54]

Although a Committee on Empire Migration was set up with Lord Astor as chairman to study the broad outlines of the problem, both the Home Office and the Scottish Office were convinced that the ₁volume of Irish immigration into Britain was not high enough to justify legislation. The growth of the Roman Catholic element in Scotland was due to 'rapid multiplication' rather than to immigration, Adamson explained to MacDonald. Thus even the complete stoppage of immigration from the Free State would not remove what appeared to be the main ground for complaints, namely the marked tendency of the Irish and Roman Catholic element in Scotland to increase in numbers as compared to the native population.[55] Similarly, Clynes reported that, as the Irish-born population in England was also decreasing, 'the damage, such as it is, caused by Irish immigration, is almost done'. Most new immigrants were women destined to become domestic servants. As in Scotland, the problem was one of the native increase of the Irish-born element. Clynes also pointed out the difficulty of controlling immigration between Great Britain and Ireland.[56] This did not satisfy MacDonald. 'We should refuse to be a dumping ground of Dominion refuse,' he sternly minuted.[57] Seven months later he was still calling the matter of Irish immigration 'a perfect scandal'.[58] But, despite the prejudice of many Protestants, the question of Irish immigration never became a political issue serious enough to galvanize the Government into action. And without the cooperation of the Free State Government, which was highly unlikely,[59] it is doubtful if much could have been accomplished in any event.

[54] Report by Adamson on Irish in Scotland, CP 229 of 21 July 1930 (CAB 24/22).
[55] Scottish Office to MacDonald, 29 July 1931 (MacDonald papers, 1/358).
[56] Clynes to MacDonald, 13 Aug. 1931 (ibid.).
[57] Minute by MacDonald (ibid.).
[58] MacDonald to Sir Archibald Sinclair, 24 Mar. 1932 (ibid.).
[59] Minutes of meeting at Dominions Office between Free State and British Officials, 27 Apr. 1931 (DO 4431/8/25).

PART II

THE IMPACT OF DE VALERA

8

The Challenge

I am afraid the whole [Irish] business will be giving you a lot of anxiety, not perhaps so much for itself as for its possible reactions.

Irwin to MacDonald, 1 April 1932

The real trouble about Ireland is that De Valera, like Gandhi, puts his reason in keeping with a mentality which simply baffles one in its lack of reason ... The position is that whenever we have tried to get him to face the real facts of the situation he refuses to do so, and his generalities about goodwill have no existence in reality ... He will do nothing except what is a step to an Irish Republic, and is undoubtedly a complete prisoner to the Irish Republican Army.

MacDonald to the Archbishop of York, 13 September 1932

I hope it may not be necessary to renew the old fight but of course it entirely depends on the strength or weakness of H.M. Government, which is always an unknown quantity, especially in relation to Ireland.

Carson to Linton-Oman (founder, British Union of Fascists), 1 February 1933

My post-bag, growing larger almost every day, proves conclusively to me that the Conservative Party throughout the country is in a condition bordering on something like open revolt.

If the policy in regard to de Valera adds fuel to what may soon be the conflagration of India, the Government's further tenure of Office may be exceedingly short.

Rothermere to Thomas, 13 April 1934

There are three people, you know, who are impossible to deal with—de Valera, Gandhi and Beaverbrook.

Baldwin to Crozier, 12 June 1934

IN August 1931, the second Labour Government collapsed. It was replaced by a 'National Government' of Conservatives, Liberals, and National Labour, formed by MacDonald to deal with the crisis in Britain's trade and balance of payments. At the general election which followed the Conservatives scored a triumph, gaining 200 seats and returning 471 strong. For the rest the election was a disaster. The Labour Party was virtually annihilated, losing over 200 seats and returning only 52 members. National Labour, as the supporters of MacDonald called themselves, returned 13 members. The Liberals, split again, returned 33 members under Sir Herbert Samuel's leadership, and 35 Liberal Nationals under Sir John Simon. Altogether the Government's supporters won 554 seats and had a majority of over 500 in the House of Commons.

The National Government came to be dominated in its early stages by the so-called 'Big Six'—MacDonald and Thomas, Baldwin and Chamberlain, and Simon and Runciman. But the man who provided the drive was Neville Chamberlain, the Chancellor of the Exchequer. Unlike his older half-brother Austen, Neville had not been trained for politics, but had pursued a business career in Birmingham after failing to make a success of a sisal plantation in the West Indies and before following in his father's footsteps to become Lord Mayor of Birmingham. In 1917 he had been appointed head of the newly created Ministry of National Service, only to resign a short time later amidst mutual recriminations with Lloyd George, whom he never forgave. Since 1918 Chamberlain had represented a Birmingham constituency in Parliament; since 1923—except for the brief Labour interludes—in high office. Unlike the easy-going and indolent Baldwin, who shunned confrontations and preferred to muddle through, Chamberlain was an intensely private man, hard-working, uncomfortable with drift, one who thrived on political clashes and revelled in his mastery of detail, continually formulating forward, aggressive policies on every conceivable issue. His defects sprang mainly from a certain aloofness of personality, which often seemed abrasiveness, and a tendency to accept too uncritically the advice of his experts, often at the expense of the wider picture. Once he had made up his mind, he generally adhered to his decision with a dogged determination, not always with sufficient regard for the consequences. But his was not always a closed mind. Like his father, he had a keen interest in imperial affairs, and would have preferred the Colonial and Dominions Office to the Exchequer had the Conservatives been returned in 1929.[1] Like his brother Austen, Chamberlain had moderate views on Ireland, and he had supported the Irish Treaty. He was the strongest man in the Government and perhaps its most innovative thinker. He was also, at sixty-two, the heir presumptive to Baldwin as leader of the Conservative Party.

For the rest, Sir Walter Runciman, who returned to his post as President of the Board of Trade that he had filled under Asquith, was a distinguished Liberal who shared Chamberlain's hatred of Lloyd George. Simon, who had also served under Asquith, was a brilliant barrister and debater who often managed to alienate while he impressed. Of Nonconformist background, he was influenced on Ireland by his wife (a niece of Alice Stopford Green), as when he had stumped the country against the Black and Tans in 1920.[2] MacDonald, who stayed on as Prime Minister, and Thomas, who returned to the Dominions Office, were the most prominent leaders of the National Labour Group, four out of thirteen of whom received posts in the new Government.

Although a coalition of Conservatives, National Labour, and Liberal Nationals, the most important thing about the National Government was the overwhelming Conservative predominance, both in MPs and ministers. Although MacDonald, Simon, and their followers received a disproportionate number of seats and possessed considerable influence as a symbol of the 'national' character of the Government, they were political prisoners. The final decision on any matter of importance rested with the Conservatives, led by Baldwin and Chamberlain.

Conspicuously absent from the new Government were Lloyd George, who had been recovering from a serious illness when the Government was formed, and Churchill, who had

[1] Iain Macleod, *Neville Chamberlain* (New York, 1962), p. 130.
[2] C.P. Scott diary, 8–9 Mar. 1923 (Trevor Wilson (ed.), *The Political Diaries of C.P. Scott, 1911–1928* (Ithaca, 1970), p. 348); and information provided by Lord Simon.

resigned from the Conservative shadow cabinet after disputes with Baldwin over India. With Labour reduced to a small but vocal rump led by George Lansbury and Stafford Cripps, Lloyd George and Churchill appeared to pose the more immediate threats to the Government. While in 1932 both men were isolated politically, the Government wished to see them remain so. Still 'apprehensive' about the 'possible fate' of its India policy,[3] the Government had good reason to be cautious lest it provide Churchill with an avenue of attack which he might use to stampede the Conservative Party against the India Bill and thus conceivably bring about the Government's collapse.

Although the National Government had to take into account the divergent views of a broadly based coalition, in practice the more liberal opinions of the Government's left wing were generally sacrificed during 1932 to those of the right. Thus Runciman's views on Ireland did not carry as much weight in the Cabinet as those of Lord Hailsham (formerly Sir Douglas Hogg), the Secretary of State for War and Leader of the House of Lords. Hailsham was a former Lord Chancellor highly regarded in Conservative circles and looked upon as a possible successor to Baldwin.[4] But more importantly, it would not have escaped his colleagues that, by deferring to the pronounced diehard views of Hailsham, they would be warding off attack by Churchill; while the corollary was also true, that by making any concessions to de Valera, they would risk incurring the Churchillian wrath. This was dangerous only when, as in 1932 on Ireland, Churchill would have the weight of public opinion on his side.

Another factor which influenced the British Cabinet in 1932 was largely concerned with Irish domestic politics. This was the desire not to weaken the position of Cosgrave's Cumann na nGaedheal Party by making hasty concessions to de Valera's more intransigent supporters. The situation in Ireland appeared especially delicate, since de Valera had to rely on the support of the Irish Labour Party to gain a majority of 79

---

[3] Sir Samuel Hoare to Lord Willingdon, 27 May 1932. Martin Gilbert (ed.), *Winston S. Churchill*, v Companion v, 2, *The Wilderness Years, 1929–1935* (London, 1981), p. 436.

[4] H. Montgomery Hyde, *Baldwin: The Unexpected Prime Minister* (London, 1973), p. 318.

against Cosgrave's bloc of 74 supporters. The very narrowness of the margin of victory and the near balance in the Dáil dictated a policy of restraint to avoid adding to de Valera's support by any precipitate action, and in the hope that de Valera might somehow undermine his own majority by such action. Following reports from William Peters, the British Trade Commissioner in Dublin, that Fianna Fáil 'had been learning sense fairly rapidly' just before the election, the Government accepted his advice not to 'bind [its] hands' before all the results were in.[5]

The initial response of the British press to the change in government in Ireland was also muted, focusing more on regret for the departure of Cosgrave than anxiety over the arrival of de Valera. Typical of this attitude was *The Times*, which attributed Cosgrave's defeat largely to the 'adventurously romantic' ideals of the younger generation, and praised the outgoing Government for its service to the Irish people.[6]

Although the Fianna Fáil election manifesto foreshadowed early action on the abolition of the oath of allegiance to the king and on withholding the land annuities, it had also indicated that de Valera intended to proceed on constitutional lines in addressing these issues. Assuming that this would be the case, Thomas expected that the Irish Senate would reject any bill aimed at abolition of the oath, thus giving the British Government eighteen months to consider its future course of action before the bill would become law.

Reporting to the Cabinet in mid-February, on the eve of the Free State elections, Thomas said that, if the Free State were to attempt to break away from the Commonwealth after the elections, it was important that it be clear that it was entirely the Free State's own doing. Although the British Government would take its stand on the Irish Treaty, he felt that the situation was very different from what it had been in 1921, when most of the population had been hostile to the British. Now there was a large party in the Free State pledged to the maintenance of the British connection. The situation demanded restraint so as not to jeopardize this support. If a

[5] William Peters to Department of Overseas Trade, 11 Jan. 1932 (BT (Board of Trade) 11/54 CRT 285).
[6] *The Times*, 22 Feb. 1932.

bill to abolish the oath became law, or if de Valera should refuse to submit the dispute over the land annuities to arbitration by an imperial tribunal, as recommended for such cases by the Imperial Conference of 1930, then Thomas felt that the British Government would have to consider the imposition of sanctions. These would probably take the form of a tariff on Irish goods to recover the loss to the British Treasury brought about by de Valera's withholding of the land annuities payments.[7]

The British had good reason to be reluctant to become embroiled in a controversy with de Valera. By 1932 the Depression had come to Britain. In February of that year there were between $2\frac{1}{2}$ and 3 million unemployed, and the number was rising. With nations turning increasingly towards Protection, British exports had fallen in value by almost half between 1929 and 1931, while imports had fallen in value at a much slower pace. The result in 1931 had been the worst balance of payments deficit since 1919, and consequent pressure on the Government to increase exports.[8] Since Ireland was, after India, Britain's best customer in 1931, receiving 60 per cent of her exports (mostly coal and industrial goods) from Britain, and sending to Britain fully 90 per cent of her exports (almost all agricultural), the British could not view with equanimity the prospect of political tensions strengthening the determination of Fianna Fáil to proceed towards its already proclaimed goal of economic self-sufficiency for Ireland. Thus the proposal for a tariff, which appeared to offer the easiest solution as to how to recoup the loss of the land annuities if de Valera withheld them, was not without drawbacks. Besides the risk of alienating some of the Government's supporters— the Liberal Free Traders—it might provoke a destructive tariff war or mutual boycott as injurious to Britain as to Ireland.[9]

Even if Britain's trade prospects might eventually improve

[7] Memo by J.H. Thomas on 'Political Situation in the Irish Free State', CP 86 of 17 Feb. 1932 (CAB 24/228).

[8] Derek H. Aldcroft, *The Inter-War Economy: Britain, 1919–1939* (London, 1970), pp. 260–1.

[9] Memos by H. Brittain on 'Irish Free State Payments to Great Britain', 23 Feb. 1932, and on 'Methods of Recovering the Irish Land Annuities', 7 May 1932 (T 160/459/5716/012/1).

as a result of going off the gold standard in 1931, the international outlook in other respects was becoming ominous. With problems looming in the Far East regarding Japan, in India with the Congress Party, and in Europe over German reparations, the risk of damage to relations with the United States had again to be taken into consideration in the event of a break with the Free State.[10]

Nor was the British Government as confident of its case in regard to the land annuities as Thomas at first assumed. Just after de Valera's Party won the elections in February, a Treasury official cast some doubt on the Free State's legal, as distinct from moral, obligation to hand over the annuities.[11] In early March, Neville Chamberlain, the Chancellor of the Exchequer, followed this up with a memorandum to his colleagues pointing out that from a 'purely legal and technical point of view' an arbitrator might hold that de Valera was right, and that it would seem 'most undesirable' to expose themselves to such a decision when they were clearly in the right.[12] The Foreign Office shared these misgivings about the legal validity of the Irish Treaty.[13]

De Valera took office in March and immediately reiterated his determination to remove the oath and to keep the land annuities in Ireland. For almost a month following de Valera's victory the British Government remained silent. In response to a query about the situation in Ireland from a worried Salisbury, Baldwin wrote lightheartedly:

He [de Valera] will have to let out the [IRA] prisoners. They will be short of practice and may practice on him. In which case he will a) be shot, or b) have to reenact the provisions he will have repealed. That dilemma does not affect us. We have an effective Cabinet sub-committee to watch Ireland and to make recommendations to the Cabinet.[14]

In a more serious vein Baldwin told Thomas Jones that he believed anything was possible. He hoped Labour would com-

[10] Foreign Office memo on 'Political Situation', 3rd ISC (32) of 8 Mar. 1932 (CAB 27/500).
[11] Memo by Brittain of 23 Mar. 1932 (T 160/459/5716/012/1).
[12] Memo by Chamberlain, 2nd ISC (32) of 8 Mar. 1932 (CAB 27/500).
[13] Minutes by W. Beckett and B.E.F. Gage, 8 Mar. 1932 (FO (Foreign Office) 627/40/1 U 139/15/750).
[14] Quoted by Keith Middlemas and John Barnes, *Baldwin* (London, 1969), p. 664.

bine with Cosgrave's Party to defeat de Valera and then a compromise candidate would emerge.[15]

During this period the Government formed the Cabinet committee to study the problem to which Baldwin referred in his letter to Salisbury. Called the Irish Situation Committee, it was set up on 2 March 1932, and continued to meet at irregular intervals for the next six years. Almost everyone of importance in the Cabinet eventually became a member of the committee, and most of the important memoranda sent to the committee were later circulated to the Cabinet. The committee first consisted of Thomas, Chamberlain, Sir Herbert Samuel (Home Secretary), Hailsham, Runciman, and Lord Snowden (Lord Privy Seal).[16] Three weeks later MacDonald, Baldwin, and Simon were added.[17] Samuel and Snowden soon resigned from the Government over the imposition of tariffs and were replaced on the Irish Committee by Walter Elliot, the newly appointed Minister of Agriculture.

From the first, domestic political considerations, spoken or unspoken, played a large part in the deliberations of the Irish Committee. Initially the committee confined itself to considering various forms of reprisal against de Valera without, however, approving any of them. Its reluctance to take quick action was due at least in part to Chamberlain's belief in the importance of keeping public opinion on its side.[18]

But there was also a danger in moving too slowly. The Government was finally forced to act not by de Valera, but by Churchill. Speaking at Plymouth on 17 March, upon his return to England from an extended tour in the United States, Churchill delivered a resounding speech on the Irish situation. For the Irish to go back on their treaty obligations, he declared, would be 'an act of perfidy'. The oath of allegiance he termed the central point around which all the discussion of the Irish Treaty focused. It was impossible that England would ever lend the slightest countenance to such violation of a solemn agreement between the British and Irish peoples. 'We stand absolutely on the Treaty,' he said. 'If Mr. de Valera

[15] Thomas Jones, *A Diary With Letters, 1931–1950* (London, 1954), p. 31.
[16] Cabinet conclusions 16(32) of 2 Mar. 1932 (CAB 23/70).
[17] Cabinet conclusions 19(32) of 22 Mar. 1932 (CAB 23/70).
[18] Minute by S.D. Waley, 21 June 1932 (T 160/459/5716/012/1).

and his Government will repudiate the Treaty they repudiate the title deeds of the Irish Free State, which becomes an anomalous body without a status at all, either in or out of the empire.'[19]

Churchill's speech was all the push the Government needed. Speaking at Birmingham the following day, Chamberlain broke the Government's long silence on Ireland by saying that it would view with the gravest concern 'any suggestion that obligations or agreements solemnly entered into by the two countries could be repudiated or varied' by either side alone 'as though it concerned that side alone', and, 'if seriously pursued', such a course 'would undoubtedly revive the bitterness and differences which it was hoped had been removed for ever'.[20] Shortly thereafter Thomas first broached the question of the oath to J.W. Dulanty, the Irish Free State High Commissioner in London, only to be informed that the oath was not mandatory in the Treaty, that it was a relic of medievalism, and that its removal was purely a domestic matter.[21] In addition, de Valera formally announced that he intended to retain the land annuities.

This was a challenge which the British Government could not ignore. Thomas made the most of it. In a 'loudly applauded'[22] speech to the Commons he made threatening noises about the seriousness with which the Government would regard the abolition of the oath or a withholding of the land annuities.

Then the Government did nothing. There followed a long series of exchanges between Thomas and de Valera in which, according to the *Annual Register*, the former showed himself to be 'firm and conciliatory', and the latter 'as intransigent as ever'.[23] The exchanges were primarily over the land annuities. De Valera insisted that the Financial Agreement of 1926, and the hitherto secret financial agreement of 1923 signed by the Cosgrave Government, were not binding since they had never been submitted to, or ratified by, the Dáil. Thomas denied the

[19] Churchill, *Complete Speeches*, v, p. 5134.
[20] *The Times*, 19 Mar. 1932.
[21] *Cmd.* 4056 (1932) xiv, p. 273.
[22] *Annual Register* (1932), p. 29.
[23] Ibid. pp. 29–30.

validity of this claim. The British refused to consider submitting the question of the annuities to the Hague Court or any other foreign tribunal, insisting instead that any arbitration be by an imperial tribunal as laid down by the Conference of 1930. This de Valera refused to accept, remembering the Free State's experience with the Boundary Commission and doubting the impartiality of an imperial tribunal.

To the British, the question of the land annuities, serious as it was, was outweighed by the issue of allegiance to the Crown. There was some disagreement in the Irish Committee as to de Valera's ultimate intentions. Some regarded the abolition of the oath as simply the first step in a planned secession from the Commonwealth. Others, including Chamberlain, were not so sure.[24] Chamberlain's views in this regard may have been influenced by a report on the Irish situation he had received in early April from Frank Pakenham (later Lord Longford), scion of a great Anglo-Irish family and a youthful member of the Conservative Research Department over which Chamberlain presided. Pakenham had interviewed de Valera and had been greatly impressed by his sincerity. His report emphasized that the abolition of the oath was not the first step on the road to separation, as many feared. Rather, his general impression was that de Valera was in a difficult position himself. Drastic action by the British Government—such as economic sanctions—would push de Valera into the hands of the IRA, throw Ireland into a depression, and might even lead to a revolution. In that event Bolshevism was more likely than surrender.[25]

Whatever its feelings about de Valera's ultimate intentions, the Government could hardly stand meekly by and acquiesce in the removal of the oath, for that would place in jeopardy the whole Treaty of 1921—still regarded as the keystone of the Government's Irish policy—and bring into question the nature of the Free State's relationship to Great Britain and the Commonwealth. But more than that, it would have been impolitic not to take some action. With Churchill beating the drums, and public opinion in Parliament and in the British

[24] 2nd Meeting of ISC of 12 Apr. 1932 (CAB 27/523).
[25] Frank Pakenham, 'Notes on Interview with De Valera and James MacNeill, the Governor General of the Irish Free State, on Mar. 30, 1932' (Baldwin papers, 9/254).

press echoing his call for a policy of firmness, failure to act would be interpreted as a sign of weakness.

Still looking for a way out, the Cabinet hesitated to act. In spite of Salisbury's entreaties, debates in either House on Irish affairs were blocked in an effort to avoid the risk of swinging Irish opinion behind de Valera as a result of a direct attack upon him. The necessity of keeping the Commonwealth behind Britain had also to be taken into consideration. The prime ministers of South Africa and Canada had already expressed concern over the way in which the situation was developing. Care had to be taken to ensure that the onus for creating a breach rested on de Valera.[26]

The situation began to alter, however, when on 28 April John MacLoughlin, the leader of the Senate and one of Cosgrave's principal supporters, crossed to London with the message that a firm and early statement by the British Government was essential if Cosgrave were to have a chance for an early return to power.[27]

MacLoughlin's views were corroborated two days later by Donal O'Sullivan, the clerk of the Senate, who was sent to London to confer with Thomas by Cosgrave and Patrick McGilligan, the former head of the Ministry of Finance, who ostensibly feared that correspondence would be tampered with. O'Sullivan brought with him more detailed instructions. Cosgrave urged that, before the third reading of the bill to abolish the oath, the British should make a declaration respecting the action which would be taken in the event of the passage of the bill. This should be done only if the Government intended to adhere to its terms and to implement them if necessary, regardless of the consequences. According to O'Sullivan, Cosgrave's change of policy was due solely to tactical considerations. The Irish Labour Party was divided on the question of the Oath Bill, and it was quite possible that a firm statement by the British Government might make the difference. In addition, Dulanty had intimated to Thomas that in de Valera's view the British Government would, as in the past, give way rather than precipitate a crisis.[28]

---

[26] Smuts also warned against drastic action. 3rd Meeting of ISC of 5 May 1932 (CAB 27/523).
[27] Ibid.   [28] Ibid.

Thomas was willing to recommend that the Cabinet follow Cosgrave's advice, but only if the latter gave him something in writing to assure him that he would not change his mind in the meantime. As Cosgrave was unwilling to do this, the Irish Committee declined to recommend any change in policy.[29]

At the next meeting of the Committee on 9 May, Chamberlain said that the Free State Government was preparing to take action on a number of matters, including pensions due to former members of the Royal Irish Constabulary. He felt that it would be unfair to Cosgrave's Party to let the situation drift, and unfair to de Valera not to give him some warning of the consequences of his actions. But Chamberlain left open the possibility of postponing action until the forthcoming Ottawa Conference on imperial trade.[30]

De Valera's first budget, as expected, imposed tariffs on a wide range of imports, mainly manufactured goods from Great Britain. In response, the British announced that they saw no point in entering into the planned trade discussions with the Free State Government in preparation for Ottawa until they were ready to observe an agreement. But the British Government went no further. Again, warnings were forthcoming from the Commonwealth cautioning against hasty action. The influential South African leader, General Smuts, wrote to say that the Empire must not be allowed to break up on account of a 'lunatic' who was merely 'a transient apparition'. Given time the Empire could defeat de Valera, but to issue threats or an ultimatum against him would be playing into his hands.[31]

For a time de Valera appeared to waver. Dulanty informed the British that de Valera's outlook had greatly altered since his coming to office, and that he was now ready to reach a solution. The difficulty was that de Valera wanted to negotiate over the land annuities, where the Government felt its case to be weakest, rather than over the oath, where they believed themselves on firmer ground. The British were reluc-

[29] Ibid.

[30] 4th Meeting of ISC of 9 May 1932 (CAB 27/523).

[31] Telegram from British High Commissioner in the Union of South Africa to Dominions Secretary, 21 May 1932, annex V of 23rd ISC (32) of 21 May 1932 (CAB 27/525).

tant even to submit the matter of the land annuities to an imperial tribunal, though they felt bound to make the offer. 'There is no room for a compromise about the Land Annuities,' a senior Treasury official, S.D. Waley, told Chamberlain.

We could not well refuse *arbitration*, but the terms of reference will need to be carefully framed so as to take into account the intentions of the governments and the inequities of the case. On the purely legal issue de Valera *might* beat us, if he contends that: (i) the Government of Ireland Act 1920 *did* come into force as regards Southern Ireland to the extent of giving away the Land Annuities; (ii) the release of the Free State from the liability to contribute to the British 'Public Debt' must imply a waiver of the Land Annuities; (iii) the 1926 Agreement could not of itself impose a *new* obligation to pay the Annuities, not having been confirmed by the Free State Parliament.[32]

With the British unwilling to risk serious negotiations over the land annuities, and prepared only to consider *a possible* alteration of the oath, little room was left for compromise.[33] Thomas and Hailsham nevertheless met with de Valera in Dublin on 8 June, and again in London two days later. The British kept the issue of the oath in the forefront of the negotiations, but offered to refer both issues to an imperial tribunal for arbitration, an offer which de Valera refused.

Although the negotiations ended in failure, the British press virtually unanimously applauded the Government for its stand. *The Times*, for example, argued that de Valera was not interested in negotiations on the oath, but only in gaining concessions for the Free State at Ottawa. It insisted that there could be no change in the attitude of the National Government:

They [the Government] hold that the Oath Bill which has been introduced by Mr. de Valera and passed by the Dáil is an arbitrary and unjustifiable breach of the terms of the Anglo-Irish settlement ... [T]heir conclusion is endorsed by the vast majority of the people of this country, that the unilateral repudiation of a solemn agreement makes it useless for them to contemplate further agreements with the Free State Government at Ottawa.[34]

[32] Memo by S.D. Waley, 6 June 1932 (T 160/458/F 5716/03).
[33] Suggested by MacDonald at 5th Meeting of ISC of 5 June 1932 (CAB 27/523).
[34] *The Times*, 11 June 1932.

Even the Liberal *Manchester Guardian* laid the blame for the breakdown of the negotiations and the upsetting of 'the friendly and harmonious relations that have existed between the Free State and Great Britain for ten years' squarely on the 'fanaticism' of de Valera. The paper did point out, however, that most people in Britain did not regard de Valera's aims as 'outrageous', but only objected to his methods. It urged the Government to 'think long' before adopting coercive measures against the Free State and to leave the way open for 'an honourable settlement and the closest political and economic co-operation, without thought of domination on our part or derogation from Ireland's rights of self-government'.[35]

With most of the British press firmly behind it after the failure of the negotiations with de Valera, the Government felt free to threaten sanctions against the Free State. On 17 June Thomas told the House of Commons that the imperial preferences enjoyed by Ireland under the recently enacted tariff legislation would not be renewed when they lapsed in November. While the Government would continue to make the payments on the land purchase bonds, it would take steps to recoup these amounts from the higher duties which would be levied on Free State products.[36]

Thomas's speech went over well in the House. Lloyd George, in his first speech of the session, praised the Dominions Secretary's performance and supported the Government's position. Churchill, who had also prepared a strong speech on Ireland, 'but found his thunder stolen by Lloyd George',[37] had to content himself with an attack on Labour's position and support for Thomas's handling of the situation.

The only opposition to the Government's policy came from the Labour benches. Speaking with Lansbury for the Labour Party, Cripps charged that 'behind the velvet glove there seemed to be a somewhat mailed fist', and said that in the Labour Party's view the removal of the oath would not make 'the slightest difference to the foundation upon which the British Commonwealth of Nations is based, it will not alter it

[35] *Manchester Guardian*, 11 June 1932.
[36] *Parl. Deb. Commons*, vol. 267, cols. 700–701 of 17 June 1932.
[37] Baldwin to MacDonald, 19 June 1932 (MacDonald papers, 2/12).

one whit, and it seems to us in those circumstances rather a pity to make a mountain out of a molehill'.[38]

Thomas's performance in the House on Ireland boosted his stock in the Cabinet, where the debate was regarded as a much needed triumph for the Government. Especially welcome were the interventions of Lloyd George and Churchill, particularly as the former had been siding steadily with Labour on other issues.[39] Not least influenced by his performance and its reception was Thomas himself. At the next meeting of the Irish Committee, on 21 June, he argued that public opinion in the House of Commons would not be satisfied unless some action was taken on Ireland. Moreover, he emphasized, decisive action would enable Cosgrave and his Party to demonstrate that they had been right in maintaining that the British Government would follow that course, whereas failure to act would greatly strengthen the position of the Irish extremists and weaken the position of Cosgrave and his supporters. Baldwin agreed with Thomas, but advised that overt action be avoided until correspondence with de Valera had definitely been terminated.[40]

But the Cabinet was still not united on the need for strong action against the Free State. While it was generally agreed that de Valera's threat to retain the land annuities had to be met firmly, there was less agreement about how that should be done. Some members of the Cabinet felt that action should be considered only after the implications of a tariff war between Britain and Ireland had been more fully studied. Concern was also expressed that, if Britain took action, the IRA might get out of control and might even attack the British garrisons at Queenstown, Berehaven, and Lough Swilly, none of which was in a position to resist organized attack.[41] Two days later these concerns had magnified and the Cabinet was awash with rumours ranging from a threatened *coup d'état* by de Valera in Ulster and the proclamation of an Irish republic, to the possibility of a *coup* by the IRA against the Free State Government.[42]

[38] *Parl. Deb.* of 17 June 1932.
[39] David Margesson (Chief Whip) to MacDonald, 22 June 1932 (MacDonald papers, 1/1/10); Jones, *Diary With Letters*, p. 45.
[40] 6th Meeting of ISC of 21 June 1932 (CAB 27/523).
[41] Cabinet conclusions 37(32) of 22 June 1932 (CAB 23/71).
[42] Cabinet conclusions 38(32) of 24 June 1932 (CAB 23/71).

On 29 June, when things had calmed down, Thomas again urged the Cabinet to take some action against the Free State 'in view of the state of public opinion in Parliament and throughout the country'. An early election in the Free State was inevitable, he told his colleagues, and if the Government did not act to recover the land annuities Cosgrave's Party would be 'in grave danger of defeat'. Immediate action was necessary if legislation were to be enacted before the convening of the Ottawa Conference.[43]

The Cabinet gave way grudgingly. The usual fears of the effects on United Kingdom trade and unemployment of a tariff war with Ireland were buttressed by a note from the Board of Trade circulated to the Cabinet a few days earlier showing that since 1929 Ireland had passed Australia, Germany, and the United States to become Britain's second-best trading partner and, moreover, one with which Britain enjoyed a favourable balance of trade.[44] Thomas answered this by pointing out that de Valera had already imposed some tariffs on British goods, and that the success of Cosgrave at the forthcoming general election in Ireland would mean a return of free trade with the Free State. Moreover, the issue went deeper than any question of trade, he emphasized, since it really involved the whole question of sovereignty.[45] In the absence of MacDonald, Chamberlain, and Runciman, who were in Lausanne attending the Disarmament Conference, decision in the matter rested finally with Baldwin. He concluded the discussion by announcing that he had with 'great regret' come to the conclusion that there was no alternative to Thomas's policy. His decision was duly ratified by the Cabinet.[46]

On 1 July de Valera withheld the £1,500,000 payment due to the British Government on the land annuities. The British responded by imposing a customs duty on Irish imports to make good the loss. De Valera, in turn, announced that he would in future withhold further payments due to England— chiefly money for pensions due to the Royal Irish Constabu-

[43] Cabinet conclusions 40(32) of 29 June 1932 (CAB 23/71).
[44] Board of Trade memo on 'Effect of Possible Retaliatory Action on United Kingdom Trade', appendix iv to CP 227 of 24 June 1932 (CAB 24/231).
[45] Cabinet conclusions 40(32) of 19 June 1932 (CAB 23/71).
[46] Ibid.

lary—as well as impose further retaliatory tariffs on British goods. On the eve of the conference called to tighten the bonds of imperial unity, Great Britain and Ireland found themselves charging headlong into a trade war.

During most of July and August Chamberlain, Baldwin, Thomas, and other important Cabinet ministers were in Ottawa for the Imperial Economic Conference. Despite hopes that the 'general Ottawa atmosphere' would somehow induce the Irish delegates to put pressure on de Valera to accept imperial arbitration of the dispute,[47] and optimism by Chamberlain as the Conference was ending,[48] it was difficult to see how there could be any easy turning back even if de Valera did accede to such arbitration. The problem, as Thomas explained it to the Irish Committee on the eve of his departure for Ottawa, was that de Valera meant by arbitration something essentially different from the meaning they themselves attached to the term. While the British wanted a purely legal answer to the question of the land annuities, de Valera meant that the tribunal should determine what was fair and reasonable for the Free State to pay, having regard for counterclaims. Among these was the claim to a share of the 'spoils' or 'partnership assets' represented by the colonies acquired by Great Britain during the period of the Union. The British Government, on the other hand, was convinced that the annuities represented a fair settlement and wanted at all cost to avoid getting itself involved with wider issues.[49]

Not long after the departure of the British delegates for Ottawa, the Labour Party launched a campaign aimed at preventing the outbreak of an economic war. In Parliament Cripps tabled a series of amendments to the Government's Bill aimed at preventing the levying of any duties on Irish goods until the matter had been submitted to arbitration. Meanwhile, Lansbury tried to rouse the British conscience against the renewal of strife with Ireland.

Neither effort met with success. Lansbury's appeals to the Archbishop of Canterbury, the President of the National Free

[47] Sankey to Thomas, 17 Aug. 1932 (PREM (Premier) 1/132).
[48] Chamberlain diary, 20 Aug. 1932, cited in Keith Feiling, *The Life of Neville Chamberlain* (London, 1946), p. 215.
[49] 7th Meeting of ISC of 5 July 1932 (CAB 27/523).

Church Council, and the Chief Rabbi fell flat. At best, the
replies were sympathetic but noncommittal; others were not
even that.[50] 'The real difficulty', wrote Cosmo Gordon Lang,
the Archbishop of Canterbury, a Scottish Protestant not noted
for his sympathy towards Irish Catholicism, 'is that de Valera
seems to be incapable of reasoning. He merely repeats his
position over and over again ... I cannot think that Christian
Principles require that the demands of a man who shows himself to be so unreasonable should be immediately granted.'[51]
Cripps was only slightly more successful on the parliamentary front. He invited William Norton, the leader of the Irish
Labour Party, to London with the approval of de Valera to
look for a way out of the impasse. Cripps had a plan. Pat-
terned apparently upon the Dogger Bank Tribunal of 1905, it
envisioned the setting up of a commission composed of two
members each from Britain and Ireland to ascertain the facts
of the situation, whereupon the two governments would then
negotiate.

From the beginning, MacDonald and Sankey, the National
Labour Lord Chancellor who was watching over the Dominions Office in Thomas's absence, viewed the Labour initiative as a trap. Without the concurrence of the Government's
'right wing' they did not feel that they could make any important decisions regarding Ireland, but neither could they
afford not to appear at least open to conciliation. On 14 July
MacDonald and Sankey met with Norton, Lansbury, Cripps,
Greenwood, and Attlee. The meeting only increased Mac-
Donald and Sankey's suspicion that the Labour leaders were
trying to pressure them into concessions. Particularly alarming
was the suggestion that MacDonald should enter immediately
into direct negotiations with de Valera, for there was concern
in the Irish Committee about the Prime Minister's ability to

[50] Lansbury to James Reid, 26 July 1932 (Lansbury papers, 10/252).

[51] Cosmo Gordon Lang to Lansbury, 21 July 1932 (ibid.). Other churchmen were
more concerned about the recurrence of bad feeling between Ireland and Great
Britain. The Archbishop of York, e.g., wrote to MacDonald expressing 'the anxiety
which many are feeling on Christian as well as on general political grounds with
regard to the possibility of economic war with Ireland. One cannot be satisfied with
a mere surrender of Ireland to economic pressure, even if such pressure leads to
surrender and not to defiance; for it would be with bitterness.' (12 Sept. 1932,
MacDonald papers, 2/35).

hold his own with the Irish leader, 'who was a notoriously difficult and procrastinating negotiator'.[52]

But the following day de Valera arrived in London and MacDonald had no choice but to face him. When they met, the Irish leader pressed MacDonald for a temporary 'truce' and the suspension of tariff duties while an independent commission was set up to consider the annuities dispute. His requests were not granted. Convinced beforehand that de Valera 'did not want a settlement' and 'proposed the enquiry to get a suspension of economic pressure which he knew once relieved could not be reimposed', MacDonald 'kept a stiff upper lip' during the negotiations and tried in vain to get the Irish leader to make some concessions of his own.[53] De Valera departed the next day, leaving MacDonald relieved that the Government had neither 'been led into a trap', nor given the impression of backing down, but worried nonetheless that de Valera might somehow still 'claim a complete victory, damage his political opponents and remain master of the Irish Free State'.[54]

The failure of the negotiations between Thomas and the Irish delegates at Ottawa, and between MacDonald and de Valera in London, led, at least in public, to a general hardening of the British Government's attitude towards de Valera. Behind the scenes, however, there was still considerable doubt as to the wisdom of launching an economic war with Ireland if it could possibly be avoided. William Peters, the Government's only reliable source on Irish affairs, opposed the policy from its inception. He doubted whether Cosgrave could be expected to benefit from any distress resulting from de Valera's policies. No amount of 'economic facts' would change the latter's attitude towards the dispute, he warned, and de Valera would simply respond by stirring up nationalist sentiment. If anything, Fianna Fáil's failure might result in a *coup d'état* by the left-wing elements in the country. Peters feared that in the meantime the prohibitive tariff imposed by the Free State on British coal might have serious repercussions on the entire British coal industry.[55]

[52] 8th Meeting of ISC of 14 July 1932 (CAB 27/523).
[53] MacDonald to Thomas, 19 Aug. 1932 (PREM 1/132).
[54] 10th Meeting of ISC of 15 July 1932 (CAB 27/523).
[55] 12th Meeting of ISC of 21 July 1932 (CAB 27/523).

The warnings of the highly regarded Peters were not without their effect, especially on the Liberals, many of whom were committed to Free Trade and did not approve of the general turn towards Protection that the Government was taking. Moreover, the attitude of the left-wing press towards the Irish developments was stronger than had been anticipated. The opposition of the Labour *Daily Herald* came as no surprise, but the reaction of the Liberal *Manchester Guardian* was cause for more concern. In an editorial denouncing the beginning of the trade war, the paper said that it 'would be hard to recall a more stupid and insane episode in the whole history of Britain's commercial relations ... Somebody has to break the deadlock, and there is every reason why it should be Mr. MacDonald.'[56]

Such criticism—plus misgivings expressed by Hankey, who was becoming increasingly disturbed over the way the Irish lobby in the United States was embittering the United States against Britain,[57] Sir Edward Harding, the Permanent Under-Secretary at the Dominions Office, and Lord Granard, a prominent Anglo-Irish peer with business interests in both countries—was enough to convince Sankey that 'the present situation cannot be allowed to go on forever'.[58]

The Foreign Office shared Hankey's fears over the international implications of a renewal of strife with Ireland, especially in regard to its effects upon opinion in the United States and the Dominions. But there was also strong anti-de Valera feeling within the department. One official, B.E.F. Gage, thought that 'as long as this obstinate fanatic [de Valera] remains in power in the Irish Free State the chances of a settlement being reached are negligible'.[59] Gage viewed with alarm de Valera's shift to the left, but could see no answer to it because of the 'Irish love of a fight and enjoyment of martyrdom'.[60]

Despite its distaste for de Valera and longing for Cosgrave's return to power, the Foreign Office was not uncritical of the Government's approach to the problem. It deemed it unfor-

[56] *Manchester Guardian*, 26 July 1932.
[57] Roskill, *Hankey*, iii, p. 52.
[58] Sankey to MacDonald, 10 Aug. 1932 (PREM 1/132).
[59] Minute by B.E.F. Gage, 20 July 1932 (FO 627/40/1 U 429/15/750).
[60] Ibid.

tunate that 'the inevitable battle between de Valera and the British Government' should have been joined on the land annuities issue, since Cosgrave himself had always regarded those as subject to revision. Furthermore, the imposition of a 20 per cent tariff on Irish goods had only closed the ranks of the Irish people behind de Valera and given the impression that the British Government was prepared to treat her late enemy Germany more liberally than the Free State.[61]

The Foreign Office urged that the only possibility of Cosgrave returning to power was if 'the greatest circumspection and moderation' were employed in dealing with Ireland. Any action 'savouring of haste or intimidation (or which can be represented in such a light)' would inevitably drive the country more completely into the hands of Fianna Fáil and Fianna Fáil itself into the hands of the IRA. Should the latter take place, it was feared that de Valera could never again break with the IRA and that the Republican issue would then be presented not as a matter of negotiation, but as a revolutionary demand 'with all that this might imply as regards Northern Ireland'.[62]

Thus, despite the considerable anti-de Valera animus within the department, the Foreign Office felt obligated to recommend a conciliatory approach. Simon, the Foreign Secretary, duly pointed out to MacDonald the danger of letting the present situation with the 'exalted lunatic who is at the head of the Government in Dublin' continue uncorrected. But he offered as a possible alternative only that the Government draw up in advance the proper terms of reference in the event of any form of arbitration being suggested by Dominions leaders.[63]

By late August, however, MacDonald was less inclined than ever towards compromise. About Anglo-American relations he cared a great deal. But he had not failed to note that the Anglo-Irish settlement of 1921 had not brought about the great improvement in Anglo-American relations so widely predicted. Moreover, when he received Simon's letter, MacDonald had just returned from a weekend visit to Mount

[61] Foreign Office Report on Ireland, n.d. (July 1932) (Simon papers, FO 800/287/32).
[62] Ibid.
[63] Simon to MacDonald, 9 Aug. 1932 (FO 800/287/4/88).

Stewart, the country house in Northern Ireland belonging to his friends the Londonderrys. Although while in Ulster he had engaged in no official discussions on the Irish situation, he had nevertheless, he told Simon, kept both his 'eyes and ears pretty widely [*sic*] open' and had 'come to the conclusion that what we have to do at present is to stand pat'. Southern Irish opinion, he continued, was 'beginning to think that de Valera had mismanaged the whole situation'; but, on the other hand, Cosgrave's Party was not 'altogether satisfied' with what the British had done. Northern Ireland, meanwhile, was 'very nervous' and its ministers 'full of misunderstandings' and worried about the possibility of concessions to de Valera. Any concessions by the British would not only embarrass Cosgrave, but would dishearten British supporters in Northern Ireland and encourage Republicans in the North to believe that the British were 'squeezable'.

MacDonald opposed any widening of the subjects to be submitted to arbitration because he was convinced that the Irish people were not interested in them, and, he noted, 'de Valera is raising them not because he thinks of a settlement regarding them, but because he wishes to raise a very wide range of grievance from which to launch a full-blooded and openly confessed demand for an independent Republic'.

Accordingly, MacDonald urged, they should 'keep hammering away' on the one issue of the land annuities because 'feeling within the South seems to be more and more influenced by the desire to have a settlement, on account of the growing distress, and we ought to push hard upon the feeling'.[64]

During the late summer and early autumn of 1932, MacDonald's strategy seemed to offer some hope of success. Reports on Ireland in the British press were full of encouragement, leaving almost unanimously the impression that de Valera was in serious trouble. Typical of these was the comment of the Irish correspondent for *The Times* in early August that after 'one of the most depressing weeks in recent Irish history the Free State citizen is bewildered almost to the point of despair'.[65] Similarly, the *Daily Telegraph*'s Irish correspond-

---

[64] MacDonald to Simon, n.d. (late Aug. 1932) (FO 800/287/4/91).
[65] *The Times*, 8 Aug. 1932.

ent reported: 'The belief is steadily growing among all sections of the community here that nothing save the supersession
of Mr. de Valera can now prevent the trade of the Irish Free
State from being completely ruined.'[66]

Even the Irish correspondent of the *Manchester Guardian*
generally gave gloomy prognostications concerning de Valera's future, as, for example, in early November, when he
reported that 'Mr. de Valera is a man hedged in with difficulties that grow every day'.[67]

Information received from contacts between official and un-
official representatives of the Government with the opposition
in Ireland also tended, not surprisingly, to present an optimistic picture of the chances for success of British policy. In this
regard, besides 'Charley' Londonderry, who was now Minister
for Air in the National Government, and whose wife was one
of MacDonald's closest friends, MacDonald relied for information primarily on his Parliamentary Private Secretary,
Major Ralph Glyn, and on Edward Hilton Young, the Conservative Minister of Health. Glyn's duties as a director of an
Irish railway company provided him with convenient opportunities for frequent trips across the Channel, during which he
generally made a point of getting in touch with Cosgrave or
his associates. Hilton Young, who had assisted Churchill on
Ireland in 1922, had renewed his interest in Irish affairs in
1931 during a brief stint as Secretary of the Overseas Trade
Department.

During the autumn of 1932 all three contributed to Mac-
Donald's belief that de Valera was 'steadily losing ground'
and that the British Government need only stand firm to
ensure the triumph of Cosgrave. After seeing Cosgrave on a
trip to Ireland in early September, Glyn informed the Prime
Minister that there was a 'feeling of uncertainty about lest we
should be knuckling down to de Valera'.[68] At the same time,
Londonderry 'got into a panic' at the prospect of British
concessions to de Valera.[69] Similarly, Hilton Young brought
back from a trip to Dublin in August further encouragement

[66] *Daily Telegraph*, 8 Aug. 1932.
[67] *Manchester Guardian*, 2 Nov. 1932.
[68] MacDonald to Thomas, 7 Sept. 1932 (MacDonald papers, 2/12).
[69] Ibid.

from Cosgrave on the strong British stand, and a warning that
any settlement with Fianna Fáil 'would be quite disastrous and
would mean the end of their constitutional Party and all hope
of working harmoniously with Great Britain'. Young returned
from Dublin convinced that Fianna Fáil was losing strength
and might be forced into using 'violent means to obtain a
position in the Dáil independent of any other Party'. He was
equally convinced that the IRA was the key to the situation.
'Nobody doubts', noted Young, 'that they have the Fianna
Fáil Government entirely in their power.'[70]

Domestic political considerations in Britain also continued
to militate against adopting a conciliatory approach towards
de Valera. Most of the Conservative press demanded that
the Government take a hard line. In July MacDonald
arranged through Young to have Sankey set up an inter-
departmental subcommittee under Walter Elliot, the Financial
Secretary to the Treasury, to keep the British press informed
on Irish developments and to counter propaganda from
the Free State Government. The line Young wanted the press
to present was that the dispute with the Free State was tragic
but absurd and required only the application of common
sense to what was in actuality nothing but a domestic Irish
dispute.[71]

The reaction of the Conservative press showed that, if anything, it felt that the Government was not being hard enough
where de Valera was concerned. While the Liberal *Daily News*
and the *Manchester Guardian* were sympathetic, and Lord Rothermere's *Daily Mail* was willing to support the Government if
it gave a strong lead, most of the Conservative papers were
less co-operative. *The Times*, in particular, was antagonistic to
Young's approach. In its view, a strengthening of the British
attitude and 'not the slightest indication of weakening' was
the only thing which would bring a change of heart to de
Valera, since it was impossible to deal in any other way with
a man like him. Similarly, the Conservative *Birmingham Post*
and the *Manchester Despatch* felt the Government was being too

[70] Memo by E. Hilton Young on 'The Political Situation in the Irish Free State',
7 Sept. 1932 (PREM 1/132).

[71] Hilton Young to MacDonald, 23 July 1932; and MacDonald to Hilton Young,
25 July 1932 (PREM 1/132).

soft and 'adopted the diehard attitude of hitting him [de Valera] as the only remedy'.[72]

Besides the hostile attitude towards de Valera taken by the Conservative British press, there remained the two other domestic political factors mentioned earlier which reinforced the Government's determination to take a hard line against de Valera: Lloyd George and Churchill. Although both men were frequently absent from the House during 1932 while writing—Lloyd George on his war memoirs and Churchill on his biography of Marlborough—each of them had denounced de Valera and endorsed the Government's firm handling of the situation. Both men would have liked to see the Government collapse. It is by no means inconceivable that, had the Government shown 'weakness' on Ireland, they would have teamed up with the diehards and other dissidents to attack it. Although in retrospect this may seem unlikely, just such a combination had been the result most feared by J.C.C. Davidson (the Conservative Party Chairman in 1932) over the Irwin declaration in 1929,[73] and the Conservative Party remained restive over India during 1932.[74] Next to India, Ireland was the most emotional imperial issue for Conservatives. Diehards like Lord Salisbury emphasized the links between the situation in Ireland and nationalist agitation in India.[75] For the National Government to have backed down in its confrontation with de Valera in 1932 would have been to risk widening the breach in the Conservative Party by adding Ireland to India, an opening which Churchill, and possibly even Lloyd George, would not have been slow to exploit. This was the thrust behind the repeated warnings delivered to the Cabinet by Thomas that public opinion in Parliament and in the country demanded a hard line on Ireland, a message that was not lost on Baldwin. Throughout 1932 Churchill, together with Salisbury and other right-wing leaders, closely monitored the Government's Irish policy to keep it 'sound' and to ensure that they had their 'part to play in confirming and also in influencing the Government's

---

[72] Memo by Lord Chancellor, CP 291 of 25 Aug. 1932 (CAB 24/232).

[73] Gillian Peele, 'Revolt over India' in Chris. Cook and Gillian Peele (edd.), *The Politics of Reappraisal, 1918–1939* (New York, 1975), pp. 121-2.

[74] Gilbert, *Churchill*, v, pp. 440-1.

[75] Lord Salisbury to *The Times*, 28 Mar. 1932.

actions'.[76] Churchill kept Thomas mindful that it was 'De Valera and the Oath together with his attitude to the British Empire' that they were fighting, adding that the 'English people are better pleased with the way the Duties are weighing on the Irish, than anything that has happened since the Government came into office and they will be very sulky if anything happens to take these duties off, and woe unto the man by whom it happens'.[77]

With the Government undecided about how to handle de Valera, the pressures of right-wing opinion proved decisive. Thomas found his jingoistic tendencies applauded and reinforced at every turn. MacDonald feared that he would get the 'blame' if there was any backing down on their part.[78] Characteristically moderate ministers like Baldwin, Chamberlain, and Runciman swallowed their considerable misgivings and fell into line with Hailsham's diehard views whenever it came to a Cabinet decision regarding Ireland.

For several months after de Valera's abortive trip to London in July, no serious effort was made by either side to break the impasse that had developed. Although de Valera offered to place the land annuities in the Bank for International Settlement pending a settlement of the dispute—provided that the British call off the tariff war—he continued to press for passage of the bill abolishing the oath. The British rejected the proposal.[79]

The Cabinet, meanwhile, was becoming progressively more Conservative in complexion. In July Sir Donald Maclean died and was replaced as President of the Board of Education by Lord Irwin (later Lord Halifax). In September the Liberal free traders, Samuel and Sinclair, resigned in protest at the Imperial tariff policy agreed upon at Ottawa, as did Lord Snowden. The most important addition to the Cabinet at that time was Walter Elliot, who was promoted to Minister of Agriculture and Fisheries.

These changes did not increase the likelihood of an early settlement with de Valera. Although now in transition to-

[76] Churchill to Salisbury, 28 Mar. 1932 (Gilbert, *Churchill, Companion* v, 2, p. 408).
[77] Churchill to Edward Marsh (for Thomas), 17 Sept. 1932 (ibid. p. 474).
[78] Minute by Harding, 17 Aug. 1932 (DO 35/397).
[79] De Valera to Thomas, 5 Aug. 1932; Thomas to de Valera, 14 Sept. 1932; and memo by Dominions Secretary, CP 303 of 14 Sept. 1932 (CAB 24/232).

wards becoming the 'prince of appeasers', Irwin had, as Edward Wood, made himself a minor diehard hero when, as
Under-Secretary to Churchill at the Colonial Office, he had
been one of those who tried to narrow the scope of the Boundary Commission in 1922, an effort he was to repeat two years
later. Elliot had in the past exhibited more liberal views on
Ireland. He had welcomed the Irish Treaty and considered it
the greatest accomplishment of the Lloyd George Government.[80] But as one of the leading promoters of British agriculture, Elliot was under strong pressures not to seek a readmit-
tance of Irish agricultural products on easy terms. Moreover,
he shared the belief that economic pressure would probably
cause de Valera to reconsider his position.[81]

During September de Valera was busy presiding over the
League of Nations Assembly in Geneva. While there he indicated to Simon a willingness to re-enter into negotiations with
the British Government on the question of the land annuities.
A meeting was accordingly scheduled for mid-October.

The Cabinet was unsure whether in seeking negotiations de
Valera was just playing politics in order to relieve some of the
pressure on him from Irish farmers to do something about
reopening the British market for unrestricted cattle exports, or
whether the economic pressure was finally having some effect
in Ireland, so that he was ready to make serious concessions
in an attempt to reach a settlement. Thinking the latter might
well be the case, Chamberlain asked his Treasury officials to
consider whether, should the occasion arise, they could invent
some face-saving device 'which without surrendering anything
of substance would enable him to say to his supporters that
he had done something, and thus perhaps relieve him from
the obligation to go to his electors for a mandate for a Republic'.[82] Whether or not de Valera was prepared to make
concessions for a settlement, the British Government clearly
was not. Domestic political considerations—both in Ireland and
at home—once again ruled that possibility out beforehand.[83]

[80] Colin Coote, *A Companion of Honour: The Story of Walter Elliot* (London, 1965),
p. 74.
[81] 9th Meeting of ISC of 14 July 1932 (CAB 27/523).
[82] Minute by R.I. Gelt to Ferguson, 15 Oct. 1932 (T 160/458 F 57716/03).
[83] Memo by Hilton Young on 'The Irish Free State Negotiations', 10 Oct. 1932
(PREM 1/132).

The mere mention of the forthcoming discussions was enough to arouse the ever-vigilant diehards.[84] Hailsham, their watchdog in the Cabinet, took offence at the very thought of British concessions. There could be no question of compromise on the oath, he insisted at a preliminary meeting of the Irish Committee, and, until that question was satisfactorily settled, he did not believe that the Government could afford to face Parliament with any plans for taking off the special duties, even should there be a satisfactory settlement of the land annuities dispute. The Committee agreed. 'It would be unthinkable, in Cosgrave's interests, as well as our own', it concluded, 'for the United Kingdom representatives to acquiesce in the repudiation of the financial provisions of the Treaty and the later Agreements.'[85]

When the discussions with de Valera opened on 4 October, the British found that he was no more prepared to make concessions than they. De Valera tried to keep the discussions centred on the financial dispute, though even there he was unyielding. The British tried to steer him back to the constitutional issues. He admitted that there were political considerations in the background, but said that, as in 1921, he had an open mind on the question of association with the British Commonwealth. Whether there was to be an association would depend on the conditions attached to it, including the question of the continued division of Ireland. When Chamberlain tried to pin him down to specifics, de Valera replied with Parnell's famous words about the futility of attempting 'to put bounds to the march of a nation'.[86]

Despite the failure of the negotiations to break the deadlock, they went well enough that they were followed up a short time later with a visit to London by Joseph Walshe, Secretary of the Free State Ministry of External Affairs. In informal talks with officials at the Dominions Office, Walshe presented what appeared to be a serious offer of a compromise, based on (1) a settlement of the financial disputes on a fifty-fifty

---

[84] Lord Selborne to Lady Selborne, 5 Oct. 1932 (Selborne papers, 106/164).

[85] 14th Meeting of ISC of 27 Sept. 1932 (CAB 27/523).

[86] 'Minutes of a Conference between British Ministers and Irish Free State Ministers', 14 and 15 Oct. 1932, CP 350 of 18 Oct. 1932 (CAB 24/233).

basis; and (2) acceptance of the agreement 'as a friendly settlement as between two members of the Commonwealth'.[87]

For the first time it appeared that the British might be open to a compromise. Despite their stern words, they still had considerable doubts about the wisdom of their policy. Both the Dominions Office and the Board of Trade, the two departments most closely involved, urged moderation and compromise as the best way of dealing with de Valera, as did the Foreign Office. Runciman consistently echoed regrets from William Peters, the British Trade Commissioner in Dublin, that the only reason that it was impossible to negotiate a trade agreement with the Irish Free State was that the political and financial dispute stood in the way. Runciman also pointed out that in general, despite the dispute, Ireland still treated British goods more favourably than did some of the other Dominions. He warned that, if the Import Duties Act was applied to the Free State as contemplated, the consequences would probably mean a shift in Irish trade to other countries, in particular Canada, a shift in trading patterns that might become permanent, even with the restoration of normal conditions.[88]

Runciman's opinions mattered. Not only were his arguments weighty, but he was highly regarded by Chamberlain. Moreover, he was important to MacDonald and Baldwin as a symbol of Liberal support. After the defection of Samuel and Sinclair over tariffs, there remained only three National Liberals and three National Labour ministers in a Cabinet dominated by thirteen Conservatives. MacDonald, whose relations with Simon were already strained,[89] and who was striving desperately to maintain the façade of a National Government, could not afford to risk alienating Runciman. With Baldwin already under heavy Tory pressure to elevate one of their own to the premiership,[90] the defection of another Liberal from the Cabinet might prove fatal.

The encounter with de Valera had also had its effect on some members of the Cabinet. Chamberlain, who had not met him before, was struck by his transparent honesty, although

[87] 15th Meeting of ISC of 25 Oct. 1932 (CAB 27/523).
[88] 14th Meeting of ISC of 27 Sept. 1932 (CAB 27/523).
[89] Hankey diary, 3 Oct. 1932. Roskill, *Hankey*, iii, p. 56.
[90] Jones, *Diary With Letters*, p. 56.

thinking that he was living 'in a world of his own'.[91] This change in attitude was immediately apparent when the Irish Committee met on 25 October to discuss Walshe's proposals. Stressing de Valera's honesty and desire for peace, Thomas—who had got on well with the Irish delegates at Ottawa—raised the prospect of British concessions and urged that there could be no greater triumph than to bring de Valera and the Irish Free State Republican Party to accept a position within the Commonwealth.[92] To Hailsham's objection that any concession on the oath would be regarded as a 'betrayal and surrender', Thomas replied that Hailsham himself had said that the Statute of Westminster left it technically open to a Dominion to abolish the oath of allegiance. Chamberlain also thought that they might consider some sort of compromise on the oath and the land annuities. He agreed with Thomas that, even if Cosgrave came back into power, the Free State would be unable to resume payments on the old scale.[93]

But Hailsham was not so easily won over. He warned that de Valera might either be attempting to get material for an election manifesto or preparing for a clear break. So strongly did he put his views that in the end he carried the Committee with him. The final answer to Walshe's proposals appeared to be made in anything but a spirit of compromise. The British Government did offer to discuss a modification of the oath, a mitigation of the financial burdens, and a trade agreement, but only on condition that the following three 'essential points on which the United Kingdom Government must insist in any settlement with the Free State' be met:

1. The acceptance by the Irish Free State Government of the 1921 Treaty as valid and to be observed according to its terms unless and until it is altered by agreement;
2. That no further question should be raised by the Irish Free State Government as to the validity of the Financial Settlement, as embodied in the Financial Agreements of 1923 and 1926 and the Boundary Agreement of 1925;
3. That the acceptance of the Treaty should be accompanied on the part of the Irish Free State Government by a) an undertaking

---

[91] Feiling, p. 217.
[92] Whiskard to Harding, 22 July 1932 (DO 121/61).
[93] 15th Meeting of ISC of 25th Oct. 1932 (CAB 27/523).

not to proceed further with the Oath Bill; b) suitable arrangements, in accordance with the Treaty, to take effect on Mr.
McNeill's relinquishing the office of Governor-General.[94]

If the Irish Committee thought that these terms would be
seriously considered by de Valera, it was mistaken. Before
leaving London Walshe made it clear that the conditions demanded by the British would be completely unacceptable;
that de Valera would not enter into negotiations about the
oath, and that pressure on the issue was the surest way of
making Ireland sever its links with the Commonwealth.[95]

This failure marked the last serious attempt to head off the
Anglo-Irish economic war before it was too late; yet, probably,
it had always been too late. The British Government—no less
than de Valera's Government—was trapped in its position in
1932. It had no real choice other than to adopt the policy it
did. The pressures of right-wing opinion were simply too
strong to surmount, even had the Government so desired.
Under the circumstances, the forces of reaction were bound to
win out over the forces of moderation. In the end, Hailsham
spoke for the Cabinet when he insisted at the last meeting of
the Irish Committee for 1932 that the offer to Walshe represented the 'last word in generosity' and that 'public opinion
in this country would not support the Government if it went
further'.[96] It was only as the passage of time revealed the
inadequacy of British policy, and the international situation
deteriorated, that the British Government could move towards
putting an end to the economic war and restoring Anglo-Irish
relations to a peaceful basis.

None of this happened very quickly, and most of what did
happen was outside the control of the British Government. By
the end of 1932 it was already beginning to appear less and
less likely that Cosgrave and his Party would be returned in
the next election, or that it would make much difference even
if he were. J.B. O'Driscoll, one of Cosgrave's leading supporters, informed Thomas in November that the oath was dead
even if Cosgrave returned to power, and that the only real

[94] Memo handed to Mr. Walshe on 'Irish Negotiations', n.d. (PREM 1/132).
[95] Earl of Longford and Thomas P. O'Neill, *Eamon De Valera* (London, 1970),
p. 285.
[96] 16th Meeting of ISC of 23 Nov. 1932 (CAB 27/523).

alternative to de Valera was not Cosgrave, but a Communist government.[97] Then in January 1933 British hopes for the quick return of Cosgrave were finally buried by the return of Fianna Fáil with an overall majority, making de Valera independent for the first time of the need of the support of the Labour Party. Yet for almost two more years neither side showed any disposition towards compromise. In the meantime the tariff war between the two countries continued unabated, and trade suffered accordingly. Throughout the British Government remained convinced that the Free State's economy had a breaking point, and that 'however untouched the facade of the Irish Free State might appear to be, a decay was proceeding at an increasing rate behind it and ... sooner or later the whole structure would probably collapse very suddenly'.[98] It therefore remained only to weather the economic storm until that point was reached.

Between 1932 and 1936 the Cabinet devoted very little time to Irish affairs. Whereas during the first nine months of its existence the Irish Committee met almost bi-monthly—sixteen meetings from March to November—during the next three and a half years it met only six times. In part this was due to the desire to see what would transpire in the economic war, where inaction was encouraged by the fact that the sector of the British economy suffering the worst strains was agriculture; hence an end to the tariff war with Ireland and the reopening of the British market to unrestricted Irish agricultural exports did not appear as an altogether unmixed blessing. But mainly it was because the rise to power of Hitler in Germany, along with further Japanese inroads into Manchuria, brought a new urgency to the question of rearmament and foreign affairs in general, and pushed the dispute with de Valera to the sidelines.

Moreover, despite the fact that the British wrote Cosgrave off, at least temporarily, as a spent force[99] after de Valera's election victory in January 1933, this did not make them any

[97] Memo by Thomas, 73rd ISC of 22 Nov. 1932 (CAB 27/526).

[98] Chamberlain's words. Note of a meeting between the Lord President of the Council and the Chancellor of the Exchequer representing the United Kingdom Government, and Lord Craigavan, Mr Pollock, and Mr Andrews representing the Government of Northern Ireland, 22 June 1934 (Baldwin papers, 21/279).

[99] W. Ormsby-Gore to Baldwin, 2 Feb. 1933 (Baldwin papers, 21/274).

more anxious to enter into discussions with de Valera. On the one hand, the Government realized that, as de Valera's position had been strengthened, he would now probably be even more difficult to deal with than before. On the other, until the autumn of 1934 the domestic political situation in Britain still militated against concessions to him. In particular, Churchill's campaign to reverse the official Government policy over India appeared to be gathering strength. Croft, Wolmer, Lloyd, and Salisbury had joined him, and in February 1933 a hostile motion was narrowly defeated at the National Union of Conservative Associations. While pronouncing himself in general accord with the Government's Irish policy, Churchill claimed that it was the Government's rejection of the Conservative amendment to the Statute of Westminster that had 'probably led to Mr. de Valera's assumption of power',[100] intimated that higher duties against Irish produce might yet be necessary, and asked Thomas to convey his 'anxieties' about the Irish situation to the Cabinet's Irish Committee.[101] As a result, until the India Bill was safe, there was little likelihood of any initiative being taken on the British side to settle the Irish dispute. The British in the meantime did little more than watch as de Valera successfully steered a course between the Blue Shirts on the right and the IRA on the left, while pursuing undeterred his goals of abolishing the oath and reducing to insignificance the office of Governor-General in the Irish Free State.[102]

The Government's policy—or lack of policy—was supported by most of the Conservative press. The exceptions were Beaverbrook's *Daily Express* and *Sunday Express*, which, reflecting their owner's sentiments, had early on begun condemning the quarrel as 'a great piece of folly'.[103] Rothermere's *Daily Mail* and *Evening News*, on the other hand, supported the Government, while Rothermere himself favoured and pressed privately for a total embargo on all imports from Ireland,

[100] Speech on 'Foreign Policy and Ireland', 24 Feb. 1933. Delivered to Constituency meetings at Buckhurst Hill and Wanstead. Churchill, *Complete Speeches*, v, p. 5226.

[101] 17th Meeting of ISC of 6 Mar. 1933 (CAB 27/523).

[102] Memo by Thomas on 'Position in the Irish Free State', CP 258 of 17 Nov. 1933 (CAB 24/244).

[103] *Sunday Express*, 25 Aug. 1932.

assuring Thomas that 'If this were done de Valera would be hunted out of Ireland within a few weeks.'[104]

The independent *Economist*, edited by Walter Layton, and the Liberal and Labour press generally condemned the Government for its handling of the Irish situation. Layton was a Cambridge economist opposed to imperialism and to autarchy. He was also a Liberal and a 'rational' radical with ties to Lloyd George. *The Economist* charged that nothing was to be gained by the clash with de Valera, 'not money, nor British prestige, nor anything but mutual impoverishment and bitterness over an issue which we could well afford to settle liberally, without futile punctilio or insistence on endlessly disputable "rights" '.[105] It believed that the tariff war was undertaken 'either in the desperate hope of fomenting an anti-Fianna Fáil *coup d'état* in Ireland, or, more probably, in order to satisfy the insistent clamour of English agriculturalists',[106] and criticized the Government for having driven Irish nationalism to the left by its campaign of 'economic frightfulness', which ultimately might have the effect of driving the Free State 'clear out of the British Commonwealth'.[107] Layton also guided the Liberal *News Chronicle*, which had been formed in 1930 by a merger between the *Daily News* and the *Daily Chronicle*, and which also appealed for a speedy end to the 'dreary Irish quarrel'.[108] Similarly, the *Manchester Guardian*, which had at first been highly critical of de Valera's actions, by 1933 was lambasting the Government for having made 'the gross mistake of believing that penal tariffs would destroy de Valera's hold on the Free State', and, once that policy had failed, for not having 'the common sense or the capacity to try to seek another way out of an intolerable situation'.[109]

The initial break in the tariff war came in the fall of 1934. For this there were at least three reasons. First, it was becoming increasingly clear that it had failed in its object. There was still no real prospect of economic breakdown in the Free State. Not only had the economic war not weakened de Val-

[104] Rothermere to Thomas, 13 Feb. 1934 (Thomas papers, C61).
[105] *The Economist*, 5 Nov. 1932.
[106] *The Economist*, 12 Nov. 1932.
[107] *The Economist*, 4 Feb. 1933.
[108] *News Chronicle*, 26 July 1933.
[109] *Manchester Guardian*, 8 Mar. 1933.

era's hold over the Irish people, but it had actually strengthened it.[110] Moreover, the war was hurting Britain almost as
much as it was hurting the Free State.[111] Certain British industrialists, especially those who, like the colliery proprietors
in Wales, had a considerable stake in Anglo-Irish trade, were
beginning to become more vocal in their demands for a settlement between the two countries. Some were even intervening
personally with de Valera in an attempt to breach the divide.[112] Secondly, the worsening international situation lent impetus to any movement towards ending the Irish quarrel. And
thirdly, having safely beaten back the diehard attack on the
India Bill, the Government was now becoming increasingly
concerned about winning the floating Liberal vote in the upcoming general election. Whereas in July 1934 Chamberlain
had considered its position 'stronger than ever', five months
later he was lamenting 'the frightfully sudden slump in the
government's stock, and the continual nagging and carping
by the young Tory intellectuals'.[113] Labour was suddenly
showing new life, capturing the London County Council and
winning hundreds of borough elections up and down the country. The Government was encountering strong opposition, not
only from Labour but from within the Conservative Party and
from the press. One of its most vulnerable points was the
failure to provide adequate aid to depressed regions like the
north of Britain and South Wales, areas particularly hard hit
by the economic war with Ireland.

Chamberlain was highly susceptible to these pressures. With
MacDonald in a state of rapid decline, and Baldwin characteristically content to let matters drift, Chamberlain now more
than ever provided the drive behind the National Government. As Chancellor of the Exchequer, he was keenly aware
of the failure of the depressed coal, steel, and shipbuilding
districts of the north of Britain and Wales to keep pace with
the economic recovery being experienced by the rest of the
country, and was sponsoring a Special Areas policy to help
bring some relief.

110 Memo by Thomas, 87th ISC of 17 Oct. 1934 (CAB 27/525).

111 Memo by Thomas, CP 273 of 14 Nov. 1934 (CAB 24/251).

112 e.g. E.A. James, Director of James and Emanuel, Ltd. (Colliery proprietors of
Cardiff) to Thomas, containing notes of an interview with de Valera, 18 Oct. 1934
(DO 35/890/xi/15).   113 Feiling, p. 239.

On Ireland Chamberlain had always been a moderate and a pragmatist. He had at first favoured compromise with de Valera. When that proved unattainable, he had relied on the economic weapon to bring the Irish leader to his senses. Now that the economic war was proving self-defeating and injuring most those areas of Britain that could afford it least, Chamberlain began to regard it as a mistake and to think that the role of constructive statesmanship called for its ending on the best terms possible.

On this, as on many other things, Chamberlain was strongly influenced by Sir Warren Fisher, the Permanent Secretary to the Treasury and Head of the Civil Service from 1919 to 1939, who was, with Hankey, one of the key figures of the inter-war period—more important perhaps than any politician with the exception of Chamberlain. Together with Chamberlain and Malcolm MacDonald, on whom he also had a profound influence,[114] Fisher ranks as one of the principal architects of Britain's appeasement policy towards Ireland during the late 1930s. He has been described by one of his juniors, who was to follow in his footsteps as Permanent Under-Secretary, as 'a man of enormous dynamic energy, quick to make up his mind, and with a great capacity to get things carried through to their conclusion ... fearless and restless in disposition and rather impatient ... given to quick enthusiasms, both for people and for causes ...'.[115]

One of Fisher's earliest and longest enthusiasms was for harmony in Anglo-Irish relations. He was nothing if not outspoken in his views. As early as July 1920, he told Bonar Law that

for centuries we exploited the country &, when we didn't do that, we prevented her development lest it shd. damage our own undertakings. And it is no answer to say that we have now ceased doing these things ... The Irish have memories like horses—I am married into them & know it—and they have something to remember. They have in the past been desperately wronged—their minds dwell on

[114] Conversation with the author, May 1974.
[115] Lord Bridges, *The Treasury* (London, 1964), p. 171, quoted by D.C. Watt, *Personalities and Politics: Studies in the Formulation of British Foreign Policy in the Twentieth Century* (London, 1965), p. 104.

that, the results remind them of it—they are revengeful and suspicious. Shd. not we be so? . . .[116]

Eighteen years later Fisher's views remained essentially unchanged. During the negotiations for a general settlement with Ireland in January 1938, he felt that the British should be the ones willing to make the big concessions. Commenting on a painstakingly calculated Treasury memorandum by one of his principals on how much Ireland might be capable of paying as its part of a financial settlement, Fisher minuted:

Statistics are a sealed book to me, and therefore I should not dream of contesting Sir F. Phillips' *mathematical* conclusion. But this is primarily a *psychological* problem. The Irish are historically on incontestable ground in their view of England as an aggressor. If we adopt a higgling, huckstering attitude we should—and will deserve to—get nowhere. The practical question is whether England thinks it to *her own* interest to start a fresh chapter with Ireland. In other words, if a showdown is forced by Germany, do we want to face both East and West? Obviously an Ireland gradually becoming less hostile to England would be to us of great value, positive and negative, alike militarily and agriculturally.[117]

As a civil servant, Fisher had only influence, not power, and therefore could take no political initiatives on his own. Fortunately in this case the initiative came from the other side. Its source was John Dulanty, the Anglophile Irish High Commissioner in London who had served as a senior civil servant in the Ministry of Munitions during the war and who had been retained, despite his previously close relationship with the Cosgrave Government, in his present post by de Valera.

Like Fisher, Dulanty had been looking for a way out of the Anglo-Irish economic war from its inception. In mid-October 1934 he thought he might have found it. Discussions with two officials of the Irish Department of Trade and Commerce, who were *en route* to Germany to arrange the barter of Irish

---

[116] Fisher to Bonar Law, 17 July 1920, quoted by Eunan O'Halpin 'Sir Warren Fisher and the Coalition, 1919–1922', *Historical Journal*, 24, 4 (1981), p. 921.

[117] Minute by Warren Fisher, 19 Jan. 1938 (T 160/747/14026/04/2).

cattle in return for German coal, iron, and steel, gave him the idea that a suitable opportunity might be taken to improve relations between Britain and Ireland by a similar arrangement 'without prejudice to the wider financial or political issues involved'. His plan was that the United Kingdom should increase the quota of Irish cattle to the fullest extent possible and that, in return, the Free State Government should arrange to divert orders for coal from Poland and Germany perhaps to South Wales, to an equivalent amount. He thought that this might appeal to the British Government because the United Kingdom's share of the Irish coal trade had been reduced from £2¼ million to £800,000 per annum, and the Free State Government was planning on the basis that Germany might take over even that amount. After winning endorsement of his idea from Sean Lemass, the Minister for Industry and Commerce, and James Ryan, the Minister for Agriculture, and more grudgingly from de Valera, Dulanty called on Thomas and Harding at the Dominions Office in late October to sound them out on his scheme. He did not propose a formal agreement; merely that each side should take a suitable opportunity to make concessions. He hoped that the psychological effect of such an agreement would be beneficial for Anglo-Irish relations in general and believed that the time was right to make some attempt in that direction.[118]

Dulanty's proposal was warmly received by the officials in the Dominions Office and the Treasury, who were anxious both to increase Welsh coal exports and prevent the Free State from forming closer trade relations with Germany. 'Dulanty would seem to have acted with courage and foresight in the interests of both countries,' minuted A.P. Waterfield, who had formerly served as head of the Treasury in Ireland from 1920 to 1922. Fisher and Waley concurred.[119] Urging the adoption of 'a liberal policy as regards the IFS in this matter', Fisher soon secured the approval of Chamberlain and the other ministers involved for the setting up of an inter-departmental committee to study Dulanty's proposals under the chairmanship

---

[118] Memo by E.J. Harding on conversation with Dulanty, 30 Oct. 1934 (T 160/673/14026/01/1).

[119] Minutes by Alexander Waterfield, 19 Nov. 1934, Warren Fisher, 24 Nov. 1934, and S.D. Waley, 24 Nov. 1934 (T 160/673/14026/01/1).

of Sir Horace Wilson, Chief Industrial Adviser to the Government.[120]

At its first meeting in late November, the Committee noted that an agreement with Ireland on coal was of great importance, since the outlook on the negotiations for the sale of additional coal to Italy was not favourable, and there was the distinct possibility that the rest of Britain's coal trade might eventually fall away. An arrangement which provided for an increased export of 750,000 tons of coal to Ireland would represent employment for about 3,000 men a year and would certainly be of considerable political value, affording as it would an opportunity for more jobs in the depressed areas of South Wales and Cumberland which had not benefited by other trade agreements. The advantage to the British shipping and slaughtering business had also to be taken into consideration.[121]

A few days later the Irish Committee met to put its stamp of approval on the work of the civil servants, whereupon secret negotiations between British and Irish representatives began in earnest.[122] Within a little more than a week an agreement was reached which called for the British Government to increase the quota of imports of Irish cattle by one-third, in return for which the Free State undertook to buy its coal from Great Britain.

The formal announcement of the Coal–Cattle Pact—as it was called—was made on 3 January. It was hailed almost unanimously in the press as the beginning of the end of the economic war between the two countries. Giving voice to the general feeling, *The Economist* welcomed 'the evidence of returning sanity in Anglo-Irish relations', and expressed hope that the agreement would be 'rapidly followed up by a general peace that would restore to a normal basis commercial intercourse with our nearest and one of our best markets'.[123]

These hopes were soon disappointed. The fault was not

---

[120] Minutes by Warren Fisher, 24 Nov. 1934, and Walter Elliot to Thomas, 2 Nov. 1934 (ibid.); and Ernest Brown to Runciman, 9 Nov. 1934 (Baldwin papers, 21/283).

[121] Minutes of Inter-departmental Conference on Exchange of Trade with the Irish Free State, n.d. (late Nov. 1934). T 160/673/14026/01/1.

[122] 22nd Meeting of ISC of 12 Dec. 1934. CAB 27/523.

[123] *The Economist*, 5 Jan. 1935.

entirely de Valera's. In April he cracked down hard on the
IRA, a step that was widely regarded in Britain 'as a preliminary to the re-opening of amicable talks for a settlement',[124]
and in May he made a conciliatory speech in the Dáil, in which
he gave an assurance that the Free State would not permit
Irish territory ever to be used by any foreign power as a base
for attacking Great Britain. At the same time he said that he
was ready to negotiate further trade agreements with Britain
on the basis of pound for pound.

But the British Government was slow to follow up on the
Coal-Cattle Pact. For this there was a number of reasons. Not
many other commodities invited the same treatment as coal
and cattle, and the Ministry of Agriculture was reluctant to
extend that agreement further because of the strong criticism
it would encounter from British farmers. The Home Office
was cool to any further agreements with the Free State without first consulting the Government of Northern Ireland,
because concessions to the Free State would generally be made
at its expense. The Board of Trade, for its part, was not
particularly concerned with a general lowering of tariffs. It
was convinced that British manufacturers could compete effectively even with them, and believed that their lowering would
only antagonize domestic industries in Ireland and embarrass
the Free State Government. What it most wanted to see concluded was an agreement guaranteeing Britain against discrimination in all administrative matters, such as public con-
tracts, import licensing, quotas, etc., in return for which it was
willing to consider the possibility of according full Dominion
treatment in quotas to all Irish products other than cattle,
which were covered by the previous agreement.[125]

The real problem was that there were obvious limits to how
much progress could be made without a political initiative.
Although the civil servants involved—Fisher, Wilson, Hankey,
and Harding—favoured an attempt at improving relations
with the Irish, by themselves they could do nothing. As Wilson
informed Thomas in February 1935, 'If therefore real progress

[124] *Sunday Express*, 7 Apr. 1935.
[125] Minutes of Inter-departmental meeting held at Board of Trade, 22 Jan. 1935
(BT 11/503/CRT 10 297/10098/4); Board of Trade memo on 'Trade with the Irish
Free State', 18 Jan. 1935 (ibid.).

is to be made (and the growing movement in the Irish Free State to set up more factories is to be countered before it is too late) there seems nothing for it but to consider again whether it is possible to make a move in the direction of general trade, financial, etc., relations.'[126] But, no real progress was likely without some long overdue ministerial changes. Although growing noticeably senile, MacDonald still clung to the premiership. Thomas also had lost much of his drive and mental agility. He lacked imagination, had never liked paperwork, had a reputation for gambling and heavy drinking, and had on occasion, with his fondness for relating ribald stories, not ingratiated himself with Dominions politicians. An imperialist at heart, with a sentimental affection for the king, Thomas found de Valera's republicanism repugnant to his deepest instincts. Moreover, he had played the role of 'the first Minister that ever stood up to Ireland'[127] for so long that he found it difficult to adapt once the billing was changed. He was almost removed from the Dominions Office in June, when MacDonald finally stepped down and exchanged places with Baldwin, but MacDonald had demanded as part of his price for turning over the premiership that Thomas remain in the Cabinet, and, after several unsuccessful attempts to remove him, Thomas ended up retaining his old post.[128] MacDonald's son Malcolm, who had been in line to become Dominions Secretary, received instead the Colonial Office, and it was six months before Thomas could be persuaded to exchange positions with him.

In other changes of note, Londonderry was removed from the Air Ministry and replaced by Sir Philip Cunliffe-Lister. Although temporarily 'promoted' to the Leadership of the Lords, Londonderry had lost all influence with the Government and was dropped in December. Also dropped were Hilton Young, MacDonald's erstwhile adviser on Ireland, and Sankey, whose place at the Woolsack was taken by Hailsham, thereby making room at the War Office for Halifax. Simon, miscast as Foreign Secretary, moved over to the Home Office, and was replaced by Hoare.

[126] Wilson to Thomas, 13 Feb. 1935 (ibid.).
[127] Thomas to Rothermere, 25 Jan. 1934 (Thomas papers, V/625/C60).
[128] Simon diary, 4 June 1935.

Another important development occurred in June when the
Judicial Committee of the Privy Council ruled that the Dominions had the right to abolish the right of appeal from their
governments to the king in Council in Great Britain, thus
resolving a dispute which had been simmering between the
Free State and Britain almost since the signing of the Treaty.
As *The Times* noted, 'The Committee has ruled, in effect, that
the Statute of Westminster means exactly what it was
generally understood to mean, and that it finally swept away
every vestige of restriction on the legislative powers of the
Dominions.'[129]

The Privy Council ruling increased pressure on the Government to move towards a settlement. While some of the Conservative press still tried to differentiate between the Free
State's 'moral' as opposed to 'technical' obligations under the
Treaty,[130] even these distinctions were swept away by the
Labour and Liberal press. 'Only hidebound political fanatics
with no sense of responsibility would miss this chance of making a lasting and honourable peace,' asserted the *Daily Herald*,
adding that the 'way lies along the path of breaking down the
stupid trade barriers'.[131] Similarly, the *Manchester Guardian*
urged the Government to undertake negotiations, saying that
it had been 'acting all along on a false basis, namely that of
the sanctity of treaties and Imperial obligations and the over-
riding of de Valera's arguments ... We should be wise to
admit that morality has nothing to do with it and try to get
at the underlying issues.[132]

The pressure on the Government was not limited to the
press. In Parliament James Maxton, the leader of the Independent Labour Party, exhorted the Government 'to do something definite, concrete and courageous with reference to the
Irish position',[133] while Cripps, speaking for the Labour Party,
pleaded with it to 'launch a fresh offensive of friendship upon
the Government of Ireland'.[134]

These demands could not be altogether ignored by the

[129] *The Times*, 3 June 1935.
[130] *Daily Telegraph*, 3 June 1935.
[131] *Daily Herald*, 3 June 1935.
[132] *Manchester Guardian*, 21 June 1935.
[133] *Parl. Deb. Commons*, vol. 303, cols. 626–634 of 20 June 1935.
[134] Ibid. cols. 678–683.

Government. With an election looming in the autumn, it was felt at high levels in the Conservative Party that the Government majority might be lost if the Liberal vote which had supported the Government in 1931 failed to do so again.[135] Nevertheless, compared to the situation on the continent, Ireland remained for the Government a minor irritant. Already Hitler had begun the rearmament of Germany, and in October Mussolini complicated the situation by invading Ethiopia. Politics revolved around the question of sanctions against Italy and Britain's role in the League of Nations. Ireland was forgotten. The general election in November returned the Government as strong as ever, with 432 seats, although both Ramsay and Malcolm MacDonald lost their seats. Liberals, except when supported by the Conservative Party, fared badly, and Labour did not do as well as expected, although it did end up with 154 members, a gain of a hundred-odd seats.

Even before the election, Fisher had begun exploring with Dulanty the prospects for a general settlement of all issues separating their two countries. At an inter-departmental meeting at the Treasury in late October Dulanty again played the German card. He told those present that German delegates were due to arrive in Dublin within a week to discuss the extension of the existing trade agreement between the two countries. Thus encouraged, the British agreed that the time was right 'for broadening the friendly front represented by the present coal–cattle arrangement, and that it would be worth some sacrifices on both sides'.[136] This decision was confirmed after the elections,[137] and reflected on the political level when Thomas was at last transferred 'screaming and kicking' from the Dominions Office[138] to the Colonial Office to make way for Malcolm MacDonald.

During December and January Dulanty continued negotiating with the British. His task was not made easier by de Valera's initial refusal to consider any real concessions, other than an assurance that he would do what was possible to

---

[135] Cowling, *Impact of Hitler*, p. 93.
[136] Board of Trade minute, n.d. (BT 11/503/CRT 11998/10098/46/2).
[137] Notes of meeting at Treasury, 27 Nov. 1935 (ibid.).
[138] Chamberlain diary, 21 Nov. 1935, quoted by Cowling, *Impact of Hitler*, p. 323.

divert Government orders from foreign countries to the United Kingdom, and possibly also encourage private Irish companies to do the same. In return, he asked that the British reduce their duties on Irish cattle by 30 per cent.[139] Still, the British remained interested, motivated in part by the desire to sell more coal, but even more by fear of the long-range effects on British interests of Germany and Ireland drawing together.[140] When Chamberlain, although conceding that other considerations had to be taken into account, balked at the prospect of having to justify 'what may seem on the face of it a one-sided bargain', his initial objections were eventually overcome by Fisher and Harding, who convinced him that the spirit in which the Irish carried out the agreement was much more important than the actual terms.[141] For his part, de Valera removed the tax on British coal, and made a few other minor concessions. On 17 February the continuance of the Coal–Cattle Pact for another year was announced. Not only was the prior arrangement for the exchange of coal and cattle on a pound for pound basis to be continued, but there was to be a mutual reduction of duties on certain specified items. As before, this new step towards ending the Anglo-Irish dispute was widely applauded by the British press.[142] The only criticism came from elements of the Liberal and Labour press who considered that the agreement did not go far enough.[143]

Up to the conclusion of the agreement for an extension of the Coal–Cattle Pact, the major effort in the drive for improved Anglo-Irish relations had come from below; on the Irish side from Dulanty, and on the British from the civil servants, in particular from Fisher, Wilson, Hankey, and Harding. So long as they did not attempt to move too far too fast, the Cabinet ministers whose departments were involved were content to leave matters in their hands. But the next logical step—a general settlement—would require a major political initiative

---

[139] Memo by Dominions Office on meeting between Dulanty and Harding, 17 Dec. 1935 (BT 11/503/CRT 11999/10098/2).

[140] Board of Trade to Ministry of Agriculture and Fisheries, 10 Jan. 1936 (ibid.).

[141] Harding to Sir Richard Hopkins (Treasury), 9 Jan. 1936, and minute on foregoing letter by Fisher (ibid.).

[142] e.g. *Daily Telegraph*, 18 Feb. 1936.

[143] *Manchester Guardian*, 10 Feb. 1936.

that could only be undertaken by ministers. In the British Cabinet, the groundwork for this initiative was laid when Malcolm MacDonald took over as Dominions Secretary.

Though just 34 when he joined the Cabinet in November, MacDonald was already an experienced politician well versed in Irish affairs. After Oxford, he had entered Parliament in 1929 and served from 1931 to 1935 as Parliamentary Under-Secretary to Thomas at the Dominions Office, where from the beginning he had favoured conciliation or arbitration rather than coercion in dealing with de Valera.[144] His arrival as Secretary of State 'was like a breath of fresh air', and 'gave the [Dominions] Office an invigorating sense of purpose it had not enjoyed since Amery's day'.[145] Capable, diligent, affable, conciliatory, and diplomatic, MacDonald was respected and liked by most of his colleagues, and made to order for dealing with a man like de Valera, with whom, indeed, he was able to establish an instant and lasting rapport. In order to safe-guard the Government against attack from the right, and particularly from Ulster while the effort was being made to seek a settlement with de Valera, Baldwin shrewdly brought in as MacDonald's Under-Secretary at the Dominions Office the Marquess of Hartington, an influential diehard and 'mania[cal] anti-Catholic',[146] willing to help achieve a settle-ment with de Valera so long as it could not be regarded as a 'betrayal of Ulster'.[147]

MacDonald's mission was to restore harmony to Anglo-Irish relations. After being returned in a by-election in Janu-ary, he set about his duties with this aim foremost in mind. In March he met secretly with the Irish leader in a London Hotel when de Valera was passing through on his way to Switzer-land to receive eye treatment. This first talk was followed by others on similar occasions. With Baldwin's assent, Mac-Donald began exploring with de Valera the possibilities of a settlement. By May he felt encouraged enough by the progress

---

[144] Joe Garner, *The Commonwealth Office 1925–68* (London, 1978), p. 113.

[145] Ibid. p. 19.

[146] Channon diary, 23 Sept. 1935 (Robert Rhodes James (ed.), *Chips: The Diaries of Sir Henry Channon* (London, 1967), p. 22).

[147] Note of conversation between Hartington and Dulanty, 28 July 1936 (PREM 1/273/114).

of the talks to submit a report on them for the consideration of the Cabinet.

In it he provided an extensive overview of the differences separating the two countries. On the constitutional issue, he felt the concessions would have to come from de Valera, since they had given about all they could, and must still insist on two fundamental principles: first, the Irish Free State would continue as a member of the British Commonwealth, which meant recognition of the constitutional position of the Crown in both internal and external affairs; and secondly, de Valera must accept that Britain could not attempt to pressure Ulster into a united Ireland. MacDonald was hopeful that de Valera's desire for a united Ireland might influence him to accept the Crown's position.

In regard to the other issues separating the two countries, MacDonald was hopeful about the chances for an eventual settlement. Progress had already been made on the issue of trade. Regarding financial matters, he suggested that the question of the land annuities might be settled by the payment of a single lump sum by the Free State. On defence, especially in regard to the Treaty ports, the question of how far the British could go would depend to a large extent on what sort of political settlement could be reached.

While recognizing that sentimentally the Irish were still republicans. MacDonald thought that public opinion in Ireland was moving steadily towards appreciation of the advantage of the imperial connection. Even de Valera seemed of late to have become more friendly towards the United Kingdom. His co-operation with Britain at Geneva during the Ethiopian crisis showed, in MacDonald's opinion, 'that he has abandoned the traditional Irish policy that Great Britain's difficulty is Ireland's opportunity'. Moreover MacDonald believed that, rather than being the supreme obstacle the British had always felt it to be, dealing with de Valera would actually be to their advantage because, 'on account of his unique position and influence in Irish politics', an arrangement concluded with him would have 'much more prospect of being permanent than one concluded with any other possible Southern Irish leader'.

Finally, as far as the Treaty of 1921 was concerned, Britain's acquiescence in Germany's recent breaches of the Versailles Treaty and the Locarno Pact made it difficult for England to insist upon its full rights by the Irish Treaty. 'We can scarcely,' MacDonald asserted, 'without ridicule and damage to ourselves, be less realistic and less generous in our treatment of a Dominion Government than in our treatment of a Foreign Government.'[148]

A few days later MacDonald had to defend his recommendations before the Irish Committee. He began by conceding that de Valera 'remained difficult and was by nature uncompromising', but argued that public opinion expected the Government to take some action. He told the Committee that de Valera was engaged in drafting a new constitution which would abolish the Crown so far as internal affairs were concerned, retaining it only as head of some form of external association. A constitution of this kind, he warned, would mean the end of the Free State's membership of the Empire.[149]

Within the Committee, Hailsham remained the largest obstacle to any concessions. On the other hand, MacDonald received support in various measures from his father, Chamberlain,[150] Elliot, Runciman, Simon, and Sir Thomas Inskip, the new Minister for the Co-ordination of Defence. Baldwin, however, remained equivocal, while the Marquess of Zetland, Secretary of State for India, opposed concessions to Ireland because of their possible effect on India.[151]

In early July MacDonald had another meeting with de Valera. 'It is perhaps an indication of his present practical mood', MacDonald later told the Irish Committee, 'that in the course of it he never mentioned Oliver Cromwell, or any character or event which troubled Ireland prior to 1921.' MacDonald thought that de Valera seemed anxious to retain a link with the Commonwealth for the sake of Irish unity, though he remained determined to abolish the Crown for internal affairs. MacDonald had expressed sympathy for de Valera's goal of achieving Irish unity, telling him that he

[148] Memo by Malcolm MacDonald on 'Relations with the Irish Free State', CP 124 of 5 May 1936 (CAB 24/262).
[149] 23rd Meeting of ISC of 12 May 1936 (CAB 27/523).
[150] Malcolm MacDonald, *Titans and Others* (London, 1972), pp. 61-2.
[151] 24th, 26th, and 28th Meetings of the ISC of 25 May, 24 June, and 22 July 1936 (CAB 27/523).

'thought that any Irish patriot should desire above all else a
United Ireland', but warned him that his actions could only
widen the breach between North and South. While the British
Government would put no obstacle in the way of their uniting,
if they desired to do so, it 'was not we who could persuade
the North. Only the people of the Irish Free State could persuade them by pursuing a policy which would ultimately incline them to come in of their own free will.' But de Valera
remained insistent that the British should use their influence
with the North to promote the cause of Irish unity.[152] Following MacDonald's report and further discussion in the Irish
Committee, the Cabinet agreed at the end of July that there
was not much that could be done to prevent de Valera from
making his expected constitutional changes, and that the only
course was to hope that the result was satisfactory enough to
justify Ireland's remaining in the Commonwealth.[153]

In early September Fisher, Harding, and Wilson began ex-
ploratory talks with Dulanty for a final settlement.[154] But before the conversations had proceeded far, they were overtaken
by the events surrounding Edward VIII's relationship with Mrs
Simpson. Hoping to turn the impending crisis to his advantage, de Valera urged the British Government to use the occasion to make a 'supreme effort' to reach the basis of a
settlement 'which would mean that for all time Ireland would
remain within the Empire'. The core of the Irish proposal was
that the king would remain 'King of Ireland'—though precisely what that meant was not spelled out—and that a joint
body resembling the old Council of Ireland would be
created.[155] The difficulty was that this would obviously require
the approval of Northern Ireland. Although Baldwin met with
Craigavon in October to brief him on the current state of the
negotiations and, in view of the delicate situation, to warn
him to 'watch and damp down the anti-Catholic demonstra-

[152] Memo by MacDonald on conversations with de Valera. Appendix I to CP 204
of 7 July 1936 (CAB 24/263).
[153] Cabinet conclusions 55(36) of 29 July 1936 (CAB 27/523).
[154] Fisher to Dulanty, 14 Sept. 1936; Minute by Harding on meeting between
Horace Wilson, Sir Grafton Bushe, Fisher, Harding, and Dulanty on 15 Sept. 1936,
and letter from de Valera commenting on the discussions of 7 Sept. 1936; note by
Batterbee on conversation between Fisher, Wilson, Batterbee, Bushe, and Dulanty on
14 Oct. 1936 (PREM 1/273/14).
[155] Memo by Batterbee, 15 Oct. 1936 (ibid.).

tions in Ulster',[156] there is no indication, despite prodding
from Wilson,[157] that he went any further than that.

By then the abdication crisis was at hand. On 28 November
Sir Harry Batterbee, the Senior Assistant Secretary in the
Dominions Office, crossed over to Dublin to brief de Valera
on the situation. Three possible scenarios were presented
should the king hold to his determination to marry Mrs Simpson: first, that she should become queen; second, that she
should not become queen but that Edward need not abdicate;
and third, that Edward should abdicate in favour of the Duke
of York. De Valera's initial reaction to the crisis was that it
presented 'a good pretext for getting rid of the Monarchy,
and if he [the King] loves the woman, why shouldn't he marry
her?' Then he favoured the second alternative. 'De Valera is
against the Monarchy', Baldwin told Hankey, 'but he is such
a gentleman he won't kick an enemy when he is down.'[158]
Finally he agreed to accept the third alternative—the one
favoured by the British Government—after Batterbee argued
that as a Catholic he would surely wish to uphold the sanctity
of marriage, but insisted that it would have to be accomplished by an act of his own Parliament.[159]

Despite concern over what de Valera's bill might actually
entail, and Ramsay MacDonald's anger at seeing his son's
work undone,[160] de Valera's willingness to go along with the
British Government and the rest of the Dominions on the
abdication question brought relief to the Government, where
some even hoped that the crisis might be used as a means of
getting a better understanding with the Free State.[161] Even
after de Valera took advantage of the situation to introduce,
along with a bill recognizing the abdication of King Edward
VIII, another eliminating the king and the Governor-General
from the Constitution of the Free State so far as internal affairs
were concerned, the feeling in the Irish Committee was one

[156] Note by Wilson for Baldwin for use in discussion with Craigavon, n.d. (October 1936) (ibid.).
[157] Wilson to Baldwin, 11 Dec. 1936 (ibid.).
[158] Roskill, *Hankey*, iii, p. 254.
[159] Wilson to Baldwin, n.d. (PREM 1/273/14).
[160] Nicolson diary, 30 Nov. 1936 (Harold Nicolson, *Diaries and Letters:* i *1930-1939* (ed.) Nigel Nicolson (London, 1966), p. 282).
[161] Wilson to Baldwin, 11 Dec. 1936 (PREM 1/273/14).

more of relief than anger. Simon thought that de Valera's objective was 'only to bring the Free State Constitution into accord with the realities of the situation'. Chamberlain said that he himself did not feel that the exclusion of the Crown from the internal affairs of the Free State was a fundamental and essential matter, or that such exclusion in itself prevented the king from being the head of the Commonwealth, and that 'far from de Valera's action having done harm, it might well have done good' if it led to a new definition of what was meant by the king as head of the Commonwealth in external affairs.[162]

The Irish Committee was further encouraged when Batterbee reported that de Valera 'regarded the recent legislation as the end of the story so far as he was concerned, and that he did not wish to alter the association with the other members of the Commonwealth unless and until the Irish people otherwise decided'. Though de Valera still believed that partition precluded a final settlement of the differences between England and Ireland, he thought the European situation reason enough 'for closing the ranks'.[163]

MacDonald accordingly recommended that the Cabinet accept that de Valera's new legislation did not alter the Free State's membership in the Commonwealth because in his opinion it represented 'the beginning of de Valera's permanent acceptance of the King as King of Ireland and head of the Commonwealth'. The worst thing about it, he thought, was the bad example it set for the rest of the Empire, particularly South Africa and India. But even here he felt that the other Dominions were 'already rather inclined to regard the Irish as curious people who must do things differently from everybody else, and an example from the Irish Free State is likely to be less infectious than an example from anywhere else'.[164] The Cabinet agreed, with only Hailsham and Zetland dissenting.[165]

In early January MacDonald had two long meetings with

[162] 30th Meeting of ISC of 15 Dec. 1936 (CAB 27/524).
[163] Batterbee to Wilson and Fisher, 6 Jan. 1937, and Batterbee to MacDonald, 7 Jan. 1937 (DO 35/890/x1/2).
[164] Memo by MacDonald, CP 15 of 17 Jan. 1937 (CAB 24/247).
[165] Cabinet conclusions 3(37) of 25 Jan. 1937 (CAB 23/87).

de Valera as the latter was passing through London. While de Valera seemed anxious for a settlement, he seemed less willing to make concessions in order to get it. For the first time, much of the discussion was concerned with defence. De Valera declined to give any guarantee that the Irish ports would be available to the British in time of war, even though he thought they should be. He said that an attack on Britain's independence would be a threat to Ireland's independence, and he believed that the Irish people would eventually understand this, even going so far as to say that, if Ireland had been independent in 1914 he would probably have been 'one of those fighting in Flanders'. But he could not make any assurances, and said that British insistence on that point would make an agreement impossible.[166]

Largely because of these impediments to a settlement on defence, Anglo-Irish relations during 1937 remained in a state of limbo. On the Irish side, de Valera was busy preparing his new constitution, which was not completed until May. On the British side, Baldwin, always the master of inaction, now in declining health and approaching his seventy-second birthday, was marking time until the coronation of the new king and the opening of the Imperial Conference at the end of May, when he would retire. Malcolm MacDonald, however, was impatient with this drift. Recognizing that the only real remaining stumbling block to a satisfactory general settlement was partition, MacDonald in April approached Craigavon with the idea of resurrecting something along the lines of the old Council of Ireland. Appealing to the Ulster Prime Minister's reputation for patriotism, MacDonald asked whether 'Northern Ireland might be able, even by a slight gesture, to perform a very valuable service to the King and the Empire. They could help to anchor the Irish Free State inside the Empire.'[167]

Craigavon was unmoved. He expressed to MacDonald 'with some force' his view that it was impossible to deal with the Southern Irish. In his speeches he had never left any loophole open which would permit co-operation with the South and he

[166] Memo by MacDonald of 17 Jan. 1937 (CAB 24/247).
[167] Memo by Malcolm MacDonald on talk with Craigavon, 7 April 1937)PREM 1/273/14).

could not now reverse his attitude. Nor was there much likelihood of any successor of his adopting a different attitude.

In his report to Baldwin, MacDonald noted that Craigavon
'showed a fundamental distrust of the Southern politicians
which seems to me to be at the root of the difficulty of getting
any cooperation'. He urged the Prime Minister to take up the
matter with Craigavon at a later date. This Baldwin declined
to do. No doubt Baldwin had a keener sense of the difficulties
involved in dealing with the men of the North than did his
Dominions Secretary. MacDonald may have seriously underestimated the problems involved, as would seem to be the case
if he actually did believe that the root of the difficulty was
Craigavon's distrust of Southern politicians. The problem ran
much deeper than that. MacDonald may have been influenced in this by his officials in the Dominions Office. Batterbee
in particular, somewhat of a romantic at heart, was prone to
underestimating the differences separating North from South.
Six years earlier he had speculated to Tom Jones about
whether there would be anyone using the Parliament Building
at Stormont within ten years.[168]

To his credit, MacDonald did not give up that easily. During the spring of 1937 he made a concerted effort to become
'good friends' with Craigavon and to get him to change his
approach to the South. In the first objective he succeeded, but
not in the second.[169]

On 28 May Baldwin finally turned over the premiership to
Neville Chamberlain. Ramsay MacDonald also resigned, and
died a short time later. He was replaced as Lord President of
the Council by Halifax. Simon stepped up to become Chancellor of the Exchequer, leaving the Home Office open for
Hoare. Duff Cooper became First Lord of the Admiralty,
while Anthony Eden remained as Foreign Secretary and Malcolm MacDonald as Dominions Secretary.

The first order of business for the new Government was the
Imperial Conference just getting under way in London. For
the first time the Irish Free State had declined to participate.
This enabled MacDonald to discuss constitutional develop-

[168] Tom Jones diary, 5 Oct. 1931. Jones, *Diary With Letters*, p. 14.
[169] MacDonald to Chamberlain, 9 June 1937 (DO 35/800/x1/54).

ments regarding Ireland informally with the other Dominion leaders. For the most part these discussions only confirmed what MacDonald already knew; that none of the Dominions considered that de Valera's constitutional changes—which were published in draft form in early May and approved by the Dáil on 14 June—should make any difference to the Free State's membership in the Commonwealth.[170] On one point where he sought reassurance—whether or not de Valera's legislation would encourage the republican movement in South Africa—MacDonald was told by Havenga, the South African Minister of Finance, that it would have the opposite effect because it would enable the opponents of the republicans to show the perfect freedom inside the British Commonwealth.[171]

Before their arrival at the Imperial Conference, all the Dominion prime ministers, including Joseph Lyons, the Prime Minister of Australia, himself of Irish-Catholic descent, had made it clear to the British that they did not wish to be drawn into the Anglo-Irish quarrel. In the past, while almost always professing sympathy with the British position, they just as often counselled caution and appeasement on the Irish question, and indeed on most other issues as well. Canada had its French minority to worry about, South Africa its Afrikaner republicans, and Australia a large Irish population, none of which groups had much sympathy with Britain's imperial pretensions. Thus in the long run the Dominions exerted a restraining influence on Britain's Irish policy. During the Imperial Conference the British found this attitude welcome, as they too were anxious to have the other Dominions keep out of the Anglo-Irish dispute as much as possible.

Although the question of Anglo-Irish relations was never formally discussed at the Imperial Conference, MacDonald did brief the Dominion prime ministers on the Irish situation at an informal discussion held on 14 June in the Prime Minister's room at the House of Commons. While he deliberately

[170] e.g. letter from W.L. MacKenzie King (Canadian Prime Minister) to the Canadian High Commissioner on 19 April 1937, stating that the Free State Constitutional proposals were 'of no great importance' and that they should 'not be taken as effecting a fundamental alteration in the position of the Free State as a Member of the Commonwealth' (DO 55/800/x1/55).

[171] Note of conversation between MacDonald and Havenga, 4 June 1937 (DO 35/891/x1/72).

played down the significance of many of the Anglo-Irish differences, including the 'minor tariff war', he admitted that the question of partition was 'particularly difficult', and might 'prove the Achilles heel in the relations between the two islands'. The Dominion prime ministers, in return, all expressed their sympathy for the British position and their desire to see Ireland remain a member of the Commonwealth.[172]

On 9 June the Irish Committee discussed de Valera's new constitution. It had, as expected, eliminated the king in internal affairs, but retained the Crown for external relations. There was general agreement in the Committee that it was out of the question for them even to contemplate the expulsion of the Free State from the Commonwealth. Halifax argued that time was the best and only healer of the differences between the two countries, and that, while he attached great importance to de Valera's undertaking to maintain the External Relations Act on a permanent footing, he considered it 'hopeless and a waste of time to discuss these constitutional niceties with de Valera himself'.[173]

Thus was settled, at least for the time being, the matter that had weighed most heavily with the British Government since de Valera had come to power in 1932: the question of the future constitutional position of Ireland within the Commonwealth. Although de Valera's constitutional legislation of 1936 and 1937 transformed Ireland into a republic in all but name, it was greeted at the time by both the British Government and the British press more with relief than resentment. Issues once thought so important had by then become 'constitutional niceties'. All that now mattered was whether or not Ireland wished to remain a member of the Commonwealth, and this was recognized as being up to her to decide.

Replacing the constitutional question as the one of paramount importance in Anglo-Irish relations by 1937, and indeed by 1936, at least when viewed from the British side, was the burning issue of rearmament and national defence. Without a solution to the question of the Irish ports a general settle-

---

[172] Minutes of an Informal Meeting of Principal Delegates, 1st Meeting of 14 June 1937, E(I) (DO 35/891/x1/82).
[173] 34th Meeting of ISC of 9 June 1937 (CAB 27/524).

ment with Ireland appeared impossible, and without a general
settlement the British could not feel secure that, in the event
of a war with Germany, they would not at the same time have
to worry about Ireland at their rear.

It was to avoid this latter possibility that in the autumn of
1937 the British began to press de Valera on the question of
the Irish ports. Discouraged by de Valera's intransigence on
financial matters, but anxious to show that he could 'get more
done in a month than he could in six when SB was on top',[174]
Chamberlain was determined to reach an agreement with Éire
(which was now the official name of the former Free State)
on defence, even if it meant postponing for the time being a
settlement on other issues. He was glad to see de Valera returned to power in the Irish elections in July, both because he
accepted MacDonald's view that 'de Valera in opposition
would be forced to move to the left so that in fact, when after
a few years Cosgrave lost office, we should have to deal with
a more difficult de Valera than ever', and because he thought
that de Valera was the only one who could keep the really
fanatical Irish in line.[175] But before he could reach an agreement on defence with de Valera, Chamberlain had to win the
acquiescence of the Chiefs of Staff to the turning over of the
reserved Irish ports to the Irish Government. In fact, the
Chiefs of Staff needed little persuading. The reasons for this
will be examined in the following chapter.

[174] Quoted by Cowling, *Impact of Hitler*, p. 149.
[175] Note on Chamberlain's interview with MacDonald, and report on MacDonald's conversation with de Valera at Geneva, 24 Sept. 1937 (PREM 1/273/14).

9

The Irish Ports

We are in the remarkable position of not wanting to quarrel with
anybody because we have got most of the world already, or the
best part of it, and we only want to keep what we have got and
prevent others from taking it away from us.

Chatfield to Sir Warren Fisher, 4 June 1934

I can well understand the anxiety that you feel with regard to
the proposal to hand over the harbours to the Government of
Southern Ireland ... the risk is not so great as it would appear,
the fact being that in a war, if the population of Southern Ireland
were hostile to Great Britain, it would be very difficult to retain
the harbours in question which are all vulnerable to land attack.
It would be necessary, therefore, to send a quite considerable
force—something between one and two divisions—to Ireland,
which we could ill afford in order to make sure that the harbours
were not captured. In these circumstances it seems wiser to hope
that it may be possible to have the good will of the Irish people
on the next occasion that we need it.

Duff Cooper to Selborne, 3 May 1938

By the terms of the Anglo-Irish Treaty of 1921, the British
retained in peacetime the ports of Berehaven, Queenstown
(Cobh), and Lough Swilly in the Free State, and in wartime
'such harbour and other facilities as the British Government
may require'. The Irish representatives at the Treaty negotiations conceded these points without much argument because
they were preoccupied with other more immediate concerns
and because it did not occur to them that they were matters
on which the British would compromise. Although these
concessions placed obvious limitations on Irish independence—Ireland was not, at least in the British view, a Dominion when it came to defence—they were not matters which
aroused much discussion in the Dáil during the debates on the
Treaty, nor were they ones over which the Cosgrave Govern-

ment later chose to make much of an issue. This situation changed, however, once de Valera came to power. Ironically, as the danger of war increased, so also did the apparent willingness of the British Government to consider turning over the control of the reserved ports to the Irish Government. Unlike Hitler, to whom the British often observed him bearing a strong resemblance, at least in his actions, de Valera did not even have to resort to threats in order to get his way (except perhaps for the veiled threat of the IRA getting out of control and attacking the ports). He had only to make known his desire for the transfer of the ports to his control; the British did the rest.

From the beginning, the question of the reserved ports and the larger question of the future role of Britain in the defence of Ireland were as much political as they were military decisions. In the highly charged atmosphere of 1921, with the memory of the previous war still fresh, the Lloyd George Government could not have made further concessions in regard to imperial defence even if it had wanted to and if the Services had been willing to accept them on strategic grounds. This is why there was so little discussion of the matter in the first place. By 1937, however, the situation had changed dramatically. During the intervening sixteen years the Irish had demonstrated beyond a doubt that they were capable of establishing a stable government. Despite the tariff war and the other attendant problems, it was by then almost impossible even for diehard Tories to picture a hostile Ireland in the event of another war, as had not been the case back in 1921 when memories of 'the Troubles' and of the Easter Rising still exercised a powerful influence. Moreover, 1937 was a different and more dangerous world than 1921. The British people no longer had the same confidence in their own strength that they had had before. Appeasement, which had its first visible manifestation with the Irish Treaty in 1921—but which had, in fact, begun almost as soon as the war had ended—was just reaching its high point in 1938, when the British Government signed away its rights to the Irish ports. Germany, Italy, and Japan were not the only ones hoping to benefit from Chamberlain's appeasement policy, and it is not surprising that de Valera remained one of its strongest supporters. Fortunately, in the case of Ireland, it led to a happier result.

The terms of the Treaty of 1921 concerning Britain's right to use certain Irish ports in peace and war were left purposely vague. This was because the Admiralty did not know in 1921 what kind of war it should be preparing for, or even who the next enemy would be. In fact, with Germany prostrate, France seemed a possible candidate. With Lord Balfour, Chairman of the Committee of Imperial Defence, warning against the menace of a French air strike,[1] and Sir Henry Wilson, the CIGS, sounding the alarm against the dangers of a foreign lodgement in a hostile Ireland, especially if Ireland possessed submarines,[2] it is hardly surprising to find the Admiralty trying to stake out as many rights as possible for itself in Ireland, or considering the possibility of war with France. Berehaven, on the south-western coast of Ireland, for example, was envisioned in the Admiralty scheme of things as occupying the same position in a war against France as that of Scapa Flow in the war against Germany.[3]

Although the Admiralty had no difficulty getting its way with the Treaty, it did run into some problems in the years which followed. These arose in disputes with the War Office and the Dominions Office. In the first instance, although the reserved ports existed for the wartime use of the Navy, it was the Army which had to maintain them in time of peace and protect them in time of war. With its budget already threadbare, the War Office demonstrated little enthusiasm for shouldering this burden. When its efforts to persuade the Admiralty to turn over the bases to the Free State proved unavailing, it responded by leaving them undermanned and neglected. When faced with the cost of renovating and maintaining the bases in 1937, the Treasury—which was a partner in this in that it had refused to allocate the necessary funds for their upkeep—quailed at the costs involved and agreed with the War Office that the time had come to transfer

[1] 147th Meeting of CID of 23 Oct. 1921 (CAB 2/3).
[2] Ibid.
[3] Draft Second Interim Report of the CID Subcommittee on the Irish Treaty, appended to minutes of the 26th Meeting of the Subcommittee, 13 July 1926 (CAB 16/70).

the ports and the expense involved in renovating and maintaining them to the Irish Government.

The other problem the Admiralty had was with the Dominions Office, which occasionally expressed the view that the Free State should be treated in defence matters in the same way as the other Dominions. The need for a special arrangement in regard to the reserved ports was questioned, since it was assumed that in the event of war Ireland, like all the other Dominions, would immediately become involved, and the use of the Irish ports would in any case be available. The Dominions Office also thought that, when the provisions of the Treaty relating to Article 6 came up for review in 1926, as provided for by the Treaty, this review might include the provisions of Article 7 concerning the reserved ports. This view was advanced by Lord Birkenhead at a meeting of the CID in October 1925.[4] Although Lord Beatty, the First Sea Lord and Chief of the Naval Staff, was able to assert successfully the Admiralty position that Article 7 was not meant to be subject to review (in fact, there never was an official review of either article), this did not extricate him entirely, as Sir Laming Worthington-Evans, the Secretary for War, took advantage of the opportunity to complain about the costs involved in maintaining the ports.[5] The matter was referred to the Chiefs of Staff (COS) Subcommittee of the CID where, after lengthy explanation by Beatty on how necessary the Irish ports would be in a war against France, the COS agreed that their retention was of sufficient importance to merit the expense of their upkeep. Lord Cavan, the CIGS, however, noted at the time that 'the value of the Southern Irish Coast Defences to the Navy as a base must, in the end, depend on the goodwill of the Irish Free State, without which their defence would become an almost impossible commitment'.[6] This same argument was used later by Worthington-Evans to justify the reduction of manpower at the bases,[7] and it had lost none of its force in 1937.

The dispute within the Government over the future dispo-

[4] 204th Meeting of CID of 29th Oct. 1925 (CAB 2/4).
[5] Ibid.
[6] Appendix 1 to 23rd Meeting of Chiefs of Staff Subcommittee of the CID (CAB 55/1).
[7] 216th Meeting of CID of 17 July 1927 (CAB 2/4).

sition of the Irish ports did not end with the decision of the COS in 1925 that they should be retained. In the summer of 1926 Amery again raised the possibility of attempting to reach an amicable agreement with the Free State regarding defence. He told a CID Subcommittee formed to study the matter, and of which he was chairman, that the goal for which they should aim was that the Free State should receive exactly the same treatment as the other Dominions. He thought that if they could establish friendly relations in time of peace they 'might presume such relations would continue in time of war'.[8]

Amery hoped that the Admiralty would at least see fit to allow the Free State to take over an increasing share of its own coastal defences. The War Office strongly endorsed this idea. At a meeting of the same CID Subcommittee in December, E.T. Humphreys, the Deputy Director of Military Operations, urged that 'the sooner the coast defences in Ireland could be handed over to the Irish Free State the better'.[9] The Admiralty, however, remained unmoved. W.A. Egerton, the Director of Plans, declined even to consider the possibility of allowing the Free State to use a destroyer or cruiser for its own coastal defence.[10]

When the CID met in February 1927 to decide the future of the Irish ports, the Admiralty had a powerful advocate in the person of Winston Churchill. Although as Chancellor of the Exchequer he was already pruning funds from each of the three Services, Churchill made it clear that he did not expect these savings to be made at the expense of the British position in Ireland. He said that the withdrawal of British garrisons from Irish ports would be 'most unwise', and insisted that consideration of any proposals to that end by the Free State should be postponed for at least ten years. Worthington-Evans denied that there was any 'present intention' of removing the British garrisons, and Amery assured Churchill that the question would not be raised with the Free State 'unless the atmosphere was favourable'.[11] When, at an informal meet-

---

[8] Ibid.
[9] 27th Meeting of the CID Subcommittee on the Irish Treaty, 16 Dec. 1926 (CAB 16/70).
[10] Ibid.
[11] 220th Meeting of the CID of 15th Feb. 1927 (CAB 2/4).

ing between Irish and British representatives in late April, held as a preliminary to the holding of the conference called for by the Treaty, the Irish asked for information that would enable them to consider the question of taking over and maintaining the three reserved ports, the Cabinet decided that they should be told that there was no reason to furnish this information. The British Government was not prepared to discuss the handing over of responsibility for the defence of the ports.[12] The Irish did not press the point, and the conference was never held.

The War Office, however, had not rid itself of the hope of relinquishing responsibility for the ports. Ten months later, Humphreys was again arguing that 'the sooner the Irish Free State was in a position to assume responsibility for the defence of all her ports the better'. He 'presumed that this was what the other service departments wished', and added that it was 'impossible to expect to keep the Irish Free State indefinitely in a different situation to the other self-governing Dominions'.[13]

This also remained the position of the Dominions Office. At a meeting of the CID in February 1928, Amery suggested that Queenstown be turned over to the Irish, as it was 'near Cork, and was the place where most American visitors landed, and for this reason the Irish probably attached a good deal of sentimental value to it'. But Churchill blocked the idea, arguing that 'it was much better to let the Irish have something which they could grumble about'.[14]

So long as Churchill was in the Cabinet there was little or no chance of the reserved ports being turned over to the Free State. Once Labour came to power in 1929, the matter was dropped altogether. Beset by other problems, the Labour Government had little time or inclination to worry about relations with the Free State. On defence questions, it relied heavily upon the advice and guidance of the Service Chiefs and of Sir Maurice Hankey, the Secretary to both the Cabinet and the CID. Usually an ardent advocate of co-operation

[12] Cabinet conclusions 28(27) of 27 April 1927. CAB 23/55.
[13] 29th Meeting of the CID Subcommittee on the Irish Treaty, 3 Nov. 1927 (CAB 16/70).
[14] Ibid.

with the Dominions on Imperial Defence, Hankey's enthusiasm tended to wane when it came to dealing with the Free State. In part, this was due to the reciprocal lack of enthusiasm evidenced by the Irish Government, which had yet to set up an effective liaison between its service departments and the British. But where Hankey energetically courted the other Dominions on defence matters, when it came to the Free State he preferred to let the initiative come from the other side, recommending meanwhile that on defence the Free State be treated as being on a par with Newfoundland.[15]

There were, in fact, some tentative steps taken towards co-operation on defence between the British and Irish Governments while Cosgrave was in power. For example, a Free State army officer in London acted as a liaison with the War Office, and there was co-operation involving the CID, such as censorship and the attendance of Free State officers at British services schools.[16] But a lingering suspicion on both sides precluded wholehearted co-operation. Moreover, especially towards the end, the shadow of de Valera loomed large in every decision made by the British regarding relations with the Cosgrave Government.[17]

The coming to power of de Valera in 1932 brought with it no immediate change in the Anglo-Irish defence relationship. Although Berehaven had been placed by the CID in Category A among British ports at home and abroad—signifying that adequate defences should be installed in peacetime, and that it should be fully manned and efficient before the outbreak of war—it had, like Queenstown and Lough Swilly (Category B—less important but still high priority),[18] and virtually all other British ports, been allowed to fall into a state of disrepair during the 1920s. When asked by the Cabinet's Irish Committee to consider to what extent a decision to apply economic 'sanctions' against the Free State would affect the garrisons of

[15] Minute by C.W. Dixon to P.A. Koppel, 13 Dec. 1929 (DO 117/167-D12257); minute by C.R. Price, 22 Jan. 1929, and memo by Hankey, 7 May 1929 (DO 117/137/D3020).

[16] S.L. Holmes to H. Batterbee, 28 Feb. 1929 (ibid.).

[17] e.g. fears voiced by Madden, the First Sea Lord, at 87th Meeting of Chiefs of Staff Subcommittee, 21 Sept. 1930 (CAB 53/3).

[18] CID memo on 'Imperial Defence policy: Defence of Ports at Home and Abroad', distributed to Cabinet as CP 248 of 25 July 1928 (CAB 24/198).

the reserved ports in Ireland, the War Office indicated that
the change in government in Ireland had had no effect on its
thinking in regard to the ports. Over the years the garrisons
in those ports had been reduced to the minimum needed to
maintain them: 425 of all ranks at Queenstown, 153 at Berehaven, and 150 at Lough Swilly. The War Office did not
think that an economic boycott of the ports would be effective,
but noted that the garrisons, 'being weak and scattered, are
not in a position to resist organized attack, more particularly
at Berehaven, without reinforcements'. Moreover

Owing to uncertainty as to the future of these ports, our present
policy is to do the bare minimum for the comfort of the isolated
garrisons. Expenditure has been pared to the limit. If it were not
essential, for reasons of security, to hold the ports, the War Office
would be glad for the occupation to come to an end and to be rid
of an awkward commitment.[19]

The Admiralty view, however, also remained essentially unchanged. It now raised the prospect that 'the situation might
even become so serious that these harbours might be open to
use by fleets hostile to this country'.[20] In any event, the general
deterioration in Anglo-Irish relations from 1932 to 1935 precluded serious discussion about the future of the ports. Not
until Malcolm MacDonald became Dominions Secretary in
the late Autumn of 1935, and the possibility of a general
settlement of all outstanding disputes with the Free State
Government began to be seriously explored, did the question
of the reserved ports again become an issue.

British policy had, in fact, already begun to change even
before MacDonald replaced J.H. Thomas at the Dominions
Office. In early November 1935 the COS Subcommittee of
the CID was asked to consider the possibility of some modification of the Irish Treaty with regard to the reserved ports,
either as a separate issue or as part of an attempt to reach a
general settlement. On Hankey's advice, the matter was referred to the Deputy Chiefs of Staff (DCOS) Subcommittee,
of which Hankey was also secretary, to be discussed in conjunction with representatives from the Dominions Office.[21]

[19] Ibid.
[20] Memo by Admiralty, ISC 21(32) of 7 May 1932 (ibid.).
[21] 154th Meeting of Chiefs of Staff Subcommittee, 7 Nov. 1935 (CAB 53/5).

The meetings of the DCOS Subcommittee soon revealed that Admiralty thinking had undergone a profound change in the previous four years. Now for the first time it was willing to consider withdrawing from the ports in the hope of improved relations with the Free State.[22] When the COS considered the situation in February 1936, Vice-Admiral W.M. James explained that the Admiralty was willing to give up the Irish ports because the reorientation in British defence policy had modified their importance. This meant the Admiralty now recognized that France was unlikely to be the next foe in a European war. The Admiralty still insisted, of course, upon retaining the unqualified right to use the ports in an emergency. While the Irish were not expected to contribute substantially to their own defence, it was hoped that they would be able to supply some minor local defence forces.[23] For their parts, Sir Archibald Montgomery-Massingberd, the CIGS, and Sir Edward Ellington, the Chief of the Air Staff, expressed themselves as 'only too glad to withdraw their personnel from the Irish Ports'.[24]

In early May 1936 MacDonald circulated his first memorandum on Irish affairs to the Cabinet.[25] In it he called for an attempt at a general settlement of the Anglo-Irish dispute. Citing quotes from de Valera indicating his willingness to undertake the expense of bringing the reserved ports up to standards set by British experts if those posts were turned over to his Government, MacDonald warned that an attempt on the British part to preserve the 1921 agreement on defence would be an obstacle to any new settlement.[26]

Appended to MacDonald's own memorandum was one by the COS expressing their willingness to turn over the reserved ports to the Irish Government as part of a general settlement, so long as they retained the right to use them in an emergency. In addition the COS were now willing to countenance an Irish navy which might include destroyers, in the hope that

---

[22] The Admiralty papers on the subject of the reserved ports are in ADM (Admiralty) 116/3657.
[23] 163rd Meeting of Chiefs of Staff Subcommittee, 4 Feb. 1936, (CAB 53/5).
[24] Ibid.
[25] CP 124 of 5 May 1936 (CAB 24/262).
[26] Ibid.

such a force 'would provide a valuable point of contact'[27] between the Free State and Britain. Noting that an improvement
in relations with Ireland would necessitate a change in policy
with regard to secret matters, and that no leakage of secrets
had ever occurred from the Free State, the COS recommended
that, should the Free State become responsible for the defence
of the reserved ports, its representatives should be allowed to
attend the meetings of the Joint Overseas and Home Defence
Committee and its officers should be admitted to schools
of instruction at which other secret matters were discussed.

The CID did not discuss the proposals presented by the
COS regarding the Irish ports until 12 May. More than three
months had elapsed since the COS had considered the matter.
The German reoccupation of the Rhineland during the interval had further impressed upon the Service Chiefs the need to
secure Britain's flank. Hankey emphasized to the Committee
the anxiety felt by the DCOS that the 'common interest of the
Irish Free State and the United Kingdom in the defence of
ports should be brought home to the Irish Free State Government'. He argued that, if they could get on better terms with
Ireland, they could afford to 'take risks' in admitting Free
State officers to British service schools, hoping that 'in this
way the spirit of camaraderie which now existed between our
defence forces and those of the other Dominions might be
extended to those of the Irish Free State'.[28]

Without dissent the CID accepted Hankey's recommendation and agreed also that, 'provided improved relations are
assured, and despite the risks involved, it would be desirable
to offer to hand over the complete responsibility of the
defences of the reserved ports to the Irish Free State'. In
return, the Committee asked that the Free State be required
to supply auxiliary vessels for defence of the ports and, if they
wished to do more, that they should not be discouraged from
supplying destroyers as well. The port facilities should also be
brought up to British specifications at Irish expense, and be
available for British use upon request.[29]

---

[27] Chiefs of Staff Subcommittee memo on 'Coast Defences in the Irish Free State',
Paper No. D, COS 9 of 4 Feb. 1936, Appendix I to CP 124 (ibid.).
[28] 278th Meeting of CID of 12 May 1936 (CAB 2/6).
[29] Ibid.

One month later the COS were asked to consider a more serious possibility: how defence relations with Ireland would be affected in the event the Irish Free State had to be regarded as a friendly foreign country. If de Valera's new constitution turned the Free State into a republic MacDonald was anxious that Ireland 'should at least leave the Empire as a friend and not as an enemy'.[30]

After first deploring the fact that de Valera was a 'fanatic by temperament', Sir Ernle Chatfield, the First Sea Lord, conceded that they were caught in a bind. Despite the strategic importance of the ports, it was doubtful if they would be of any use to the Royal Navy if Ireland were hostile in time of war, as they were landlocked and impossible to use or maintain without the co-operation of the Irish unless the whole country was conquered. He then speculated about the danger that might arise in a war with Germany in which the Germans might persuade the Irish to co-operate with them in return for complete independence. The rest of the Committee considered this a rather remote possibility.

Sir Charles Deverell, the new CIGS, said that 'there could be no greater disaster than the loss of the Irish Free State'. But if Ireland were to secede, both he and Ellington thought that the best that could be hoped for would be an offensive-defensive alliance. Hankey said that they really had only two options. One was to hold on to the ports as outposts in a foreign country, like Gibraltar. The other was to say to the Irish that they could hold the ports as an independent republic, but must guarantee that the British could use them. He thought that there was some hope for the second proposal because the Free State did not want to be over-run by any foreign power and therefore it was in de Valera's interest to ensure them their use. Considering also the savings that would be realized if the ports were turned over, the COS agreed that they should be given up even if the Free State left the Commonwealth. But the COS also asked that a covering memorandum be drawn up calling 'attention to the disastrous effect on our security of an independent Irish Free State, and to the necessity of making every effort to avoid such a contingency arising'.[31]

[30] 180th Meeting of Chiefs of Staff Subcommittee, 6 July 1936 (CAB 53/6).
[31] Ibid.

Three weeks later the COS again considered and deplored the possibility of Ireland leaving the Empire.[32] In the meantime, the Joint Planning Subcommittee of the CID had also been looking into the question. It too reported that Irish secession would be disastrous, for the added reason that there was a considerable number of Irish officers in the armed services who might become aliens if the Free State seceded. Moreover, the Army could ill afford to lose its annual intake of Irish recruits, which in 1936 had risen about 520 men from the previous year. If the Free State did secede, the Subcommittee likewise recommended the conclusion of an offensive–defensive alliance. In return for a guarantee of its territory and communications, the Free State would guarantee to Great Britain every facility required by British forces in time of war, including the free use of Irish ports, Irish aerodromes, and freedom of movement for British forces in the South.[33]

The political difficulties in the way of an offensive–defensive alliance on the basis suggested by the Joint Planning Subcommittee were obvious. The COS also raised the possibility that an independent Ireland might repudiate an alliance with Britain. On one point the COS and the Joint Planning Subcommittee were in complete agreement: that the strategic interests of the Empire could best be served by the existence of a friendly Ireland within the Commonwealth. So long as Ireland remained within the Empire there was always the hope that a less extreme government might come into power in the Free State—one more favourably disposed to co-operate with Britain.[34]

On 1 September 1936 MacDonald circulated to the Cabinet a memorandum setting out in some detail the use the Admiralty intended to make of the Irish ports in the event of war. That use, of course, depended upon the nature of the war. Against France the ports would be of the most use, in which case the Admiralty envisioned using both Queenstown and Berehaven as bases for the Main Fleet, with Lough Swilly serving as a convoy assembly port. In a war against Germany,

[32] 183rd Meeting of Chiefs of Staff Subcommittee, 27 July 1936 (ibid.).
[33] Report of Joint Planning Subcommittee of CID, COS 403 of 23 July 1936 (CAB 53/28).
[34] Memo by Chiefs of Staff, COS 405 of 30 July 1936 (ibid.).

on the other hand, it was thought that the three ports would only be necessary as bases for auxiliary vessels.[35]

Although not prepared to consider these bases as anything less than 'vital' in any war, it was clear that their priority was much lower in the Admiralty's opinion when Germany was regarded as the most likely adversary. This perhaps accounts in part for the reluctance of the Admiralty to dismiss the possibility of war with France.[36]

Once MacDonald had secured the acceptance of the COS and the CID for turning the reserved ports over to the Free State, his problem became that of persuading de Valera to accept them as long as there were conditions attached. Whether de Valera's refusal to guarantee that the British could use the ports in time of war if they were turned over to the Free State in the meantime was 'purely a matter of politics',[37] as MacDonald first thought, it soon became clear that the refusal was final. In the meantime, with the risk of war growing, the War Office was becoming ever more insistent that something should be done about preparing the ports for war. Both the Treasury and the Dominions Office remained hopeful that the Free State could be made to shoulder the burden as part of a general settlement, though they realized that a decision on the ports could not be deferred much longer.[38]

In September 1937, in an attempt to pick up the threads of their earlier conversations, MacDonald met with de Valera in Geneva. He found the latter's position no different from what it had been the previous January. The atmosphere was not improved by de Valera's 'extremely tiresome intervention' on the subject of Palestine to the General Assembly due, Mac-Donald believed, to his grievance about partition. De Valera would give no assurance that the British could use the Irish ports in case of war.[39]

[35] Memo by Chiefs of Staff, COS 405 of 30 July 1936 (ibid.).
[36] Ibid.
[37] Note of conversation between MacDonald and Dulanty, 4 Feb. 1937 (DO 35/894/x1/15).
[38] Minute by Stephenson, 5 Mar. 1937; minute by Hartington, 7 Mar. 1937; Batterbee to R.H. Haining (War Office), 10 Apr. 1937; and Haining to Batterbee, 10 July 1937 (DO 35/894/x/31/2-4).
[39] Report on MacDonald's conversations with de Valera at Geneva, 24 Sept. 1937 (PREM 1/273/14).

Disappointed by de Valera's intransigence, but convinced of the need to secure some sort of an agreement on defence, Chamberlain began to consider the possibility of attaining a separate agreement on defence, even if de Valera refused to make any definite assurances regarding the right of the British to use the ports in wartime. But here, he cautioned MacDonald, 'we should have to be careful as the absence of any assurance that we could use these ports in war rendered our arrangements very vulnerable to criticism from those who suspected de Valera's good faith'.[40]

For several reasons, Chamberlain placed more value on obtaining Ireland's goodwill than he did on retaining the reserved ports. Not least was his desire to save the British Treasury the expense of bringing the ports up to war standards. Convinced that, if war came, Britain's chances for survival would depend in the long run as much upon her economic strength as upon her military strength, Chamberlain, as Chancellor of the Exchequer during the first two years of British rearmament, had kept a tight reign on defence expeditures and had tried to keep the budget as close to being balanced as was feasible. Favouring the needs of the Royal Air Force as a first priority over the needs of the other services, including the Royal Navy, the Treasury under Chamberlain had been parsimonious about allocating the funds necessary to bring up to standard and maintain even British ports. The reserved ports in Ireland had been neglected entirely.

More important, Chamberlain underestimated the importance of the ports to the Royal Navy in time of war, and perhaps also the chances of securing the goodwill of the Irish people in time of war even if a settlement had been made only on financial and trade matters, leaving Britain in control of the reserved ports. Unlike Churchill, his opposite number in almost every respect, Chamberlain was a great peace minister who was unlucky in his timing. Unlike most of his colleagues, he had had no direct military experience of the First World War, either at the Front or in one of the Service ministries. Despite his long career, he had never presided, even in peacetime, over one of the Service ministries. Given a choice, he

---

[40] Note on talk between Chamberlain and MacDonald, Sept. 1937, and minute by Chamberlain on draft memo by MacDonald, 5 Oct. 1937 (ibid.).

preferred the Ministry of Health, the Dominions Office, or the Exchequer to any of those. Plotting military strategy was not something that he enjoyed, or at which he was very good. Although no one in 1937 could have foreseen the fall of France three years later, everyone in the Cabinet, including Chamberlain, knew how close Britain had come to defeat by submarines in 1917. Yet he does not seem to have grasped the importance of the Irish ports in dealing with that menace. 'I am not sure that I appreciate the use which the general staff think we should want to make of the reserved ports in war,'[41] Chamberlain noted on a draft memorandum for the Irish Committee, which MacDonald submitted to him for his perusal after another session on defence with de Valera in early October.

I fully understand the danger if they were used by enemy forces, but of course there would be a wide difference between an assurance that no enemy should use them and one that we should have the use of them for any purpose we liked. I think any reference to the Chiefs of Staff should bring out this point. We would get the first assurance but not the second and I should like to feel satisfied as to the importance of the difference.[42]

Whatever the value of the reserved ports in wartime, Chamberlain was convinced that their value to Britain would be negated if Ireland were unfriendly in such a war. He believed that the potential goodwill to be won by turning over the ports as part of a general settlement outweighed any advantages to be secured by retaining the ports without that goodwill. On the whole, the Cabinet and the COS agreed with him.

On 6 October MacDonald circulated a memorandum to the Cabinet on his recent talks with de Valera. These conversations had reaffirmed his belief that the latter was 'really genuine in desiring whole-hearted friendship and co-operation between the Irish Free State and Great Britain, but would rather like to get that friendship on his own terms'.[43] MacDonald noted with satisfaction that de Valera now regarded the constitutional question as settled. Reaching a financial

[41] Note on talk between Chamberlain and MacDonald, Sept. 1937, and minute by Chamberlain on draft memo by MacDonald, 5 Oct. 1937 (ibid.).
[42] Ibid.
[43] CP 228 of 6 Oct. 1937 (CAB 24/271).

settlement, however, might yet prove difficult. De Valera was still unwilling to recognize as valid the financial agreements the British had reached with Cosgrave. While he was prepared to start with a 'clean slate' to make a new agreement, his real hope was that the British Government would waive all money owed to it, in exchange for an Irish expenditure of a few hundred thousand pounds on the reserved ports if they were turned over to Ireland.[44]

With regard to the ports, de Valera also told MacDonald that he regarded the British occupation as an infringement of Ireland's sovereignty. If Britain should be involved in war under these circumstances, de Valera warned that feeling in Ireland would be so strong that there would be land attacks on the ports by irresponsible but considerable Irish forces. Britain might then find itself involved in the reconquest of Ireland. On the other hand, if Britain were to give up the ports, then there was much more likelihood that if war came Ireland would come in on the British side, and also of the British being invited to use the ports in the common defence of the two countries.[45]

De Valera also raised the question of Anglo-American relations with MacDonald, saying that a settlement of the Anglo-Irish dispute would make an immense difference in feeling in America, and emphasizing that 'real unqualified friendship' with the United States would be vastly more valuable to Britain than the satisfaction of a claim for a sum of money, or than continued occupation of the Irish ports against the will of almost the whole Southern Irish population.[46]

While conceding to de Valera the importance of American friendship, MacDonald did not feel constrained to make any concessions on account of it. Nor would he admit the right of one member of the Commonwealth to remain neutral if the others were at war. He warned de Valera that, if he did not give the assurance the British Government required, it might decide not to negotiate any new defence agreement with him.

[44] Ibid.
[45] Ibid.
[46] De Valera had been making a concerted effort to appeal to American public opinion by means of radio broadcasts to the United States and interviews with the American Press. Although annoying, this did not have any overt effect on British policy.

Nor could the British Government consider turning over the use of the ports if its military advisers said that their use was essential to Britain's existence, as it 'would be criminal for a Government to surrender a point which was of the greatest possible importance to its people'. De Valera countered by saying that military advisers were 'notoriously conservative and limited in outlook' and that, even it it were true that the use of the ports had been vital in the last war, that was no criterion as the next war would be totally different. Military advisers were always thinking in terms of the last war. In the end, MacDonald conceded that the question of whether or not to turn over the ports would be a political decision to be made by the Cabinet.[47]

In November 1937 MacDonald suggested to de Valera that the discussions which had been taking place between British and Irish civil servants periodically since 1935 be expanded to include the situation that might arise in the event of a major war. De Valera responded on 24 November, saying that a piecemeal discussion between civil servants such as that suggested could achieve no useful purpose until some prior understanding had been reached between the two Governments. He proposed instead negotiations between ministers from each Government on the outstanding issues dividing them. The British Government welcomed the proposal, and agreed that negotiations should begin in January.[48]

The question of the reserved ports remained the biggest problem. Because of domestic difficulties, MacDonald thought that de Valera would be unwilling to give any promise regarding British use of the ports in time of war. The most the British could hope for would be a repetition of the assurance which he had already given, that he would take all necessary measures to deny the use of Irish territory to an enemy of Britain, and that, if his own forces were inadequate for this purpose, he would invite the assistance of British forces.[49]

Despite the obvious drawbacks, MacDonald nevertheless

---

[47] CP 228 of 6 Oct. 1937 (ibid.).
[48] De Valera's dispatch of 24 Nov. 1937 and the British reply of 4 Dec. 1937 are quoted in part in Cabinet conclusions 300(37) of 15 Dec. 1937 (CAB 24/273).
[49] Memo by Secretary of State for Dominions of 10 Dec. 1937, ISC 128(32), Appendix III to Cabinet conclusions 300(37) (ibid.).

saw 'distinct advantages' for Britain in such arrangements. There appeared to be certain military advantages, though as a layman he declined to assess them. On the political side, he thought that co-operation in defence matters 'might well in time help in appeasement between the two countries'. There were also financial advantages to be gained if Ireland took over the cost of modernizing the equipment of the ports, estimated to involve capital expenditure of some £747,000, besides annual maintenance charges thereafter of £230,000.[50]

If the COS, who were currently considering the matter, advised the Government to maintain its existing rights in the ports under these circumstances, then a new defence agreement with the Irish Government would clearly be out of the question. In that case, MacDonald warned, 'any chance of getting de Valera to reach a reasonable settlement on the financial and trade disputes would vanish'. But if, on the other hand, the COS advised the Government to take the risks involved in withdrawing from the ports, then there was some possibility of agreement on the other matters.[51]

For his part, MacDonald left no doubt that he was willing to accept those risks, and to make financial and trade concessions in an effort to reach a settlement with de Valera. He admitted that he did not regard a settlement on the lines indicated as in any way ideal, and maintained that the 'only satisfactory final settlement would be one in which the Irish Free State Government accepted frankly, freely and ungrudgingly loyalty to the King and full association with the British Government'. But 'owing to the attitude of de Valera and the introduction of the New Constitution', MacDonald could not see that any such settlement was possible 'for a very long time to come', if indeed it could ever be achieved. But any substantial improvement in relations between the two countries would 'not only prevent further estrangement and hostility', he concluded, but would also 'positively help to bring about gradually that real friendship and co-operation which should be natural on account of the common interests of the two countries', and which he felt certain 'de Valera himself genuinely desires in principle'.[52]

[50] Ibid.   [51] Ibid.
[52] Ibid.

The Cabinet agreed with the Dominions Secretary.[53] In fact, on the previous day, the Cabinet's Irish Committee had already begun planning strategy for the forthcoming negotiations. It is clear from the record that Germany was very much on the minds of those present. Simon compared the coming negotiations with de Valera to dealing with Germany, in that the concessions proposed to be made by Britain were of a concrete and largely financial character, whereas the concessions hoped for from the other side were largely of an imponderable character. Another danger was that, if the January negotiations failed, de Valera would be certain to use whatever offer was made as a starting-point when he next came over. Nevertheless Simon was in favour of running the risks involved, 'for success would mean the ease of many of our present anxieties'.[54]

Hoare, who was feeling pressure from the Government of Northern Ireland,[55] cautioned his colleagues against appearing 'too forthcoming'.[56] He suggested instead a discussion similar to that which Halifax had just had with Hitler.[57] In general, they should take the line that they were 'doing de Valera a favour by consenting to negotiate'.[58]

This advice was ignored by Chamberlain, who thought that the Goverment of Northern Ireland was very likely 'over sanguine' in its view that de Valera was in such difficulties that he would accept almost any terms. Chamberlain conceded that in order to obtain an agreement on defence they might have to abandon their claim to the land annuities payments, but urged that they should use every endeavour to conclude a defence agreement with Ireland, even if it were impossible to reach one on finance. He added that de Valera's prestige would be greatly increased if he achieved an agreement and that this would be an inducement to him to be reasonable.[59]

In order to reach such an accord, however, the acquiescence

---

[53] Cabinet conclusions 300(37) (ibid.).
[54] 35th Meeting of ISC of 14 Dec. 1937 (CAB 27/524).
[55] Memo by Home Secretary on interview with J.M. Andrews, Acting Prime Minister of Northern Ireland, 9 Dec. 1937, Appendix II to Cabinet conclusions 300(37) (CAB 24/273).
[56] 35th Meeting of ISC (CAB 27/524).
[57] Halifax had met with Hitler at Berchtesgaden on 19 Nov.
[58] 35th Meeting of ISC (CAB 27/524).
[59] Ibid.

of the COS had yet to be won in turning over the reserved ports to Ireland without any assurance that they would be available to the British in time of war. This acquiescence was largely a formality, though a necessary one, as no defence agreement with de Valera could be presented to Parliament with any chance of approval, without their prior approval. Hankey, for one, thought it unfair to put the onus on the COS for what was, in essence, a political decision. 'The decision ought ...' he told Sir Thomas Inskip, the Minister for the Co-ordination of Defence, adding that there were 'no new military factors: only new political factors'.[60] Inskip agreed that the COS had gone 'to the utmost limit'[61] in the answers which they had given in their earlier report.

For their part, the COS were only too aware that it was impossible to separate the strategic aspects of any decision regarding Ireland from the political implications involved. Lord Gort, the new CIGS, did not, in any event, put much store in any assurances that they might be given in time of peace. He argued that they could not afford to send garrisons to the reserved ports in time of war if Ireland were ill-disposed; while, if Ireland were well-disposed, they would be able to send garrisons anyway, even lacking an Irish promise to grant facilities in time of peace.[62]

In order to ensure a favourable answer from the COS, Chamberlain saw to it that the questions were sufficiently precise so as to exclude the possibility of their speculating too widely on the political as well as the military aspects of the policy under consideration. At the request of the Cabinet, the Chiefs were asked to give an estimate of the military significance of the reserved ports to Britain during a major war, which would cover four possible situations:

1. a situation in which the ports are retained in our hands, and the Free State remains friendly;
2. a situation in which the ports are in the hands of a friendly Free State;
3. a situation in which the ports are retained in our hands, but the Free State is hostile; and

[60] Hankey to Inskip, 10 Dec. 1937 (CAB 63/34).
[61] Inskip to Hankey, 13 Dec. 1937 (ibid.).
[62] H.L. Ismay to Inskip, 10 Dec. 1937 (ibid.).

4. a situation in which the ports are in the hands of a hostile Free State.[63]

The Cabinet also concluded that, subject to further consideration in the light of the report from the COS, they should, as
a part of a general settlement with the Free State, indicate
their willingness to withdraw from the ports on condition that
the Irish Government bring the ports up to defence standards
at its own expense, and thereafter maintain the defences at
that level. The Irish must also agree to provide small naval
vessels and airplanes for coastal defence, as well as to increase
considerably the number of their defence forces generally. In
addition, they would be asked to co-operate closely with the
British in defence matters, and to purchase any defence equipment that might be needed and that could not be locally
manufactured from the United Kingdom, as well as to arrange
for the erection and operation of one or more munitions factories in consultation with British experts.[64]

Under the circumstances it was obvious that, whatever
answers to the four questions the COS might give, the Government would be able to do what it had already determined
upon. Especially unpalatable were possibilities 3. and 4. When
the COS met to discuss the matter, Gort said that they would
be confronted with 'an almost intolerable situation if Ireland
were hostile'.[65] He estimated that at least a division would
then be required for the defence of each port, while the situation would be even worse if the ports had already been handed
over to the Free State.[66]

Chatfield thought that a hostile Ireland might have to give
way quickly, but the prospect of Irish bases for German submarines and aircraft drove him to the conclusion that 'they
should urge upon the Government that it must never be allowed to happen'. Gort tried to persuade Chatfield that Belfast

[63] Cabinet conclusions 300(37) (CAB 24/273).

[64] Ibid.

[65] 276th Meeting of Chiefs of Staff Subcommittee, 21 Dec. 1937 (CAB 59/8).

[66] Ibid. Though the CIGS had no need to say so, the dispatch of three divisions
to Ireland in the near future was out of the question. Five months later the Chiefs of
Staff had to warn the French that the best they could do in the event of war would
be to provide *two* divisions. Nothing more could be provided for a year or more after
the outbreak of hostilities. See Donald Cameron Watt, *Too Serious a Business: European
Armed Forces and the Approach to the Second World War* (Berkeley, 1975), p. 102.

and Milford Haven might be made to serve the same purpose as the Irish ports. Similarly, Sir Cyril Newall, the Chief of the Air Staff, argued that their loss 'would be a nuisance but their importance was not sufficient to warrant the extensive effort necessary to hold them against a hostile Ireland, still less to effect their capture'. Eventually, Chatfield conceded that the most important consideration was to avoid provoking Irish hostility, but he stressed that under some future circumstances ship losses might become so serious as to necessitate drastic measures to regain the ports.[67]

[67] 276th Meeting of Chiefs of Staff Subcommittee (CAB 59/8).

10

The Settlement

We are signing the Agreement with Dev and his colleagues to-day. All that I have done since I came into office is to take advantage of the better relations which you had already established between Southern Ireland and this country by the negotiation of the coal-cattle pacts. When I came here I found the Irish as ready as ourselves to discuss the whole thing in a friendly spirit. You will see that besides the trade agreement we are settling the financial dispute and the question of the Treaty Ports. On both of these we on our side are being very generous. If you had been given a chance by the Cabinet when yourself Dominions Secretary to make such a generous offer you could have got this Agreement long ago. But time had to pass before the United Kingdom Cabinet evolved into the frame of mind to make this gesture.

MacDonald to Thomas, 25 April 1938

THE negotiations which began on 17 January were long and difficult. De Valera personally conducted all the important bargaining for the Irish delegation. Assisting Chamberlain, on the British side, were MacDonald, Simon, Hoare, Inskip, Stanley, and Morrison. Although Ulster declined to participate, its representatives were present in spirit, if not in person. To statements by de Valera that partition would be one of the questions which would be discussed in the forthcoming talks, Craigavon had responded by calling a snap election in the North to support his policy of 'Not an Inch'.

The British press welcomed the talks wholeheartedly, though there were differences of opinion on how far the Government should be prepared to go in making concessions and on the subject of partition. For the most part, the Conservative press warned against 'unrequited concessions' to Ireland, and urged the Government to stand by Ulster.[1] The

---

[1] *Daily Telegraph and Morning Post*, 13 Jan. 1938; *Yorkshire Post*, 30 Dec. 1937. An exception was the *Spectator*, which could see no reason why the British Government should not try to persuade Northern Ireland into an All-Ireland federation. 21 Jan. 1938.

Liberal and Labour press, on the other hand, exhorted the Government to be generous in its treatment of Ireland, and to consider sympathetically de Valera's case regarding partition.[2] The *Manchester Guardian* was characteristically forthright in its views on both partition and the Ulster Government:

Everyone knows that the Northern Government comes nearer to being a 'totalitarian' State than any other part of the Commonwealth. The treatment of the religious minority is a scandal. The whole electoral machinery has been twisted to its disadvantage; there is an extraordinary apparatus of penal legislation denying elementary liberty of the subject ... There is a religious discrimination in public employment. So long as these things continue there will be no peace in Ireland. The British Government cannot end them by direct interference—that would be 'coercion', even if it were in a good cause,—but it could bring moral pressure on Lord Craigavon to behave differently. It was the British Government that put the Ulster minority—a third of the population—under Lord Craigavon's Government, and the fair treatment of that minority is an Imperial concern.[3]

The raising of the issue of partition prompted the first significant investigative reporting by the British press since 1922 on conditions in Northern Ireland, conducted largely by correspondents of the Liberal press. The political correspondent of the *News Chronicle*, for example, asserted that 'for 17 years Craigavon's Tory Government has ruled the Six Counties with a rod of reaction', and warned that, unless the Nationalist minority in the North were given civic justice, a new 'trouble' would break out in time.[4]

Although the British emphasized from the beginning that there could be no question of their using pressure or coercion against Ulster, de Valera nevertheless pressed them to use some sort of moral suasion to end partition, and charged that the presence of British troops in Ulster, combined with various British subsidies, constituted a powerful inducement

---

[2] *News Chronicle*, 13 Jan. 1938; *Manchester Guardian*, 17 Jan. 1938; *New Statesman and Nation*, 21 Jan. 1938; *The Economist*, 22 Jan. 1938; *Daily Herald*, 11 Feb. 1938. This spirit was not limited to the press. Some of the trustees of the National Gallery, with the support of its director, Kenneth Clark, suggested the return of the disputed Hugh Lane pictures to Ireland as a gesture of reconciliation. The suggestion was turned down (DO 35/899/x/54/4).

[3] *Manchester Guardian*, 11 Feb. 1938.

[4] *News Chronicle*, 28 Jan. 1938.

to Northern Ireland to remain part of the United Kingdom. He also made it clear that British failure to make any concessions regarding partition would affect his negotiating stance on other issues. When asked by Chamberlain whether he would have given a different response on the use of the ports, had the British ministers met him over partition, de Valera answered that this would have been so. 'The hatchet would have been buried', he added, 'and things would have been fundamentally different.' On the question of the ports, de Valera would not, despite repeated promptings by the British, give any assurances. He said that the British Government should base its plans on the assumption that the ports would not be available to them. Although they should provide for the possibility of switching over to them at a later stage, he emphasized that it 'would be the height of unwisdom for the United Kingdom Government to make any more favourable assumption'.[5]

On the ports, the British were prepared to give way; on partition, they were not. This intransigence regarding partition was based on political expediency, not moral principle. Chamberlain's own view was that 'ultimately there would have to be a united Ireland just as there was a united Canada', but that de Valera and his colleagues were not approaching it in the right manner.[6] During the first day's talks Chamberlain was struck by the fact that, contrary to what he had previously assumed, de Valera's attitude toward Northern Ireland was not that he wished to coerce her by means of penalizing commercial measures, but that he was anxious to secure her goodwill and to promote a better understanding.[7] This marked the beginning of a transformation in his attitude towards the Irish leader. When MacDonald first briefed his colleagues on what to expect in de Valera's negotiating style—saying that his characteristics as a hard bargainer might be summed up in the words 'friendliness', 'frankness', and 'obstinacy'—Chamberlain was prompted to compare de Valera's mentality to Hitler's in that 'it was no use employing with them the arguments which appealed to

---

[5] 1st Meeting of Anglo-Irish Negotiations, 17 Jan. 1938 (CAB 27/642).
[6] 1st Meeting of Irish Negotiations Committee, 17 Jan. 1938 (ibid.).
[7] 2nd Meeting of Irish Negotiations Committee, 18 Jan. 1938 (ibid.).

the ordinary man'.[8] But as the negotiations wore on, Chamberlain and de Valera developed a high level of trust and regard for each other which proved lasting.

During the first round of negotiations, which ended on 19 January, virtually all the concessions came from the British. The biggest was an offer to drop their demand for the settlement of the financial dispute from a single lump sum payment of £26 million to £10 million.[9] This reflected the determination of the British to pay any reasonable cost for a settlement. If they 'could really get an all-round agreement and a new spirit in Irish relations', Simon was prepared to 'throw the money into the scale without a pang'.[10] Chamberlain likewise noted in his diary on 23 January:

I shall be grievously disappointed if we don't get an all-round agreement, on everything except partition. This is a difference that can't be bridged without the assent of Ulster and her assent won't be given unless she has confidence in the Government of Eire, and that cannot be attained except slowly and step by step. But if de Valera will heed the good advice I gave him, I should not despair of ultimate agreement on unity, and in the meantime I am satisfied that, queer creature as he is in many ways, he is no enemy of this country.[11]

This spirit was not shared by everyone on the British team. Discontent with the way Chamberlain was handling the negotiations surfaced during the month's interval before the beginning of the second round of negotiations scheduled for late February. It took the form of sympathy for Ulster and fear of a Conservative backlash if pressure of any kind were brought against her. Loudest in opposition were Morrison, the Minister of Agriculture and Fisheries, and Hailsham. Sitting on the fence was Hoare—making no secret of his dissatisfaction with the direction in which the talks were headed, but reluctant to confront Chamberlain head-on.

Morrison launched the attempted revolt at a meeting of the Irish Committee on 17 February by suggesting that they defer the trade agreement until a later date, unless they were pre-

[8] 1st Meeting of Irish Negotiations Committee, 17 Jan. 1938 (ibid.).
[9] Minute by S.D. Waley to F. Phillips, 18 Jan. 1938 (T 160/747/14026/04/2).
[10] Simon diary, 23 Jan. 1938.
[11] Chamberlain diary, 23 Jan. 1938.

pared to accept the Irish point of view in every respect, even
to the extent of putting pressure on Ulster to abandon partition. He objected strongly to extending to Ireland the same
trade terms granted to the other Dominions by the Ottawa
Agreements. Hoare joined Morrison in deploring a situation
in which Irish goods would have free entry to the United
Kingdom, while United Kingdom exports to Ireland would
still be subject to restriction. Added to this was Hailsham's
fear that a trade agreement would leave de Valera 'with a
lever to use against Northern Ireland in order to force the
termination of partition. Ulster manufacturers might in fact
get into such desperate straits that they would either vote for
inclusion in Eire or more their factories into Eire.'[12]

Supporting the trade agreement, on the other hand, besides
Simon, MacDonald, and Chamberlain, was Oliver Stanley,
Derby's son and Runciman's successor at the Board of Trade,
who disputed Morrison's contention that they would have the
Irish 'at their mercy' if the trade war were to resume. Mac-
Donald warned that they were dealing with a 'strange people
who were more influenced by sentimental than by logical and
economic considerations'. Any attempt to draw back from a
trade agreement would arouse intense suspicion in the minds
of de Valera and his colleagues and might even drive the
present Government in Ireland from power, substituting for it
a more extreme one which would refuse to sign a defence
agreement. Chamberlain agreed, adding that British public
opinion wished the negotiations to succeed and would blame
the Government for a breakdown.[13]

The matter did not end there. The resignation of Eden on
20 February, after a dispute with Chamberlain over Italy,
provoked a ministerial crisis which was, however, quickly resolved when Halifax replaced Eden as Foreign Secretary,
Hailsham succeeded Halifax as Lord President, and Lord
Maugham became Lord Chancellor. But as a result both
Chamberlain and Halifax were absent when the Irish Committee next met on 22 February. Hoare and Morrison exploited the opportunity to broaden their attack on the trade
agreement and, by extension, Chamberlain's whole conduct

[12] 36th Meeting of ISC of 17 Feb. 1938 (CAB 27/524).
[13] Ibid.

of the negotiations. Warning that the proposed trade agreement would 'meet with very strenuous opposition from the agricultural interests throughout the United Kingdom' and be 'violently' opposed by Ulster, Morrison urged the Committee to 'take care to be guided by the Cabinet's collective voice'. He also objected to an earlier suggestion of MacDonald's that the British Government should make some statement regarding partition, arguing that it could serve no useful purpose and would cause 'great astonishment and deep resentment among the Government's supporters throughout the United Kingdom'.[14]

Like Morrison, Hoare during the previous few days had been conferring with ministers from Northern Ireland, who had told him that, if the Government entered into the projected trade agreeement with Ireland without 'substantial compensation' for Northern Ireland in the form of financial assistance from the Exchequer, they would be 'bound to come out in the Parliament of Northern Ireland with a root and branch condemnation of the whole arrangement'. Hoare agreed with Morrison that Conservative opinion throughout the country and in the House of Commons would be 'upset and alarmed' at the magnitude of the sacrifice which they had to make in the defence, finance, and trade agreements, and by the uncertainty whether Britain would get any substantial advantages in return. As a compromise, the Committee decided that they should seek an agreement with the Irish for a 'break clause' should the final terms negotiated by the officials prove unsatisfactory.[15]

When talks resumed during the last week of February, de Valera again insisted that the British Government do something about partition. But the British ministers were more concerned with winning the approval of the House of Commons for what seemed on the face of it a one-sided agreement than they were in discussing the evils of partition with de Valera. The proposed defence and trade agreements appeared most vulnerable to attack.

On the Irish Committee, only Hailsham and Morrison strongly opposed turning the Irish ports over to Ireland as

[14] 37th Meeting of ISC of 22 Feb. 1938 (CAB 27/524).
[15] Ibid.

part of a defence agreement. Hoare and Simon were undecided to the end, not because they thought the ports were of
much military value, but because they were worried about
domestic repercussions in Britain. But Chamberlain remained
determined to give up the ports, even though de Valera had
indicated a willingness to make a financial and trade agreement without the ports being surrendered. Chamberlain insisted that this would be unwise. The British could not afford
to re-equip the ports and provide money for garrisons, and
Irish goodwill would be sacrificed. When war came the ports
would be of no use and any money spent would have been
wasted. Far better, in his opinion, to turn the ports over to
Ireland in order to secure, perhaps for the first time in history,
the goodwill of the Irish people, so that 'no more would be
heard of the old cry "England's difficulty Ireland's opportunity" '.[16]

Inskip agreed that it would be 'fantastic' from their point
of view to be spending money on ports in Ireland 'which for
us had only a sentimental or a paper value' when the defence
of ports in Britain itself was no longer assigned a high order
of priority. He argued that public opinion would take the
arrangement with de Valera as tantamount to a gentleman's
agreement on the right to use the ports in wartime. If de
Valera asserted that there was no understanding between
them, he would not be taken seriously. The very absence of
a written agreement on defence would be taken as showing
that the essentials of a written agreement existed. He and
MacDonald helped carry the Irish Committee for Chamberlain. In the end, only Hailsham held out against surrendering
the ports.[17]

With the question of the ports settled, there remained only
the problem of winning Ulster's consent to a trade agreement.
At first, Chamberlain hoped to persuade de Valera to make
some special trade concessions to Northern Ireland.[18] When
he refused, it looked as though the negotiations might yet end
in failure. Like Hailsham, Chamberlain thought that Northern Ireland's biggest fear was that Ulster industrialists might

[16] 40th Meeting of ISC of 1 Mar. 1938 (CAB 27/524).
[17] Ibid.
[18] 7th Meeting of Anglo-Irish Negotiations, 3 Mar. 1938 (CAB 27/642).

decide to relocate their factories in the South.[19] But the real root of the problem was that the Ulster Government simply did not trust Britain to safeguard its interests. Londonderry characteristically took it upon himself to voice these doubts to the Cabinet. The biggest fear concerned partition. Mindful of 1935 (when he had been Air Minister), when the Civil Aviation Act 'behind my back, with poor Craigavon properly hoodwinked' had chosen Shannon over an airfield in Northern Ireland as the terminus for trans-Atlantic flights, he warned Hoare that the British Government might in a similar fashion cave into pressure from de Valera and take measures to end partition.[20]

Londonderry took Hoare's refusal to address the Ulster Unionist Council in early March as 'further evidence of the antagonism of the Cabinet towards Ulster'. Nor did he trust Chamberlain, who was 'comparatively new to politics', and had 'naturally been influenced by the post-war attitude' which 'unfortunately had brought about the Treaty and particularly had given independence to Southern Ireland with all the disasters attending that independence which we prophesied before the War'. Londonderry objected to the 'Liberal point of view', which Austen Chamberlain had acquired and with which MacDonald was 'thoroughly impregnated'. He was also suspicious of Oliver Stanley and the 'pusillanimous spirit in the Government which appears to be ready to give up anything for the hope of a great life'. What Northern Ireland feared most, according to Londonderry, was neither de Valera nor the Nationalists in Ulster, but a change in attitude of the British people. 'Coercion of Ulster, if it came', he told Hoare,

would come from ignorant people in England who cannot see the value of maintaining Ulster as part of the British Empire. This would make itself felt at election times, and the Free State would go on applying pressure which I have no great faith in the British Government's resisting. The British Government can always put on a squeeze, as you know, without appearing to coerce, and a Socialist Government would certainly do this.[21]

---

[19] 3rd Meeting of Irish Negotiations Committee, 3 Mar. 1938 (ibid.).
[20] Londonderry to Hoare, 6 Mar. 1938 (Templewood papers, X:4).
[21] Ibid.

Londonderry's opinions, in so far as they reflected the real insecurity of Ulster, could not be ignored. This placed the British Government in a difficult position. The situation, as MacDonald outlined it for the Irish Committee on 8 March, was that, if de Valera failed to secure an agreement, he would probably be defeated by extremist elements in Ireland. If, on the other hand, the British Government gave in to de Valera, it would face the threat of a joint attack from both Ulster and British public opinion which might make its own position untenable.

For the next few days the opposing positions were debated in Cabinet and Irish Committee meetings. On the one hand, Hoare urged his colleagues to make concessions to Ulster.[22] He warned that Northern Ireland might be on the brink of a 'very serious political upheaval', as Craigavon and Andrews had both assured him that if the proposed agreement went through they would either have to launch an attack on the British Government for its surrender of Ulster's vital interests, or they themselves would have to resign. MacDonald, on the other hand, advocated the acceptance of the trade agreement despite the objections from Northern Ireland. He maintained that all parties in the House of Commons, not excluding the Conservatives, were in favour of a settlement and would be critical if a break occurred on an issue of merely secondary importance. He also warned of the effect on opinion in the Dominions if a break took place on an issue of 'comparatively minor' importance.[23]

Chamberlain tried to stike a balance. He too objected to being 'blackmailed' by Northern Ireland, and would have agreed with MacDonald had he been convinced that the

---

[22] 41st Meeting of ISC of 8 Mar. 1938 (CAB 27/524). Sir Wilfrid Spender, the Permanent Secretary at the Ulster Ministry of Finance and head of the Northern Ireland civil service, recorded in his diary that Hoare told him at this time that, if the Northern Ireland Cabinet stood firm regarding trading privileges, 'a majority of his colleagues would see that Ulster was not let down'. Later, after Craigavon had 'astounded' his colleagues by acquiescing in de Valera's refusal to grant trade privileges to Northern Ireland, Hoare 'felt that he and his Unionist supporters in the British Cabinet had been so let down by the volte face of the Ulster Government that he could no longer act as their protagonist in the future' (quoted by Fisk, p. 47). Spender's account was written more than two years afterwards, and he may even at the time have failed to catch the nuances in Hoare's position.

[23] Cabinet conclusions 11(38) of 9 Mar. 1938 (CAB 23/92).

Northern attitude was due 'solely to obstinacy and unreason-
ableness'. But he was satisfied that the attitude of Northern
Ireland was 'based on honest motives held with all sincerity'.
Moreover, even more than the 'bitterest opposition from
Northern Ireland and the supporters of Northern Ireland in
this country', he would contemplate 'with great anxiety and
apprehension' an arrangement which strengthened rather
than weakened the existing barriers between Northern and
Southern Ireland, and which would only intensify the ill-feeling, suspicion, and distrust between them.[24]

Simon thought the arguments advanced by MacDonald
and Chamberlain evenly balanced, but said that, since Northern Ireland's objections to the settlement were due more to
political than to economic difficulties, there had to be some
point at which they must be prepared to stand firm and tell
Northern Ireland that they had done their best for her, but
they were not prepared to sacrifice an agreement with Ireland
in order that Northern Ireland should obtain 100 per cent of
her *desiderata*. To this Chamberlain and the rest of the Irish
Committee generally agreed.[25]

Simon's intervention in this instance reflected both his own
feelings on the matter and opinion within the Treasury, especially that of Fisher. While the Treasury under Fisher had
been sympathetic to Southern Ireland from the inception of
the Free State in 1922, its attitude towards Northern Ireland
had been more equivocal, primarily because Fisher regarded
it as a damaging obstacle in the path of Anglo-Irish harmony.
Though realist enough to know that under the circumstances
no British Government could try to pressure Ulster into ending partition, he was adamant that no unnecessary obstacles
should be placed in the way of eventual union in Ireland. As
S.D. Waley, Principal Assistant Secretary at the Treasury, put
it: 'This means we favour the marriage, but the young lady's
consent is required.'[26]

While Fisher was not insensitive to the great economic
deprivation Northern Ireland was suffering during the
1930s—again, in Waley's words, 'The Treasury have a very

[24] 42nd Meeting of ISC of 10 Mar. 1938 (CAB 27/524).
[25] Ibid.
[26] Note by Waley for use in discussing partition, Jan. 1938 (T 160/747/14026/04/2).

lively interest in the prosperity of Northern Ireland—which comes to us when bankrupt'[27]—he disagreed with Northern officials on the best remedy. Fisher felt that Northern Ireland 'would gain greatly from the termination of the present wholly uneconomic partition',[28] and was annoyed when officials from Northern Ireland blamed their troubles on the Anglo-Irish trade war but then complained loudly when any attempt was made to end it.[29]

Fisher could see little positive about the Government of Northern Ireland, and resented its political power. When Chamberlain suggested that they should try to persuade de Valera to make special tariff concessions to Northern Ireland that would allow its goods to enter Ireland more cheaply than those of the rest of the United Kingdom, Fisher wryly pronounced it 'an admirable idea, appealing to de Valera's heart and to Lord Craigavon's pocket'.[30]

But Fisher's patience was limited. When it appeared for a time that Ulster might by its intransigence derail the course of the negotiations, he acted decisively to stiffen the British ministers, in particular his chief, Simon. The Treasury had already challenged as 'misleading' the trade figures produced by the Northern Government showing a calamitous drop in trade between Belfast and the South since the beginning of the economic war. It questioned the value of these statistics, since no attempt was made to differentiate between Ulster goods and British goods passing through Ulster on the way to the South. Thus a very large part of the loss in sales was born by British exporters. Nor would the Treasury accept the Northern charge that a low tariff on goods coming from the South to Ulster would constitute any real threat, since Southern goods were too expensive to compete in the North. The real objection to the proposed settlement, as Waley pointed out and Ulster officials conceded privately, 'was *political* and not economic'.[31] Fisher did his best to ensure that Simon understood this and did something about it. On a

[27] Minute by Waley, 14 Jan. 1938 (ibid.).
[28] Minute by Fisher, 14 Jan. 1938 (ibid.).
[29] e.g. note by Government of Northern Ireland on 'Renewal of Coal–Cattle Pact', Jan. 1938 (ibid.).
[30] Minute by Waley, 24 Feb. 1938 (ibid.).
[31] Minute by Waley to Fisher, 7 Mar. 1938 (ibid.).

memorandum on the subject being prepared for the Chancellor
of the Exchequer, Fisher pencilled a few stern comments
of his own: 'Are we never to be allowed by Ulster to come
to terms with the South? Is the tail always going to wag the
dog?'[32]

Fisher's urging was not wasted. On 10 March, when
Chamberlain appeared nearly to have given up hope for a
successful conclusion to the negotiations with de Valera,
Simon at last intervened forcefully and secured the Irish Committee's assent that the agreement with the South should not
be sacrificed solely on account of the intransigence of Northern
Ireland.[33]

But Simon's intervention, timely as it was, in no sense was
meant to be taken as a suggestion that the British Government
should adopt a strong line against Ulster. Indeed, his very
choice of words, that the proposed treaty with Ireland should
not be sacrificed 'in order that Northern Ireland should obtain
100 per cent of her *desiderata*',[34] was an obvious indication that
he was keeping the doors of the Exchequer wide open for a
compromise. Nor was anyone in the Treasury under any illusions on that score. The most obvious solution appeared to
be another amendment to the Unemployment Insurance
Agreement between Great Britain and Northern Ireland, in
particular the waiving of the British right to reopen the agreement when their contribution exceeded £1 million. The Treasury hoped, however, that there would be no question of any
concession until Ulster asked for it, and promised 'to call off
their blackmail in return'.[35]

In the meantime, events transpiring in Europe did nothing
to diminish the importance of a rapid solution to the Anglo-
Irish dispute. Since early February a crisis over Austria had
been looming. On 12 March—the day the Irish delegates
returned to Dublin to consider the latest British proposals—
the situation in central Europe reached a climax. The following day Hitler entered Vienna in triumph and Austria was
incorporated into the Reich.

[32] Minute by Fisher, 7 Mar. 1938 (ibid.).
[33] 42nd Meeting of ISC of 10 Mar. 1938 (CAB 27/524).
[34] Ibid.
[35] Minute by Waley to Woods, 10 Mar. 1938 (T 160/747/14026/04/2).

Chamberlain did not react to these events passively. Unable to do anything about Germany, he became all the more determined to reach agreement with Ireland. He remained characteristically optimistic about the eventual outcome. 'I shall be accused of having weakly given way when Eire was in the hollow of my hand,' he recorded in his diary.

Only I and my colleagues (who are unanimous) can judge of this, but I am satisfied that we have only given up the small things (paper rights, and revenues which would not last) for the big things—the ending of a long quarrel, the beginning of better relations between North and South Ireland, and the co-operation of the South with us in trade and defence. It is possible that the Austrian incident may help me in bringing home to people here and in Ulster, that there is no time for keeping open old sores.[36]

Chamberlain had good reasons for wanting to be done with Ireland. Not only would it leave him free to concentrate on more important things, but it would have been difficult for him, both personally and politically, to have gone so far and then not succeed. References to his famed 'rigidity of mind' were already creeping back into the press, such as this comment of *The Economist*:

The hopes for a comprehensive settlement which animated both sides at an earlier stage have faded. It is difficult to avoid the reflection that if Mr. Chamberlain could spare for Ireland a little of the optimistic zeal that he has lent to the chance of a settlement with Italy he might be rewarded with a far greater return in strategic and economic advantage, and in friendship that would stand the test of time.[37]

The proposals that the Irish delegates took back to Dublin for consideration contained nothing very new, although the terms of the financial settlement had been softened. On partition, the British still could offer no more than their usual assurance not to object should Ulster desire closer relations with the South. On defence, the British expressed their willingness to turn over the Treaty ports and give up their rights under the Treaty of 1921. On finance, the British offered to settle for a lump sum of £10 million, with a continuation of

---

[36] Chamberlain diary, 13 Mar. 1938.
[37] *The Economist*, 10 Mar. 1938.

the current annual payment of £250,000. Trade was the difficulty. The British offered to accept the draft agreement, but only on condition that the Irish make certain additional concessions to Ulster.[38]

Informing the Cabinet of these latest proposals on 16 March, MacDonald warned that, if nothing could be obtained which would commend itself to Northern Ireland, then it would be necessary to realize that the negotiations had broken down. Privately he told Chamberlain they must face the fact that, even if it so desired, it would be impossible for any Irish government without a majority in the Dáil, and with its own supporters strongly opposed to concessions to Ulster, to get the trade provisions through its parliament. 'This is a hard political fact which we cannot escape.' Although agreeing with Chamberlain that it would be impossible politically to defend a settlement if the Northern Government were actively opposing that part of it which concerned itself,' MacDonald won his agreement that they should use all their influence with the Ulster Government to get them to concur with the present draft agreements minus free entry or any other concessions.[39]

In a more general vein, MacDonald noted that the discussions of the last two months had shown that the difficulty between North and South still lay at the root of the Anglo-Irish problem. But for that, they might not only have already won the agreements which were at present in draft, but also have gotten a much better pact on defence. 'Unless we make a beginning', he continued,

this difficulty is going to upset all our efforts to settle the old quarrel at any time in the reasonably near future. We have got to try and break through the suspicions and distrust which at present exist, just as we are trying to break through the suspicions and distrust which have existed between Italy and this country. If we could now conclude the series of agreements which are in prospect, with the result not only that Northern Irish trade with Eire would improve over the next few years, but also that greater friendliness and co-operation between Eire and this country would become manifest, (and Eire's association with the British Commonwealth be stabilized) it

[38] Cabinet conclusions 14(38) of 16 Mar. 1938 (CAB 23/93).
[39] MacDonald to Chamberlain, 16 Mar. 1938 (PREM 1/274/14).

is possible that better relations between the North and South would gradually grow. We ourselves might do a good deal to foster these better relations by taking opportunities to bring Northern Irish and Southern Irish Ministers together occasionally for the discussion of common problems ...

But if, on the other hand, the present negotiations were now to break down because of Northern Ireland, warned Mac-Donald, 'there will be mutual recrimination across the border and this root difficulty of the whole problem will become greater instead of less'.[40]

In conclusion MacDonald urged Chamberlain to appeal to Craigavon and his colleagues to give their consent, even if reluctant, to the best agreement possible at that time. He rather thought that the Northern Government believed that, if the British pressed hard enough, they could get free entry for Northern Ireland's goods into the South. This had been one reason for their pushing so persistently for it. Now that it was quite clear that no amount of pressure would get the additional concession for them, he though that they might be persuaded to alter their attitude and to accept the benefits which would come to them and the rest of the United Kingdom from the proposed agreements. This acceptance might also be abetted by some timely financial concessions.[41]

MacDonald was not mistaken about the Government of Northern Ireland. Behind the implacable façade there lurked some semblance of rationality. By now it had become apparent even in Belfast that the British had gone as far as they could go in extracting concessions for the North from the South. Nothing could now be gained and much lost in terms of public opinion by pushing the confrontation with the British Government too far. For Craigavon the course was clear: he hurried over to London, wiring ahead to Chamberlain that he was coming 'to help and not to hinder'.[42] It did not turn out that way. Following MacDonald's advice, Chamberlain appealed first to Craigavon's patriotism, emphasizing the importance of the defence treaty and the value of showing the world at such a time that disputes between large countries

[40] Ibid.
[41] Ibid.
[42] Cabinet conclusions 14(38) of 16 Mar. 1938 (CAB 23/93).

and small ones could still be settled by friendly discussions.[43]
When that got him nowhere, he turned to finance. There he
fared better. Craigavon agreed to accept the trade agreement
with Ireland, but only after expressing 'a desire to receive as
large a financial bribe as possible'.[44]

It was clear that the Northern ministers wanted something;
it was less clear what. As they appeared to have no proposals
of their own to make, the British tried first to buy them off
with an offer to increase their contribution to Northern Ireland's Unemployment Insurance Fund. This failed, since
Craigavon expected to receive that in any event. Inskip then
proposed to increase defence spending by £400,000 a year in
Northern Ireland. Unfortunately, neither Inskip nor Andrews
had any idea how the money should be spent, and both feared
it might create more problems than it would solve. In desper-
ation, the British tried to win the Northern ministers' acceptance of the agreement with Ireland 'on the understanding
that the question of a financial bribe can be considered later
on'. Even this failed. Craigavon's only proposal—that something be done to modify the land annuities payments in
Northern Ireland—was not considered very practicable by the
Treasury, as it could only end up costing the Northern
Government revenue it already received.[45]

When the negotiations with the Treasury failed to reach an
immediate conclusion, Craigavon suddenly announced that
he had changed his mind and decided not to accept the agreement with Éire after all. Instead, he planned to spend the next
fortnight preparing a memorandum setting forth their objections to the treaty.

Such behaviour did nothing to endear him to the Treasury.
'In the circumstances it is difficult to regard Northern Ireland
as particularly deserving of any financial concessions,'[46] minuted Waley. Fisher was even more blunt. Dismissing Craigavon's proposals with a curt 'preposterous', he characteristically
cut to the heart of the matter:

The problem is only in a minor degree a financial one. The real
issue is whether Northern Ireland is to be allowed to veto a settle-

[43] 'Rough note on points which might be made to Lord Craigavon' 16 Mar. 1938
(PREM 1/274/14).   [44] Minute by Waley, 21 Mar. 1938 (T 160/747/14026/04/1).
[45] Minute by Phillips, 21 Mar. 1938 (T 160/747/14026/04/1).
[46] Minute by Waley, 21 Mar. 1938 (ibid.).

ment between us and Southern Ireland. In the present state of Europe it is a vital interest of ours to reduce the number of possible dangers; in consequence a less hostile Ireland is a matter of real importance. Blackmail and bluff (oddly enough called Loyalty) have for many years been the accepted methods of Northern Ireland. It is high time these parochial die-hards were made to face up to a touch of reality.[47]

While Simon may well have shared these sentiments, he knew better than to express them in Cabinet. Instead, when the Cabinet discussed the situation on 23 March, he professed himself 'not unsympathetic' to Northern Ireland. Although some of Craigavon's proposals were 'not helpful', he suggested there 'might be ways in which help could be given'.[48]

As a Liberal in a Conservative-dominated Cabinet, Simon had to be circumspect in dealing with Ulster. As a National Labour representative, MacDonald suffered under the same disadvantage. In discussing Ulster in Cabinet, neither could be too forthright in expressing their views for fear of jeopardizing their careers, which is why MacDonald generally expounded his views on partition to Chamberlain privately. Now, in explaining the current situation to the Cabinet, Mac-Donald took care to echo Hoare's expressions of sympathy for Ulster and to emphasize the positive aspects of Craigavon's recent behaviour. But however he explained the situation, it was now clear to everyone that the onus for failure in the Anglo-Irish negotiations no longer rested upon themselves and de Valera, but had been shifted to the Government of Northern Ireland.

This was too much for the long-suffering Hailsham. The necessity for a settlement with de Valera he had been forced grudgingly to accept, but it was one thing to settle with de Valera, and quite another to win that settlement by putting pressure on Northern Ireland. It was this latter threat which Hailsham read into MacDonald's careful exposition of the Irish situation on 23 March. His disappointment on learning that the 'final offer' to de Valera agreed to by the Irish Committee had proved to be not so final after all was now compounded by his alarm on hearing 'that we are now occupied in trying

[47] Minute by Fisher, 22 Mar. 1938 (ibid.).
[48] Cabinet conclusions 16(38) of 23 Mar. 1939 (CAB 23/93).

to bribe the Ulster Government from the British Exchequer'. Fearing that he might be confronted with a *fait accompli*, yet reluctant to take the matter up in Cabinet, Hailsham unburdened himself the following day in a letter to the Prime Minister. 'I realise', he wrote,

that some of my colleagues regard Ulster as an obstinate and stubborn people who are wholly unreasonable in preferring their loyalty to the King and their inclusion in the Empire to adhesion to a disloyal Republic; but I understood that we are all agreed that if the negotiations were started with Eire it would be made clear to Eire that we should not bring any form of pressure on Ulster on the Partition issue. To agree to free entry for Eire products into the United Kingdom without ensuring free entry to Ulster products into Eire seems to me to be doing indirectly what we have resolved not to do directly, namely, to give Eire the power to bring economic pressure on Ulster in order to compel its people to secede from the United Kingdom and to become a part of Eire.... No doubt the pill can be gilded so attractively from the resources of the United Kingdom Exchequer as to conceal the poison which lurks within it, but I don't believe that ... the Ulster Government would have anything to do with the Treaty, whatever financial inducements are offered, if they appreciated that its effect would be to enable Eire to compel Ulster to secede from her allegiance. Ulster loyalty is not for sale!

Like those of his friends in the North, these brave words scarcely masked grave doubts. While declining to recapitulate the 'overwhelming' arguments against the treaty, Hailsham wound up by begging Chamberlain 'not to agree to using the British taxpayers' money to try and coax a reluctant Ulster into the stranglehold of this Treaty'.[49]

Chamberlain's reply left little room for further argument. While acknowledging that Ireland had it in her power to put considerable economic pressure on the North, the Prime Minister saw this as 'the inevitable result of their separation'. The effect of the treaty would be 'to reduce this power of pressure and not to increase it'. Chamberlain also reminded Hailsham that the special duties were not put on to protect Northern Ireland or British farmers, but to provide a revenue for the loss of the land annuities, 'and if we choose to abandon them

[49] Hailsham to Chamberlain, 24 Mar. 1938 (PREM 1/274/14).

for the sake of a general financial settlement our people may complain, but Ulster would have no such ground'.[50]

The imputation that he had stooped to bribing Craigavon especially aggrieved Chamberlain.

I never suggested a bribe to him [Craigavon] nor did anybody on this side. It is he who has put forward a number of financial demands, some of which, I must say, I think extremely unreasonable. Others, on the other hand, I think not unreasonable and I think we can go some way to meet him. But it is altogether libellous to suggest that we are trying to bribe him to accept something which he would otherwise be reluctant to do.

If, in fact, we come to an arrangement satisfactory to Craigavon, it will be entirely voluntary on his part and not owing to any pressure from us.[51]

Whether because his grievance was political rather than financial, as the Treasury thought, or because he expected more resistance from the British, or simply because his Government was disorganized, Craigavon had not bothered before leaving Belfast to formulate a detailed list of financial demands to put to the British. He and Andrews were not even agreed on what it was they wanted. After several days of negotiations, the gist of Craigavon's demands appeared to be: first, a desire for a subsidy of £400,000 a year for the Northern Ireland Exchequer; second, a negative contribution whereby, if the Northern Ireland budget showed a deficit, the United Kingdom would make up the difference; and third, agricultural subsidies. Even Andrews conceded that the first demand was 'nonsensical', while the Treasury dismissed the third demand as 'entirely illogical' since agriculture was a 'transferred subject' for which Northern Ireland was responsible. The second demand was viewed by the Treasury as 'quite reasonable', as 'the implication of the settlement of 1922 is that Northern Ireland should have a social expenditure on the same scale as Great Britain and should not be more heavily taxed'.[52]

In fact, Craigavon's tactics were beginning to bear fruit. MacDonald and Hoare were already preparing a list of concessions for Ulster, including benefits for the Northern In-

[50] Chamberlain to Hailsham, 28 Mar. 1938 (ibid.).
[51] Ibid.   [52] Minute by Waley, 24 Mar. 1938 (T 160/747/14026/04/1).

surance Fund, Northern agriculture, and an assurance that the British Government would be prepared to consider as sympathetically as possible any difficulty which might arise in the future regarding Northern Ireland's financial arrangements with the United Kingdom. Although the Treasury refused to accept Craigavon's demand for an annual payment of £400,000 for the duration of the treaty, and balked at making some of the agricultural concessions, these points, as well as a promise to place as many armaments orders as possible in the future in Ulster and to withdraw the British declaration about partition, formed the basis of the eventual settlement with Northern Ireland. Even Fisher bowed to the inevitable: 'If yielding to Lord Craigavon will carry with it Ulster's permission to us to reach a settlement of an enduring kind with Southern Ireland, I advocate our being blackmailed (assuming we continue the policy of allowing a veto to Ulster).'[53]

When, despite these concessions, Ulster continued to raise objections, the British attitude began to stiffen. The American Ambassador, Joseph Kennedy, called on Halifax to stress the importance to Anglo-American relations of a speedy settlement of the Anglo-Irish dispute.[54] At a meeting of the Irish Committee on 8 April, Chamberlain, Simon, and MacDonald expressed strong regret at the prospect of further delay. Even Hoare felt that Ulster had 'overstated its case', though he did think that further armaments expenditure could be directed towards Belfast, where the firm of Harland and Wolff was already at work on an aircraft carrier. Only Hailsham continued to speak unreservedly in support of the Northern Government.[55]

Frustrated by the delay, Chamberlain resolved to cut through the maze by once again intervening personally in the negotiations with Ulster. That same day he sent a personal appeal to Craigavon asking him

to implement what you said to me when you came over last term, namely that you meant to help and not to hinder. In my anxieties

[53] Minute by Fisher, 26 Mar. 1938 (ibid.).
[54] Halifax to MacDonald, 7 Apr. 1938 (FO 800/310/206); minute by MacDonald, 26 Mar. 1938 (DO 35/893 Part I/xii/135).
[55] 43rd Meeting of ISC of 8 Apr. 1938 (CAB 27/524).

over the international situation it has become almost essential for me to show some evidence that the policy of peace by negotiation can be successful. I have good hope that I shall be able to bring forward an Anglo-Italian agreement as evidence of this, but if I can accompany that with an Anglo-Irish agreement it would add greatly to the impression made upon the world. And it is very necessary that an impression of solidarity here should be made and not least in Berlin.

While expressing sympathy for Craigavon's difficulties, the Prime Minister left his Northern counterpart in no doubt that he wanted the matter concluded within a week 'one way or the other'.[56]

Chamberlain was not to be disappointed. A few more financial concessions from Simon was all it took, and on 22 April the Prime Minister was able to announce that accord with Ireland had been reached. A week earlier the Cabinet had set its final stamp of approval on the agreement. The finalized Treaty had three main provisions. The first, covering defence, abolished the provisions of the Treaty of 1921 and provided for the transfer of the reserved ports to Ireland, which, in turn, agreed to maintain them up to British standards. The second ended the financial dispute by requiring Ireland to pay a lump sum of £10 million. It also called for the abolition of the special duties imposed in 1932 by the two governments at the outset of the economic war. The third, concerning trade, provided for the virtual lifting of British customs duties on Irish goods, and lightened corresponding Irish duties on British goods, without removing Ireland's right to protect its infant industries.

In explaining the final terms to the Cabinet, MacDonald had to admit that the agreement did not look good on paper. Though it had its good points, such as serving as a check to Irish industrial development, most of its expected value would be in intangibles, such as goodwill. He hoped that it would open a new chapter in Anglo-Irish relations.[57]

On 25 April, following a luncheon at 10 Downing Street, the new Anglo-Irish Treaty was signed. At the conclusion of the ceremony, Chamberlain returned to de Valera the pair of

[56] Chamberlain to Craigavon, 8 Apr. 1938 (PREM 1/274/14).
[57] Cabinet conclusions 19(38) of 13 Apr. 1938 (CAB 23/93).

field-glasses which he had handed over upon surrendering his command at Boland's Bakery to the British at the end of the Easter Rising, more than twenty years before. It was a fitting tribute. A few days later de Valera paid a tribute of his own to Chamberlain in a speech to the Dáil:

It is a good British policy to have an independent Ireland. It is fortunate both for this country and Britain that the present Goverment does take that view. It is a fortunate circumstance, also, that the present British Prime Minister is Prime Minister, because there is no doubt that the agreement could not have been made were it not for the fact that he believes in the policy in Britain's interest, and that at a critical time he himself used all his influence to try to get the difficulties overcome.[58]

The Treaty with Ireland was welcomed almost unanimously by the British press. The only misgivings on the right concerned the ports, and on the left the failure to make progress on partition.[59]

In Parliament the only serious attack came from Churchill, whose views on Ireland had not changed since 1921. Not only did he see the new Treaty as a repudiation of his own earlier accomplishment, but he also regarded the men who made it—on both sides—as his personal enemies. Churchill's speech to the House focused on the surrender of the Irish ports, but it was excessively alarmist and consequently only served to diminish his reputation again at a time when that reputation had been on the upswing.[60]

Writing about these events ten years later, when he was intent upon building up what may be called the 'guilty men syndrome'—whereby the blame for the events leading up to the Second World War is fixed squarely on Chamberlain and his colleagues, without regard to the circumstances of the time—Churchill condemned the surrender of the British rights to the Irish ports by saying that a 'more feckless act can hardly

---

[58] Reported in *Manchester Guardian*, 28 Apr. 1938.
[59] The *Daily Telegraph and Morning Post*, 26 Apr. 1938, for instance, expressed concern about the ports, and the *Spectator*, 6 May 1938, on partition. The *Yorkshire Post*, 26 Apr. 1938, was the most critical of the Treaty in general, calling it 'a decidedly one-sided agreement, which might doubtless have aroused vigorous criticism if it had been entered into in different circumstances'.
[60] Robert Rhodes James, *Churchill: A Study in Failure, 1900–1939* (New York, 1970), p. 364.

be imagined', and that he 'never saw the House of Commons more completely misled'.[61] The answer to this, of course, is that, whether or not in retrospect they were right, the Chamberlain Government and the House of Commons knew full well at the time what they were doing and had valid reasons for doing so. At the time, not even Churchill's natural allies, the Tory press, could accept his case. 'Mr. Churchill impressively marshalled a number of dire possibilities which cannot be lightly dismissed,' commented the *Daily Telegraph and Morning Post*. 'The answer to them is that the *defeat* of the present agreement would not avert those possibilities, but would help to realise them. The acceptance of the agreement offers at least the chance of banishing them forever. It is an act, not only of faith, but of prudence.'[62]

This was the view of the Chamberlain Government and of the House of Commons. There is little reason to doubt that it also represented accurately the attitude of the great majority of the British people.

---

[61] Churchill, *Second World War*, i, p. 277.
[62] *Daily Telegraph and Morning Post*, 6 May 1938.

The Debate Over
Partition

The Irish Treaty, following so closely upon the conclusion of
an Anglo-Italian accord, carried Chamberlain to a height of
prestige and popularity in England he had never known before. Even Beaverbrook began touting him as 'the best P.M.
we've had in half a century'.[1] Beaverbrook was especially
pleased by the Irish settlement, for which his papers had long
been pulling: 'The Irish Treaty has given him [Chamberlain]
splendid credit. Added to his Italian triumph, he now appears
to be a mighty man—even to his opponents.'[2]

This euphoria did not prove lasting; within six months
Anglo-Irish relations were again at a low ebb. The reason for
this, as MacDonald had foreseen, was the failure of the settlement to contain anything on partition. Chamberlain, no
doubt rightly, did not consider this practical politics. As soon
as the Irish negotiations were completed, he transferred Mac-
Donald to the Colonial Office to replace Ormsby-Gore, who
had just resigned his post over the proposal to partition Palestine. Derby's favourite son, Edward Stanley, was appointed to
take MacDonald's place at the Dominions Office. Though
only forty-four, Stanley was rather deaf and unwell, and died
within a few months. Meanwhile, the Duke of Devonshire
(formerly Hartington) stayed on as Parliamentary Under-
Secretary of State at the Dominions; a further indication, if
any were needed, that nothing serious was intended about
partition.

During the sixteen months that separated the conclusion of
the Irish Treaty from the outbreak of war, foreign affairs
dominated the Cabinet's attention. Irish affairs were generally

[1] Beaverbrook to R.B. Bennett, 9 Mar. 1938, cited in A.J.P. Taylor, *Beaverbrook*
(New York, 1972), p. 379.
[2] Beaverbrook to Governor Cox of Ohio, 28 Apr. 1938 (ibid., p. 382).

ignored, even by Chamberlain. But the problem of Ireland did not vanish with the signing of the Treaty. No sooner did de Valera leave London than he began to agitate about partition. The British response, such as it was, came not from the Cabinet, which was too preoccupied with other issues, but from the various departments involved, in particular from the Dominions Office, the Home Office, and the Board of Trade; and to a certain extent from the British press. So-called 'bureaucratic imperatives' are involved here, and although they did not ultimately amount to much it is worth having a brief look at them and at how the politicians reacted to them.

While partition was viewed primarily by the British Government as a political issue—and an explosive one at that, which partially explains why nothing serious was ever done about it—it also was marked with pretty obvious moral overtones, involving as it did the forcible subjection of a considerable Catholic minority to the Protestant majority. The Home Office, whose duty it was to oversee the situation in Ulster, never took as a serious part of its responsibility a need to look out for the welfare of the Catholic minority. Not until the Irish negotiations in 1938 did it even begin to investigate their situation, and then only because MacDonald, alarmed lest de Valera use the excuse of the mistreatment of Northern Catholics as a reason for breaking off the negotiations, managed to prod a reluctant Hoare into having his officials look into the matter.[3]

The resulting investigation was not intended to be far-reaching. Nor was it. After taking note of complaints appearing in the press and elsewhere alleging discrimination by the Northern Government, and of statements 'said to have been made' by members of that Government, such as 'we have a Protestant Parliament for a Protestant People', one Home Office official nevertheless noted that the Northern Government had never admitted that any religious discrimination was practised, and that therefore 'in the absence of any means of securing an impartial investigation into the position it is impossible to reach a reliable conclusion as to the facts'. He singled out for praise the almost totally segregated Ulster school system—which happened to be headed by a Catholic—

[3] Minute by Stephenson, 7 Mar. 1938 (DO 35/893/X11/123).

for the way the greatest care had always been taken to secure strict impartiality in administering educational policy.[4]

The senior official in the department concerned with Northern Ireland was equally good at rationalizing the situation existing there. He conceded that in one sense it was of course obvious that Northern Ireland was, and had to be, a 'Protestant state', otherwise it would not have come into being and would certainly not continue to exist. It was equally obvious that in such conditions the number of Catholics in positions of public importance would be small and, apart from those who were already in such positions before the partition, few new entrants could be expected into the ranks of the civil service, the higher ranks of the police, etc. Similarly, he found it difficult to believe that there was any widespread movement against employing Catholics among Protestants, since in the nature of the case the majority of Catholics had to be employed by Protestants. While conceding that from time to time 'incidents had occurred' in the dockyard and elsewhere [there had in fact been bloody riots in Belfast in 1935, which left eleven people killed and nearly six hundred injured: a Catholic demand for a commission of inquiry was refused], he believed that in the intervals feeling always improved. 'In any case,' he concluded, 'all the evidence I have seen goes to show that the Government of Northern Ireland do their best to protect Catholics against victimization, but are, in certain instances, powerless.' There was no reason whatever, in his opinion, to believe that they encouraged victimization and disorder, 'except to the extent that flamboyant speeches on the 12th of July[5] might conceivably have that effect'.[6]

This satisfied Hoare, who informed the Dominions Office that he was 'impressed' by the defences of the Northern Government which he had received from his officials. The officials in the Dominions Office were less impressed. While acknowledging the difficulties involved in getting at the truth when there was so much bitter feeling and prejudice on both

[4] Note by Martin Jones on the 'Treatment of the Catholic Minority in Northern Ireland', n.d. (ibid.).

[5] Anniversary of the Battle of the Boyne (1689), celebrated each year by the Protestant Orange Order in Northern Ireland to commemorate the defeat of the Catholic forces under James II by the Protestants under King William III of Orange.

[6] Note prepared by Markbreiter for Hoare, Mar. 1938 (DO 35/893/XII/123).

sides, and recognizing that an impartial investigation was not practicable in the present atmosphere, Batterbee nevertheless urged that the Home Office be asked to furnish information and figures to substantiate whether or not the government services in Northern Ireland were practically closed to Catholics. Granted that the head of the Northern Ireland Education Department was a Catholic, he wondered whether or not that was 'the exception which proves the rule?' In addition, Batterbee wanted information on gerrymandering in the Nationalist counties, refusing to accept the argument that the Nationalist refusal to co-operate absolved the Government of all responsibility for the result.[7]

Batterbee found himself over-ruled. Although Harding agreed that the information received from the Home Office was 'sufficient to show that what de Valera said to the Press was not without justification', he recommended against pressing the Home Office further at the moment.[8] His reasons are not difficult to guess. The negotiations with Ireland were entering the crucial stage, and Ulster's co-operation would be necessary if they were to be a success. Then was not the time to pry into its internal affairs. Moreover, Northern Ireland was the Home Office's concern, and Hoare and his Conservative colleagues would not appreciate any intrusion by MacDonald and the Dominions Office.

There was also a reason closer to home. Hartington, reasonable on most matters, became a man of strong prejudices when it came to Catholics and Ulster. Between Batterbee and the officials of the Home Office, he had no trouble choosing when it came to determining the relative merits of the case concerning Ulster. He felt that British ministers had been 'unduly impressed' by de Valera's allegations about the unfair treatment of the minority in the North and the 'so-called gerrymandering' of the constituencies. He could not comprehend how anyone could complain about persecution of Catholics in the North when the facts showed that there had been a steady and continuing decrease of Protestants in the South, and an equally steady increase of Catholics into the North, an increase which had 'seriously alarmed Northern Ireland minis-

[7] Minute by Batterbee, 7 Mar. 1938 (ibid.).
[8] Minute by Harding, 9 Mar. 1938 (ibid.).

ters and others anxious to maintain the Protestant character of the country'. He rejected charges of gerrymandering— which was 'very largely the fault of the Catholics, who boycotted the whole business'. With regard to employment in the public service, he asserted that broadly speaking 'Catholicism was the religion of the masses and Protestantism of the classes', and that it was therefore almost inevitable that a large majority of posts requiring educated men should be occupied by Protestants.[9]

What really concerned Hartington was not the condition of the impoverished masses in the North—Catholic or Protestant—about which he knew and cared little, but the gradual vanishing of the aristocratic Anglo-Irish way of life in the South, about which he knew and cared a great deal. He bemoaned the steady and continuing decrease of Protestants in the South, and imagined that the failure of former Unionists to play any role in the government there was due not to the fact that they would not receive adequate support, but because they would be 'exposed to every form of intimidation, persecution, arson and possibly assassination'.[10]

Hartington's attempt to demonstrate that it was the Protestant minority in the South rather than the Catholic minority in the North whose persecution deserved looking into was not apt to impress anyone in the Dominions Office. For his part MacDonald was 'convinced that as soon as the present Irish talks are over we must go quietly and carefully into the position of the minority in the North'.[11] While he never really got that chance, there is no reason to think that it would have made any difference. MacDonald also believed that something should be done about partition in general, as did Chamberlain, who later even got the opportunity, under circumstances perhaps as fortuitous as could be hoped, to do something about it. All was in vain. Contrary to what de Valera and other Irish nationalists thought at the time, and some no doubt still believe, the power and influence of the British Government over the Protestants of the North is not now, and never has been, as strong as it would have liked.

*   *   *

[9] Minute by Hartington, 10 Mar. 1938 (ibid.).   [10] Ibid.
[11] Minute by MacDonald, 5 Mar. 1938 (DO 35/892/X11/118).

Upon his return to Ireland after signing the Treaty, de Valera renewed his campaign against partition. By the end of the year he had set up an Irish Anti-Partition League, for which he was the chief spokesman. His efforts met with some encouragement from the British press. When Fianna Fáil was returned with an overall majority in June, for instance, the *Manchester Guardian* applauded the election results as 'hardly less gratifying to us than to Mr. de Valera'.[12] Similarly, when de Valera appointed the eminent Protestant scholar and founder of the Gaelic League, Douglas Hyde, as Éires's first President, the choice was widely applauded in the British press as an indication that he was turning in a liberal direction.[13]

The *Manchester Guardian*, in particular, once so critical of de Valera, was now his loudest and strongest champion in England, and thus, by extension, the sternest critic of partition and of the Ulster Government; so much so that officials in the Dominions Office were sometimes surprised at the harshness of its attacks on the latter. For example, after Eamonn Donnelly, an Ulster Nationalist, was arrested for agitating against partition and interned by the Northern Government under the Special Powers Act, the *Manchester Guardian* immediately took up the case and used it as an excuse for lambasting the Ulster Government.

Our Statesmen today are fond of boasting of our freedom and attachment to liberty. A case reported today is a reminder that one part of the United Kingdom is still in the Dark Ages. Northern Ireland has lived for the last sixteen years under a legal framework that set the example to the totalitarian state in repressive legislation. Its Civil Authorities (Special Powers) Acts were in flagrant denial of all the canons of British justice ... However the face of such things, can we regard the Government of Northern Ireland, which practises these miserable, smallminded tyrannies, as a loyal and worthy partner in the Empire?[14]

The Donnelly case, predictably, led to new demands by the Dominions Office that the British Government do something to protect the Catholics in Northern Ireland. For the first time, the Home Office evinced some willingness to co-operate. Sir Alexander Maxwell, the new Permanent Under-Secretary,

[12] *Manchester Guardian*, 21 June 1938.   [13] *The Times*, 27 June 1938.
[14] *Manchester Guardian*, 29 July 1938.

discreetly sounded out officials in Ulster on the possibility of getting rid of some of their repressive legislation.[15] This led nowhere, as all the blame was heaped on to Dawson Bates, Ulster's Home Secretary for the past sixteen years, about whom apparently nobody could do anything.[16]

In the meantime, Devonshire was taking umbrage at Batterbee's support for the Irish Government's 'unreasonable request' for British intervention in the Donnelly matter, viewing it as a political subterfuge by de Valera to set a precedent for increased British involvement in Northern Ireland's affairs. The Duke could see 'no good whatever encouraging de Valera in views of this kind'. In his opinion de Valera had 'taken no steps whatever to woo the people of the North', and they should therefore 'lose no opportunity of making it quite clear to him that we are not prepared to act as his catspaw in forcing the people of Northern Ireland out of an allegiance and a form of Government to which the majority of the people are sincerely attached'.[17]

This was also Stanley's view. He complained that 'Not only has de Valera taken no steps since our agreements with him to woo the North; he has done the very opposite.' He cited as examples 'of how not to help any movement away from Partition', de Valera's speech at the inauguration of Hyde (which he viewed as 'unnecessarily provocative to Northern sentiments'), and de Valera's refusal to allow a British warship to take part in a recent regatta at Cobh. 'We are ready to help our friends in Eire in any way that we properly can,' he concluded. 'But it is up to them to assist occasionally; the two barriers to a United Ireland at the moment are Eire and Northern Ireland; the United Kingdom is no bar.'[18]

While Batterbee and Harding were doing their best, with some help from the Home Office, to reduce tension between the North and the South, the Board of Trade was also doing its small part. T.G. Jenkins, the Assistant Secretary whose assignment it was under the terms of the Treaty to check on Irish good faith in regards to the price commission, attempted

[15] Minute by Stephenson, 29 July 1938 (DO 35/893/X11/229).
[16] Minute by Batterbee, 6 Sept. 1938 (DO 35/893/X11/236).
[17] Minute by Devonshire, 21 Aug. 1938 (DO 35/893/X11/234).
[18] Minute by Stanley, 21 Aug. 1938 (ibid.).

to foster better relations between the North and the South by encouraging officials of both Governments to discuss matters of common interest, including some which did not arise directly out of the trade agreement. He tried even to get them to consider such matters directly, without a British intermediary, hoping that this might eventually foster direct contact on the ministerial level.[19] Although Jenkins's efforts did not bear much fruit—mainly because the Northern officials were unable to win the co-operation of their ministers for tripartite talks in London[20]—they are at least one further indication that the British were beginning to view the ending of partition as being in their own interest, and that they did take some tentative steps in that direction.

The reason for this belated recognition by the British of some of the disadvantages of partition was directly related to the worsening diplomatic situation in which Britain found herself, or, as one high Dominions Office official put it at the height of the Munich crisis, 'the extreme undesirability of an incident in Ireland at present, having regard to the general international situation'.[21] It was this state of affairs which lent Batterbee's views about the evils of partition added weight, and which encouraged the Home Office and the Board of Trade to do their parts in attempting to foster amicable Anglo-Irish relations. It was also a situation which de Valera, despite his obvious and sincere admiration for Chamberlain's policy, was hopeful of exploiting for the advantage of Irish unity.

The role of Ireland in the drama of Munich has not been the object of close scrutiny by historians. This is hardly surprising, as the Dominions as a whole have not generally been credited with being much of a factor in British policy formulation before and during the crisis.[22] But as the so-called

[19] Memo by T. G. Jenkins, 16 June 1938 (DO 35/893/X11/227).
[20] Jenkins (Board of Trade) to John Leydon (Ministry of Industry and Commerce, Dublin) 22 Nov. 1938 (DO 35/893/X11/250). Jenkins also found de Valera's attitude unhelpful. Jenkins note of talk with de Valera, 1 Feb. 1939 (DO 35/893/x11/276).
[21] Minute by Sir Eric Machtig, 17 Sept. 1938 (DO 35/893/X11/230).
[22] e.g. D.C. Watt, 'The Influence of the Commonwealth on British Foreign Policy: the Case of the Munich Crisis' in *Personalities and Politics*, pp. 159–74, seeks to re-evaluate the role of the Dominions, but virtually ignores Ireland. For Ireland's role

'Guilty Men' thesis gives way to Chamberlain's conception of British weakness in face of the combined threats of Germany, Italy, and Japan as the main explanation for Munich,[23] the importance of the Dominions in British policy-making becomes correspondingly more important. Chamberlain and the rest of the Cabinet knew that if Britain went to war over Czechoslovakia in the autumn of 1938, she would be doing so without a united Empire behind her. It appeared almost certain that Ireland and South Africa would not go to war then, at least not immediately, and improbable that Canada would do so.[24] At the very least, this knowledge must have contributed to and reinforced Chamberlain's determination to avoid war if at all possible.

In September 1938 de Valera was elected President of the League of Nations Assembly. Although it no longer meant much, this put him in a position to view Chamberlain's ventures in personal diplomacy from near at hand and to keep in close contact with the British as the crisis developed. On most matters concerning foreign affairs during the 1930s—Ethiopia, collective security, non-intervention in Spain—de Valera and the British Government had tended to think alike. Although de Valera did not hesitate to pursue his own policy whether or not it was in accord with British policy—as when he decided to recognize the fact of the Italian conquest of Ethiopia before the British had made up their minds to do so—Geneva had on the whole provided a forum where British and Irish delegates could agree in mutual harmony on various issues concerning foreign policy at a time when often there was very little else upon which they could agree.

Munich proved to be no different. Throughout de Valera was a strong supporter of Chamberlain's attempts to avert

---

in the crisis, see Deirdre McMahon, 'Ireland, the Dominions and the Munich Crisis', *Irish Studies in International Affairs* (1979).

[23] See Michael Howard, *The Continental Commitment* (London, 1972).

[24] See Watt, *Personalities and Policies*, pp. 159-74, and Roskill, *Hankey*, iii, pp. 383-4. There is, however, some uncertainty on this point. The Dominions Office, and perhaps also the War Office, appear to have thought as late as early July that if war came that year, while Canada and South Africa might take some weeks to decide to come in, Ireland would almost certainly join immediately. Minute of conversation between Robinson (War Office) and C.W. Dixon (Dominions Office), 8 July 1938 (INF (Ministry of Information) 528 CN16/5).

catastrophe.[25] 'The best thing England's ever done,' he told Lady Diana Cooper.[26] Not surprisingly, the British hoped to turn de Valera's support into concrete assurances that the Irish ports would be available for use by the British Navy in the event of war. In this, despite some progress, they were ultimately unsuccessful, largely because partition still stood in the way.[27]

The British learned two things from their dealings with de Valera during the Munich crisis. The first was that Ireland, while perhaps remaining technically neutral in a future war, could be expected to co-operate in a number of important respects. The second was that de Valera, although he might sincerely desire to be of help in an emergency, could not be expected to move ahead of Irish public opinion when it came to co-operation with Britain. This did not prevent the Services from making their plans on the assumption that events would soon carry Ireland into a war on the British side.[28]

In Ireland the Munich Settlement served to recharge old hopes and fears that the question of partition might now be looked upon in a new light by the British. Lest the similarity between the position of the Catholic minority in Ulster and that of the German minority in Czechoslovakia had escaped Chamberlain, de Valera took care to bring it home to him. When congratulating him on Munich, de Valera suggested that the time had now come for the power possessed in Ulster by the Imperial Government to be transferred to an all-Ireland parliament, with the control of local affairs being left to Northern and Southern Ireland respectively.[29] A motion to this end was even moved at Westminster by an Irish Labour MP.

[25] Feiling, p. 364.

[26] Diana Cooper, *The Light of Common Day* (Boston, 1959), p. 243.

[27] Note of conversation between Inskip and de Valera, 8 Sept. 1938; summary of talk between Inskip and de Valera, 16 Sept. 1938; report of conversation between R. A. Butler and de Valera at Geneva, 26 Sept. 1938 (DO 35/894/x31/18).

[28] The War Office expected that within a month Ireland would join Britain in a war. The Admiralty, while more realistic about the possibility of Ireland remaining neutral in the event of a war, still laid plans for the immediate occupation and complete defence of the Irish ports in the event of an emergency. Report by MO1 on 'Dominion Opinion', 30 Aug. 1939 (WO 193/104/1A); Admiralty minutes on 'Defence of Ports' (ADM 1/9874/939/39).

[29] Note of telephone conversation between de Valera and Chamberlain 4 Oct. 1938 (PREM 1/349).

The prospect, however remote, of the British Government making some move towards restoring Irish unity, was sufficient to produce the usual alarums in Belfast. 'It is obvious from the statements made at Stormont Castle and in the Ulster Unionist press that there is a growing fear here of the reactions in Ireland to Britain's attitude in handing over the Sudetenland to Germany,' wrote the Belfast correspondent of the *Manchester Guardian*.

Already Lord Craigavon has found himself assailed from several quarters for sending a telegram to Mr. Chamberlain congratulating him on the Munich Agreement. One Unionist critic told him bluntly that he had 'cut the ground from beneath his feet' in answering any future agitation for the restoration of the Northern Nationalist areas to Eire. Another described the telegram as 'a colossal blunder'.[30]

While the alarm in Belfast was exaggerated as usual, the *Manchester Guardian* did its best to lend it credence. In a leader of 10 October entitled 'Nearer Home', the paper bemoaned the failure of the Boundary Commission to do anything about ending partition and suggested that 'now, however, that self-determination is once more in fashion we might expect a demand for a new Boundary Commission—on the Anglo-French plan (for Czechoslovakia)'.[31] But this demand failed to materialize. De Valera himself, in an interview published in the *Evening Standard* a week later, rejected the idea of a plebiscite in Ulster, urging instead that Britain persuade Ulster to join an all-Ireland parliament.[32] This was going too far for most of the British press. Even the *Evening Standard*, generally sympathetic to de Valera, could see nothing to be gained in raising anew the question of partition. 'In race, religion and culture the people of the North differ from the South. Given a free choice they would vote steadfastly against any plan of absorption. And so long as that is true, no British Government could approve the surrender of their independence.'[33]

Aside from the *Manchester Guardian*, the only real support from the British press for de Valera's campaign against partition came from the Labour press. The Labour Party itself had little love for Ulster's sectarian ways, which almost always

---

[30] *Manchester Guardian*, 10 Oct. 1938.   [31] Ibid.
[32] *Evening Standard*, 17 Oct. 1938.   [33] Ibid.

worked to the advantage of the Unionists. The obvious solution seemed to lie in a united Ireland. During the 1920s this fact was obscured by MacDonald's sympathy for the Ulster Protestants and distaste for the Catholic South, and by the weakness and divisiveness of the Northern Ireland Labour Party. The expulsion of MacDonald from the Labour Party solved the one problem, but the other remained. In September 1937 Cripps decided to test the waters and crossed over to Belfast to spread the gospel of the British Labour Party. Upon arrival he announced that the ultimate solution of the economic difficulties of both the North and the South lay in a united Ireland, and in a lecture on 'Socialism and Imperialism' he exhorted Irish workers to strive for the overthrow of the Craigavon Government just as the working classes in Great Britain would strive in the future to overthrow the British National Government.

Cripps's visit was not a success. The Northern Ireland Labour Party Conference responded to his appeal by rejecting by a vote of 90 to 20 a resolution from the Armagh Branch pledging co-operation with the workers of Éire in achieving the unity of Ireland and condemning the sectarian policy of the Craigavon Government.[34] Cripps himself departed embittered, never to return. The first and last serious attempt by a prominent member of the British Labour Party to mobilize support against the Unionist Party in Northern Ireland had failed. Henceforth British Labour would rail against partition from afar, primarily in the Labour press. A year later, for instance, the *Daily Herald* commented favourably on de Valera's proposals for granting Ulster autonomy in an all-Ireland parliament, and warned that

the British partition of Ireland is a dangerous anachronism which must be ended. These three hundred miles of artificial frontier separating the North from the rest of Eire is the deepest wound which the English people have inflicted on the Irish people—a wound which keeps alive ancient antagonisms between the English, morally responsible for the existence of the divisions, and the overwhelming majority of the Irish race.[35]

[34] *Irish Independent* interview with Cripps, and report in the *Irish Times* on Cripps's lecture on 'Socialism and Imperialism', contained in reports nos. 265 and 267 on news comment prepared for the ISC, Sept. 1937 (CAB 27/543).
[35] *Daily Herald*, 18 Oct. 1938.

By the autumn of 1938 partition indeed appeared likely to be the reef upon which British hopes for Irish co-operation in wartime would founder. The forthcoming spirit evinced by de Valera at Geneva did not long outlast his return to Dublin. In early October, when Devonshire crossed over to Dublin for conversations with him, he was told that while Chamberlain had done splendidly at Munich there still remained 'other minorities to be considered'. De Valera also warned that, if conscription were introduced in Britain if war broke out, 'it would be morally wrong to apply conscription to Northern Ireland, and he would be almost bound to take some action'.[36] A month later, while congratulating MacDonald upon his return to the Dominions Office, de Valera again warned that the question of partition was 'bound to assume more and more importance and become increasingly urgent as the months pass', and that the solution would not be made easier by delay.[37]

After Munich the Dominions Office and the Home Office resumed their argument over partition. In response to one of de Valera's charges—that Northern intransigence was due either directly or indirectly to British financial support—the Home Office concluded that it was 'quite unfounded' since a comparison of the contributions from Northern Ireland to imperial funds with grants from imperial funds to Northern Ireland from November 1921 to date showed that Northern Ireland had paid £28,687,300 to the United Kingdom Exchequer and had received back only £20,783,800, leaving a balance of £7,903,500 in favour of the United Kingdom.[38]

The Dominions Office officials reluctantly came to the same conclusion. While noting that de Valera unfortunately appeared sincerely to believe his own allegations, as well as pointing out the 'very great generosity' with which Northern Ireland had been treated by Britain, Batterbee nevertheless conceded that 'it must, however, be remembered that the North had no desire for an independent position—they would have been quite content to have been left part of the United

[36] Minute of conversation between Devonshire and de Valera, 4 Oct. 1938 (DO 35/893 Part II/x11/265).
[37] De Valera to MacDonald, 5 Nov. 1938 (DO 35/893 Part II/x11/254).
[38] Memo by Home Office, n.d. (DO 35/893 Part II/x11/251).

Kingdom'.[39] Harding was more critical of the Home Office report. Arguing that de Valera's assertion that Northern Ireland only exists through subsidies from the United Kingdom was 'not wholly unreasonable', he pointed out that, after allowing for the cost of services in which Ulster had a share in the benefits with other parts of the United Kingdom, it certainly seemed that it received from, rather than gave to, the rest of the country. He also noted that the War Office spent approximately £650,000 a year in Ulster, a sum which had not been included in the Home Office figures. On the other hand, Harding observed, the reason that Ulster did not contribute its fair share to the United Kingdom Exchequer was due to its economic problems, which placed it in 'much the same position' as the depressed areas in Britain. Moreover, Harding agreed with Batterbee that Northern Ireland would have been 'quite happy' to have remained as an integral part of the United Kingdom and not to have been given a separate government.[40]

Upon the urging of Harding, the Home Office once again looked into the various allegations that had been made by de Valera and others about the mistreatment of the Catholic minority in Northern Ireland, and again gave short shrift to such charges. Regarding the alleged gerrymandering of local government constituencies, it conceded that 'there may be a grievance', but ventured that it did 'not seem to be as great as represented', and that the minority themselves were 'largely to blame for not availing themselves of opportunities which were offered of making representation'. On the Special Powers Act, it allowed that the regulations were in form 'exceedingly drastic', but claimed that in practice they appeared to be administered 'with great moderation'.[41]

While Batterbee remained convinced that in respect to matters like gerrymandering and discrimination in employment de Valera in many instances had 'justice on his side', and that the whole system of the Special Powers Act 'wants overhauling', even he agreed that there was no reason to suppose that there was deliberate injustice to the Catholics on the part

[39] Minute by Batterbee, 18 Nov. 1938 (ibid.).
[40] Minute by Harding, 18 Nov. 1938 (DO 35/893 Part II/x11/257).
[41] Minute by Home Office, n.d. (DO 35/893 Part II/x11/251).

of the Northern Government. He thought that the bias of the
Ulster authorities was bound to be in favour of those who
were supporters of the regime, but added that it was 'everywhere inimical to good and impartial administration where
Government and Party are as closely united as in Northern
Ireland'. De Valera, he noted, had at one time been largely
dependent on the IRA for support, but had been able to
throw off reliance on that body—in a way which the Northern
Government had not been able to throw off their dependence
on the Orange Lodges. 'If the Government of Northern Ireland wish partition to continue,' Batterbee concluded, 'they
must make greater efforts than they have made at present to
win over the Catholic minority, just as on his side de Valera,
if he wishes to end partition, can only do so by winning over
the Northern Protestants. At present both sides are showing a
lamentable lack of statesmanship and foresight.'[42] Harding
agreed. Noting that all their efforts to improve relations between North and South in recent months had been 'blocked',
he suggested the appointment of a United Kingdom High
Commissioner as the most practical step which the British
could take in the direction of helping towards the establishment of better relations between the two states.[43]

In the uncertain state in which Anglo-Irish relations were
suspended at the end of 1938, even the appointment of a
United Kingdom High Commissioner in Ireland was more
than de Valera was willing to countenance. Evidence from
the British side of the cooling in Anglo-Irish relations since
the signature of the Treaty in May—the reverse of what
Chamberlain had predicted at the time—came on 13 December, when Chamberlain was cataloguing his achievements of
the year to the House of Commons. Wild applause from the
Conservative benches greeted his mention of each accomplishment until he reached the Treaty with Ireland, for which
there was, as Harold Nicolson noted in his diary that night,
only 'slight applause'.[44]

Under the circumstances, as the Dominions Office recognized, there was little the British could do to respond to de

[42] Minute by Batterbee, 5 Dec. 1938 (ibid.).
[43] Minute by Harding, 5 Dec. 1938 (ibid.).
[44] Nicolson diary, 13 Dec. 1938. Nicolson, *Diaries and Letters*, i, p. 382.

Valera's anti-partition campaign. Coercion of Ulster was out of the question, both for political reasons and because it would have seemed suicidal on the probable eve of a second world war to risk a repeat performance of that selfsame crisis which had threatened to paralyse Britain on the eve of the first. In vain did MacDonald repeatedly emphasize to de Valera that his anti-partition campaign was 'bound to have the effect of stiffening people on all sides', and would thereby in the process undo some of the good which had been accomplished by the Treaty. De Valera could, with equal justice, insist that 'no man sitting in his chair could stand out of the partition campaign', and that 'if he did not enter into it and keep some sort of control over it it would get into unconstitutional channels'.[45] In the event, whether despite of or because of de Valera's agitation, the anti-partition campaign did spill over into unconstitutional channels. In so doing it effectively derailed whatever chance de Valera might have had of getting the British to do something about partition.

In the light of recent events in Northern Ireland, the IRA campaign against Britain, which began in early 1939, did not amount to much,[46] but at the time it was a cause of considerable consternation both in Britain and Ireland, and it was in a real sense a prelude to current troubles. The campaign began on 12 January, when the IRA issued a formal ultimatum to Lord Halifax, the Foreign Secretary, demanding the withdrawal of all British armed forces and civilian representatives from every part of Ireland. This was followed by sporadic bombings throughout England, culminating in an explosion in Coventry in August 1939 in which five people were killed and about seventy others wounded. Thereafter it gradually wound down until finally being discontinued in 1941.

The IRA offensive did not have the hoped for results. Anglo-Irish relations remained on a fairly amicable footing, as both sides condemned the acts of violence. Nor, despite the professed anxiety of Londonderry and a few of his friends,[47]

[45] Minute of conversation between MacDonald and Dulanty, 23 Dec. 1938 (DO 35/893 Part II/x11/265).

[46] See J. Bowyer Bell, *The Secret Army* (New York, 1970), pp. 145–95.

[47] Londonderry to Chamberlain, 21 Jan. 1939, and draft reply from Chamberlain to Londonderry, Jan. 1939 (DO 35/893/Part II/x11/278).

did the IRA campaign do anything to weaken the link between Great Britain and Northern Ireland. In fact, as might
have been expected, the reverse was the effect. Outraged by
the attacks, British public opinion rallied behind Ulster, whose
Government was provided with a convenient opportunity to
crack down hard on the leading Republicans. The British
quickly shelved their plans for intervening with the Northern
Government with regard to the Special Powers Act,[48] not to
revive them again for almost thirty years.

For his part, de Valera did not let the IRA activity deter
him from his efforts to persuade the British to take some step
toward ending partition. On 25 March he met with Chamberlain at Chequers, and again 'dilated upon the alleged ill-treat-
ment of the populations in the Southern part of the Northern
area'. He also invoked the danger that, in the event of Britain
being engaged in a European war, 'his position might rapidly
come to resemble that of Mr. Redmond in the Great War,
when the latter lost the support of the majority in Ireland
through his loyalty to the Empire'. Chamberlain agreed to do
his best with the Ulster Government, but said that he was not
very hopeful of the result in the current state of feeling.[49]

Chamberlain was especially anxious to placate de Valera at
that time because his Government was then preparing to introduce the first peacetime conscription bill in modern British
history—which it did on 26 April—and was worried about
the response this might evoke from de Valera if Ulster were
included under its provisions. The situation was especially
delicate in light of the fact that de Valera was planning a trip
to the United States in the near future for the opening of the
Irish pavilion at the New York World's Fair, where the temptation to raise the issues of partition and conscription in an
embarrassing way might prove overpowering. Chamberlain
had already drafted a letter to Craigavon imploring him to
make some concession to Ireland 'in the interests of national
safety',[50] but instead he invited Craigavon over to London for
consultations. The Ulster leader proved as unwilling as ever

---

[48] A.S. Hankinson (Home Office) to Cleverly (Prime Minister's Office), 23 Jan.
1938, and Hoare to Chamberlain, 25 Feb. 1939 (PREM 1/348).
[49] Minute by Chamberlain on conversation with de Valera, 25 Mar. 1939 (ibid.).
[50] Draft letter from Chamberlain to Craigavon, 25 Apr. 1939 (ibid.).

to make even a symbolic gesture of friendship towards the South, pressing instead for the enforcement of conscription in Ulster. De Valera, meanwhile, had cancelled his projected trip to the United States in order to combat the extension of conscription to the North, informing Chamberlain that such an act 'would raise the temperature to a white heat, and that he would not be answerable for the consequences'.[51]

De Valera's intrusion into what were regarded as the United Kingdom's internal affairs was resented by the Cabinet. Hoare and Inskip argued that it would be 'indefensible' to exclude Ulster from the conscription bill, at any rate without the agreement of the Northern Government, claiming that such action

would be represented as tantamount to an admission that de Valera can veto proposals affecting a part of the United Kingdom and also to a recognition that the Northern Ireland boundary is an artificial division, and that on major matters of policy the six counties have to be recognized as part of Ireland rather than as part of the United Kingdom.

But they recognized the danger if de Valera were allowed to use the issue to stir up anti-British feeling in the United States, and conceded that 'the American reaction to the contention that Great Britain is exercising a tyrannical coercion over Irishmen is a greater danger than the reaction in Eire itself'.[52]

Most damaging of all, the Catholic hierarchy in Ulster came out strongly against any attempt to impose conscription. This convinced the British Labour Party that the whole thing was a bad idea.[53] On 4 May Chamberlain announced to the House of Commons that it had been decided not to include Northern Ireland in the conscription plan, giving as his reason that it would have been difficult enough to enforce in Northern Ireland with the acquiescence of de Valera, and that without his acquiescence it was impossible.

[51] Minute of telephone call from Dulanty, n.d. (ibid.).
[52] Memo by Hoare and Inskip on 'the Application of the Military Training Bill to Northern Ireland', Apr. 1939 (ibid.).
[53] Attlee to Chamberlain, 27 Apr. 1939 (ibid.).

PART III

THE TEST OF WAR

12

The Outbreak
of War

On 1 September 1939 German troops invaded Poland. Two days later, after the failure of a series of diplomatic interventions, Great Britain and France declared war against Germany. Shortly thereafter Chamberlain replaced the existing Cabinet with a War Cabinet which, except for being somewhat reduced in size, bore a striking resemblance to his peacetime Cabinet. The old inner circle of appeasers was still there, although whatever solidarity had ever existed between them was greatly diminished. Chamberlain reluctantly offered Hoare the Privy Seal.[1] Simon, though 'very much deteriorated',[2] remained at the Exchequer, but his influence had also declined. Halifax, as close to Chamberlain as ever, stayed on as Foreign Secretary. The most important addition was Churchill, brought on by popular demand, who returned to his old seat at the Admiralty as First Lord. In his wake came Eden, as Dominions Secretary, though without a seat in the War Cabinet, forcing Inskip to abdicate to the Woolsack as Viscount Caldecote. Hankey was brought out of retirement and installed as Minister without Portfolio in order to 'keep an eye on Churchill'.[3]

Between Churchill and Chamberlain there were bound to be strong differences of opinion. In part this reflected a dissimilarity in temperament which had marred their relationship in the past. While not blind to Churchill's good points, Chamberlain felt that these were outweighed by his faults. He regarded Churchill as a 'brilliant wayward child who compels admiration but who wears out his guardians with the constant strain he puts upon them'.[4]

---

[1] Hankey diary, 23 Aug. 1939 (cited by Roskill, *Hankey*, iii, p. 413).
[2] Ibid.   [3] Hankey diary, 3 Sept. 1939 (ibid. p. 417).
[4] Chamberlain to Irwin, 12 Aug. 1928 (quoted by Gilbert, *Churchill*, v, p. 295).

Contrasting personalities were not all that separated the two men; they also disagreed fundamentally over how vigorously the war should be prosecuted. Chamberlain resented Churchill's refusal to see virtue in inaction, and to share the War Cabinet's collective view that 'time was on our side', and not the Germans.[5] Believing that he was fighting a war of politics and economics rather than direct military force, Chamberlain trusted in the economic blockade to defeat Germany. He considered his past blamelessness one of his chief assets, and was not prepared to sacrifice this moral superiority by intervening in the affairs of neutral states if it could possibly be avoided. This seemed all the more essential as it appeared that, unless the war was shortened by the internal breakdown of Germany, the ultimate issue might once again depend on the United States.[6]

Over Ireland there was certain to be controversy between Churchill, on the one hand, and Chamberlain and the rest of the War Cabinet on the other. Upon the outbreak of war de Valera immediately informed Chamberlain that his policy was to maintain the neutrality of Ireland, but that he would not tolerate any German activities, including propaganda, on Irish soil.[7] On 4 September, when the subject was first discussed by the War Cabinet, the importance of the Southern Irish ports as bases for British naval forces was emphasized, probably by Dudley Pound, the First Sea Lord.[8] The following day Churchill announced that the Admiralty was preparing a statement of its case. While conceding that negotiations 'would need very tactful handling', he suggested that it should be stressed that it was in Ireland's interest that the ports be available for naval use, and that without them Britain would be severely handicapped in protecting Ireland's trade and communications, which she was unable to do on her own.[9]

The main objectives of the Admiralty in regard to the Irish

---

[5] Cowling, *Impact of Hitler*, p. 369.

[6] Smuts to Hankey, 26 Jan. 1940, and note by Hankey (Hankey papers, 4/32).

[7] Cabinet conclusions 47(39) of 1 Sept. 1939 (CAB 23/100).

[8] WM (War Cabinet Minute) 2(39) of 4 Sept. 1939 (CAB 65/1). The Chiefs of Staff had agreed to stress to the War Cabinet the importance of securing the Irish ports. COS 3(39) of 4 Sept. 1939 (CAB 79/1).

[9] WM 3(39) of 5 Sept. 1939 (CAB 65/1).

ports were set out in a memorandum on Irish neutrality circulated to the War Cabinet by Eden on 16 September. As a
minimum, the Admiralty wanted an adequate coast-watching
service on shore in Ireland to keep a look-out for German
submarines and to report immediately to the Admiralty any
information collected. In addition, it wanted British naval
vessels to be allowed to enter Ireland's territorial waters to
search out and destroy submarines. Finally, it desired the use
of certain Irish ports by British ships and aircraft as bases for
operations against German submarines on the high seas.[10]

It was already clear, however, that the Admiralty might
have to be content with a good deal less than its stated objectives. On 12 September Dulanty had handed Eden a memorandum informing him that 'in order to insure and maintain
the neutral status of Ireland during the present state of war in
Europe', the Irish Government had decided to place immediate restrictions on the use of Ireland's territorial waters and
ports by surface or submarine craft belonging to any of the
belligerent powers.[11] Under the circumstances, Eden did not
see how they had any choice but to acquiesce in de Valera's
decision. To refuse 'might have unfortunate reactions on neutral and particularly United States opinion', he argued, and
would presumably eliminate any prospect of securing assistance which the Irish authorities might otherwise be willing to
give through their coast-watching service. Moreover, naval
action by itself might not prove safe or adequate without shore
facilities 'which could only be obtained by force, involving a
still greater risk of serious conflict with Eire'.[12]

Churchill contested Eden's recommendations, arguing on
18 September that the existing position in regard to Ireland
was 'profoundly unsatisfactory' from the Admiralty's point of
view. From his colleagues in the War Cabinet he received
sympathy but no support. Most were as anxious as Eden to
avoid an 'open difference' with Ireland, trusting instead in the
'course of events' to bring Ireland into the war on Britain's
side. In the meantime it was agreed that any approach to de

[10] Memo by Eden on 'Neutrality of Eire', WP (War Cabinet Paper) (39)34 of 16
Sept. 1939 (CAB 66/1).
[11] Dulanty to Eden, 12 Sept. 1939 (CAB 65/1).
[12] Memo by Eden, WP 39(34) of 16 Sept. 1939 (CAB 66/1).

Valera on the basis of a deal over partition was 'out of the question'.[13]

Churchill made no effort to conceal his distaste for the War Cabinet's decision with regard to the Irish ports.[14] But meanwhile the outlook for Anglo-Irish relations was improved considerably by de Valera's acceptance of Sir John Maffey as British Representative to Ireland. The British had long felt the need for a high level official—preferably a High Commissioner—in Dublin. With the outbreak of war, de Valera finally saw the need for one (although he was willing to accord to Maffey only the title of British Representative to Ireland, and then only after a personal appeal from Chamberlain).[15] Maffey, a former Permanent Under-Secretary at the Colonial Office, was brought out of retirement to fill the post.[16]

Maffey soon proved himself an astute diplomat. He came back from his first visit to Dublin—carried out in great secrecy, under the pseudonym of Harrison—convinced that de Valera's goodwill was genuine and that the only line possible at present was for them to try to retain that goodwill and to render Ireland's neutrality as benevolent as possible. De Valera had told him that there was a time when he would have done anything in his power to help destroy the British Empire, but that his position had changed and he now believed, at least in part because of the change in spirit in the British Government he had seen in the Treaty negotiations, that a 'united and independent Ireland' might well find a relationship within that Empire.[17]

Although he gradually assumed many of the ordinary diplomatic functions of a minister or High Commissioner, from the beginning it was understood that the main purpose of

---

[13] WM 19(39) of 18 Sept. 1939 (CAB 65/1).

[14] WM 28(39) of 26 Sept. 1939 (CAB 65/1).

[15] For the appointment of Maffey and for de Valera's finickiness over the title accorded him, see John T. Carroll, *Ireland in the War Years 1939–1945* (New York, 1975), p. 17.

[16] Batterbee, who would have liked the assignment, was sent instead to New Zealand as High Commissioner. Granard was briefly considered, but it was decided that he was 'too Irish', and 'although great fun, might not be entirely reliable'. The Duke of Norfolk, the premier Catholic peer in the realm, was also considered for the post and then rejected, most likely because of his age (31) and lack of experience. Horace Wilson to Eden, 7 Sept. 1939, and T.L.D. to Wilson, 7 Sept. 1939 (PREM 1/340).

[17] Report by Maffey on his visit to Dublin of 14 Sept. 1939. Appendix II to WP (39)34 of 16 Sept. 1939 (CAB 66/1).

Maffey's mission was a military one: to co-ordinate Irish coastal defences as closely as possible with those of Britain. One of his main functions was to provide the link through which information on German submarine activity obtained from coast-watching services in Ireland could be relayed to the Admiralty. By deciding 'tacitly to acquiesce in' Irish neutrality, rather than formally to agree to it, the British intended to serve notice that, while hoping to avoid a breach with Ireland over the issue, they nevertheless intended to use their influence to try to persuade the Irish Government to strain its interpretation of neutrality as far in the direction of British interests as it was possible for it to go. In particular, the British wanted the Irish Government to prohibit German submarines from entering its territorial waters, while allowing British naval forces to do so to search for enemy submarines in order to prevent their using Irish territorial waters or ports as bases for attacks on British shipping.[18]

De Valera had mixed feelings about these demands. While his personal sympathies were not in doubt,[19] he had his own position to consider. Though 'known to be pro-British in sentiment on the question of the war', he did not feel strong enough to co-operate openly with the British. He warned Maffey that if he went it was utter nonsense to think that a government of the right more favourable to Britain would replace him. 'The only alternative to his government was a government of the left.'[20]

On the whole, Maffey was pleased with de Valera's attitude, describing it as 'more forthcoming than anything I had dared to hope for'. He thought this showed that 'some of the seed sown has not been wasted', and claimed that 'the whole fabric of neutrality is beginning to look healthier from our point of view'. De Valera accepted, for instance, the need for a British liaison officer in Dublin representing the Admiralty and having under him three or four men whose purpose it would be to promote the efficiency of the Irish coastal service. But Maffey's high spirits were due at least in part to the fact that during the course of a conversation with de Valera on

[18] Note for guidance of Sir John Maffey, 19 Sept. 1939 (DO 1107/h/x/15).
[19] De Valera to Chamberlain, 20 Sept. 1939 (PREM 1/340).
[20] Report by Maffey, 24 Sept. 1939 (PREM 1/340).

20 September the two men had scarcely touched upon the two most obvious problems confronting their governments: the Irish ports and partition. The former topic Maffey tactfully avoided raising with de Valera, having been warned beforehand by Walshe that any mention of the ports at present would 'upset the applecart'. Regarding the latter: 'As I left the room', Maffey reported, 'he [de Valera] led me to his black map of Eire, with its white blemish on the North East corner, and said: "There's the real source of all our trouble." He could not let me go without that.'[21]

While satisfied that he had handled the negotiations with de Valera in the best way possible, Maffey was clearly apprehensive about what Churchill's reaction might be. 'I hope the First Lord will understand', he said, that action at Berehaven 'would undoubtedly shake the President's position. If such action is vital we shall have to take it. But we must think twice and count the gain and the loss.'[22]

While Maffey was right in thinking that Churchill would not like his report, the War Cabinet nevertheless agreed for the time being to leave matters in his hands.[23] Churchill let off steam by updating his instructions to the Admiralty for dealings with Southern Ireland.

All this talk about partition and the bitterness that would be healed by a union of Northern and Southern Ireland will amount to nothing. They will not unite at the present time and we cannot in any circumstances sell the loyalists of Northern Ireland ...

There seems to be a good deal of evidence, or at any rate, suspicion that the U-Boats are being succoured from West of Ireland ports by the malignant section with whom de Valera dare not interfere. [In fact, the internment of sixty-four republicans had been announced the day before.] If the U-Boat campaign becomes more dangerous we should coerce Southern Ireland both about coast watching and the use of Berehaven etc.[24]

But even within the Admiralty there was little sense of urgency regarding the need for the Irish ports—other than that generated by the First Lord himself.[25] The Director of Plans,

[21] Ibid.
[22] Ibid.
[23] WM 28(39) of 26 Sept. 1939 (CAB 65/1).
[24] Quoted by Carroll, p. 27.
[25] 2nd meeting of First Lord's staff, 18 Sept. 1939 (ADM 205/4).

for example, indicated at this time that 'the use of Berehaven and Lough Swilly would be a considerable convenience but is not vital'.[26] Similarly, George Dunn, the head of M (Military Branch, Admiralty), felt that the line of action in regard to the ports 'seems mainly political: do we wish to conciliate Irish susceptibilities or are we indifferent to them? ... From the Naval point of view, there seems little to be gained by taking a drastic line.'[27]

Churchill did not take such opposition gracefully. Although determined to play the loyal colleague and not provide Chamberlain with any grievances, he regarded his defeat in the War Cabinet as merely temporary, and awaited only a suitable opportunity to reopen the question. This occasion presented itself in mid-October, when a German submarine penetrated the defences of Scapa Flow—a feat never accomplished in the First World War—and sank the battleship *Royal Oak*. The loss of the ship and over 800 men was a severe jolt to British pride and sense of security which left the Government considerably shaken. On the following day the Germans bombed Rosyth, another major British naval base on the coast of Scotland. Though this latter attack was without much effect, it added fuel to rumours already rife in Whitehall that the Germans either had already launched or were on the verge of launching their western offensive.[28]

Churchill reacted to the attack on Scapa Flow characteristically by becoming even more belligerent than before. Augmenting his natural pugnaciousness was the fear that he might be made the scapegoat for the disaster and thus be branded with Scapa Flow as he had been with the disaster at the Dardanelles in the First World War.[29] on 15 October, the day after the sinking of the *Royal Oak*, Churchill raised anew the need for the Irish ports.[30] Two days later, following the bombing of Rosyth, he was more adamant, admonishing his colleagues that the incidents of the past twenty-four hours had 'brought to a head' the question of the use of Lough Swilly

[26] Minute by George Dunn, head of M, 10 Sept. 1939 (ADM 1/10366/271/40).
[27] Ibid.
[28] Cadogan diary, 15, 16, 17 Oct. 1939 (David Dilks (ed.), *The Diaries of Sir Alexander Cadogan, 1938–1945* (New York, 1972), pp. 224–55).
[29] Cowling, *Impact of Hitler*, p. 370; Churchill, *Second World War*, ii, p. 491.
[30] WM 48(39) of Oct. 1939 (CAB 65/1).

and Berehaven. The fleet had to be provided with safer alternative harbours, and 'the time had come to make it clear to
the Irish Government that we must have the use of these
harbours, and intended in any case to use them'.[31]

For the first time it now appeared that there might even be
some chance of Churchill getting his way. But while most of
the War Cabinet seemed to think that some action was necessary, if only to appease the First Lord, there was little agreement on what should be done. There was talk of Chamberlain
meeting with de Valera, but no agreement on where that
should take place. Finally the War Cabinet agreed only that
the ports were of the 'utmost importance', and that Churchill
should formulate reasons for proving that this was so, while
Eden would advise the Cabinet on the best way of approaching de Valera on the subject.[32]

Churchill was not slow to exploit this opening, small though
it was. The next day he circulated to the War Cabinet a
memorandum by the Deputy Chief of Naval Staff showing
why the need for ports in Ireland had become 'imperative'.
The reason given was that destroyers and other escort vessels
operating from Plymouth and Milford Haven had since the
beginning of the war been running at capacity, and that
'many of the vessels themselves are now beginning to show the
signs of strain, and their crews are worked to the extreme of
human endurance from lack of sleep and rest. Winter will
make it worse.'[33] Noticeably absent from the report was any
reference to the need for the Irish ports as anchorages for the
British fleet, the ostensible reason why the First Lord had
raised the issue anew in the first place. On this point Churchill
was forced to retreat slightly, admitting to the War Cabinet
that he had 'perhaps rather over-stated this part of the case,
since other anchorages were available'.[34] But he still insisted
that the Irish ports were needed as bases for escort vessels,

[31] WM 50(39) of 17 Oct. 1939 (CAB 65/1).

[32] Ibid.

[33] Memo by Deputy Chief of Naval Staff on 'Need for Berehaven'. WP (39) 93 of
18 Oct. 1939 (CAB 66/2).

[34] In fact, the attacks on Scapa Flow and Rosyth had only further convinced
Admiral Sir Charles Forbes (Commander in Chief, Home Fleet) that they had only
to provide reasonable defences to enable the Home Fleet to make undisturbed use of
its chosen base at Scapa Flow. See S.W. Roskill, *White Ensign: The British Navy at
War, 1939-1945* (Annapolis, 1960), p. 50.

including battleships, and pressed Eden to 'do everything in his power to persuade de Valera to meet us over the question of Berehaven as soon as possible'.[35]

It is a measure of the ascendancy that Churchill was establishing over the War Cabinet that none of his colleagues challenged him on any of the inconsistencies in his statements over the previous two days. Not only was the need for Berehaven as a base for the main fleet purely an invention of Churchill's, but, if anything, the need for the Irish ports as bases in the anti-submarine campaign had been diminishing rather than increasing since the outbreak of the war. The amount of British tonnage lost by enemy action in October totalled only 72,000 tons, less than half the amount lost in September.[36] Much of this loss was due to magnetic mines in the English Channel rather than to U-Boats, and was easily replaced by buying and building. By 1940 Great Britain had actually more shipping than at the outbreak of war.[37] Moreover, though they did not know it, the British were sinking U-Boats faster than they could be replaced, and the reason they were not destroying even more of them was due more to faulty anti-submarine measures and to the fact that coastal command crews had received no training at all in anti-submarine warfare, than to their being denied use of Irish bases from which to operate.[38]

Eden himself was under no illusion in regard to what he termed privately 'our woolly plans' to secure the Irish ports. 'I fear that it becomes every day clearer that it is scarcely possible for de Valera to square neutrality with the grant of the facilities for which the Admiralty asks,' he wrote to a senior Foreign Office official on 20 October.[39] For his part, Maffey was convinced that de Valera was already bending Irish neutrality as far as possible under the circumstances. Arrangements were in force for the immediate signalling to the Admiralty of any information on German submarine activity off the coast of Ireland, and a British naval attaché was

[35] WM 51(39) of 18 Oct. 1939 (CAB 65/1).
[36] *Annual Register* (1939), p. 116.
[37] Taylor, *English History 1914-1945*, p. 462.
[38] Roskill, *White Ensign*, p. 456.
[39] Eden to H.W. Malkin (Foreign Office), 20 Oct. 1939 (Halifax papers, FO 800/310/228).

in Dublin with full travelling facilities for checking on the efficiency of this coastal service. A British salvage tug was also operating at Berehaven. In addition, at Maffey's request, de Valera had withheld certain orders implementing Irish neutrality in detail so as not to embarrass Great Britain, and Chamberlain in particular. Moreover, the Irish Government was accepting the fact that, whatever the regulations might be, British surface craft would pursue and attack hostile submarines in Irish territorial waters. Similarly, Irish coastal organizations were not monitoring the flights of British aircraft, which were allowed to fly over Irish territory without anything being said. Given that the policy of neutrality 'commands widespread approval among all classes and interests in Eire', Maffey did not feel that there was any more de Valera could do. 'There is no gainsaying de Valera's view', he warned Eden, 'that any tampering with the neutrality of the ports would raise a storm here, the consequences of which are beyond computation, and which would certainly bring him down. There is a general consensus as to that.' Maffey included in his report a personal message from de Valera to Chamberlain, assuring him of his genuine friendship, but telling him that 'he could not grant what was impossible'.[40]

No doubt anticipating such a report from Maffey, Churchill looked to Halifax for support. But the Foreign Secretary took refuge behind a smokescreen of 'morality', which in this case translated into 'legality'.[41] Churchill refused to accept the legality of Ireland's neutrality, telling Halifax that 'legally I believe they are at war but skulking'.[42]

On 24 October the War Cabinet considered Maffey's latest report. It showed, Eden pontificated, 'the rigid and unsatisfactory attitude adopted by de Valera'. The Dominions Secretary saw three possible courses open to them:

1. To seek further discussion with de Valera: he did not think this would serve any useful purpose. .
2. To acquiesce in de Valera's attitude and endeavour to secure what we could, bit by bit: he feared, however, that this would produce only minor concessions of comparatively little value.

[40] Maffey to Eden, 21 Oct. 1939 (ibid.).
[41] Malkin to Eden, 19 Oct. 1939 (ibid. 227).
[42] Churchill to Halifax, 20 Oct. 1939 (ibid. 238).

3. To make forcible use of the harbours. If we did so, he did not think that de Valera would oppose us with military force, but he would indict us before the world and rally his people against us. There would be serious repercussions in the United States and in the Dominions, and the passive support which we now received from great numbers of Irish people would be alienated. In addition, Eire might grant facilities to the enemy.[43]

Churchill immediately dismissed the first two alternatives as the 'easiest course', and reverted instead to his idea of challenging the constitutional position of Éire's neutrality. While conceding that it might be advisable to postpone action until the United States had repealed its Neutrality Act, he argued that they 'should then, having set out the juridical position and made clear to the world that we are not committing a violation of neutrality, insist on the use of the harbours'.[44]

Churchill's suggestion did not gain any backers. Eden pointed out that Canada and South Africa would not support a challenge of Ireland's neutrality on legal grounds, since they held that they also were entitled to decide whether or not to join Britain in war. Similarly, Chamberlain, while granting that the First Lord had presented a 'powerful case', nevertheless said that at the moment it was difficult to maintain that the use of the Irish ports was a matter of life and death. 'De Valera's attitude', he said, 'had been only what he had expected', and he 'did not doubt the truth of de Valera's assertion that the creed of Ireland was neutrality and that no Government could exist that departed from that principle'. Chamberlain thought that, if they put the case as they saw it to the Dominions, they should obtain complete sympathy. 'Seizure of the ports, on the other hand,' he said, 'would undoubtedly have the reverse effect. It would have most unfortunate repercussions in the United States and India, where it would be hailed as a high-handed and unwarranted action.' He felt that the risks resulting from seizure of the ports were so great that they were not justified in taking them until the situation became much worse. Instead, they should share their view with the Dominions of the 'intolerable attitude adopted

[43] WM 58(39) of 24 Oct. 1939 (CAB 65/1).
[44] Ibid.

by Eire and the dangers for the whole Empire resulting from
that attitude ... If Great Britain went down, the Dominions
would go down with her.'[45]

Emboldened perhaps by Chamberlain's intervention on his
behalf, Eden volunteered that, at the present stage, they
should not make use of any threats to de Valera, or make any
further statements to him, as he was well aware of their attitude. This only provoked Churchill's ire all the more. Saying
that they should 'take stock of the weapons of coercion', he
wanted to know 'what would be the consequences to Ireland
as regards trade, employment, and so forth of her being declared a foreign country?' Perhaps in an attempt to soothe
him, Halifax ventured that, if they reached the stage of informing Ireland that she was no longer a member of the
British Commonwealth, 'it might not appear so long a step to
demanding the return of ports essential to our security'. In
the end, the War Cabinet agreed:

1. to invite the Dominions Secretary to take every opportunity of
   bringing home to the Dominions that the use of ports in Eire by
   the Royal Navy was essential for the security of the Empire, and
   that the present attitude adopted by Eire in that matter was
   intolerable;
2. to invite the Lord Chancellor and the Law Officers of the Crown
   to prepare a memorandum setting out the legal and constitutional issues involved in the termination of Eire's membership of
   the British Commonwealth;
3. to invite the Dominions Secretary, in consultation with the Departments concerned, to prepare a memorandum on the financial, economic and political considerations involved in the termination of Eire's membership of the British Commonwealth.[46]

The discussion of Ireland on 24 October was the closest the
War Cabinet had yet come to an internal crisis. On no other
issue were the views of Chamberlain and Churchill so dia-
metrically opposed. And yet neither man could afford an open
breach—Chamberlain because he needed Churchill as a symbol of his determination to go on until Hitler was eliminated,
and Churchill because he still did not possess anywhere near

the backing in the Conservative Party necessary to challenge Chamberlain for the Party leadership. The conclusions reached by the War Cabinet were a stalemate. For Chamberlain and Eden they represented a reprieve from Churchill's emotional onslaught about the Irish ports. But Churchill could take satisfaction in having carried the War Cabinet with him for the first time into considering the coercion of Ireland. He had, moreover, met serious opposition only from Chamberlain and Eden, and had received what sounded like qualified support from Halifax.

Much depended upon the nature of the proposed memorandum to be drawn up by the Dominions Secretary. Here Eden and Chamberlain were at an advantage, since it was Eden who was supposed to draw it up. But this was to be done in consultation with the other departments, and Churchill was determined that the views of the Admiralty should carry special weight. Moreover, Eden himself was caught in a quandary. He was the leader of the so-called 'Eden Group', whose avowed aim was the replacement of Chamberlain by Churchill as Prime Minister.[47] He even owed his post as Dominions Secretary to Churchill. But since his return to office, his relations with Chamberlain had been 'very cordial'.[48] The differences that separated the two men have often been exaggerated, not least by Eden himself.[49] In fact, both in temperament and in outlook, Eden was closer to Chamberlain than he was to Churchill. In addition, peering into the future, should Chamberlain falter, and Churchill's age or judgement betray him, Eden must have appeared, even to himself, as a likely candidate for the top post.

Like Chamberlain, Eden viewed Churchill's fixation on the Irish ports as something akin to insanity. Although he knew that he could count on the Prime Minister's support if it came to a show-down, it was he who would have to bear the brunt of the First Lord's displeasure in the meantime. Eden's greatest ally was time. Churchill could not keep his emotions at fever pitch indefinitely. Accordingly, Eden dawdled for almost two weeks before circulating a memorandum on the matter to

[47] Nicolson diary, 3 Oct. 1939 (Nicolson, *Diaries and Letters*, ii, p. 38).
[48] Nicolson diary, 14 Sept. 1939 (ibid. p. 32).
[49] Anthony Eden (Earl of Avon), *The Reckoning* (Boston, 1965), p. 80.

the War Cabinet, doing his best in the meantime to keep the
matter on the departmental level.

This was not easy. For one thing, most of the suggestions
with which the Admiralty bombarded the Dominions Office
during this period had a strong Churchillian ring to them. For
instance, it suggested, among other things, that they take the
dispute to the public, showing that the British Government
had expected to be able to use the ports in time of war when
they made the decision to surrender them.[50] The difficulty
with this was that, besides being untrue, the last thing that
the Dominions Office wanted was for the question of the ports
to erupt into a public controversy.[51] Churchill, moreover, not
being content to leave the drafting of such a memorandum to
civil servants, impressed his views on the Dominions Secretary
personally. Writing on 26 October, two days after confronting
him on the matter in the War Cabinet meeting, Churchill
lectured Eden as to whether he was 'fully conscious of the
grave wrong that has been done to us and to our vital interests
and of the urgent need to repair it. If I were to let the public
know the facts about how we are being hampered,' Churchill
continued, 'there would be such a storm of wrath against de
Valera and his adherents, not only in Great Britain but in
Southern Ireland, as have [*sic*] never been seen. The British
nation has a right to know who are the enemies who are
hampering our efforts to feed them.' Among Churchill's
suggestions was for Eden to examine the possibilities that
might be opened up if Ireland were driven from the Empire.
'What', he queried,

is the maximum of evil consequences and penalties which we could
enforce against them—having regard to the fact that we need their
food as much as they need our trade? What would be the position
of Irishmen domiciled in Great Britain, including many thousands
drawing our Unemployment Benefits, or of Irish immigrants who
come over? What pressures could we put upon them economically

[50] Minute by T.S.V. Phillips (Director of Plans, Admiralty), 9 Nov. 1939 (ADM
1/10366/271/40).
[51] Stephenson (Dominions Office) to Phillips, 8 Nov. 1939 (ibid.). Stephenson
insisted that there was nothing in the records of the negotiations on the Irish ports on
which to base any claim that the use of the ports in time of war by Britain was part
even of a gentlemen's agreement.

and financially? Would our relations with them become more precisely defined, if they were a foreign country?

Can anything be collected from the foregoing to enable us to confront them with pressures which would lead to their ceasing to pursue their malignant policy of strangulation now in force?[52]

Eden defended himself by asserting his right to determine the final wording of the memorandum. His feelings at the time were recorded by his *alter ego*, Oliver Harvey.

A.E. dined last night. He is most disappointed with Winston's attitude over Eire—latter wishes to seize the ports and drive Eire out of the Empire! A.E. says de Valera is doing all he can for us and it would be madness to drive him further and start up all the trouble again. And what would U.S.A. say? Apart from that, Eire even now is our best recruiting ground. Winston's attitude over India is just as bad. Here he is up against Halifax. A.E. is beginning to doubt whether W.C. could ever be P.M. so bad is his judgement on such matters.[53]

Besides time, Eden had one other asset in his struggle with Churchill: common sense. Churchill could carry his emotional arguments only so far before they ran up against a wall of hard facts. In this instance, as so often before in the past, it was the civil servants who wielded the axe. In an inter-departmental meeting held on the afternoon of 30 October to consider the effects on trade, shipping, recruiting, etc. if Ireland ceased to be a member of the Commonwealth, it was decided that the taking of coercive action against Ireland was likely to be self-defeating. As the official representing the Treasury later reported:

Practically everyone present agreed that on the short view any inconvenience that could be caused to Eire if she left the Commonwealth would only be at the cost of considerable inconvenience to ourselves; and that while in the long view the pressure that we could exert would no doubt be very unpleasant for her (if no worse) the immediate consequences might, if anything, be the other way round.[54]

---

[52] Churchill to Eden, 26 Oct. 1939 (ADM 1/10366).
[53] Oliver Harvey diary, 30 Oct. 1939 (Lord Harvey of Tasburgh papers, 56395 vol. xvii).
[54] Minute by E. Hauser, 30 Oct. 1939 (T 160/884/16430).

Especially worrisome to the Treasury were the possible effects if Ireland were to retaliate in such an eventuality by separating her financial system from Britain's by converting sterling into dollars. While such action would create difficulties for Ireland as well as for the United Kingdom, and 'might even in the long run prove disastrous to her,' noted Waley, 'in the short run however the over-riding consideration is that Eire being a creditor of this country for a substantial sum has the power to cause us considerable embarrassment by calling us to repay at a most inconvenient time.'[55] At a time when Britain needed all the financial strength she could muster to purchase arms and other supplies in the United States, this consideration was likely to carry a great deal of weight in the War Cabinet, especially with that erstwhile Chancellor of the Exchequer, Chamberlain, who had long held that Britain's real strength lay not in her military might on the battlefield but in her superiority in financial and economic power over Germany.

Churchill did not surrender gracefully. On 30 October he complained to the War Cabinet about the failure to censor telephone conversation between Britain and Ireland, calling it 'an inexplicable gap in our defences'.[56] The following day he again called for 'more drastic measures' against Ireland. But the rest of the War Cabinet was no longer listening. Eden patiently explained—what Churchill already knew—that the Irish authorities were already co-operating with their British counterparts on censorship. Not only was the German minister in Dublin not permitted to send cypher messages, but the Irish authorities were also giving the British copies of all messages sent by cable to the United States—the presumed route for messages from the German legation in Dublin to Berlin.[57]

On 7 November Eden's memorandum and that prepared by the Lord Chancellor and the Law Officers of the Crown on the probable effects of termination of Ireland's membership in the Commonwealth were submitted to the Cabinet. Each concluded that it would be a mistake to expel Ireland from

[55] Memo by Waley, 31 Oct. 1939 (ibid.).
[56] WM 65(39) of 30 Oct. 1939 (CAB 65/1).
[57] WM 66(39) of 31 Oct. 1939 (CAB 65/1).

the Commonwealth.[58] The two memoranda were not discussed by the War Cabinet for almost two weeks, and even then rather cursorily. By then Churchill had long since given up on bringing the War Cabinet around to his point of view, though privately he continued to accuse the Dominions Office and the War Office of 'untruthfulness' and—what was even worse in his eyes—of taking 'the side of Mr. de Valera in the controversy'.[59] But the very success of the anti-submarine campaign had robbed Churchill of his best argument for seizing the ports. This Caldecote duly pointed out, asserting that 'it could not be said that, in present circumstances, the use of Berehaven constituted a vital interest'.[60] The matter was allowed to drop, not to be resurrected again seriously until a year later when Churchill could do so under his own authority as Prime Minister.

By the end of 1939, Anglo-Irish relations seemed to be on an even keel. The British had accustomed themselves to Irish neutrality, which the Irish did their best to bend in Britain's favour. The extent of this unneutral cooperation was a closely guarded secret. For instance, the Irish Government permitted British airplanes which had to make forced landings in Ireland to refuel and get away.[61] They also agreed to the re-routing of the two cables to the United States through London because of British concern over the possible use by the Germans of their legation as a channel for espionage reports to Berlin. A third cable linking Ireland with Le Havre was also censored by the British, as were telephone conversations between Britain and Ireland.[62]

The press in both countries was also heavily censored throughout the war. In Britain this task fell to the Ministry of Information, whose main concern in regard to Ireland was to

[58] Memos by Caldecote, D.B. Somervell, and T.J. O'Connor on 'Eire: Termination of Membership of the British Commonwealth', WP (39) 759 of 7 Nov. 1939 (CAB 67/2); and by Eden on 'Eire: Termination of Membership of the British Commonwealth', WP (39)102 of 7 Nov. 1939 (ibid.).

[59] Churchill to J.H. Godfrey (Director of Naval Operations), 10 Nov. 1939 (ADM 205/2).

[60] WM 92(39) of 23 Nov. 1939 (CAB 65/2).

[61] Minute by Admiral Osborne, 22 Sept. 1939 (INF 528 CN16/5).

[62] WM 66(39) of 31 Oct. 1939 (CAB 65/1).

avoid offending de Valera and inflaming opinion on both sides by preventing the publishing of any adverse comment on the neutrality policy of the Irish Government, or any action by the Irish Government which might be inconsistent with that policy. While the Ministry of Information was willing to permit a 'moderate amount of criticism of the apparent ingratitude of Mr. de Valera and his Government',[63] most newspapers declined even to go that far. The *Daily Telegraph and Morning Post*, for example, in an editorial at the beginning of the war entitled 'The Empire Decides', simply omitted any mention of Ireland altogether.[64]

The Ministry of Information's handling of censorship was guaranteed not to please everyone all the time. At first it allowed speculation in the press on the possibility of Ireland entering the war if partition were ended. *The Times*, for example, published in late October an article from its Irish correspondent reporting that

Anti-British feeling, where it exists, is nourished almost entirely by partition. If the Irish border could be removed the people of this island would be wholeheartedly on the British side because, probably for the first time in history, the British and Irish peoples are in complete ideological concord. So long as the six counties are cut off from the rest of Ireland, however, much of the old bitterness will remain.[65]

But after complaints on the matter were received from the Ulster Government, it was decided that nothing should be published in the British press which might embarrass either Irish Government.[66]

More than anything else, it was the IRA that seemed to threaten the continuation of peaceful Anglo-Irish relations into the new year, not so much for what it might be capable of achieving on its own—for, despite its German contacts and a great deal of publicity, this did not appear to be much—but

---

[63] A.D. Waterfield (Ministry of Information) to Dulanty, 16 Sept. 1939 (INF 528 CN16/5).

[64] *Daily Telegraph and Morning Post*, 5 Sept. 1939.

[65] *The Times*, 31 Oct. 1939.

[66] Northern Ireland censorship representative to Ministry of Information, 3 Nov. 1939, Walter Monckton to R.M. Barrington-Ward, 9 Nov. 1939, and Monckton to Osborne, 15 Nov. 1939 (INF 528 CN16/5).

for the possible effects on public opinion of its repression. In December de Valera had permitted the release of an IRA man on a hunger strike as a concession to public opinion in Ireland. The British Government, however, had to weigh the effects of its actions not only on Irish but also on English public opinion. The real test came over the sentencing to death of two Irishmen for their part in the Coventry explosion in August 1939 that had accidentally taken five lives. The execution, scheduled for 7 February, evoked wide sympathy in Ireland and repeated warnings from de Valera. Chamberlain was deluged with appeals for clemency, ranging from Smuts and President Roosevelt (who cautioned that the execution of the IRA men might transform them into martyrs, as had happened to the leaders of the Easter Rising), to ordinary MPs and Cardinal Hinsley, the Catholic primate of Britain.[67]

Despite the serious misgivings of Eden,[68] Halifax,[69] and MacDonald,[70] the War Cabinet agreed with Sir John Anderson, the Minister of Home Security, that they had no choice but to go ahead with the executions because of the 'peculiarly brutal and callous nature' of the Coventry murders and because of the outcry from British public opinion that could be expected if the convicted men were reprieved.[71]

Although Ireland went into its obligatory national mourning, complete with flags at half-mast, masses, theatres and cinemas closed—all of which Maffey characterized as 'a vast deal of humbug'[72]—when it was over Ireland emerged as seemingly pro-British as ever. De Valera—who earlier had warned Chamberlain that he considered the moment to be 'one of the turning points in the history of Anglo-Irish relations'[73]—had misjudged the situation; 1916 was not to be repeated.

Maffey also thought the situation blacker than it was. By moving sharply to the left, de Valera succeeded in keeping

---

[67] The appeals are in PREM 1/416. Also Eden to Chamberlain, 5 Feb. 1940 (ibid.).

[68] WM 4(40) of 5 Jan. 1940 (CAB 65/1).

[69] Halifax to Chamberlain, 1 Feb. 1940 (ibid.).

[70] MacDonald to Chamberlain, 5 Feb. 1940 (PREM 1/386).

[71] WM 24(40) of 26 Jan. 1940, Confidential Annex (ibid.).

[72] Maffey telegram to Dominions Office, 8 Feb. 1940 (CAB 63/147).

[73] De Valera to Chamberlain, 5 Feb. 1939 (ibid.).

Irish reaction to the executions within constitutional re-
straints. The 'frequent acts of violence' that Maffey anticipated did not materialize, nor did de Valera resort to raising
the question of partition 'more vehemently', as Maffey also
feared would be the case. And de Valera's administration was
neither as unpopular nor as incompetent as Maffey reported
it to be.[74] Despite his rapidly failing eyesight, de Valera remained firmly at the helm, where he would remain throughout the rest of the war.

Aside from a few minor disturbances created by the IRA,
there was little to disturb the relative harmony of Anglo-Irish
relations during the early spring of 1940. Indeed, tranquillity
reigned supreme across the whole of western Europe during
those balmy spring days. The only serious fighting was taking
place far to the east, where the Finns had against all odds
been resisting the Russians since late November. For lack of
anything better to do, the British and French began formulating plans for aiding the Finns. These schemes came to
naught when Finland gave in to the Soviet demands and
made peace on 12 March. But rather than abandon their
project altogether, the British decided instead to go ahead
with their earlier plans for mining Norwegian territorial
waters to prevent shipments of Swedish iron ore to Germany.
And while they were contemplating infringing upon the neutrality of Norway and Sweden, Pound could see no reason
why consideration should not 'be given at the same time to
the question of occupying Berehaven?'[75] Such logic was difficult to confute; on 26 March the Chiefs of Staff agreed to
have the Joint Planning Subcommittee of the COS reconsider
the matter.[76] But events determined otherwise. The date to
mine Norwegian waters was set for 8 April. The COS were
scheduled to consider the report of the Joint Planning Subcommittee on the feasibility of the plan to seize Berehaven
four days later. Unbeknownst to the British, Hitler had also
selected 8 April as the date for a full-scale assault on Denmark
and Norway in order to forestall just such a move as they

[74] Maffey telegram to Dominions Office, 8 Feb. 1940 (CAB 63/147).

[75] COS 59(40) of 26 Mar. 1940 (CAB 79/3).

[76] Ibid. Churchill, however, 'deprecate[d] loading Narvik with this just now'.
Churchill note on letter from Pound to Ismay, 26 Mar. 1940 (ADM 116/4471).

were contemplating. By 12 April the Germans had over-run Denmark and most of Norway, and rumours were sweeping through Whitehall that the Low Countries were next. Under the circumstances, the plans for seizing Berehaven were quietly shelved.[77] The time for day-dreaming was past. The 'phoney war' was over; the real war was about to begin.

[77] COS 75(40) of 12 Apr. 1940. CAB 79/1.

13

The Rise of Churchill

WHEN the Germans launched their sudden invasion of Holland and Belgium on 10 May 1940, the Chamberlain Government was already under attack from its own supporters in the House of Commons because of dissatisfaction with its prosecution of the war in general, and of the Norwegian campaign in particular. That very evening Chamberlain was forced to resign, and Churchill became Prime Minister.

The change in government was more one of spirit than of personnel. Of the pre-war appeasers, only Hoare was removed—soon to be sent to Madrid as ambassador. Despite his dethronement, Chamberlain—as Lord President of the Council—remained popular among Conservatives and was clearly number two in the Government, with authority over the home front. Halifax—who, despite his peerage, had been for many, including the king, the Conservative Party, sections of the Labour Party and Chamberlain himself, their first choice to succeed Chamberlain as premier[1]—stayed on as Foreign Secretary. Outside of the War Cabinet, Simon became Lord Chancellor, Caldecote returned to the Dominions Office, and Eden went to the War Office. In addition, Labour now entered the Government to make it truly National: Attlee as Lord Privy Seal, Arthur Greenwood as Minister without Portfolio, and Ernest Bevin, the powerful Secretary of the Transport and General Workers' Union, as Minister of Labour. All three eventually held seats in the War Cabinet. But the biggest change of all was that Churchill was now in control—swept into power by a wave of national emotion—and becoming Prime Minister, Minister of Defence, and Leader of the House of Commons.

During the next few days confusion reigned supreme. With

[1] Cowling, *Impact of Hitler*, p. 383.

France collapsing with such astonishing rapidity, anything seemed possible. A recurring nightmare, frequently voiced by Halifax, was that the Germans were preparing for an air-borne assault on Ireland 'which would then become their base for land and sea operations against the United Kingdom'.[2]

Halifax had reason to be concerned. The Irish Government was in no position to resist a concerted attack by the IRA with German reinforcements. Although the Irish Army was believed to be 90 per cent loyal to the Government, and without any general sympathy with the Germans, it numbered only 8000 regulars, together with 6,000 reserves. The loyalty of an additional 16,000 volunteers was more suspect, as it was believed that the IRA had infiltrated their ranks. Moreover, while there were coast defences at Lough Swilly, Cork Harbour, and Berehaven, the regular Irish Army was short of field artillery, light machine guns, and ammunition of all types; while the Volunteer Force was equipped only with rifles. The condition of the other Services was even worse. There was no Irish Navy worthy of the name; only three small vessels in all, two of which were but armed fishing craft. The Air Force was not much better, comprising some 14 obsolescent aircraft and 6 Ansons. All in all, the Irish could not be expected to count for much in an emergency. The British concluded not only that the Irish Army would be unsuitable for action against the defended ports, should the Germans seize them, but doubted even whether it would be able to hold its own against the IRA.[3]

In fact, the actual strength of the IRA was a mystery in Whitehall. The War Office, remembering 'the Troubles', knew only that they were strongest in the south-west and west of Ireland, that they had a considerable number of sympathizers in Northern Ireland, and that its members were equipped with rifles and possibly light automatics. So long as the IRA was operating alone and in defiance of the Irish Government, the War Office felt that the existing one-division garrison in Northern Ireland, assisted by the Royal Ulster Constabulary, would be sufficient to maintain law and order throughout the

[2] WM 121(40) of 14 May 1940, and WM 131(40) of 20 May 1940 (CAB 65/7).
[3] Memo by CIGS of 20 May 1940 (WO 193/761 MO(A)/1A).

province and to prevent external aggression by the IRA. But if the IRA were supported by the Irish Army, as might conceivably happen if de Valera's Government were toppled by an IRA revolt aided by the Germans, then the situation would become serious and further reinforcements would be necessary.

To preclude such an eventuality, the British did not intend to intervene until invited to do so by the Irish Government. In preparation, General Cameron, the General Officer Commanding-in-Chief (GOC-in-C) in Northern Ireland, was ordered to draw up plans for using the 53rd Division then in the North to provide immediate assistance to the Irish Government and to secure the Irish ports, while reinforcements from Great Britain would be dispatched to take its place in Northern Ireland. These plans were based on a number of assumptions: that the IRA would do almost anything to attain its object of unifying Ireland and destroying English influence there, even to the extent of giving German troops every assistance should they land in Ireland; that the Irish Government would resist strongly any attempt by the Germans to use their country against England; and that the Germans would back the IRA against the Irish Government so as to force the British to withdraw some of their forces from the main theatre of operations in order to support the Irish Government.

Exactly how the Germans would go about invading Ireland was never made altogether clear. Approximately 600 miles of direct flight separated German bases in Holland from southwest Ireland. This would take the Germans over some of the best defended localities in England. An alternate route south of the English coast would add considerably to the distance and probably make a return flight without landing and refuelling impracticable. Any attempt by the Germans to form an airbase in Ireland from which to attack England's 'back door' was discounted by the War Office because of the difficulties involved in supplying it and protecting it from British counterstrokes. But it was thought possible that the Germans might use troop-carrying aircraft which they could land in Ireland without access to aerodromes as they had done in Holland. A cadre of leaders and NCO's might be sent in that manner, together with a considerable amount of equipment and ammunition if that had not already been brought in by sea and hidden in caches on the west coast. They might also drop parachutists in an attempt to seize strategic points in conjunction with the IRA. The estimated eighty-three German residents in or near Dublin were not considered a threat, as they would be quickly interned if evidence were found of their complicity in the machinations of the IRA or of their direct activity in German interests.

Aside from the intervention of the 53rd Division, and the sending of reinforcements to Ulster, it had yet to be determined what measures should be taken immediately in the event of a German invasion of Ireland. Air power would be the most decisive weapon, but there British resources were severely limited, as was being demonstrated in their reluctance to comply with French requests for additional air support on the Western Front for fear of leaving the island denuded of air defence. Effective defence of Ireland might require the transfer of several bomber squadrons from England to Ulster. 'The use of bomber aircraft for these purposes would undoubtedly be playing into the enemy's hands,' Sir John Dill, the new CIGS, conceded, 'but on the other hand it could hardly be avoided since the defence of one of the Dominions could not honourably be neglected.'[4]

Whether or not the War Cabinet would have agreed with this assessment is another question. In any event, Dill could see little other choice. The only real alternative, in his view, would be to strengthen the Irish Army with aircraft and other military supplies from Britain, as de Valera was urging; but this could only be accomplished by withdrawing them from other more vital areas. And, while it would be welcome if the Irish Government would act against the IRA before the arrival of the Germans, he could see few political or economic measures which could be taken to force it to do so. As Ireland was more or less self-supporting, 'a blockade would only result in the loss to the United Kingdom of large quantities of food, cattle and other imports, which are badly needed'.[5]

In Dublin, meanwhile, de Valera, unnerved by the rapid collapse of Holland, had taken to badgering Maffey at all hours of the night for military aid to prevent the Germans

---

[4] Memo by CIGS of 20 May 1940 (WO 193/761 MO(A)/1A).
[5] Ibid.

from establishing contacts with the disaffected elements in Ireland by air or otherwise.[6] A week earlier, on the opening day of the German offensive on the Western Front, Maffey had tried in vain to stir de Valera with a dramatic appeal for assistance—'Where did Ireland stand? Why not send an Irish brigade to France?'—only to be confronted with the usual arguments.

De Valera at once invoked the old bogey of Partition. De Valera said 'I cannot understand why Mr. Chamberlain does not tell Craigavon to fix up his difficulties with us and come in. That would solve the problem. I said 'If the Partition question were solved to-day would you automatically be our active Ally?' He replied 'I feel convinced that that would probably be the consequence.' But de Valera held to his narrow view. He seems incapable of courageous or original thought and now on this world issue and in every matter he lives too much under the threats of the extremists.

Unfortunately, he is a physical and mental expression of the most narrow-minded and bigoted section of the country. In all circumstances great difficulties surround the path of the leader there, but de Valera is not a strong man and his many critics know that well.[7]

De Valera nevertheless finally agreed to a secret military liaison between the Irish and British Armies in order to co-ordinate joint defence plans against a German invasion.[8]

In London, the chain of disasters on the Western Front was causing some in the War Cabinet to become more amenable to de Valera's strictures against partition. Since the outbreak of war Lord Lothian, the British Ambassador in Washington, had been urging that the only way to secure the Irish ports and at the same time keep the Irish-Americans pro-British would be for Britain to initiate a movement of reconciliation between North and South, perhaps by setting up a board for the discussion of common war problems.[9] Others who held similar views, like Waldorf Astor, owner of *The Observer*, had no doubt impressed them upon members of the Government when the occasion allowed.[10]

[6] Maffey telegram to Caldecote, 16 May 1940, appended to memo by Caldecote on 'Attitude of Eire', WP (40) 128 of 18 May 1940 (CAB 67/6).
[7] Memo by Maffey, 10 May 1940 (ibid.).   [8] See Carroll, pp. 41-4.
[9] Lothian to Halifax, 21 Sept. 1939 (FO 371/2083/400).
[10] Waldorf Astor to Lothian, 1 June 1940 (Lothian papers, G D.40/17/398/228-229).

Halifax was by no means immune to such arguments. At heart he was a conciliator, as he had demonstrated in dealing with men as different as Hitler and Gandhi. Unlike the Cecils, with whom he shared an aristocratic High Church background, Halifax bore no antipathy to the Catholic Church, nor did he see any special virtue in the Orangemen. Representing in many ways a twentieth-century Conservative alliance between education, wealth, and social standing, Halifax was a man of many parts and much experience who could not be ignored.

In rethinking his views on Ireland at such a perilous time, Halifax was encouraged by W.K. Hancock, a distinguished historian at the University of Birmingham who, like himself, was a Fellow of All Souls. Australian by birth, and long interested in Commonwealth affairs, Hancock was personally acquainted with de Valera and on friendly terms with other Irish leaders. Convinced that there had to be a better way of achieving Irish unity than by Nazi conquest, Hancock penned a short memorandum to this effect to send to de Valera, but which he decided at the last minute to send instead to Halifax. In it he urged some form of collaboration between North and South, Catholic and Protestant.[11]

Halifax was sufficiently impressed by Hancock's memorandum to discuss it in the War Cabinet on 18 May and later to send it to Churchill, together with a note of his own saying that the 'root of the matter' was in the section on partition.[12] Baldwin was also recruited to make a personal appeal to Craigavon 'to be helpful at this time of national danger'.[13]

In raising this question at the highest level of the British Government for the first time in almost twenty years, Halifax was sailing into uncharted seas. Besides the usual difficulties which made it difficult for the British openly to discuss partition, there was now the added obstacle of the Prime Minister himself, to whom any course of action which smacked of coercion against the 'loyal' Ulstermen in favour of the 'traitorous'

---

[11] Hancock's letter to Halifax of May 1940 and his memo on 'The Effects of the War on Ireland's Destiny as a European Nation: Reflections by an Australian' are in PREM 4/53/2/135–138.

[12] Halifax to Churchill, 19 May 1940 (ibid. 134).

[13] Baldwin to Craigavon, c. 23 May 1940, quoted in Lady Craigavon's diary. John Bowman, *De Valera and the Ulster Question 1917–1973* (Oxford, 1982), p. 221.

Southern Irish was anathema. Churchill at first tried to put Halifax off, telling him that they would have to consider the matter later, 'when we get a little breathing space'.[14] Halifax, however, was insistent, and soon enlisted the equally alarmed Chamberlain on his side. Although the discussion leading up to the decision went unrecorded, the War Cabinet was able to reach a compromise. On 27 May it invited Chamberlain, in consultation with Caldecote,

1. To make an immediate approach to de Valera in order to bring home to him the danger facing Eire, and the need, in order to combat it, for early and full cooperation with this country. In particular he should ask for the use of Berehaven for the Navy.
2. To invite Lord Craigavon to agree that the Government of Northern Ireland should take part in an All-Ireland Council *during the period of the present emergency*.[15] [Emphasis added.]

By watering down '2' in an attempt to make it palatable to Craigavon, the War Cabinet virtually assured that it would be unacceptable to de Valera, and that therefore '1' would be lost. This concerned Halifax and Chamberlain—who were agitated by recent reports warning that the Germans might be preparing for descent on Ireland at any moment[16]—more than it did Churchill.

Meanwhile, secret conversations had already commenced in London and Dublin on plans for concerting military action to counter a German invasion of Ireland. On 24 May Walshe and Colonel Liam Archer, the head of the Army's military intelligence section, met with Sir Eric Machtig (who had recently replaced Harding as Permanent Under-Secretary at the Dominions Office) and others from the Dominions Office and the Services.[17] From the outset, the British were anxious to impress upon their Irish counterparts the gravity of the situation, especially as they felt initially that 'the Irish were inclined to view somewhat light-heartedly the possible scale of German attack'.[18] That same day Walshe and Archer crossed

[14] Churchill to Halifax, 20 May 1940 (PREM 4/53/2/133).

[15] WM 141(40) of 27 May 1940 (CAB 65/7).

[16] WP (40)183 of 30 May 1940 (CAB 66/8).

[17] 'Minutes of a Meeting Between Irish and British Representatives', 24 May 1940 (PREM 3/130/37/23).

[18] 'Minutes of a Meeting Between Representatives of the Dominions Office and Service Departments', 28 May 1940 (PREM 3/130/37/3). The British estimated the

over to Belfast with Lieutenant Colonel Dudley Clarke, a young staff officer just returned from Norway who was assigned by the War Office to co-ordinate Anglo-Irish defence measures. The following day, accompanied by two staff officers from the headquarters of General Sir Hubert Huddleston, the new GOC-in-C in Northern Ireland, the three journeyed down to Dublin for talks with General McKenna, the Irish Army Chief of Staff. He and the other Irish officials were completely forthcoming in giving all the details of their military organization and equipment—insisting as always on absolute secrecy—while the British just as frankly set forth their plans for sending a flying column south from Ulster in the event of a German attack. On the whole, Clarke found the talks with Walshe and McKenna 'most encouraging'. Although the Irish made it clear that there could be no intervention except in the event of a German attack, they nevertheless left it entirely up to the British to decide what form that intervention should take. While unable to get the Irish to concede that the threat of a successful invasion was anything more than 'remote', Clarke left Dublin feeling that he had at least impressed upon them the danger of a German invasion in force.[19]

While encouraged by the results of these staff talks, the War Office remained concerned that the Irish might be 'somewhat too confident in their ability to deal with internal subversive activities, which if exploited by the German agents might well reach formidable proportions'. Moreover, 'until she [Eire] abandons her attitude of neutrality she cannot fully safeguard herself against danger of enemy activities within her territory ... Unless this security can be achieved, Eire will remain a serious weakness in the defence of these Islands'.[20]

Germans to have 4,000 to 5,000 trained parachutists, and the aircraft (30 4-engine JU 90s and FU 200s) with which to get them to Ireland. Although probably exaggerated, this may not have been too far off the mark. Almost exactly a year later the Germans were able to seize Crete by means of a massive airborne invasion involving some 3,000 parachute troops followed by some 22,000 other troops brought in by air. Even this, however, was a difficult and costly operation for the Germans which succeeded only because they had complete control of the air. See B.H. Liddell-Hart, *The History of the Second World War*, i, (New York, paperback edn, 1972), pp. 135-6.

[19] Ibid.

[20] WP (40)183 of 30 May 1940 (CAB 66/8).

In fact, the Germans did not have plans drawn up for the invasion of England, much less Ireland, though the British did not know this at the time. Nor, unlike during the First World War, did the Germans intend to make even a half-hearted effort to aid the more fanatical Irish Nationalists like the IRA in a serious uprising against either the Irish or the British Governments; although on this the German Foreign Office and the *Abwehr* (German intelligence department) were characteristically divided, the former feeling that German interests were best served by Irish neutrality, and the latter advocating support of the IRA for its nuisance value.[21] Nevertheless, coming as these reports did during the beginning of the invasion scare in Britain—the evacuation of Dunkirk was then in progress—and in view of the British experience in Norway, it is not surprising that Halifax and Chamberlain should have taken the threat of a German attack on Ireland seriously, nor that they would insist that the War Cabinet take measures to prevent it, as they did on 30 May.[22]

Churchill refused to share in this alarm. Not only could he not see what the Germans stood to gain by starting a civil war in Ireland, but he thought that the possible advantages accruing to the British from such an attack outweighed the risks— including the opportunity to reoccupy Berehaven with or without the consent of de Valera.[23]

Churchill imparted these views to General Ismay, the Deputy Secretary to the War Cabinet and head of the military wing of the War Cabinet Secretariat (which had replaced the pre-war CID). With his colleagues in the War Cabinet he had to be more circumspect. After the disaster in Norway, neither Chamberlain nor Halifax had much faith in Churchill's abilities as a military strategist. Moreover, together they stood a good chance of over-riding him in the War Cabinet, as was demonstrated on 29 May when they forced him to yield to a considerable extent on the question of what instructions to

[21] Bell, pp. 184–95.

[22] WM 147(40) of 30 May 1940 (CAB 65/7). The Admiralty was equally alarmed at the possibility of the Germans reaching the Irish ports before them. Pound to A.V. Alexander (First Lord of the Admiralty), 4 June 1940 (Alexander papers, 5/4/20). For a discussion of German plans for a projected invasion of Ireland, code-named Operation 'Green', see Fisk, pp. 189–239.

[23] Minute by Churchill to Ismay, 25 May 1940 (PREM 3/129/1/3).

send to General Gort for the evacuation of Dunkirk. Sir
Alexander Cadogan, the Permanent Under-Secretary at the
Foreign Office, who recorded the 'horrible discussion' in his
diary that night, feared that relations were becoming 'rather
strained', which he blamed on Churchill's 'theatricality'.[24]

Churchill may have sensed that he was getting into trouble.
He was not yet the hero of the Battle of Britain. When the
War Cabinet discussed Ireland on 30 May he remained silent.
With France on the verge of collapse, and the remains of the
British Expeditionary Force surrounded on the beach at Dunkirk, he probably saw little point in getting involved in an
argument with Chamberlain and Halifax over the relative
advantages versus the disadvantages of a German attack on
Ireland. Perhaps also he was no longer as confident about the
situation as before. The previous day Ismay had warned him
that information from 'secret sources' indicated that the Germans had 'concerted detailed plans with the IRA and that
everything is now ready for an immediate descent upon the
country'.[25] Although still emphasizing the advantages a 'civil
war in Ireland arising out of a German descent would bring',
Churchill conceded that much would depend 'on prompt
attack upon the enemy Air Force who have invaded, or are
on the way there'.[26]

While Churchill remained relatively unperturbed by rumours of an impending German invasion of Ireland, others
were less at ease, despite assurances from Sir Cyril Newall, the
Chief of the Air Staff, that measures to meet such an attack
were already well in hand.[27] On 3 June—shortly after the last
of the British Expeditionary Force had been safely withdrawn
from Dunkirk—Halifax drew the War Cabinet's attention to
a telegram he had just received from Sir Percy Loraine, the
British Ambassador in Rome, warning that large numbers of
Germans were passing through Naples on their way to Cadiz,
where they were to form an expeditionary force which would
attempt to seize Ireland. While admitting that it was difficult
to know what degree of importance to attach to such reports,

---

[24] Cadogan diary, 29 May 1940 (Dilks, p. 292).
[25] Ismay to Churchill, 29 May 1940 (PREM 3/130/37/21).
[26] Minute by Churchill to Ismay, 31 May 1940 (PREM 3/129/1/3).
[27] WM 157(40) of 1 June 1940 (CAB 65/7).

Halifax agreed with Loraine that it was unwise to ignore them.[28]

Chamberlain shared this concern, his sense of urgency heightened by every new rumour that came in. Major Desmond Morton, Churchill's personal intelligence adviser, warned, for instance, that 'the German Gauleiters of Eire are already there [in Ireland], known by name and functioning in a certain way'. The local Quisling, according to Morton, was Sean Russell, who had already formed a shadow government and was only awaiting German assistance to seize power. In addition, Morton conveyed word from a seemingly reputable source—Sir Charles Tegart, a former Chief of Police in Bombay who was later to serve with the Ministry of Food—claiming that up to 2,000 Germans had already been landed in Ireland from German U-boats and other methods since the outbreak of war, 'many ostensibly studying Irish Folk Lore'. According to Tegart, these and other Germans had been buying up interests on the West and South coasts of Ireland, rooting up hedges, and levelling suitable fields for landing grounds.[29]

Wildly exaggerated as these rumours undoubtedly were,[30] that they could have so alarmed Chamberlain and others, including Caldecote and the officials at the Dominions Office, who perhaps might have been expected to know better, is a measure of the uncertainty and confusion over German intentions which prevailed at the highest levels of the British

[28] WM 151(40) of 3 June 1940 (CAB 65/7). The Admiralty took the threat of a German invasion seriously enough to order units of the fleet to stand off the coast of Ireland in order to intercept merchant ships sighted off Iceland which might be conveying enemy troops to Ireland, and to be in a position to proceed quickly to the West Coast of Ireland if the news of an enemy landing were received. HMS *Newcastle* to HMS *Sussex II*, 9 June 1940, and C.-in-C. Home Fleet to HMS *Newcastle*, 9 June 1940 (WO 193/761/MO1(a)/8A).

[29] WM 168(40) of 16 June 1940 (CAB 65/7).

[30] Instead of 2,000 agents, the German *Abwehr* had then only one agent in Ireland, Captain Hermann Goertz, who had parachuted into Ireland a few weeks earlier with the mission of using the IRA for sabotage operations in Northern Ireland and making contacts with Irish people of pro-German sympathies. His mission was not a success. Although Goertz managed to elude capture for several months, his contact in Ireland, a Dublin businessman named Stephen Held, was apprehended almost immediately along with most of Goertz's equipment. And Sean Russell, the IRA leader, who was in Berlin at the time, died on 14 Aug. while *en route* to Ireland in a German submarine.

Government during the days immediately following the fall of France. After a conference at the Dominions Office, during which Tegart did nothing to allay Chamberlain's 'grave anxiety' regarding the situation in Ireland, the Lord President passed on the substance of his fears to Churchill. While conceding that Tegart's reports lacked proof 'and might therefore be inaccurate in some particulars' he was convinced that 'the general picture presented is a true one'. He and Caldecote had therefore decided that the only solution was to urge de Valera and Craigavon to come to London for a conference as soon as possible.[31]

Acting accordingly—and hoping no doubt that Craigavon had not gone unmoved by the dramatic events of the past month—Chamberlain met with him on 5 June and appealed to him to consider 'what conciliatory gesture under the circumstances the people of Northern Ireland would be prepared to make'.[32] When no response was immediately forthcoming, Chamberlain wrote again a week later 'reproaching' Craigavon for the delay, and telling him that if de Valera could be persuaded to come to London it was essential that he also be present.[33] This indication that the British Government might actually mean business did not go over well in Belfast, which was already in a state of 'panic' from the whole affair.[34] Craigavon, whose grip on the situation was being undermined by old age and ill health (though his condition in both respects was no worse than Chamberlain's), replied caustically, telling Chamberlain that he was not impressed by his sense of urgency, and that he would not meet with de Valera unless there was a prior announcement by the British Government that (1) de Valera had determined to drop his neutrality; and (2) that de Valera had agreed to the reservation contained in a letter from the Dominions Secretary on 24 May, 'putting aside all questions of a constitutional nature and considering only matters of common concern between your two parts of Ireland, i.e. Defence'.[35]

[31] Chamberlain to Churchill, 12 June 1940 (PREM 3/131/2/17).
[32] WM 168(40) of 16 June 1940 (CAB 65/7).
[33] Ibid.
[34] W.B. Spender diary, 8 June 1940 (cited by Bowman, p. 221).
[35] Craigavon to Chamberlain, 14 June 1940 (PREM 3/131/2/17).

Craigavon's 'wholly unexpected response' was matched by a reply from de Valera to a similar invitation which was hardly more forthcoming. De Valera feared that a visit by him to London would either give rise to suspicions which might jeopardize the existing friendly staff discussions between the two countries, or, if the question of partition were thought to be involved, 'then nothing but the complete disappearance of partition would satisfy the Irish', and ensuing disappointment on that score would probably result in the visit causing more harm than good'.[36]

Undaunted by these rebuffs, Chamberlain first considered going to Ireland himself, only to be persuaded against it because he 'could not hope to travel unrecognized, and his visit would cause the same publicity and have the same disadvantages as a visit by de Valera to London'. He then decided to send MacDonald to Dublin, as he might pass unrecognized and was on very friendly terms with de Valera. The mission's object, Chamberlain informed the War Cabinet on 16 June, would be to convince the Irish leader that adequate defensive precautions must be taken before a German invasion had begun. De Valera had to be made to realize 'that it would be too late to do anything after the invasion had started, when bridges would be blown up to impede troop movements, and de Valera himself probably shot. The whole thing might be over in a matter of hours.' Accordingly, de Valera should 'throw neutrality aside and invite British troops to assist in the Defence of Ireland.' If that was impossible for the moment, MacDonald should 'insist on the rounding up of the IRA and the internment of the Germans'; and if that precipitated a rebellion, as it well might, so much the better. The Éire Army would then be fighting the IRA and upsetting German arrangements. At the same time, MacDonald was to propose the establishment of a 'council for the defence of all Ireland', which would 'not only consider matters of defence, but would form a bridge for eventual discussion of partition'. If de Valera could be persuaded to accept the proposition, then MacDonald was to see Craigavon and try to persuade him to accept it as well.[37]

In urging such a course, Chamberlain was not motivated

solely by his genuine alarm about the strength of the IRA; he was also concerned that Churchill might use the IRA threat as an excuse to seize the Irish ports. Here Chamberlain's fears were also exaggerated. Although Churchill opened the discussion on Ireland in the War Cabinet on 16 June with a reference to a suggestion from Smuts that the Irish Atlantic ports be occupied at once, even in the face of Irish opposition, in order to prevent them suffering the same fate as the Norwegian ports,[38] as Prime Minister, Churchill perforce had to exercise a wider vision than he had as First Lord of the Admiralty—even when it came to Ireland. England was also in a far more precarious position than had been the case nine months earlier. Along with everyone else, Churchill now looked across the Atlantic for England's ultimate salvation. He was still awaiting word from Roosevelt on his request for forty or fifty older American destroyers for use against the U-boats. At the time he had also urged the President to send an American fleet to Irish ports.[39] Under the circumstances, any action which might serve to alienate Irish-Americans clearly had to be avoided. Churchill recognized this. While asserting that as a 'last resort' they should not hesitate to secure the Irish ports by force, he told the War Cabinet that it would be 'unwise at this moment to take any action that might compromise our position with the USA in view of the present delicate developments'.[40]

MacDonald's mission was foredoomed to failure. Upon his arrival in Dublin the next day he was greeted by the announcement over the radio that Pétain had formed a government and asked for an armistice. While this development—coupled with uncertainty about the fate of the French fleet—gave added weight to his argument that Ireland was in serious danger of a 'lightning attack' from Germany, it only reinforced the grave doubts in de Valera's mind about Britain's ability to ensure her own survival, much less that of neighbouring countries.[41]

[38] Telegram no. 304 from United Kingdom High Commissioner in South Africa, appended to WM 168(40) (ibid.).
[39] Churchill to Roosevelt, 15 May 1940 (cited in Churchill, *Second World War*, ii, pp. 24-5).
[40] WM 168(40) of 16 June 1940 (CAB 65/7).
[41] Hempel, the German Minister, had already reassured de Valera that Germany

De Valera left the British under no illusions as to his future course of action. To MacDonald's suggestion that the 'wisest course' for Ireland would be to abandon immediately her neutrality and co-operate with Britain in resistance to Germany, he returned an 'emphatic negative'. He held out no possibility of British use of the Irish ports, and would not consider a joint council for defence. Nor, refusing to accept MacDonald's argument that the Held papers constituted sufficient documentary evidence of a German conspiracy against his government, would he agree to arrest prominent IRA members in Dublin. Instead, he emphasized to MacDonald his 'determination to resist either belligerent to the utmost limit of his powers'. This resistance, MacDonald warned the War Cabinet upon his return from Dublin, 'would be directed against any attempt on our part to seize the Atlantic ports by force'. De Valera also taunted the British by adding that the 'position might have been different if there had been a united Ireland'.[42]

With the fall of France the British were suddenly confronted by their worst strategic situation since Napoleon. For the first time in modern history, moreover, they had to face a continental adversary without the use of the Irish ports.[43] All of this was profoundly unsettling to the War Cabinet and its military advisers. Fearing a German attack on Ireland in the wake of the French collapse, and warning that there could be no security for Ireland or Britain unless British or Dominion troops and air forces were stationed in Ireland and British ships allowed to use Irish ports,[44] the Chiefs of Staff began to reconsider their earlier decision that operations in Ireland should be undertaken only by the invitation of the Irish Government on the assumption that Irish neutrality had already been violated by the Germans. On 18 June the Director of Plans ordered the Inter-Service Planning Staff to carry out a tactical and administrative examination of the problems

---

would not invade Ireland, besides hinting that a German victory would bring an end to partition in Ireland. Longford and O'Neill, *de Valera*, pp. 363–4.

[42] WM 173(40) of 20 June 1940 (CAB 65/7).

[43] The British still had the use of the ports in Northern Ireland, of course.

[44] Memo by ACIGS on 'Anti-Aircraft Requirements for Eire', 18 June 1940 (WO 193/761/MOI(a)/7A).

involved in British occupation of Queenstown, Berehaven, the Shannon River Estuary, and the airbases at Foynes and Rineanna. In this examination, 'Irish hostility was to be assumed'.[45]

Yet despite this strong language, the COS remained determined to avoid a collision with the Irish if it could possibly be avoided. On 19 June the Joint Planning Subcommittee of the COS warned that it was 'almost a foregone conclusion that, simultaneously with air attack, and perhaps also seaborne invasion on our East and South coasts, we shall be faced with a Nazi descent upon Eire'. While recognizing that this was a political problem of a 'supremely explosive quality', the planners nevertheless considered it their duty to impress upon the War Cabinet that the continuation of the partition deadlock was producing a 'very dangerous' military situation. They went on to make two forceful suggestions:

1. We suggest that the strongest possible pressure should be brought upon the Northern Ireland Government, coupled with the necessary conditions to be undertaken by Eire and guaranteed by His Majesty's Government. The latter should include the occupation by British forces of the Irish Atlantic ports, and the immediate adoption of all possible measures to ensure the defence of Eire, such as the internment of German and IRA personnel and the reinforcement of Eire by British land and sea forces.

2. We suggest that the people of the North should be told in the plainest terms that if we win the war we shall see to it that a united Ireland is ruled within the Empire as a true dominion with all that it implies, but that if we lose the war—as we may well do if the enemy succeeds in subjugating Ireland—they will have a united Ireland in any event, but unified under the German jackboot instead of the British Crown.[46]

Chamberlain and the COS were not the only ones who were beginning to think that pressure would have to be brought on the North in regard to partition. On 18 June Ernest Bevin, whose first-hand knowledge of Ireland exceeded that of any other man in the Government, raised the matter directly in a letter to Churchill. Unlike Churchill, whose connections with Ireland were mainly aristocratic, Bevin's ex-

[45] JP 40(5)(ISPS) of 18 June 1940 (WO 193/761/MOI(a)/4A).
[46] COS 473(40)(JP) of 19 June 1940 (CAB 80/13).

perience of Ireland was mainly in the slums of Cork, where he had worked as a union organizer before the First World War.[47] During the 1930s, while in his fifties, Bevin had taken an active lead in trying to prevent the English-dominated Transport and General Workers' Union from being subverted by Irish nationalists and sectarian bitterness, or by the rival Irish Transport and General Workers' Union. In the process, he became convinced that 'there was no desire on the part of the work people particularly of the North and South to be divided from the rest of the union membership in Britain'. With Ireland now in danger he urged that nothing should be allowed to stand in the way of Irishmen coming together to defend their own soil, and believed that 'so far as the work-ingmen are concerned they would welcome it, particularly if the politicians could be compelled to play the game'. On partition, that 'other matter which has always agitated the people in Ireland', Bevin felt Irish feeling was 'if they served the purposes of the British Empire now that they would be let down at the end'. De Valera, he maintained, had 'always been willing to settle the matter if someone was brought in outside of the British Empire to preside'.[48]

Bevin characteristically did not content himself with general advice, but followed it up with a definite plan of action. The blueprint for the plan was actually the work of Lionel Curtis, who had been approached by Bevin for advice. Now back at All Souls with Hancock, Curtis, after consulting with five other academics, including Arnold Toynbee, had come up with advice for Bevin similar to that given by Hancock to Halifax.[49] Bevin took the substance of Curtis's proposal and passed it on to Churchill for 'immediate consideration', arguing that 'resolute action to dispose of this matter once and for all' would bring a tremendous volume of opinion on to their side in the United States, and would 'alter the whole aspect of the defence effort in Australia'. He suggested:

1) that the two Governments in Ireland should immediately have a joint Defence Council;

[47] Alan Bullock, *The Life and Times of Ernest Bevin*, i, (London, 1960), p. 86.
[48] Bevin to Churchill, 18 June 1940 (PREM 4/53/2/118).
[49] Bowman, p. 223.

2) that the General Staff should be ordered to consult by the two Governments immediately;

3) that we should enter into an agreement with Ireland that there should be a statement that we are willing to accept a new constitution on the basis of a united Ireland at the end of hostilities;

4) that the Chairman of the constitution working body should be selected by the President of the United States.[50]

In response, Churchill said that, although he would welcome any approach to Irish unity, he 'could never be a party to the coercion of Ulster to join the Southern counties'. While he was 'much in favour of their being persuaded', the key to this was 'de Valera showing loyalty to Crown and Empire'.[51]

Meanwhile, on 19 June, after considering the recommendation of its Joint Planning Subcommittee, the COS asked that the dangers of the situation in Ireland be brought before the War Cabinet. Admiral Tom Phillips, the Vice-Chief of the Naval Staff, pointed out that the fact that the Germans had established themselves along the French Atlantic coast made it all the more imperative that the British fleet should secure early occupation of the Irish ports.[52] The COS met again on the morning of 20 June, just before the meeting of the War Cabinet. By then the Inter-Service Planning Staff was well advanced in its preparations for the seizure of the Irish ports. In a short discussion, Pound briefed his colleagues on 'certain projects which the Admiralty were now considering, as a matter of urgency' in regard to the Irish ports.[53]

Chamberlain saw the preliminary draft of the *aide-memoire* from the COS before the meeting of the War Cabinet. What he saw disturbed him. Unlike Churchill, Chamberlain tended to take the advice of military experts seriously. It now seemed to him that the choice came down to either forcibly seizing the Irish ports or putting pressure on Ulster to make some gesture regarding partition. The first possibility he ruled out because of the 'possibly unfavourable reaction which would be caused in the USA by any forcible measure against Ireland',[54] but he was prepared to embrace the second. The

[50] Bevin to Churchill, 18 June 1940 (PREM 4/53/2/118).
[51] Churchill to Bevin, n.d. (PREM 4/53/2/120).
[52] COS 186(40) of 19 June 1940 (CAB 79/1).
[53] COS 187(40) of 20 June 1940 (ibid.).
[54] WM 173(40) of 20 June 1940 (CAB 65/7).

refusal of Craigavon to make even the slightest concession at such a critical juncture in the fate of the nation had clearly annoyed him. He was also upset by MacDonald's belief that de Valera had not passed on to his colleagues the assurances he had given him that a declaration of a united Ireland should settle the issue once and for all, and that there would be no going back on that, for de Valera had told MacDonald that one of the principal reasons why his Cabinet refused the British offer was that they believed that a united Ireland would not result from it.[55] Chamberlain accordingly suggested that

MacDonald should go to Dublin and ask whether, in return for ports and occupation of Ireland, and internment of IRA, de Valera would be content to accept a declaration stating that His Majesty's Government were, in principle, in favour of the establishment of a United Ireland. This would naturally have to be followed by an approach to Lord Craigavon, who would have to be told that the interests of Northern Ireland could not be allowed to stand against the vital interests of the British Empire. Lord Craigavon would naturally ask whether the United Ireland would form part of the British Empire. The answer to this was clearly in the affirmative, though of course full Dominion status carried with it the right to secede from the Commonwealth.

If de Valera still maintained a negative attitude, Chamberlain urged that MacDonald should insist that the proposition be put to his Government, some members of which he understood were likely to take a less rigid view. Only if this were done did Chamberlain think that they could be on stronger ground *vis-à-vis* the United States, should they be compelled to use force later on.[56]

In making 'proposals that looked like coercion of N. Ireland',[57] Chamberlain knew that he was in for an unequal struggle. Earlier Churchill had made it clear that any deal MacDonald could work out with de Valera would be 'contingent upon Ulster agreeing and Ireland coming into the war'.[58]

---

[55] Note by MacDonald of a conversation between himself and de Valera, Aiken, and Lemass on 18 June 1940 (PREM 3/131/2/25).

[56] WM 173(40) of 20 June 1940 (CAB 65/7).

[57] Cadogan diary, 20 June 1940 (Dilks, p. 305).

[58] Minute by Chamberlain on report by MacDonald of conversation with de Valera, n.d. (PREM 3/131/2/32).

Now, in a 'passionate speech',[59] Churchill voiced his opposition to Chamberlain's proposals, objecting to the putting of 'undue pressure on the loyal province of Ulster' and stressing that he 'would not urge those who had worked self-government loyally within the Empire to join with those who wished to stay outside it'. Churchill then went on to play down the seriousness of the military situation and to argue in favour of allowing the Germans to make the first move. 'If they succeeded in establishing themselves in Ireland', he concluded, 'our forces should be ready to pounce on them. The whole of Ireland, including de Valera, would in those circumstances be on our side.'[60]

Chamberlain was beaten. While his influence in the War Cabinet and Conservative Party was rapidly waning,[61] Churchill's moment had finally arrived. Only two days earlier Churchill had stirred the nation with his 'This was their finest hour' speech, and his authority in the War Cabinet was now unchallenged. Chamberlain tried to temper Churchill's tirade by explaining that he had suggested the possibility of 'urging this very strong course upon Northern Ireland' only because of the danger of the situation. Even this did not win him much support. Attlee agreed with Churchill that a German invasion would furnish the best chance of securing a united Ireland, and saw no advantage in attempting to coerce either Northern or Southern Ireland. Even Bevin agreed that coercion was 'impossible', and considered it unlikely that any substantial advance could be made towards the prospect of a united Ireland. In the end, the War Cabinet adopted a proposal of Halifax's that MacDonald should return to Dublin and continue educating de Valera as to the danger of invasion, while at the same time exploring to what extent any advance towards a united Ireland would help de Valera in dealing with Irish opinion. If anything useful came out of the discussion, it could then be put to Craigavon. But no undue pressure would be put on Northern Ireland to consent to union with the

---

[59] Cadogan diary, 20 June 1940 (Dilks, p. 305).
[60] WM 173(40) of 20 June 1940 (CAB 65/7).
[61] For the growing feeling against 'the old gang' and in particular against Chamberlain, Kingsley Wood, and Inskip, see Nicolson diary, 6 June 1940 (Nicolson, *Diaries and Letters*, ii, p. 94).

South; nor would steps be taken to occupy ports in Southern Ireland in advance of an aggression by Germany.[62]

Having imposed his will on the War Cabinet, Churchill next turned to the military. The Joint Planning Subcommittee of the COS had concluded that a German sea-borne expedition to Ireland would probably consist of more than a division. Although recognizing that the Germans would be running very great risks in sending such an expedition, it was felt that they were prepared to take such risks. In addition, the Germans might be able to land an airborne contingent of about 1,000 men, while the IRA, numbering approximately 2,000 well-armed men, were expected to rise against the Government. As the Irish were not expected to put up much effective resistance, the Subcommittee recommended that the British go to their assistance immediately 'with all the forces which could be spared'.[63]

This the COS were prepared to do. Although Britain itself was now virtually denuded of effective combat troops—most of the Army's equipment having been abandoned on the Continent—much of what was available was nevertheless earmarked for dispatch to Ireland. A Royal Marine Brigade together with loaded transport was stationed at Milford Haven in order to be ready immediately to seize a bridgehead at Foynes and other naval bases should the Germans invade. The 3rd Division would then provide the reinforcements which would pour over from Britain. In addition, as previously planned, the 53rd Division, although not yet fully trained and equipped, would sweep down from the North, while the even less fully trained and equipped 61st Division would then take its place in Northern Ireland.[64] On Ismay's suggestion it was also decided that for British intervention to be effective it would be 'out of the question' to delay in waiting for a request for assistance from de Valera.[65] General Huddleston, the Commander in Northern Ireland, was instructed 'to take action forthwith' without even waiting for confirmation from the War Office if he felt that a serious

[62] WM 173(40) of 20 June 1940 (CAB 65/7).
[63] JP 478(40) of 20 June 1940, and JP 479(40) of 20 June 1940 (CAB 80/13).
[64] COS 188(40) of 20 June 1940, and COS 189(40) of 21 June 1940 (CAB 79/5).
[65] COS 191(40) of 24 June 1940 (ibid.).

invasion of Ireland had taken place, provided that he first made every effort to obtain confirmation from Maffey.[66]

Churchill was more alarmed by the measures prepared by the COS to meet the supposed German threat to Ireland than by the threat itself. Objecting strenuously to the 'undue risk' involved in removing the only two thoroughly equipped divisions out of Britain at such a time, he argued in proper Clausewitzian fashion that 'nothing that can happen in Ireland can be immediately decisive'.[67] He then returned to his old seat at the Admiralty for two meetings on 20 and 21 June during which it was decided because of the heavy losses to move all trade to the Northern Approaches.[68] At a stroke this greatly reduced the pressure on the British fleet and fighter command to protect British trade, thus making less imperative the need for bases in Ireland. The Joint Planning Subcommittee also revised its earlier predictions and concluded that there was no longer much chance of the Germans successfully launching an organized seaborne invasion of Ireland from Norway, Spain, or France.[69] The COS nevertheless remained so concerned about the seriousness of the threat that would be posed by a successful German landing in Ireland, and of the need to clear up such a landing as soon as possible, that the question of troop dispositions was eventually referred to the War Cabinet for a final decision. It agreed with Churchill that the 3rd Division should not be sent to Northern Ireland or to Ireland immediately in the event of a German attack, but should remain in England for the defence of the United Kingdom.[70]

Although fears of a German invasion of Ireland gradually receded after 21 June, Chamberlain did not desist in his efforts to resolve the Irish question. From Maffey he learned that the Irish would have agreed to the British proposals three months earlier, but that their views had been 'somewhat influenced by the recent German successes'. Maffey nevertheless thought that the chief reason for de Valera's unwillingness to give a

[66] WO (cipher) to Huddleston, No. 75889(MO8) of 9 July 1940 (WO 193/1761/MOI(a)9A).
[67] Minute by Churchill to Ismay, 30 July 1940, COS 509(40) (CAB 80/4).
[68] Minutes of meetings at Admiralty on 20 and 21 June 1940 (ADM 205/7).
[69] Revised draft JP 485(40) of 22 June 1940 (CAB 80/4).
[70] WM 191(40) of 2 July 1940. Confidential annexes (CAB 65/14).

definite assurance that Ireland would enter the war immediately in exchange for the promise of a united Ireland after
the war was the fact that Ireland was almost completely unprepared for war. Chamberlain accordingly drafted the following proposals for MacDonald to submit to de Valera:

1. A declaration of a United Ireland in principle.
2. A joint body including representatives of the Government of Eire
   and Northern Ireland to be set up at once to work out the
   constitutional and other practical details of the Union. The
   Government in London to give such assistance as might be desired.
3. A joint Defence Council to be set up immediately.
4. Eire to join the war on our side forthwith, and, for the purposes
   of the defence of Eire, permission to be given for British naval
   vessels to have the use of Southern Irish ports and for British
   troops and aeroplanes to be stationed in Eire as may be agreed
   with the Eire Government.
5. The Eire Government to intern all German and Italian aliens in
   the Country and to take any steps necessary to suppress Fifth
   Column activities.
6. The British Government to provide equipment as early as possible to the Eire Government ...[71]

MacDonald presented these proposals to de Valera on 26
June. That same day Chamberlain wrote to Craigavon informing him of this latest initiative, expecting, as he told the
War Cabinet, that the Ulster Government would want 'to
play their part in bringing about so favourable a development'.[72]

Whether Chamberlain really expected much to come from
these proposals is doubtful. The 'most unsatisfactory' reply he
received from de Valera came as no surprise. 'MacDonald's
report of his visit is discouraging—the de Valera people are
afraid we are going to lose, and don't want to be involved
with us,' he recorded dolefully in his diary on 28 June.[73] The
reply from Ulster was even more blunt. This too should not
have surprised him. Within the House of Lords, their Lordships had begun stirring at the first rumours of overtures to

---

[71] Memo by Chamberlain on 'Eire: Negotiations with de Valera', WP (40)223 of
25 June 1940 (CAB 66/9).
[72] Ibid.
[73] Chamberlain diary, 28 June 1940 (Chamberlain papers NC2/24A).

de Valera, and Caldecote's reassurances were having little effect. Londonderry had already written to Churchill telling him that he was convinced that no gesture that could be made by Craigavon would have any effect on Southern Ireland, and that even if Craigavon were persuaded to make one, he would only undermine his own support in Northern Ireland. Londonderry was unimpressed with Maffey, who,

like so many of those who have known nothing about Irish history, believes that there is a possibility of a rapprochement between Craigavon and de Valera with far-reaching results. Of course, this is all nonsense, and the proper rapprochement would be between your General Staff and the Armed Forces of Eire, and if Eire was unwilling to accept our protection or the reinforcement of their forces by British Forces for the purposes of withstanding any attempted invasion, I would suggest that you go still further and take over the defence in the South as you have done in the North.[74]

Londonderry was not alone in arguing against concessions to de Valera. Letters in a similar vein poured into the Prime Minister's office from all directions. Josiah Wedgwood, an influential Labour MP, wrote warning Churchill against repeating the mistake of Belgium in Ireland. 'We can do very well on our own', he maintained, 'but we cannot carry any more half-hearted allies. A dose of Nazi-ism will do Southern Ireland all the good in the world.'[75] This no doubt was also Craigavon's opinion. In response to Chamberlain's letter requesting his co-operation in trying to persuade Ireland to enter the war, he telegraphed back: 'Am profoundly shocked and disgusted by your letter making suggestions so far reaching behind my back and without any preconsultation with me. To such treachery to loyal Ulster I will never be a party.'[76]

Chamberlain was considerably taken aback by this 'entirely unjustified' accusation. 'All that the Government had done', he complained to the War Cabinet the following day, 'was to enquire what would be the attitude of the Government of Eire towards a certain plan. It had throughout been made clear that it would be necessary to obtain the assent thereto of the

[74] Londonderry to Churchill, 21 June 1940 (PREM 4/53/2/120).
[75] Wedgwood to Churchill, 8 July 1940 (PREM 4/53/2/409).
[76] Craigavon to Chamberlain (telegram), 27 June 1940 (ibid.).

Government of Northern Ireland.' Rather than risk a row with Craigavon, the War Cabinet quickly agreed that Chamberlain should send him a reassuring reply 'emphasizing that Northern Ireland's position was entirely protected'. It also decided that MacDonald should continue his negotiations with de Valera over the ports because it would place them in a stronger position in regard to American opinion if they were compelled later to resort to force.[77]

Craigavon was not mollified by the assurance that he would have every opportunity of making his own views known before any decision affecting Northern Ireland was taken. 'Your telegram only confirms my confidential information and conviction that de Valera is under German dictation and far past reasoning with,' he wired back to Chamberlain. 'He may purposely protract negotiations till enemy has landed. Strongly advocate immediate naval occupation of harbours and military advance south.'[78]

Nor did things go smoothly for MacDonald. Despite his assurances to the contrary, the Irish Government remained convinced that, as far as a united Ireland was concerned, the British Government would not be able to deliver on its promises after the war was over. Nor was pressure from the United States likely to have much effect. Ambassador Kennedy assured Halifax that the British effort was futile, as the Irish were convinced (as was he) that the British were going to lose the war, and that it would be a mistake to throw in their lot with them.[79]

As negotiations with de Valera dragged on inconclusively, Chamberlain became progressively more discouraged. On 2 July he informed the War Cabinet that it looked as though the Irish Government was taking the view that Germany was invincible. 'It might well be that, not only would they not be prepared to invite our forces into Eire before a German invasion, but that if and when an invasion took place their forces would offer no real resistance.'[80] When, four days later, the British gave up on the negotiations, the only good that

---

[77] WM 184(40) of 28 June 1940 (CAB 65/7).
[78] Craigavon to Chamberlain (telegram), 29 June 1940 (PREM 3/131/2/10).
[79] WM 184(40) of 28 June 1940 (CAB 65/7).
[80] WM 191(40) of 28 June 1940 (ibid.).

had resulted from their efforts was a tacit agreement from the Irish Government to 'turn a blind eye' to British attacks on German warships of any kind if discovered in Irish territorial waters.[81]

The failure of his efforts regarding Ireland came as a hard blow to Chamberlain. It proved also to be the last major political initiative of his life. He fell ill in July, resigned in November, and died shortly thereafter. With him went much of the spirit of accommodation in British policy towards Ireland, to be replaced by the more belligerent attitude of Churchill. Once Chamberlain's protective mantle had been withdrawn, those apt to disagree with this change, in particular Halifax (who was also a possible rival), MacDonald (whom Churchill regarded as 'rat-poison' for his connection with the surrender of the Irish ports in the first place),[82] and Caldecote (whom Churchill may not have forgiven for being chosen over himself as Minister for the Co-ordination of Defence in 1936), were soon exiled or banished—Halifax as Ambassador to the United States. MacDonald as British High Commissioner to Canada, and Caldecote as Lord Chief Justice.

In July Churchill received his first reliable report on the situation in Ireland from British intelligence. It said that, while the majority of the Irish people did not expect a British invasion, there was 'complete unanimity on the viewpoint that the Irish Forces must repel the first invader, whether British or German'. It cited as evidence for this the fact that trees had been felled and other precautions taken close to the Ulster border. It also said that the Irish parties were more united than ever before, and that, although the Irish forces could not do anything to repel an invader, 'they were determined to make things as difficult for him as possible'.[83]

As for the IRA, it was not believed that the Germans had any control or communication with it in Ulster, and it was considered very doubtful that they had any control over it in the South except for one *small but extremely intelligent* body on the lines of the *Irish Republican Brotherhood*'. Sean Russell was

---

[81] WM 195(40) of 6 July 1940 (ibid.).
[82] Cadogan diary, 18 Dec. 1940 (Dilks, p. 341).
[83] 'General Report on Ireland', July 1940 (PREM 3/129/2/15).

assumed to be its leader, and, while believed to be still in Berlin, it was thought that he might soon attempt to land in Ireland. 'It is from this body that British forces, should they have to enter Eire at any time, will receive the greatest opposition such as the blowing-up of railways, roads, etc.' But the Irish authorities were satisfied that they would be able to deal effectively with the 'perpetrators of such outrages'. As for the main group of the IRA, the great majority of the younger leaders had already been arrested and interned, both in the North and the South. Of the old IRA, many of the veterans of the 1916–1921 War, like Dan Breen, had already joined the new Local Security Force and would probably obey the Dublin Government for the time being.

The report was not free from prejudice. The Irish Security Force, for example, was said to be increasing in numbers (135,000) and in efficiency, 'the latter fact being largely due to the number of the Protestant Community who are co-operating, subject to the proviso that they will not fight against the British under any circumstances. The result of this co-operation means that the men will be led by a good type of officer.' The report also noted that 'some of those who think further ahead are wondering what will ultimately happen to all the rifles now being handed out indiscriminately should there be no invaders to fight against. An Irishman does not like to give back firearms once he is in possession of them.' More blatantly, after noting that the *Altmark* incident[84] had been praised in Ireland, the report gratuitously adds: 'The breaking of any law naturally appeals to all Irishmen.'

Apart from these brief asides, the report was a fairly good one. It stated that the Irish Security Force was prepared to carry on guerrilla warfare indefinitely if attacked. McKenna, the Chief of Staff of the small Irish Army of 25,000 men, was reported to be a 'good type of man who does not dabble in politics and will not allow politics to be discussed in the Army'. In conclusion, the report expressed scepticism about the ability of the 53rd and 61st Divisions to hold down Northern Ireland and assist the South in the event of an invasion. It was estimated that it would take about three days to get to

---

[84] On 16 Feb. 1940 a British force stopped the *Altmark*, a German ship, in Norwegian waters and rescued the British prisoners of war which she was carrying.

Queenstown or the Shannon from Ulster, and even this would only be practicable with a friendly Ireland. Thus it was all the more important that the Navy have forces ready complete with landing parties to deal with any possible German attempt to seize ports in Ireland.[85]

Following the fall of France, the British had been faced with three alternatives in regard to Ireland: they could try to persuade Ireland to enter the war on their side; they could try to coerce Ireland into entering the war; or they could resign themselves to continued Irish neutrality. Chamberlain had tried the first approach and failed; Churchill now felt free to try the second. But, like Chamberlain, he was constrained by the need to retain the goodwill of the United States and by the fact that it was in Britain's obvious self-interest to keep a friendly Ireland. An awareness of the former had persuaded Churchill against the wisdom of seizing the Irish ports by force; the latter he was prone to forget.

In attempting to bring pressure on Ireland, Britain had few means at her disposal. With political pressure unlikely to have much effect, and economic coercion apt to be self-defeating, the only remaining alternative was a refusal to supply the Irish Government with the arms it so sorely needed. But even here, it was questionable whether it was in Britain's own interests to keep Ireland defenceless, and it might only drive her to seek arms elsewhere. Churchill eventually resorted to all three ways to bring pressure to bear on Ireland, none with much success.

Churchill first attempted to impose an arms embargo on Ireland. In the summer of 1940 Ireland was virtually defenceless against air attack. The Irish Army had only one under-equipped anti-aircraft battalion, including two medium batteries, for the defence of the whole island. At the height of the invasion scare the War Office recommended that the long-standing demands of the Irish Government for more anti-aircraft guns and other war material be met.[86] But a week later the COS rejected this recommendation and decided that no

---

[85] Ibid.

[86] Memo by ACIGS on 'Anti-Aircraft Requirements for Eire', 18 June 1940 (WO 193/761/MOI(a)/7A).

material should be supplied to Ireland unless an agreement was first reached with de Valera.[87]

This decision, plus the publication in the British press of a number of articles commenting unfavourably on Ireland's neutrality, brought Anglo-Irish relations to their wartime nadir. Nor were Irish fears assuaged by the standing ovation Churchill received from the House of Commons on 4 July when he announced the implementation of 'Operation Catapult' the seizure or destruction of all accessible French warships to prevent their falling under German control. In a conversation with Maffey, de Valera talked of the unpredictability of war, asking him who would have guessed three months earlier that Britain would attack the French Fleet. Warning that a 'premature move by British forces in Ireland would spell disaster', de Valera said that the staff work of the Irish Army had in recent years been directed at meeting an attack from Britain. With the outbreak of war they had switched over completely to planning against Germany. He now felt that once again the greater danger came from Britain. While he regretted that he had had to turn down the British scheme for a united Ireland—'the dream of his life'—he feared that in the present circumstances acceptance would have meant civil war. He now asked only that the British trust him enough to supply anti-tank guns, anti-aircraft guns, and airplanes that were needed for home defence.[88]

Alarmed by Maffey's report on his conversation with de Valera, and by the deterioration in Anglo-Irish relations in general, Caldecote urged the War Cabinet on 19 July to endeavour to 'damp down the Press campaign', make a public declaration that they had no intention of invading Ireland, and give more munitions to Ireland.[89] While declining to make a public statement disclaiming any intention of invading Ireland, the War Cabinet did agree to soften the press campaign, which had not been instigated by the Government in the first place, as de Valera supposed.[90] The question of

[87] COS 192(40) of 24 June 1940 (CAB 79/5).

[88] Maffey to Dominions Office, 17 July 1940. Annex I to WP(40)274 of 19 July 1940 (CAB 66/10).

[89] Memo by Caldecote on 'Relations with Eire', WP (40)274 of 19 July 1940 (ibid.).

[90] WM 209(40) of 22 July 1940 (CAB 65/8). While it was recognized that occa-

whether or not to resume arms shipments to Ireland was less easily resolved. Supporting the Dominions Secretary's request were Chamberlain[91] and, in yet another reversal, the COS;[92] opposed was Churchill.[93] On 26 July the War Cabinet overrode the Prime Minister's objections and determined to resume the shipments of arms to Ireland.[94] But for Caldecote it may well have been a Pyrrhic victory. Within three months not only had the decision been reversed, but he had been replaced as Dominions Secretary by the more amenable Lord Cranborne.

sionally newspapers like the *Daily Mirror* and the *Daily Sketch* published items which caused resentment when reproduced in Ireland, the Ministry of Information tried to discourage the British press from doing so, and to publish instead material on Ireland which showed 'understanding of the difficulties facing de Valera'. John Betjeman, who was then serving in the Films Division of the Ministry of Information, and who had been sent to Ireland in June to observe the situation, reported back that de Valera was 'Britain's best friend in Ireland' because, although he put Ireland before anything else and thought that the allies were beaten, there was still no doubt that he and his ministers felt that the best interests of Ireland would be served by a British victory. Like Maffey, Betjeman had quickly become convinced that partition was the key to the problem, and that the British Government should do something about it. His advice was that the British press should be encouraged to take a sympathetic line towards de Valera, but that 'everything should be done towards voicing in the press an outcry for the abolition of partition'. The first part of his advice was accepted; not the second. Crozier interview with Dulanty of 26 July 1940 (Crozier papers); Cecil Thomas (editor, *Daily Mirror*) to Walter Monckton (Deputy Director General of the Ministry of Information), 11 June 1940; H. Hodson (Empire Division) to Monckton, 21 June 1940; Betjeman to Hodson, 21 June 1940 (INF 258/CNI/615).
    [91] WM 208(40) of 19 July 1940 (CAB 65/8).
    [92] COS 229(40) of 22 July 1940 (CAB 79/5).
    [93] WM 209(40) of 22 July 1940 (CAB 65/8).
    [94] WM 213(40) of 26 July 1940 (CAB 65/8).

14

The Ascendancy
of Churchill

THE Battle of Britain—which raged from approximately
mid-July to mid-September 1940—provided de Valera with a
brief respite from Churchillian pressure. But once the battle
was over, Ireland again became a focus of attention. This time
the question was how Britain could avoid defeat in the submarine war. With shipping losses on the Atlantic convoys,
even though now routed around the north coast of Ireland,
reaching a record level in October, the Admiralty began to
raise anew the possibility of having to seize the Irish ports by
force.[1] Nor had the defeat of the Luftwaffe banished altogether
the spectre of a German invasion of Ireland, as Dill, the CIGS,
made clear in late October.[2] On 5 November, Churchill, re-
sponding to these pressures, for the first time spoke out publicly on the issue to the House of Commons, calling the denial
of the Irish bases a 'most heavy and grievous burden ... which
should never have been placed on our shoulders, broad though
they be'.[3]

The public response was overwhelming. Both the British
and American press, which had hitherto for the most part
discussed the subject in muted terms if at all, suddenly joined
in unison in condemning de Valera for denying the use of the
ports to British forces. *The Economist*, for example, wrote:

[1] Memo by Chief of Naval Staff, COS (40)868 of 25 Oct. 1940 (CAB 80/14). COS
(JP)(40)878 on 'Irish Ports: Possible use of', is closed for fifty years. See also ADM
205/2.
[2] Memo by CIGS, COS (40)877 of 29 Oct. 1940 (CAB 80/14). Two days earlier,
however, on 27 Oct., the interpreters of MI 14, basing their views on Enigma de-
crypts, had commented that 'it appears that the Invasion of UK and/or Eire is not
imminent'. This conclusion was supported by photographic reconnaissance which
indicated a considerable movement of shipping eastwards out of the Channel. See
Martin Gilbert, *Winston S. Churchill*, vi, *Finest Hour 1939–1941* (Boston, 1983), pp. 878-
9; and F.H. Hinsley et al., *British Intelligence in the Second World War: Its Influence on
Strategy and Operations*, i, (London, 1979), p. 189.
[3] Churchill, *Complete Speeches*, vi, p. 6299.

If the ports become a matter of life and death—for Ireland as well as England—there can be only one way out; we must take them. That would of course revive the old bitterness. But if bitterness there must be, let us have the bitterness *and* the bases, not the bitterness alone—which is all mere retaliation would provoke.[4]

Similarly, the diplomatic correspondent for the *Daily Telegraph* warned that recent sinkings in the Atlantic made it imperative for new steps to be taken at the earliest moment.[5]

In fact, Churchill had meant nothing in particular by his remarks; he was simply letting off steam. In his memoirs, he later wrote: 'We could of course at this time have descended upon de Valera's Ireland and regained the southern ports by force of modern arms. I had always declared that nothing but self-preservation would lead me to this.'[6] This was an exaggeration. On 6 November, the day after making his provocative speech in the House of Commons, Churchill told the COS that the time had come for approaching the United States to bring pressure to bear on the Irish Government, as Britain could not itself afford to spare the forces necessary to coerce Ireland into granting the bases.[7]

Since Churchill's statement concerning the Irish ports had not been intended to herald any change in British policy, the resultant public outburst caused almost as much alarm in Whitehall as it did in Dublin. Deprecating its effect on Anglo-Irish relations, the Dominions Office argued that the importance of the Treaty ports should not be exaggerated for fear of distracting the Americans from the far more important goal of getting them to convoy their own ships.[8] The Foreign Office was no less convinced of the need for prudence on the subject of Anglo-Irish relations. While acknowledging that it was well for Roosevelt to realize Britain's vital need for the Treaty ports, J.V. Browne, an official in the American Department, warned that the Americans must be left to draw their own conclusion. 'Even more important,' he added, 'no one on this side of the Atlantic should suggest that Mr. Roos-

4 *The Economist*, 10 Nov. 1940.
5 *Daily Telegraph*, 10 Nov. 1940.
6 Churchill, *Second World War*, ii, p. 600.
7 COS 376(40) of 6 Nov. 1940 (CAB 79/5).
8 Minute by P. Mason, n.d. (FO 371/24249/A4811/434/45).

evelt might bring pressure to bear on Eire. To suggest this
would be to put the President in the embarrassing position of
taking his orders from Downing Street.' Moreover, 'in emphasizing the importance for us of the Treaty ports it would
be a serious mistake to seem to be threatening the Irish in any
way, nor should our remarks be addressed directly at the
Americans'.[9]

Cranborne, who had recently replaced Caldecote as Dominions Secretary, passed on the substance of these views to
Churchill and the War Cabinet on 21 November.[10] Although
concerned about the 'inflamed' nature of public opinion, the
War Cabinet decided against any immediate statement.[11] For
his part, Churchill was not averse to letting de Valera 'stew
in his own juices for a while'. He told Cranborne that nothing
could be more harmless or more just than the remarks in *The
Economist*. The claim being made for de Valera, he added, was
'that we are not only to be strangled by them but to suffer
our fate without making any complaint'. He said that Maffey
should be made aware of the rising anger in England and
Scotland, and especially among the merchant seamen, and
that he should not be encouraged to think that his only task
was to mollify de Valera 'and make everything, including our
ruin, pass off pleasantly. Apart from this, the less we say to de
Valera at this juncture the better, and certainly nothing must
be said to reassure him.'[12]

Rather than argue with Churchill, Cranborne sent him 'a
shrewd appreciation of the position' by the Anglo-Irish nov-
elist Elizabeth Bowen, who was then working at the BBC and
who kept the Ministry of Information abreast of the situation
in Ireland. Writing from Ireland just after Churchill's speech,
Bowen decried the 'flare-up of resentment and suspicion' it
had caused, 'all the more to be regretted because, since August, pro-British feeling and sympathy for the British cause
had been steadily on the increase here'. While conceding that
the 'childishness and obtuseness of this country cannot fail to
be irritating to the English mind', she nevertheless agreed with

[9] Minute by J.V. Browne, 16 Nov. 1940 (ibid.).
[10] Cranborne to Churchill, 21 Nov. 1940 (PREM 3/127/1/14).
[11] WM 293(40) of 21 Nov. 1940 (CAB 65/9).
[12] Churchill to Cranborne, 21 Nov. 1940 (PREM 2/127/1/12).

de Valera that it would be 'a disaster for the country, with its uncertain morale, to be involved in war'.[13]

Although outwardly impenitent, Churchill was not impervious to these arguments. Not until VE Day almost five years later did he again publicly address the question of the Irish ports. Not that he gave up his attempts to secure their use. Rather, he immediately embarked on two alternate strategies. On the one hand, he tried to get the United States to bring pressure to bear on de Valera.[14] Although the American Minister in Dublin, David Gray, did his best, de Valera proved as impervious to American pressure as he had been to British.[15]

On the other, not content to rely solely on the Americans, Churchill determined to try some methods of his own on de Valera. On 6 November, the day after he made his speech in Parliament referring to the Irish ports, the COS considered the possibility of sending the 5th Division to Northern Ireland to increase British strength in case of a German invasion of Ireland. Reversing his earlier position, Churchill encouraged the transfer, but with a different object in mind. On 12 November he directed Eden, the Secretary of War, to ask General Pownall, the newly appointed Commander of the British troops in Northern Ireland, to have the Joint Planning Staff study the question of a large increase in the garrison of Northern Ireland 'with a view to a decisive move on a broad front, should this at any time become necessary'. While it should be made clear to Pownall that this was merely an exercise in staff planning and in no way implied a policy decision, Churchill nevertheless wanted it assumed that the equivalent of six divisions lightly equipped—not on the continental scale, but containing a number of independent mobile and mechanized brigades—would be employed, and that 'very large forces would be used so as to obviate serious opposition'. Two months were to be allowed for the concentration in the North, the 'effect of which in itself might produce the result desired'.[16]

Meanwhile, a new idea for bringing pressure to bear on de Valera had come to Churchill's attention. The inspiration for

---

[13] 'Notes on Eire' by Elizabeth Bowen, 9 Nov. 1940, and Cranborne to Churchill, 25 Nov. 1940 (PREM 4/536/374/5).

[14] Churchill, *Second World War*, ii, p. 564.

[15] Longford and O'Neill, *de Valera*, pp. 372–6.

[16] Churchill to Eden, 12 Nov. 1940 (PREM 3/127/3/11/78).

this plan appears to have come from Hankey, but it was also the result of the failure of the British and Irish Governments, despite months of haggling, to come to a wartime trade agreement. The root of the problem, from the British point of view, was that the Irish wanted to enjoy all the benefits resulting from the war (i.e. British subsidies for increased agricultural production) without paying any of the price in terms of rationing. Before they would strike a trade agreement with them, the British wanted the Irish to accept the principle of 'equal sacrifice' as regarded imports from overseas and Britain of goods which were in short supply. On the British side, however, there was something less than unanimity of outlook. On the one hand, the Dominions Office and the Board of Trade were in favour of acceding to most of the Irish demands for fear that too hard a bargaining stance on their part might imperil the Trade Agreement of 1938 and encourage the Irish to return to a policy of self-sufficiency. A new *rapprochement*, it was feared, might then be both more difficult to attain and be on less advantageous terms.[17] This also was Maffey's view. The 'crux of the whole matter, the key to our future economic and political relations lies in the answer to this question,'[18] he argued; 'prosperous agriculture in Eire implies good relations with the United Kingdom ... It throws her into our arms and must tend to recreate the strategic unity of the islands,' while 'a policy of industrial development based on tariffs must lead to estrangement, frictions and loss of business'.[19] On the other hand, while the Ministry of Shipping was content simply to see the matter settled amicably as soon as possible so that it could make its plans accordingly, the Ministry of Food was strongly opposed to any increase in prices offered to the Irish for agricultural goods over and above that paid to other Dominions, based on anything other than commercial grounds or on the grounds of necessity.[20]

In November, when Hankey himself finally took up the matter, the negotiations which had begun the previous spring

[17] The documents covering the trade negotiations with Ireland are in BT 11/1023/CRT 1880 and T 160/974/16022.
[18] Maffey to Eden, 6 May 1940 (BT 11/1417/CRT 81918/8840).
[19] Maffey to Horace Wilson, 4 May 1940 (ibid.).
[20] T. Jenkins (Ministry of Shipping) to Hutton (Ministry of Food), 5 Apr. 1940 (ibid.).

were still going on with no end in sight. Hankey's intervention
was prompted by a letter he received from W.B. Spender, the
Secretary to the Cabinet of Northern Ireland, praising Churchill's 'fine speech', but complaining that it had not gone far
enough. What Spender found upsetting was the availability in
Ireland of 'unlimited supplies of petrol and practically all
other imports from Overseas', while those goods were severely
rationed in the United Kingdom. He thought that Churchill
should have made it clear that the closure of the Irish ports to
British ships 'must inevitably have a serious reaction upon the
inhabitants of Eire'.[21]

Impressed with this logic, Hankey in his methodical way
began checking into the situation. Until then, the dispute over
how best to conduct the trade negotiations with Éire had been
conducted mainly on the departmental level, largely because
the ministers concerned were reluctant to become openly involved in any contention concerning Ireland. For instance,
while agreeing with Hankey that the administration of petroleum in Ireland was lax, Geoffrey Lloyd, the Secretary for
Petroleum, advised him to limit himself to verbal communication on the subject, warning that 'Eire is such political dy-
namite particularly at present that I am inclined to lie low'.[22]
At the Dominions Office Hankey fared better. While the permanent officials in the department tended to take the position
that a rationing scheme as stringent as Britain's would produce more serious hardships and difficulties in Ireland
because, not being at war, she was in a far worse situation to
cope with the ensuing dislocation, Cranborne was more recep-
tive. He agreed with Hankey that the Irish 'did not seem to
appreciate that increased sinkings should hit them at least as
hard as ourselves', and he thought that 'sooner or later we
will have to find a means of bringing this home to them'.[23]
With Churchill's encouragement, Cranborne secured the War
Cabinet's agreement to 'defer for a month the renewal of a
new comprehensive trade agreement with Eire, and that it
should be made clear to the Irish Government that Britain
would be driving a hard bargain on the matter'.[24]

[21] W.B. Spender to Hankey, 9 Nov. 1940 (ibid.).
[22] Lloyd to Hankey, 25 Nov. 1940 (ibid.).
[23] Cranborne to Hankey, n.d. (ibid.).
[24] WM 293(40) of 21 Nov. 1940 (CAB 65/9).

Though determined upon action, Churchill and Cranborne
were as yet uncertain in what that action should consist. The
answer, ironically, was supplied by an Irishman. In late November, Maffey routinely forwarded to the Dominions Office
a memorandum from a 'hundred percent Irishman', who suggested that Britain's mistake in the past had always been to
expect from de Valera a generous response to a generous
action. While allowing that de Valera would not give way
before a threat of physical force, he claimed that 'no country
in the world would re-act more readily to economic pressure',
and advised the British Government to adopt one of three
courses:

(1) Refuse to receive from Ireland any further cattle, farm produce
or manufactured goods, on the ground that they do not need them.
(2) Decide to pay a very reduced price for these goods, which would
make it uneconomical for Ireland to export them.
(3) Prohibit the sailing of all ships other than the passenger Mail
Boat to Holyhead, on the ground that they cannot spare warships
to protect them.[25]

Seizing upon it at once as just the sort of blueprint for action
for which he had been searching, Churchill forwarded the
memorandum to Lord Woolton, the Minister of Food, for his
opinion as to the likely effect on Britain if Irish supplies of
food were to be cut off for about six months. On guard as
always against interference from civil servants, Churchill
cautioned Woolton against circulating the memorandum to
his department.[26]

After receiving an encouraging reply from his Minister of
Food,[27] Churchill ordered copies of the memorandum and
Woolton's reply circulated to the departments concerned.
'The straits to which we are being reduced by Irish action
compels a reconsideration of these subsidies,' Churchill told
Kingsley Wood, the Chancellor of the Exchequer, who had
been promoted to the War Cabinet two months earlier. 'It
can hardly be argued we can go on paying them till our last
gasp. Surely we ought to use this money to build more ships

25 Cranborne to Churchill, enclosing the memo from an Irishman, 22 Nov. 1940
(PREM 3/128/114).
26 Churchill to Woolton, 23 Nov. 1940 (PREM 3/128/113).
27 Woolton to Churchill, 26 Nov. 1940 (PREM 3/128/111).

or buy more from the United States in view of the heavy sinking off the Bloody Foreland.' Although he did sound one note of caution, asking what relaliatory measures could be taken in the financial sphere by the Irish, Churchill again hoped to be spared from the depredations of the civil servants: 'Do not assemble all the pros and cons for the moment, but show what we could do financially and what would happen.'[28]

Cranborne, meanwhile, was busy laying out a rationale for the change in policy.[29] In a memorandum to the War Cabinet, the Dominions Secretary portrayed Ireland as a 'Gideon's Fleece' in a devastated continent, immune from the misfortuntes that afflicted the other peoples of Europe. 'In Eire alone', he wrote.

the ordinary life of peace is still carried on. There are no bombs, no blackout, no conscription, no disturbance of normal existence. People still hunt and shoot and race, dine out, and go to the theatres and cinemas in the evenings. Rationing has indeed been instituted, but it is of a very mild kind, and all reports that reach this country speak of abundant food, lashings of cream, and practically unlimited petrol. Is it surprising that the Irish people should want so desirable a state of things to go on? Dimly they realize that they owe it to the British Fleet. But they give us no thanks for that. They think that we do it purely out of self-interest, because Eire is indispensable to us.[30]

Cranborne saw only two ways to break the deadlock and convince the Irish of their dependence on Britain. The 'first and most obvious was to march in, horse, foot and artillery' and occupy the country and seize the ports. That approach would only be used as a last resort because it would be expensive and 'not very edifying'. The preferable alternative was economic pressure. Since the Irish were 'living in a world of illusion', they would have to be brought back to reality and made aware of the fact that they were dependent upon Britain, rather than the other way around. To accomplish this, he suggested that they should refrain so far as possible from purchasing in Irish markets, explaining if they were challenged that they felt an obligation to buy first from those countries that were allied to them rather than from neutrals.

---

[28] Churchill to Wood, 1 Dec. 1940 (PREM 3/128/109).
[29] Cranborne to Churchill, 3 Dec. 1940 (PREM 3/128/96).
[30] Memo by Cranborne, 3 Dec. 1940 (PREM 3/128/93-5).

They should also make it as difficult as possible for the Irish Government to charter ships, indicating that they required them for their own needs. They might even, in the last resort, refuse to admit ships trading with Ireland in their convoys. While this would cause considerable irritation against them, it would also inevitably sow doubts in the minds of wide sections of opinion in Ireland as to the wisdom of de Valera's policy. Such a policy would not arouse opposition in the United States or elsewhere, where the probable reaction would be that the Irish deserved such treatment.

While conceding that the outlined course of action was not likely to alter de Valera's policy, Cranborne thought that it might tend to weaken his hold on the Irish people instead of strengthening it, which would be the case if they invaded. Once 'the bubble of Irish complacency' had been pricked, it would then be up to Britain to make concessions. Besides offering some measure of protection for Irish ports and cities against the danger of German bombing, and restoring full facilities for trade and commerce, Cranborne suggested that they might even take the opportunity offered by the more conciliatory atmosphere created by the negotiations to tackle the thorny question of partition.[31]

Encouraged by Cranborne's memorandum, Churchill next turned to Robert Spear Hudson, the Minister of Agriculture and Fisheries, for support in his campaign. Hudson assured him that the Irish were powerless to damage British agriculture. Even a total ban on the export of Irish cattle and other agricultural products would have no serious effect.[32] Only Oliver Lyttelton, the newly appointed President of the Board of Trade, sounded a discordant note. Although willing to accede to economic pressure on Ireland as a short-term measure, Lyttelton cautioned against the unpredictable long-term effects of such a policy, warning that it might make Britain rather than de Valera unpopular with the Irish people. Moreover, he asked that exports to Ireland be only gradually curtailed in order to allow time for a smooth transition of the affected labour and plant into war production.[33] Satisfied by

---

[31] Memo by Cranborne, 3 Dec. 1940 (PREM 3/128/93-5).
[32] Spears to Churchill, 4 Dec. 1940 (PREM 3/127/3/11/81).
[33] Memo by Lyttelton, 4 Dec. 1940 (ibid.).

this, Churchill asked the Chancellor of the Exchequer the following day to prepare a good workable scheme 'with as much in it as possible that does not hit us more than it does the others'.[34] Wood hastened to comply with his chief's wishes, assuring him that, 'If we waged a real economic war the matter would be speedily finished.'[35]

Not that there was any prospect of their waging such a war. Churchill knew this. Indeed, there is a certain characteristic element of childishness about the whole business: in the way that Churchill from the outset tried to exclude the civil servants from becoming involved, and in the way he purposely excluded Halifax and Eden from the preliminary meeting on the matter, knowing that they, too, were likely to raise objections. From Cranborne, Woolton, Hudson, and Lyttelton, on the other hand, he knew he could count on support. All owed their positions to him; Wood, in particular, owed his present lofty status more than anything else to his having abandoned Chamberlain at the right time.[36] For Cranborne, who also had been rewarded for his prominent role in the movement to oust Chamberlain, opposition to Irish aspirations was a family tradition. The eldest son of Lord Salisbury, his own views on Ireland were probably closer to Churchill's than were those of anyone else in the Cabinet. But even he soon had second thoughts as to the wisdom of trying to use the economic weapon against Ireland.[37]

On 6 December Wood submitted two plans to the War Cabinet for consideration. The first, rather mild, was designed only to make the Irish population 'begin to feel uncomfortable in a few weeks'. The second, similar but more drastic—'in effect economic war'—called for the Ministry of Shipping to cut off almost entirely Irish access to shipping by denying insurance on ships going to Ireland and by refusing to convoy shipments made by sympathizers in the United States. Other than perhaps to expropriate Guinness or the National Stud, there appeared little Ireland could do by way of retaliation. The principal fear seemed to be that a glut of imports of Irish

---

[34] Churchill to Wood, 5 Dec. 1940 (ibid.).
[35] Wood to Churchill, 5 Dec. 1940 (ibid.).
[36] Cowling, *Impact of Hitler*, p. 385.
[37] The officials in the Dominions Office opposed the policy of squeezing Ireland, and sought in any way possible to lessen its severity. Garner, p. 244.

livestock might occur if the first plan were adopted and Irish exports not restricted.[38]

Cranborne successfully urged the adoption of the first plan. This mild embargo specifically excluded any action on coal (as some 10,000 men in Britain were dependent upon its export to Ireland for their jobs) or the freezing of Ireland's sterling balances to prevent their conversion into dollars.[39] A short time later, the COS tentatively agreed to deny with a few minor exceptions further military equipment to Ireland on the pretext that they needed it themselves.[40]

With the War Cabinet and the COS behind him, Churchill next consulted Roosevelt. On 8 December, in what he later described as 'one of the most important letters I ever wrote', he asked the President for the assistance that came to be known as Lend-Lease. He also asked for American support in securing the use of the Irish bases. In return, he promised that the British would undertake to protect Ireland from German attack and, though they could not compel Northern Ireland against its will to leave the United Kingdom, he again held out the hope that, if Ireland were to join in the war, 'a Council for defence of all Ireland could be set up out of which the unity of the island would probably emerge in some form or other after the war'.[41]

Although Roosevelt eventually responded to this appeal by submitting the Lend-Lease Bill to Congress, he made no immediate reply to Churchill's letter. Even though Gray was already putting more pressure on de Valera regarding the ports than Maffey would ever have dreamed of doing, Churchill was reluctant to act before hearing from the President.[42] Moreover, Churchill's attention was now distracted by events in Africa, where Wavell had finally launched an offensive aimed at driving the Italians out of Egypt. His victory at Sidi Barani on 11 December was followed by the invasion of Libya, which resulted in the virtual elimination of the Italian Army as a serious factor in North African operations. Churchill was greatly excited by these events, as he always was by great

---

[38] Memo by Wood, (40)475 of 6 Dec. 1940 (CAB 66/14).
[39] WM 301(40) of 6 Dec. 1940 (CAB 65/9).
[40] Memo by Dill (CIGS), COS (40)1031 of 16 Dec. 1940 (CAB 80/14).
[41] Churchill, *Second World War*, ii, p. 564.
[42] WM 304(40) of 12 Dec. 1940 (CAB 65/9).

initiatives, whether his own or the enemy's; it was the waiting in between that drove him to distraction.

Another reason for delaying a final decision on Ireland was the sudden death of Lothian, who had been in England for consultations during November. He was replaced by Halifax, who did not arrive in the United States until the end of the year. Sir Alexander Cadogan, the Permanent Under-Secretary at the Foreign Office, who did not in any case have much confidence in the efficacy of economic pressures upon de Valera, cautioned against any precipitate action until Halifax had time to put the British case to the American public.[43]

In the meantime, others cautioned against the use of force against Ireland. Sir Percy Loraine, formerly Ambassador to Italy, who had just returned from a visit to Ireland, told Halifax that, despite Southern Ireland's being more pro-British than at any time since the previous war, there was nevertheless a disposition to think de Valera right in insisting on Irish neutrality.[44] Similarly, on 23 December Maffey wrote of growing Irish disenchantment with Germany as reflected in a conversation he had recently had with Walshe, and warned that 'it must be realised that in the minds of the people here there is no feeling of having let England down, no admission that England can make demands as of right and justice. A lack of restraint on our part merely stirs the old passions and works against us.'[45]

These warnings were not lost on Cranborne, who was beginning to reconsider his earlier position. Following Maffey's advice, he asked the Ministry of Information to try to tone down the hostile press comments about Ireland. He then sent a copy of Maffey's telegram to Churchill, commenting that it looked as if the Irish Government might be beginning to see some of the errors of their ways, and suggesting that 'no doubt you will wish to take into account the more favourable trend of Southern Irish opinion in coming to any decision to put into force the economic measures which the Government has had under consultation'. Cranborne thought that it 'might be wise to delay action for the moment, especially as there are

[43] Minute by Cadogan, 20 Dec. 1940 (FO 371/24249/A481/434/45/416).
[44] Loraine to Halifax, 21 Dec. 1940 (Halifax papers, FO 800/310/-207).
[45] Maffey to Dominions Office, 23 Dec. 1940 (PREM 3/128/121/35/53).

indications that Mr. Gray, the American Minister, is bringing very useful influence to bear'.[46]

Churchill, however, was 'not at all impressed' by Cranborne's arguments for restraint. 'I do not think that a strong conversation of this kind should alter the very carefully considered conclusion to which the Cabinet came,' he told Cranborne.

Sir John Maffey naturally wishes to keep everything pleasant, but meanwhile we are suffering cruelly ... I do not see any reason for cooling down the Press. We must be very careful that inertia, delay and weakness do not dress themselves up as 'patience'. You have only just come into this business. I have been 'patient' for sixteen months. You are more likely to get an invitation [Cranborne had not yet received a customary invitation to meet de Valera] when they see there is something we can do and are going to do.[47]

Churchill was waiting only to see that 'the timing of this action fitted in with President Roosevelt's financial performances and the Congress decision thereupon'.[48] On 29 December, satisfied that Lend-Lease aid was assured, he finally ordered the Treasury to proceed with economic sanctions against Éire.[49]

Despite fears in the Dominions Office and the Board of Trade that this second economic war would be as disturbing to Anglo-Irish trade as the first, this did not prove to be the case. In part, this was because in 1941, unlike 1932, the British Government made every effort to avoid having its economic measures seem like reprisals. The British press was informed that the measures had been taken 'with profound regret' and only because the pressure on British shipping was so severe. Nor did the Government ever impose any of the drastic measures against Ireland that had been considered at the outset. The Ministry of Shipping was authorized to withdraw vessels engaged in Anglo-Irish trade as the need arose, and food supplies to Ireland were gradually reduced, but there was no sudden cut-off of supplies such as tea. Similarly, Irish

---

[46] Cranborne to Churchill, 23 Dec. 1940 (PREM 3/128/121/35/51).
[47] Churchill to Cranborne, 23 Dec. 1940 (PREM 3/128/121/35/50).
[48] Churchill to Wood, 27 Dec. 1940 (PREM 3/128/121/35/46).
[49] Churchill to Wood/Sir Edward Bridges, 29 Dec. 1940 (PREM 3/128/121/35/46).

ships and neutral ships engaged in trade with Ireland were
still allowed to sail in British convoys, and ships chartered by
the Irish Government were still allowed to be insured.[50]

These restrictions ensured that the sanctions would have no
real effect, at least in so far as the ostensible object of bringing
pressure to bear on de Valera was concerned. Thus, while the
measures taken did force the Irish to share in some of the
hardships and deprivations of wartime, such as petrol and tea
rationing, and did help slightly to reduce the congestion in
the western ports, that is about all they accomplished. The
goal of Irish ports remained as elusive as ever. The Admiralty
realized this almost at once,[51] and by April was chalking up
the economic war as a failure.[52]

Churchill, at least at first, was more optimistic about the
possible outcome. He deputized Cranborne, together with
Wood and Cross, the Minister for Shipping, to keep him informed every few days 'as to how the screw is being applied
to Southern Ireland'.[53] This Cranborne dutifully did. Each
succeeding report was in turn minuted by Churchill with an
encouraging 'Press on'. But there was little cause for optimism.
Instead of becoming more forthcoming about the ports, as the
British had hoped, de Valera responded to the British move
to cut off supplies by attempting to buy ships from the Americans. 'The fact is that de Valera still seems entirely to blind
himself to any connection between our need of the ports and
the shipping situation,' Cranborne reported to Churchill on
12 January 1941. 'To the Eire Government, apparently, the
question of the ports is still a political one. We must hope that
our new economic action will do something to open their eyes.
At the present moment, it is perhaps symbolic that the President of Eire is paralytic and the Prime Minister blind.'[54]

A week later, thinking he detected a hint of moderation in
de Valera's favourable reply to a request for the use of an
Irish base for British civil air service and for the use of an air
corridor over Ireland for military planes, Cranborne suggested
that a relaxation on arms shipments might be a fitting British

[50] WM 1(41) of 2 Jan. 1941 (CAB 65/17).
[51] Minute by C.L. Daniel, 6 Jan. 1941 (ADM 1/11104).
[52] ADM 1/11330.
[53] Churchill to Cranborne, 3 Jan. 1941 (PREM 3/128/4).
[54] Cranborne to Churchill, 12 Jan. 1941 (PREM 4/53/6/350).

concession in return.[55] Churchill did not agree. 'Until we are so satisfied (about S. Ireland's intention to enter war) we do not wish them to have arms, and certainly will not give them ourselves', he admonished Cranborne.

The concession about Lough Swilly is important and shows the way things are moving. No attempt should be made to conceal from Mr. de Valera the depth and intensity of feeling against the policy of Irish neutrality. We have tolerated and acquiesced in it, but juridically we have never recognized that Southern Ireland is an independent Sovereign State, and she herself has repudiated Dominion Status. Her international status is undefined and anomalous. Should the present situation last till the end of the war, which is certainly unlikely, a gulf will have opened between Northern and Southern Ireland, which it will be impossible to bridge in this generation.[56]

This reference to a gulf opening between Northern and Southern Ireland was to become a recurring theme in Churchill's minutes. While in a sense this can be interpreted simply as a frank and accurate assessment of what the future held under the circumstances he described, the feeling is difficult to escape that the words were meant to be as much in the nature of a threat as of a warning.

Throughout the spring the British remained hopeful that the partial blockade of Ireland was having some effect. At the beginning of January there was a sudden and acute shortage of petrol in Ireland which left motorists stranded when the pumps went dry. The shortage was caused by the sinking of two tankers carrying fuel to Ireland, and it compelled the Irish Government to reduce the basic gasoline ration, which had been double the British level, to one-quarter of its previous level. Although the British quickly saw to it that another tanker was sent to Dublin, they took care to limit future supplies to Ireland to a quantity sufficient to maintain only the reduced ration.[57]

Throughout Churchill's chief concern was that his ministers might 'fall into the error of becoming too tender-footed in this policy'. He reminded them that the 'intention was to make

[55] Minute by Cranborne on note by Maffey re conversation with de Valera, 20 Jan. 1941 (PREM 3/131/3/1).
[56] Churchill to Cranborne, 21 Jan. 1941 (PREM 3/131/4).
[57] 'Progress Report' sent by Cranborne to Churchill, 21 Jan. 1941 (PREM 3/128/30).

Southern Ireland realize how great a wrong they were doing to the cause of freedom by the denial of the ports. We must expect they will make some complaints from time to time. A stern mood should prevail in view of the ordeals to which the British nation is exposed.'[58]

On 20 February Wood assured Churchill that their plans were 'making Eire progressively more uncomfortable with daily accelerating effect', and he predicted that Ireland would 'very possibly come to us in three or four weeks'.[59] Similarly, on 19 March, Cranborne announced that 'The bubble of Irish complacency has effectively and we may hope finally been pricked.' But, despite such wishful thinking and Churchill's exhortations, the 'economic war' did little but make Ireland share in the hardships of wartime. She remained resolutely neutral yet pro-British, while de Valera remained firmly in control of affairs in Dublin.

While the War Cabinet pariently awaited the results of the economic war against Ireland, a potentially far more serious threat to the stability of Anglo-Irish relations arose when, in early May, Bevin reintroduced the question of extending conscription to Northern Ireland. Bevin did so because the figures for voluntary recruitment in Ulster had fallen embarrassingly low—much lower than had been expected—to a total of only 25,000 men, of whom an unknown but it was thought substantial number had come from the South. One of the main reasons for the reluctance to volunteer, according to Bevin, was that the fear of substantial unemployment in Northern Ireland after the war curbed enlistments, as reinstatement in employment after the war did not extend to volunteers. And, as always in Northern Ireland, the problem was further exacerbated by religious differences.[60]

Churchill, ignoring the experience of the previous war,

---

[58] Churchill to Wood and Cranborne, 17 Feb. 1941 (PREM 3/128/22).

[59] Wood to Churchill, 20 Feb. 1941 (PREM 3/128/21).

[60] Memo by Bevin on 'Application of Conscription to Northern Ireland', WP (41)107 of 1 May 1941 (CAB 66/16), and WM 49(41) of 12 May 1941, Confidential Annexes (CAB 65/18). Despite the claims of the Ulster Government that its citizens desired to make an 'equal sacrifice' with those in Britain, enthusiasm for the war was noticeably lacking in Northern Ireland both in the Catholic Nationalist and in the Protestant Loyalist communities. For the remarkable reluctance of Ulster Loyalists to join the forces, despite an unemployment rate which remained at depression levels of over 20% even with the wartime boom, see Fisk, pp. 386–99.

backed Bevin from the start. When Herbert Morrison, the Minister of Labour, tried to remind Churchill of this earlier folly by sending him extracts from his own book, *The World Crisis*, describing in detail the difficulties encountered in trying to impose conscription during the First World War, Churchill denied that it had any bearing on the current situation, 'except in so far as it favoured decided action. We irritated the Irish', he added, 'but did not push our plans through out of fear of their objections. We must at all costs avoid having toyed with the subject and given it up through weakness.'[61]

Despite Churchill's determination, a repetition of the earlier episode would have been almost inevitable had Bevin's plan been adopted. Fortunately, Churchill was over-ruled by the War Cabinet before the Government had irrevocably committed itself to the extension of conscription to Ulster. The arguments against adopting such a course of action were many and weighty. Most obvious was that enforcing it would have been more trouble than it was worth. Besides trouble with the IRA, there would probably have been a wholesale refusal to register, necessitating the setting-up of concentration camps for thousands of resisters. There would also have been the possibility of a renewal of strife between Protestant and Catholic workmen, which could have had an adverse effect on production.[62] Moreover, as expected, de Valera was vociferous in his protestations against the introduction of conscription in the North. Gray wrote to Washington that the measure would be 'madness' and 'a repetition of the same blunder made during the last war'. Maffey similarly warned that conscription would strengthen de Valera's position and weaken the growing opposition to him.[63]

As usual when American susceptibilities were involved, Churchill moved cautiously at first. A committee was set up under Morrison to study the question. It had its first meeting at Chequers on 24 May. Despite the obvious risks involved, most of the committee appeared determined to proceed with

[61] Churchill to Morrison, 5 May 1941 (PREM 3/237/114/2).
[62] Memo by Morrison on 'Application of Conscription to Northern Ireland', WP (41)108 of 22 May 1941 (CAB 66/16). Production in Northern Ireland, marked by delays and inefficiency, was already far below British standards. Fisk, pp. 400-4.
[63] Maffey to Dominions Office, 25 May 1941, appended to WP (41)113 of 24 May 1941 (CAB 66/16).

conscription. Besides Bevin, Sir Henry Pownall, the Vice-CIGS, and Sir John Anderson, Chamberlain's successor as Lord President of the Council (to whom Churchill increasingly was turning over responsibility for the civil side of running the country), argued in favour of extending conscription to Ulster.[64] If anything, de Valera's opposition seemed to harden the Government in its resolve to impose conscription on the North. This resolve weakened, however, when a telegram arrived from the Prime Minister of Canada on 26 May warning of the effects a controversy over conscription might have on Canadian unity, and urging Churchill to consult with the American Ambassador on the possible effects of such a controversy on Irish–American opinion. The reply from Winant, the new American Ambassador, forced Churchill to concede that it might be best to consult with Roosevelt before making a final decision. The *coup de grâce* came when Morrison announced that even the Ulster Government was beginning to have second thoughts on the matter.[65]

Churchill was beaten, though he did not like to admit it. It fell to his old friend Beaverbrook, the Minister for Aircraft Production, to bring this home to him. Cadogan recorded the results in his diary:

... Then a discussion on conscription in Ulster. Cabinet against Winston (rightly). He made passionate appeal: to back down now, in face of clamour, would show that the mainspring of resolution was broken ... That is all very well. But what he does is to jump to decisions—ill-considered—and then say that it shows weakness to recede. It shows stupidity to jump to them. A very gloomy and unpleasant Cabinet. Max [Beaverbrook] was on edge and very pugnacious (on the surface). Bevin was almost the only supporter of the P.M. on Ulster. But he made a most timid and rambling statement ...[66]

The next day Churchill conceded that to apply conscription to Northern Ireland would be 'more trouble than it was worth'.[67]

[64] Confidential Annex I to WM 53(41) of 26 May 1941 (CAB 65/18).
[65] Ibid. and Confidential Annex III (ibid.).
[66] Cadogan diary, 26 May 1941 (Dilks, p. 381).
[67] WM 54(41) of 27 May 1941 (CAB 65/18).

Conclusion

By the summer of 1941, a consensus had been arrived at which would govern British policy towards Ireland throughout the remainder of the war and for more than two decades thereafter. It represented a compromise of sorts. After his defeat over extending conscription to Northern Ireland in May, Churchill, in June 1941, gave up trying to win his way over Ireland except for one belated attempt to block the annual migration of Irish labourers to Britain to help harvest the potato crop.[1] Although he remained a stubborn opponent of any concessions to Ireland, his heart was no longer in it. In part this was due to an alteration in the nature of the war. British fortunes sank very low indeed in the spring of 1941. Yugoslavia and Greece were over-run, Crete seized from the air, Egypt and North Africa were in peril, and the sinking of merchant ships in the North Atlantic had reached the crisis point. But the situation was dramatically transformed after Hitler's invasion of Russia on 22 June. The Battle of the Atlantic, in particular, changed for the better. Sinkings dropped off drastically during October and declined into virtual insignificance for November and December. Not only were the ships and airplanes of coastal command performing better than before, but by then virtually all ships were sailing in well-protected convoys. All of this greatly reduced the need for the Irish bases.

There was another reason why Churchill gave up on trying to coerce the South. The events of the previous year had convinced him that he could do nothing which involved Ireland without the co-operation of the United States. This became more evident as time wore on. During the summer and autumn of 1941 American involvement in the Battle of the Atlantic progressively increased as Roosevelt gradually extended the range of the patrols of the American Navy. Amer-

---

[1] Churchill to Bevin, 19 June 1941, and Bevin to Churchill, 23 June 1941 (PREM 4/53/3/18-19).

ican entry into the war in December was followed within a few weeks by the landing of American troops in Northern Ireland. With American involvement in the war came greater American influence and control. After Pearl Harbor, Ireland could never again for the duration of the war be treated as a purely British concern.

Churchill recognized this. That is why, though he encouraged Roosevelt to do so, he himself lost interest in trying to coerce Ireland. He was determined, however, that de Valera would pay a price for his triumph; that Ireland would suffer for having, as he thought, lost her soul and abandoned Britain after so many concessions had been granted to her. The price she would have to pay was that de Valera's dream of a united Ireland would not be realized, at least not for another generation, and not if Britain had anything to say about it. Whether this was served up as 'satisfy[ing] the essential requirements of Ulster', or as 'guarantee[ing], once and for all, our strategic security',[2] the result would be the same.

The rest of the War Cabinet had no trouble in going along with this. They too were perturbed by what they perceived as the base ingratitude and selfishness of Ireland in adhering stubbornly to her neutrality when Britain was in mortal peril. Even Labour leaders like Attlee, Bevin, and Morrison felt this way. They no longer felt that they owed Ireland anything. All guilt for the past was washed away by resentment at the present. Their sympathies were now entirely with the Ulster Protestants, with whose loyalty they were deeply impressed.[3] In this way, for the first time since 1921, British policy towards Ireland became truly bi-partisan; hence, when Labour finally achieved a majority in 1945, it made no difference as far as Ireland was concerned. This change in attitude was also reflected in the British press, which no longer spoke in terms of the eventual reunification of Ireland or, in the case of the Liberal press, of the mistreatment of the Catholic minority in the North.

This apparent change in British policy towards Ireland during 1940 and 1941 signified as much as anything else a final

---

[2] Memo by Cranborne, WP (41)64 of 19 Mar. 1941 (CAB 66/15).
[3] See e.g. Bernard Donoughue and G. W. Jones, *Herbert Morrison: Portrait of a Politician* (London, 1973), pp. 327-8.

acceptance of post-1921 reality. The politicians who had grown to manhood before the First World War, and who were accustomed to think of Ireland in terms of a geographic unity, were gradually giving way to politicians in their forties and thirties, for whom the most salient fact about Ireland was Irish disunion. The politicians who made peace with Ireland in 1921 thought of the division of the country as a temporary measure based on political expedience and expected Ireland eventually to be reunited within the Empire. The politicians who dealt with Ireland after the Second World War thought of it as an entirely separate country—though one with close ties to the United Kingdom—which indeed it was soon to become.

This transition, from thinking of Ireland as a sister-nation, into regarding her as an independent country, was a difficult one to make, particularly for the older politicians. For Churchill it was especially hard. Not only was he the only surviving signatory of the Irish Treaty of 1921 still active in politics (Lloyd George was in virtual retirement), but he felt a keen sense of personal betrayal by the Irish. Nor did it help any that his erstwhile enemy was now in power in Dublin. Yet, disillusioned as he was, Churchill was not by nature a vindictive man. It seems possible that if at any time during the war—or at least before the very end—de Valera had given in, Churchill would have welcomed him with open arms and all would have been forgiven (such, after all, had been the case with Collins twenty years earlier). Evidence for this came in the immediate aftermath of Churchill's receiving the news of the Japanese attack on Pearl Harbor. He was, of course, elated by the news: 'So we had won after all!' After making plans for an immediate British declaration of war against Japan, Churchill goes on to record how 'This done, my thought turned at once to what has always lain near my heart. To Mr. de Valera I sent the following message: Now is your chance. Now or never! A nation once again! I will meet you wherever you wish.'[4]

These sentiments no doubt reflect at least something about Churchill's still deeply ambiguous feelings towards Ireland at the end of 1941. They are, however, exaggerated somewhat

[4] Churchill, *Second World War*, iv. p. 606.

for effect. Having condemned the Irish in the first four volumes of his memoirs on the *Second World War*, and preparing to ignore them in the subsequent two volumes, Churchill doubtless felt the urge to take his leave of Anglo-Irish relations on a suitably magnanimous note. More so, it appears, than the facts of the case would seem to allow. According to the official records, the actual text of the message Churchill sent de Valera after Pearl Harbor reads: 'Now is your chance. Now or never. "A nation once again." Am very ready meet you *at any time*.' (Emphasis added.) The difference is significant. It is almost inconceivable that Churchill would have been willing to fly to Dublin to meet with de Valera unless he already had some sort of prior commitment from him about entering the war, although he would certainly have been willing to meet with him in Britain or perhaps on some neutral ground. Moreover, it is virtually certain that Churchill was not suggesting that Britain would herself endeavour to do anything about partition in return for Ireland entering the war, although this is what de Valera took the message to mean, and it certainly seems to be implied. Nor did Churchill make any effort to clear up the confusion in his memoirs; in fact, he only added to it by misquoting the text of the telegram.

What Churchill actually meant in that moment of euphoria will probably never be known for certain. The closest approach to interpreting it lies in the interchange that took place between himself and Cranborne on the following day. Upon re-reading de Valera's reply to the telegram, Cranborne wrote:

I see that there is one sentence to which I feel that I ought to draw your attention. In your message to him you quoted the words 'A nation once again.' I had taken this to mean that, by coming into the War, Ireland would regain her soul. Mr. de Valera seems to have read it quite differently to mean that Northern and Southern Ireland should be reunited, and comments that 'neither he nor anybody else would have a mandate for entering the war on a deal over partition'. Ought we to leave him under this misapprehension? His Cabinet, on reconsideration, might accept your invitation on this basis, and then feel that we had led them up the garden path. May I have authority to inform Sir J. Maffey of the true interpretation of the phrase? I feel that not to do so may lead us into serious embarrassment later on.[5]

⁵ Cranborne to Churchill, 8 Dec. 1941 (PREM 3/131/6).

Churchill gave his assent, adding that he 'certainly contemplated no deal on partition. That could only come by consent
arising out of comradeship between N and South.'[6]

The First World War left the British Empire fundamentally
weakened; the Irish were but the first to exploit this weakness.
The Second World War—Churchill's determination to the
contrary notwithstanding—undermined most of what was left
of Britain's imperial greatness. In marked contrast to 1921,
when Ireland dropped out of the British Commonwealth to
become a Republic in 1949, the event passed almost unnoticed
in Britain. Of course, much had happened in the intervening
years. British efforts to persuade the Irish to assume for themselves a role within the Commonwealth ultimately had gone
for naught. The burdens of history and circumstance had
proved too great.

But it cannot be said that these efforts were wasted. While
the inter-war years did not entirely efface the resentment and
prejudice built up over centuries, they went a surprisingly
long way towards doing so. For this much credit is due to the
innate good sense of the British and Irish peoples, who gradually came to realize that the common interests uniting them
far outweighed any differences which they might have. Credit
also is due, on the British side, to politicians like Lloyd George,
Malcolm MacDonald, and Neville Chamberlain, as well as to
civil servants like Curtis, Thomas Jones, and Sir Warren
Fisher, who recognized that it was in Britain's own interest to
treat the Irish fairly and as equals and to accept Irish aspirations for national independence. Chamberlain was right in
thinking that this was the only way in which no more would be
heard the old cry: 'England's danger Ireland's opportunity.'

The biggest failure, of course, was over partition. Perhaps
the problem was insoluble, as the failure of Sunningdale and
the violence of recent years would seem to indicate. But one
may question whether the British Government might have
tried harder to do something about it during the inter-war
period. The inhibitions which restrained ministers from moving in this direction are clear. While British policy towards
Ireland in the 1920s and 1930s was determined by a complex

---

[6] Minute by Churchill to Cranborne, 8 Dec. 1941 (ibid.).

interplay of forces, interests, personalities, and events, the most
basic fact of the whole period was the dominance of the Conservative Party. Whatever the personal views of a man like
Neville Chamberlain (who, it should be remembered, had
started out in politics as a Liberal), as Prime Minister of the
National Government ultimately he and his colleagues depended for their power and position on the support of those
elements that dominated and controlled the Conservative
Party. In weighing conflicting considerations and striving to
formulate policies suited to the political, economic, and strategic realities of the time, this was the one thing they dared
never forget. At no time during these years would Conservatives have allowed the British Government to coerce 'loyal'
Ulster into reaching some sort of accommodation with the
South concerning partition; indeed, there was an implicit
assumption that no British Government would even attempt
to do so. Even when Chamberlain and Halifax felt that
over-riding strategic considerations necessitated forceful
British action regarding partition, as in 1940 after the fall of
France, they were unable to bring any serious political pressure to bear on Ulster.

This also reveals the limitations when it comes to formulating policy of powerful civil servants like Sir Warren Fisher.
Probably Fisher had more influence on ministers regarding
Ireland than anyone else, yet neither he nor Sir Horace Wilson could persuade Chamberlain and his colleagues in the
National Government to move faster towards resolving the
'economic war' with Ireland in the 1930s than the practicali-
ties of the domestic political situation would allow. Nor,
despite his strong sympathies for the South and antipathy
towards the North, could Fisher do more than try to prevent
the British Government from setting up obstacles to eventual
Irish union, and even here he was merely fighting a delaying
action, as by 1938 the British Government had virtually
conceded that henceforth social spending in Ulster would be
on a par with that of the rest of the United Kingdom.

The British failure to do anything regarding partition was
reinforced by their acquiescence in the oppression of the Catholic minority in the North by the Protestant majority. Again,
the reasons behind this are not difficult to trace. Fairly or

unfairly, the Catholic population in the North was tainted by its association with the IRA. In so far as they knew or cared about it at all, most Englishmen probably felt that the Catholics in Ulster were somehow deserving of the treatment they received for their disloyalty. In the absence of an effective spokesman for their cause, the British Government took the path of least resistance and ignored their plight.

This lack of effective opposition to its policy best explains why the British Government did nothing about partition or the mistreatment of the Catholics in the North. What opposition there was came mainly from politicians in the South, in particular de Valera. The only real domestic opposition came largely from the Liberal and Labour press, such as the *Manchester Guardian* and the *Daily Herald*. This was not serious enough to affect Government policy. Liberal and Labour politicians also provided little effective opposition to Government policy. Ramsay MacDonald and J.H. Thomas, who largely determined the Labour Government's policy towards Ireland during the short intervals when Labour was in power, were more sympathetic to the views of Ulster Loyalists than Irish Nationalists. They also shared with the Conservatives and Liberals a determination to keep Ireland from ever again becoming a divisive issue in British politics, which meant in effect the acceptance of the *status quo* regarding Ireland.

The most effective pressure group influencing the British Government's Irish policy during the 1920s and 1930s was not of the left, but of the right. This consisted mainly of the diehards, supported by right-wing organs like the *Morning Post*. In 1925 the diehards and their supporters almost provoked a rupture in Anglo-Irish relations over the Boundary Question. After de Valera returned to power in Ireland in 1932, pressure from Churchill and the diehards contributed to the strong British reaction to his demands which helped precipitate the Anglo-Irish 'economic war' of 1932–8. And it was diehard pressure, as much as de Valera's intransigence, which prevented the British Government from moving towards putting an end to the quarrel sooner.

The contribution of Churchill to Anglo-Irish relations during this period is almost evenly balanced on the positive and negative sides. His handling of Irish affairs during the critical year of 1922, which saw the birth of the Irish Free State and the outbreak of the Irish civil war, was masterly. He tried to balance fairly the interests of the Free State and Ulster, seeing in this the most likely outcome of eventual Irish unity within the Empire. In 1926, as Chancellor of the Exchequer, he helped reach an agreement resolving the Boundary Crisis on terms acceptable to both sides. But Churchill tended to regard the Irish Treaty as a final settlement of relations between the two countries. While out of government during the 1930s, he used his influence to hinder an amicable settlement of Anglo-Irish differences. During the war, initially as First Lord of the Admiralty and then as Prime Minister, Churchill endeavoured to pressure de Valera to compromise Ireland's neutrality by turning over the use of Irish ports to the Royal Navy. When this failed, he resolved that the British Government would do nothing then or later to encourage Ulster to move towards ending partition.

In the end, however, one must question whether there was anything the British Government could have done about partition even if it had had a popular mandate to intervene. Again, the experience of recent years leaves little ground for optimism. For better or worse, the British Governments of the 1920s and 1930s accepted the continued division of Ireland. Instead, they concerned themselves primarily with trying to reconcile British interests with Ireland's continuing drive towards national self-assertion. While the final result was not all that they had bargained for it did establish a new and stable basis for Anglo-Irish relations which has stood the test of time. This compensates to a considerable degree for what was probably the inevitable failure to resolve the partition problem. The answer to that final major thorn in Anglo-Irish relations lies ultimately in Dublin and Belfast rather than in London.

Bibliography

I. UNPUBLISHED SOURCES

1. *Private Papers*

1st Viscount Alexander of Hillsborough	Churchill College, Cambridge
Wilfred William Ashley, Baron Mount Temple	Shropshire Records Office, Winchester
1st Earl of Oxford and Asquith	Bodleian, Oxford
1st Earl of Baldwin	Cambridge University Library
1st Earl of Balfour	British Library
1st Lord Beaverbrook	Beaverbrook Library; now transferred to House of Lords Library
Lord Carson	Public Record Office of Northern Ireland, Belfast
1st Viscount Cecil of Chelwood	British Library
Sir Austen Chamberlain	Birmingham University Library
Neville Chamberlain	Birmingham University Library
1st Baron Chatfield	Royal Maritime Museum, Greenwich
1st Marquess of Crewe	Cambridge University Library
Sir Stafford Cripps	Nuffield College, Oxford
1st Lord Croft	Churchill College, Cambridge
W.P. Crozier, interviews with politicians	Beaverbrook Library; now House of Lords Library
Sir Andrew Cunningham, Admiral of the Fleet	British Library
1st Lord Dalton, diary	London School of Economics and Political Science
1st Viscount Davidson	Beaverbrook Library; now House of Lords Library
1st Viscount Lee of Fareham	Beaverbrook Library; now House of Lords Library
H.A.L. Fisher	Bodleian, Oxford
1st Earl of Halifax	Churchill College, Cambridge; FO 800, Public Record Office, Kew
1st Lord Hankey	Churchill College, Cambridge

Lord Harvey of Tasburgh	British Library
Thomas Jones	National Library of Wales, Aberystwyth
1st Lord Keyes	Churchill College, Cambridge
George Lansbury	London School of Economics and Political Science
Andrew Bonar Law	Beaverbrook Library; now House of Lords Library
1st Earl Lloyd George	Beaverbrook Library; now House of Lords Library
7th Marquess of Londonderry	Durham County Record Office
11th Marquess of Lothian (Philip Kerr)	Scottish Public Record Office, Edinburgh
James Ramsay MacDonald	in possession and by permission of David Marquand, and now in the Public Record Office, Kew
1st Viscount Milner	Bodleian, Oxford
Gilbert Murray	Bodleian, Oxford
1st Baron Quickswood (Hugh Cecil)	Hatfield House, by permission of Lord Salisbury
1st Viscount Runciman	Newcastle University Library
4th Marquess of Salisbury	Hatfield House, by permission of Lord Salisbury
1st Viscount Samuel	House of Lords Library
1st Viscount Sankey, diary	Bodleian, Oxford
C.P. Scott, diary	British Library
3rd Earl of Selborne	Bodleian, Oxford
1st Viscount Simon	in possession and by permission of Lord Simon; FO 800, Public Record Office, Kew
Sir Archibald Sinclair (1st Viscount Thurso)	Churchill College, Cambridge
Sir Arthur Steel-Maitland	Scottish Public Record Office, Edinburgh
John St. Loe Strachey	Beaverbrook Library; now in House of Lords Library
1st Earl of Swinton	Churchill College, Cambridge
1st Viscount Templewood (Sir Samuel Hoare)	Cambridge University Library
J.H. Thomas	Kent Record Office, Maidstone
Sir Charles Trevelyan	Newcastle University Library
Sir Robert Vansittart (1st Lord Vansittart)	Churchill College, Cambridge

Beatrice Webb (Lady Passfield),   London School of Economics
    diary   and Political Science
1st Lord Weir   Churchill College, Cambridge

2. *Interviews*

Lord Longford
Malcolm MacDonald

3. *Official Records*

The following Record Classes, all now kept at the Public Record Office, Kew, proved most valuable for this study:

Admiralty Papers

    ADM 1   Admiralty and Secretariat papers
    ADM 16   Admiralty and Secretariat cases
    ADM 205   First Sea Lords' papers

Board of Trade Papers

    BT 11   Commercial Department: Correspondence and papers

Cabinet Office Papers

    CAB 2   CID minutes
    CAB 4   CID memoranda
    CAB 16   CID subcommittees
    CAB 21   Cabinet Secretariat files
    CAB 23   Cabinet minutes and conclusions (1919–39)
    CAB 24   Cabinet memoranda (CP series, 1919–39)
    CAB 27   Cabinet committees
    CAB 32   Imperial Conferences to 1939
    CAB 53   Chiefs of Staff Committee
    CAB 65   War Cabinet minutes and conclusions (WM series, 1939–45)
    CAB 66   War Cabinet memoranda (WP series, 1939–45)
    CAB 79   Chiefs of Staff Committee minutes (1939–45)
    CAB 80   Chiefs of Staff Committee memoranda

Colonial Office Papers

    CO 537, 739, 906   Dominions, Conferences, and Miscellaneous Records

Dominions Office Papers

    DO 35   Original correspondence
    DO 114   Confidential print
    DO 117   Conferences
    DO 121   Private Office papers

Foreign Office Papers
   FO 371, 800   Correspondence relating to Dominions and Private
   Collections

Home Office Papers
   HO 45

Ministry of Information Papers
   INF 258

Prime Minister's Office Papers
   PREM 1, 2, 3, 4   Correspondence and papers

Treasury Papers
   T 160   Finance files

War Office Papers
   WO 137   Derby correspondence
   WO 193   War Office files relating to the Dominions

II. PUBLISHED SOURCES

1. *Parliamentary Debates*
Hansard   Parliamentary Debates: House of Commons
Hansard   Parliamentary Debates: House of Lords

2. *Newspapers* (consulted primarily from clippings and extracts contained in the Lloyd George papers and in the Dominions Office Reports on the British Press)

Birmingham Daily Post	*Liverpool Daily Post*
Daily Chronicle	*Manchester Guardian*
Daily Express	*Morning Post*
Daily Herald	*News Chronicle*
Daily Mail	*The Observer*
Daily Mirror	*The Scotsman*
Daily News	*Sunday Express*
Daily Telegraph	*Sunday Times*
Evening News	*The Times*
Evening Standard	*Westminster Gazette*
Glasgow Herald	*Yorkshire Post*
Irish Times	

3. *Periodicals*
Contemporary Review   *Edinburgh Review*

Fortnightly Review	*Punch*
Nation and Athenaeum	*Round Table*
New Leader	*Spectator*
New Statesman	*The Economist*
Nineteenth Century and After	

4. *Works of Reference*

Annual Register
British Political Facts by David Butler and Jennie Freeman
Dictionary of National Biography
Dod's Parliamentary Companion

5. *Books and Articles*

Akenson, Donald, *Education and Enmity: The Control of Schooling in Northern Ireland 1920-1950*, New York, 1973.

Aldcroft, Derek, *The Inter-War Economy: Britain 1919-1939*, London, 1970.

Amery, L.S., *My Political Life*, vols. ii & iii, London, 1955.

Ash, Bernard, *The Lost Dictator: A Biography of Field Marshall Sir Henry Wilson*, London, 1968.

Avon, Earl of (Anthony Eden) *The Eden Memoirs*, 4 vols., i, *The Reckoning*, Boston, 1965.

Ayerst, David, *The Manchester Guardian: Biography of a Newspaper*, Ithaca, 1971.

Barnett, Correlli, *The Collapse of British Power*, New York, 1972.

Barrett, D. and Curtis, C.F., *The Northern Ireland Problem*, Oxford, 1962.

Bateman, John, *The Great Landowners of Great Britain and Ireland*, London, 1883, rep. New York, 1970.

Beaverbrook, Lord, *The Decline and Fall of Lloyd George*, London, 1963.

Bell, J. Bowyer, *The Secret Army*, New York, 1970.

Benewick, Robert, *Political Violence and Public Order: A Study of British Fascism*, London, 1969.

Bew, Paul, Gibbon, Peter, and Patterson, Henry, *The State in Northern Ireland 1921-72: Political Forces and Social Classes*, New York, 1979.

Birkenhead, 1st Earl of, *Contemporary Personalities*, London, 1924.

Birkenhead, 2nd Earl of, *F.E.: The Life of F.E. Smith, First Earl of Birkenhead*, London, 1959.

Birrell, Derek, and Murie, Alan, *Policy and Government in Northern Ireland: Lessons of Devolution*, New York, 1980.

Blake (Lord), Robert, *The Conservative Party from Pitt to Churchill*, London, 1970.

—— *The Unknown Prime Minister: The Life and Times of Andrew Bonar Law, 1858-1923*, London, 1955.

Blaxland, Gregory, *J.H. Thomas: A Life for Unity*, London, 1964.

Bolton, G.C., *Britain's Legacy Overseas*, Oxford University Press, 1973.

Bond, Brian, *British Military Policy Between the Two World Wars*, Oxford University Press, 1980.

—— (ed.), *Chief of Staff: The Diaries of Lieutenant-General Sir Henry Pownall*, 2 vols., London, 1973.

Bowman, John, *De Valera and the Ulster Question 1917-1973*, Oxford University Press, 1982.

Boyce, D. George, *Englishmen and Irish Troubles: British Public Opinion and the Making of Irish Policy 1918-1922*, Cambridge, Mass., 1972.

—— *Nationalism in Ireland*, Baltimore, 1982.

—— 'Normal Policing: Public Order in Northern Ireland Since Partition', *Éire-Ireland*, xiv, 4 (1979), 35-52.

Bridges, Lord, *The Treasury*, London, 1964.

Bromage, Mary C., *De Valera and the March of a Nation*, New York, 1956.

Buckland, Patrick, *The Factory of Grievances: Devolved Government in Northern Ireland, 1921-1939*, Dublin, 1979.

—— *Irish Unionism*: i, *The Anglo-Irish and the New Ireland 1885-1922*; ii, *Ulster Unionism and the Origin of Northern Ireland, 1886-1922*, Dublin, 1972, 1973.

—— (ed.), *Irish Unionism 1885-1923: A Documentary History*, Belfast, 1973.

Bullock, Alan, *The Life and Times of Ernest Bevin*, 2 vols., London, 1960.

Burridge, T.D., *British Labour and Hitler's War*, London, 1976.

Callwell, C.E., *Field Marshall Sir Henry Wilson: His Life and Diaries*, 2 vols., London, 1927.

Campbell, John, *Lloyd George: The Goat in the Wilderness*, London, 1977.

Camrose, Viscount, *British Newspapers and Their Controllers*, Andover, Hants, 1947.

Canning, Paul, 'The Impact of Eamon de Valera: Domestic Causes of the Anglo-Irish Economic War', *Albion*, 15, 3 (1983), 179-205.

—— 'Yet Another Failure for Appeasement? The Case of the Irish Ports', *International History Review*, iv, 3 (1982), 371-92.

Carroll, John T. *Ireland in the War Years 1939-1945*, New York, 1975.

Chamberlain, Sir Austen, *Down the Years*, London, 1937.

Churchill, Randolph S., *Lord Derby: 'King of Lancashire'*, London, 1959.

Churchill, Winston S., *His Complete Speeches 1897-1963*, 8 vols., ed. Robert Rhodes James, New York, 1974.
—— *The Second World War*, 6 vols., Boston, 1948-53.
—— *The World Crisis: The Aftermath*, London, 1929.
Close, David, 'Conservatives and Coalition after the First World War', *Journal of Modern History*, 45, 2 (1973), 240-60.
Coghlan, F., 'Armaments, Economic Policy and Appeasement: Background to British Foreign Policy 1931-7', *History*, 57, 190 (1972), 205-16.
Cole, Margaret (ed.), *Beatrice Webb's Diaries*, 2 vols., London, 1956.
Cook, Chris, *A Short History of the Liberal Party*, London, 1978.
—— and Gillian Peele (edd.), *The Politics of Reappraisal: 1918-1939*, New York, 1975.
Cooper, Diana, *The Light of Common Day*, Boston, 1959.
Coote, Colin, *A Companion of Honour: The Story of Walter Elliott*, London, 1965.
Costigan, Giovanni, 'The Anglo-Irish Conflict, 1919-1922', *University Review* (Dublin), v, 1 (1968), 64-86.
—— *A History of Modern Ireland*, Indianapolis, 1969.
—— *Makers of Modern England*, New York, 1967.
Cowling, Maurice, *The Impact of Hitler: British Politics and British Policy, 1933-1940*, Cambridge University Press, 1975.
—— *The Impact of Labour, 1920-1924: The Beginning of Modern British Politics*, Cambridge University Press, 1971.
Cronin, Sean, *Irish Nationalism: A History of Its Roots and Ideology*, New York, 1981.
Cross, J.A., *Sir Samuel Hoare, A Political Biography*, London, 1977.
Cullen, L.M., *An Economic History of Ireland Since 1660*, London, 1972.
Curran, Joseph M., *The Birth of the Irish Free State 1921-1923*, University of Alabama Press, 1980.
Curtis, Edmund, and McDowell, R.B. (edd.), *Irish Historical Documents, 1172-1922*, New York, 1968 edn.
Curtis, L.P., *Anglo-Saxons and Celts: A Study of Anti-Irish Prejudices in Victorian England*, University of Bridgport Press, 1968.
Dallek, Robert, *Franklin D. Roosevelt and American Foreign Policy, 1932-1945*, New York, 1979.
Dalton, Hugh, *Memoirs:* i, *Call Back Yesterday 1887-1931*; ii, *The Fateful Years 1931-1945*, London, 1951, 1953.
Dangerfield, George, *The Damnable Question: A Study in Anglo-Irish Relations*, Boston, 1976.
Dilks, David (ed.), *The Diaries of Sir Alexander Cadogan, 1938-1945*, New York, 1972.
Donoughue, Bernard, and Jones, G.W., *Herbert Morrison: Portrait of a Politician*, London, 1973.

Dwyer, T. Ryle, *Irish Neutrality and the USA, 1939-47*, Totawa, N.Y., 1977.

Eden, Anthony (Earl of Avon), *The Eden Memoirs*, 4 vols., i, *The Reckoning*, Boston, 1965.

Elliott, W.Y. and Duncan Hall, H. (edd.), *The Commonwealth at War*, New York, 1943.

Ervine, St. John Greer, *Craigavon: Ulsterman*, London, 1949.

Fanning, Ronan, *The Irish Department of Finance 1922-58*, Dublin, 1978.

Feiling, Keith, *The Life of Neville Chamberlain*, London, 1946.

Ferris, Paul, *The House of Northcliffe*, London, 1971.

Fisk, Robert, *In Time of War: Ireland, Ulster and the Price of Neutrality 1939-45*, London, 1983.

Garner, Joe, *The Commonwealth Office 1925-68*, London, 1978.

Gibbs, N.H., *Grand Strategy: i, Rearmament Policy*, London, 1976.

Gilbert, Martin, *Winston S. Churchill: iv, The Stricken World 1916-1922; v, The Prophet of Truth, 1922-1939; vi, Finest Hour 1939-1941*, Boston, 1975, 1977, 1983.

—— (ed.) iv, *Winston S. Churchill, Companion, Part III: Documents 1921-1922; v, Parts I-III: Documents 1922-1939*, London, 1978-82.

Glynn, Sean, 'Irish Immigration to Britain 1911-1951: Patterns and Policy', *Irish Economic and Social History*, viii (1981), 50-69.

Gollin, Alfred M., *The Observer and J.L. Garvin, 1908-1914*, New York, 1960.

Graubard, Stephen R., *British Labour and the Russian Revolution, 1917-1924*, Harvard University Press, 1956.

Greaves, C. Desmond, *Liam Mellows and the Irish Revolution*, London, 1971.

Gretton, Sir Peter, *Winston Churchill and the Royal Navy*, New York, 1969.

Gwynn, Denis, *The History of Partition, 1912-1925*, Dublin, 1950.

Hancock, W.K. *Survey of British Commonwealth Affairs: i, Problems of Nationality, 1918-1936; ii, Problems of Economic Policy, 1918-1939*, London, 1937, 1942.

—— and Gowing, M.M., *The British War Economy*, London, 1949.

Hand, Geoffrey, 'MacNeill and the Boundary Commission' in F.X. Martin and F.J. Byrne (edd.) *The Scholar Revolutionary: Eoin MacNeill, 1867-1945, and the Making of the New Ireland*, Shannon, 1973, pp. 201-75.

—— (ed.), *Report of the Boundary Commission*, Shannon, 1969.

Handley, James Edmund, *The Irish in Modern Scotland*, Cork University Press, 1947.

Harkness, David, 'England's Irish Question' in Chris Cook and

Gillian Peele (edd.), *The Politics of Reappraisal 1918–1939*, New York, 1975, pp. 39–63.

Harkness, David, 'Mr. de Valera's Dominion: Irish Relations with Britain and the Commonwealth, 1932–1938', *Journal of Commonwealth Political Studies*, viii, 3 (1970), 206–20.

—— *The Restless Dominion: The Irish Free State and the British Commonwealth of Nations, 1921–31*, London, 1969.

Hindle, Wilfred, *The Morning Post, 1772–1937: Portrait of a Newspaper*, London, 1937.

Hinsley, F.H., Thomas, E.E., Ransom, C.F.G., and Knight, R.C., *British Intelligence in the Second World War: Its Influence on Strategy and Operations*, London, 1979.

The History of the Times: iv, *The 150th Anniversary and Beyond, 1912–1948*. London, 1952.

Holland, R.F., *Britain and the Commonwealth Alliance 1918–1939*, London, 1981.

Holt, Edgar, *Protest in Arms: The Irish Troubles, 1916–1923*, London, 1960.

Howard, Michael, *The Continental Commitment*, London, 1972.

Huxley, Gervas, *Both Hands: An Autobiography*, London, 1970.

Hyde, H. Montgomery, *Baldwin: The Unexpected Prime Minister*, London, 1973.

—— *Carson*, Kingswood, Surrey, 1953.

Inglis, Brian, *West Briton*, London, 1962.

Johnson, D.S., 'Northern Ireland as a problem in the economic war 1932–38', *Irish Historical Studies*, xxii, 86 (1980), 144–61.

Jones, Thomas, *A Diary with Letters, 1931–1950*, London, 1954.

—— *Whitehall Diary*, ed. Keith Middlemas, i, *1916–25*; ii, *1926–31*; iii, *Ireland 1916–26*, London, 1969–71.

Keith, Arthur Berriedale (ed.), *Speeches and Documents on the British Dominions, 1918–1931: From Self-Government to National Sovereignty*, London, 1961.

Kendle, John E., *The Round Table Movement and Imperial Union*, Toronto, 1975.

Kinnear, Michael, *The Fall of Lloyd George: The Political Crisis of 1922*, Toronto, 1973.

Lawrence, R.J., *The Government of Northern Ireland: Public Finance and Public Service, 1921–1964*, Oxford, 1965.

Lee, J.M., *The Churchill Coalition 1940–1945*, Hamden, Conn., 1980.

Lewin, Ronald, *Churchill as Warlord*, New York, 1973.

Liddell Hart, Sir Basil H., *The History of the Second World War*, New York, 1972.

—— *The Liddell Hart Memoirs*, 2 vols., New York, 1965.

Loewenheim, Francis, Langley, Harold, and Manfred, Jonas, (edd.),

Roosevelt and Churchill: Their Secret Wartime Correspondence, New York, 1975.

Londonderry, Marchioness of, *Retrospect*, London, 1938.

Longford, Lord (Frank Pakenham, *q.v.*), and O'Neill, T.P., *Eamon de Valera*, London, 1970.

—— and McHardy, Anne, *Ulster*, London, 1981.

Low, D.M., *Low's Autobiography*, London, 1956.

Lyons, F.S.L., *Culture and Anarchy in Ireland 1890–1939*, Oxford University Press, 1979.

—— *Ireland Since the Famine*, London, paperback edn., 1973.

Macardle, Dorothy, *The Irish Republic*, London, 1937.

McColgan, John, 'Implementing the 1921 treaty: Lionel Curtis and constitutional procedure', *Irish Historical Studies*, xx, 79 (1977), 312–33.

McCrachen, J.L., 'Northern Ireland, 1921–46' in T.W. Moody and F.X. Martin (edd.), *The Course of Irish History*, Cork, 1967, pp. 313–41.

MacDonald, Malcolm, *Titans and Others*, London, 1972.

McEvoy, Fred, 'Canadian-Irish Relations During the Second World War', *Journal of Imperial and Commonwealth History*, v, 2 (1977), 206–26.

McIntyre, W. David, *The Commonwealth of Nations, Origins and Impact, 1869–1971*, Minneapolis, 1977.

Mackintosh, John P. (ed.), *British Prime Ministers in the Twentieth Century*, 2 vols., New York, 1977, 1978.

Macleod, Iain, *Neville Chamberlain*, New York, 1962.

McMahon, Deirdre, 'Anglo-Irish Relations: 1923–38', (Ph.D. Thesis, Cambridge University, 1979).

—— 'Ireland, the Dominions and the Munich Crisis', *Irish Studies in International Affairs* (1979).

MacNeill, Ronald J., *Ulster's Stand for Union*, London, 1922.

Macready, General Sir C.F.N., *Annals of an Active Life*, 2 vols., London, 1924.

Mansergh, Nicholas, *The Commonwealth Experience*, London, 1969.

—— *The Government of Northern Ireland: A Study in Devolution*, London, 1936.

—— *The Irish Free State: Its Government and Politics*, London, 1934.

—— *Survey of British Commonwealth Affairs: iii, Problems of External Policy, 1931–9*, London, 1952.

Marder, Arthur J., *Old Friends, New Enemies: The Royal Navy and the Imperial Japanese Navy. Strategic Illusions, 1936–1941*, Oxford University Press, 1981.

Marquand, David, *Ramsay MacDonald*, London, 1977.

Massey, Vincent, *What's Past is Prologue*, New York, 1964.

Mayer, Arno, *Political Origins of the New Diplomacy, 1917-1918*, New Haven, 1959.
—— *Politics and Diplomacy of Peacemaking: Containment and Counter-revolution at Versailles, 1918-1919*, New York, 1967.
Middlemas, Keith, *The Clydesiders*, London, 1965.
—— and Barnes, John, *Baldwin*, London, 1969.
Moran, Lord, *Churchill: Taken from the Diaries of Lord Moran: The Struggle for Survival, 1940-1965*, Boston, 1966.
Morgan, Kenneth O., *Consensus and Disunity: The Lloyd George Coalition Government, 1918-1922*, Oxford University Press, 1979.
Mowat, Charles Loch, *Britain Between the Wars, 1918-1940*, Boston, paperback edn., 1971.
Neeson, Eoin, *The Civil War in Ireland*, Cork, 1966.
Nevin, Donal, 'Radical Movements in the Twenties and Thirties' in T. Desmond Williams (ed.), *Secret Societies in Ireland*, New York, 1973, pp. 166-79.
Newsam, Sir Frank, *The Home Office*, 2nd edn., rev., London, 1955.
Nicolson, Harold, *Curzon: The Last Phase 1919-1925*, London, 1934.
——*Diaries and Letters*: i, *1930-1945*; ii, *1939-1945*, ed. Nigel Nicolson, London, 1966, 1967.
—— *King George V: His Life and Reign*, London, 1952.
O'Connor, Kevin, *The Irish in Britain*, London, 1972.
O'Farrell, Patrick, *England and Ireland since 1800*, London, 1975.
—— *Ireland's English Question: Anglo-Irish Relations, 1534-1970*, London, 1971.
O'Halpin, Eunan, 'Sir Warren Fisher and the Coalition, 1919-1922', *Historical Journal*, 24, 4 (1981), 907-27.
Ovendale, Ritchie, *'Appeasement' and the English Speaking World*, Cardiff, 1975.
Overy, R.J., *The Air War 1939-1945*, New York, 1980.
Pakenham, Frank (Lord Longford, *q.v.*), *Peace by Ordeal*, London, 1935.
Peden, G.C., *British Rearmament and the Treasury 1932-1939*, Edinburgh, 1979.
Peele, Gillian, 'Revolt over India' in Chris. Cook and Gillian Peele, (edd.) *The Politics of Reappraisal, 1918-1939*, New York, 1975, pp. 114-45.
Petrie, Sir Charles, *The Life and Letters of Sir Austen Chamberlain*, 2 vols., London, 1940.
Phillips, Gregory D., *The Diehards: Aristocratic Society and Politics in Edwardian England*, Cambridge, Mass., 1979.
Pollard, Sidney, *The Development of the British Economy*, 2nd edn., rev., New York, 1969.
Postgate, Raymond, *The Life of George Lansbury*, London, 1951.

Ramsden, John, *The Age of Balfour and Baldwin, 1902–1940*, London, 1978.

Reynolds, David, *The Creation of the Anglo-American Alliance 1937–41: A Study in Competitive Co-operation*, Chapel Hill, 1982.

Rhodes James, Robert, *The British Revolution: 1880–1939*, New York, 1977.

—— (ed.), *Chips: The Diaries of Sir Henry Channon*, London, 1967.

—— *Churchill: A Study in Failure, 1900–1939*, New York, 1974.

—— (ed.), *Memoirs of a Conservative: J.C.C. Davidson's Memoirs and Papers, 1910–37*, London, 1969.

Rosenberg, Joseph L., 'Irish Conscription, 1941', *Eire-Ireland*, xiv, 1 (1979), 16–25.

Roskill, Stephen, *Churchill and the Admirals*, London, 1977.

—— *Hankey: Man of Secrets* 3 vols. ii, *1919–31*; iii, *1931–1963*, London, 1972, 1974.

—— *Naval Policy Between the Wars:* i, *1919–1929*; ii, *1930–1939*. London, 1968, 1976.

—— *White Ensign: The British Navy at War, 1939–1945*, Annapolis, 1960.

Rubenstein, William D., 'Henry Page Croft and the National Party, 1917–22'. *Journal of Contemporary History*, 9 (1974), 129–48.

Savage, David W., 'The Attempted Home Rule Settlement of 1916', *Eire-Ireland*, 2, 3 (1967), 132–45.

—— ' "The Parnell of Wales has Become the Chamberlain of England": Lloyd George and the Irish Question', *Journal of British Studies*, xii, 1 (1972).

Shay, Robert Paul, Jr., *British Rearmament in the Thirties. Politics and Profits*, Princeton, 1977.

Shinwell, Emanuel, *I've Lived Through it All*, London, 1973.

Skidelsky, Robert, *Politicians and the Slump: The Labour Government of 1929–1931*, London, 1967.

Strachey, John St. Loe, *The Adventure of Living*, New York, 1922.

Taylor, A.J.P., *Beaverbrook*, New York, 1972.

—— *English History 1914–1945*, Oxford University Press, 1965.

—— (ed.), *Lloyd George: A Diary by Frances Stevenson*, New York, 1971.

—— *Lloyd George: Rise and Fall*, Cambridge University Press, 1961; reprinted in *Politics in Wartime and Other Essays*, London, 1964.

—— (ed.), *Lloyd George: Twelve Essays*, London, 1971.

—— (ed.), *Off the Record: Interviews With W.P. Crozier*, London, 1972.

Thompson, Neville, *The Anti-Appeasers: Conservative Opposition to Appeasement in the 1930s*, Oxford University Press, 1971.

Tierney, Michael, *Eoin MacNeill: Scholar and Man of Action, 1867–1945*, Oxford University Press, 1980.

Towey, Thomas, 'The reaction of the British government to the

1922 Collins-de Valera pact', *Irish Historical Studies*, xxii, 85 (1980), 65-76.

Townshend, Charles, *The British Campaign in Ireland, 1919-1921*, Oxford, 1975.

Turner, John, *Lloyd George's Secretariat*, Cambridge University Press, 1980.

Vansittart, Lord, *The Mist Procession*, London, 1958.

Watt, David (ed.), *The Constitution of Northern Ireland: Problems and Prospects*, London, 1981.

Watt, D.C., *Personalities and Policies: Studies in the Formulation of British Foreign Policy in the Twentieth Century*, London, 1965.

—— *Too Serious a Business: European Armed Forces and the Approach to the Second World War*, Berkeley, 1975.

Wertheimer, Egon, *Portrait of the Labour Party*, London, 1929.

Wheare, K.C., *The Statute of Westminster and Dominion Status*, 4th edn., London, 1953.

Wheeler-Bennett, Sir John W., *John Anderson, Viscount Waverly*, London, 1962.

Wigley, Philip G., *Canada and the Transition to Commonwealth. British-Canadian Relations 1917-1926*, Cambridge, 1977.

Wilson, Trevor, *The Downfall of the Liberal Party, 1914-1935*, London, 1966.

—— (ed.), *The Political Diaries of C.P. Scott, 1911-1928* Ithaca, 1970.

Wrench, Sir John Evelyn, *Geoffrey Dawson and Our Times*, London, 1955.

Younger, Carlton, *Ireland's Civil War*, New York, 1969.

Index

abdication crisis 168-70

Act of Union 54

Adamson, William 116-17

Admiralty 36, 46, 54, 69, 112, 178-80, 183-4, 187-8, 230 n., 241-9 *passim*, 253-4, 272 n., 279, 283, 292, 305

Africa, Northern, in Second World War 302, 310

agrarian disturbances 20

Air Ministry 161

All Souls College, Oxford 4, 267, 278

Altmark incident 288 and n.

America, *see* United States of

Amery, Leopold Charles Maurice Stennett (1883-1945)
- and fall of Coalition 68
- advises Bonar Law on policy 69
- as First Lord of Admiralty (1922-4) 73
- in opposition 96-7
- as Colonial and Dominions Sec. (1925-9) 101, 165, 180-1; and Boundary Crisis 103; at Imperial Conference (1926) 111-12

Anderson, Sir John (later Viscount Waverley) (1882-1958)
- as Perm. Under-Sec., Home Office (1922-32) 54, 103, 106, 109-10
- as Home Sec. and Minister of Home Security (1939-40) 259
- as Lord Pres. of the Council (1940-3) 309

Andrews, J.M. 206, 213, 216

Anglo-American relations, *see* United States

Anglo-Irish economic war 315-16
- outbreak of 136-75 *passim*
- effect on British coal industry 139, 155, 158-60, 164, 177
- effect on British agriculture 147, 152, 154, 158-60, 203
- effect on Northern Ireland 207-8
- negotiations for final settlement 168, 174-5, 192-6, 198-220 *passim*, 222-5

Anglo-Irish Treaty (1921) vii, ix, 3-15 *passim*, 20, 22, 24-5, 29-30, 32, 38-41, 43, 45-6, 49, 55, 58-9, 61, 68-9, 71-2, 75-6, 80-1, 83-4, 86, 89, 90, 94-6, 98, 103-4, 106-8, 110-12, 123, 125, 127-30, 133, 141, 147-8, 150-1, 162, 166-7, 176-81, 183-4, 203-5, 210, 218, 312, 317

Anglo-Irish Treaty (1938) 218-22, 226-7, 235-6, 244, 296

Anglo-Irish War (1919-21) vii, 3-5, 177, 263

Anglo-Italian agreement (1938) 218, 221

Annual Register 4 n., 98, 129

anti-Catholicism 19 n., 21-2, 33, 87, 115-17, 165, 224, 232

Anti-Partition League 226, 236

Anti-Socialist Union 23-4

appeasement, policy of ix, 156, 167, 173, 177, 193, 229-30

Archbishop of Canterbury 4, *see* also Lang, Cosmo Gordon

Archbishop of York 121

Archer, Col. Liam 268

Argyll, Duke of 45

Armagh, county 91, 105

Ashley, Sir Wilfred William (later Baron Mount Temple) 23, 45, 71

Asquith, Herbert Henry (later 1st Earl of Oxford and Asquith) (1852-1928) vii, 53, 87, 89, 91, 95, 123

Astor, W. Waldorf, 2nd Viscount 117, 266

Attlee, Clement Richard (later Earl) (1883-1966)
- as Deputy Leader of the Labour Party in the House of Commons (1931-5) 138
- as Leader of the Opposition (1935-40) 238
- as Lord Privy Seal (1940-2) 262, 281, 311

Australia 136, 173, 278

Austria, incorporated into Germany 209, 210